Parachute Rigger Handbook

August 2015

Change 1 (December 2015)

U.S. Department of Transportation
FEDERAL AVIATION ADMINISTRATION
Flight Standards Service

Preface

The Parachute Rigger Handbook introduces the basic skills necessary for acquiring a Parachute Rigger Certificate. It is developed by the Flight Standards Service, Airman Testing Standards Branch, in cooperation with various aviation educators and industry.

This handbook is primarily intended to assist individuals who are preparing for the parachute rigger airman knowledge test and the oral and practical test. The material presented in this handbook is appropriate for senior and master parachute riggers. The handbook contains information on regulations and human factors, design and construction, materials, operations, inspection and packing, hand tools, sewing machines, the parachute loft, repairs, alterations, and manufacture.

This handbook conforms to training and certification concepts established by the Federal Aviation Administration (FAA). There are different ways of teaching, as well as performing specific rigging procedures, and many variations in the explanations of repairs, alterations, and manufacture of parachutes. The discussion and explanations reflect commonly used practices and principles. This handbook provides a basic knowledge that can serve as a foundation on which to build further knowledge. Occasionally the word "must" or similar language is used where the desired action is deemed critical. The use of such language is not intended to add to, interpret, or relieve a duty imposed by Title 14 of the Code of Federal Regulations (14 CFR).

It is essential for persons using this handbook to also become familiar with and apply the pertinent parts of 14 CFR and appropriate technical standards. Performance standards for demonstrating competence required for parachute riggers are prescribed in the appropriate practical test standard.

The FAA greatly acknowledges the valuable assistance provided by many individuals and organizations throughout the aviation community whose expertise contributed to the preparation of this handbook. This handbook contains material and pictures of various products often used by industry. It is presented here as a means of communicating information to be used for training purposes only. The FAA neither endorses nor recommends any specific trademark item in this handbook.

This handbook is published by the U.S. Department of Transportation, Federal Aviation Administration, Airman Testing Standards Branch, AFS-630, P.O. Box 25082, Oklahoma City, OK 73125.

Comments regarding this publication should be sent, in email form, to the following address: AFS630comments@faa.gov.

/s/ John Barbagallo, for

John S. Duncan
Director, Flight Standards Service

Acknowledgments

The Parachute Rigger Handbook was produced by the Federal Aviation Administration (FAA) with the assistance of Safety Research Corporation of America (SRCA). The FAA wishes to acknowledge the following contributors:

Parachute Labs, Inc., for images used in Chapters 1, 2, and 4

Ilse Ungeheuer, for images used in Chapters 3 and 5

Tim Taykalo, for images used in in Chapter 6

Tom Dolphin, for images and content used in Chapter 7 and the Appendix

Record of Changes

Change 1 (December 2015)

This is an updated version of FAA-H-8083-17A, Parachute Rigger Handbook, dated August 2015. This version contains error corrections, revised graphics, and updated performance standards. All pages containing changes are marked with the change number and change date in the page footer. The original pagination has been maintained so that the revised pages may be replaced in lieu of repurchasing or reprinting the entire handbook. The changes made in this version are as follows:

- Updated Table of Contents page numbers (page ix).

- Replaced Figure 2-12 (page 2-8) with version from previous version of the handbook (FAA-H-8083-17, Figure 2-10).

- Revised the third sentence in the second paragraph in the left column of page 2-14: changed "⅜"" to "½"."

- Revised the caption for Figure 3-17 (page 3-7): changed "Tape" to "Webbing."

- Revised the caption for Figure 3-18 (page 3-7): changed "Tape" to "Webbing."

- Revised the last sentence in the first paragraph in the right column of page 7-2: changed "FAA-licensed" to "FAA-certificated."

- Revised the third bullet under Square Canopy – Rib Repair in the right column of page 7-25: added "—mains and reserves; FAA Senior Parachute Rigger—mains."

- Revised Figure G at the bottom of page 7-82: removed "+2"" after "X = Required length."

- Revised Appendix A Table of Contents (page A-1): revised titles of new documents and updated page numbers.

- Revised Appendix A: replaced *PIA TS-100—Standardized Nomenclature for Ram-Air Parachutes* with latest version (pages A-3 – A-10).

- Revised Appendix A: replaced *SAE AS 8015B—Minimum Performance Standards for Parachute Assemblies and Components* with *Personnel PIA TS 135—Performance Standards for Personnel Parachute Assemblies and Components* (pages A-26 – A-43)

- Revised Appendix A: updated page numbering for all documents (pages A3 – A-65).

Table of Contents

Chapter 1

Introduction to Parachute Rigging

Regulations and Human Factors

A parachute rigger has a critical responsibility to anyone who uses a parachute. For many, a special meaning can be attributed to ensuring the safety of a piece of equipment that may save their life or that of a friend. For others, attention to detail may keep a stranger safe during recreational activities, such as skydiving or aerobatic flying. This chapter explains what parachute riggers do and what is required to earn a Parachute Rigger Certificate. In addition, this chapter covers relevant human factor issues and ethical standards.

The term "rigger" originated in the 16th Century and referred to a person who organized, repaired, and maintained sails and lines aboard sailing ships. The rigger was not a high-ranking individual aboard the ship, but he was an essential technician that could not be done without. Likewise, parachute riggers, as indispensible as they are, must operate within strict boundaries set forth by the Federal Aviation Administration (FAA). When parachutes were developed in the early 20th Century, those who sewed the canopies and lines became known as "riggers." In those first decades, anyone with some knowledge of sewing and materials could make or repair parachutes. As the aviation industry grew and matured, the need for trained individuals to pack and maintain the parachutes grew as well. In order to protect the pilots and public who flew in airplanes and relied on parachutes, the government began to license these individuals. Rigging, in reference to parachutes, came to mean: the final adjustment and alignment of the various component sections to provide the proper aerodynamic reaction.

Parachute Rigger Certificates

Parachutes intended for emergency use in civil aircraft in the United States, including the reserve parachute of a dual parachute system to be used for intentional jumping, must be packed, maintained, or altered by a person who holds an appropriate and current Parachute Rigger Certificate. The certificate is issued under Title 14 of the Code of Federal Regulations (14 CFR), part 65, subpart F. These regulations do not apply to an individual who packs the main parachute of a dual parachute pack to be used for intentional jumping. These regulations also do not apply to parachutes packed, maintained, or altered for use by the Armed Forces.

Any person who holds a Parachute Rigger Certificate must present it for inspection if requested by the Administrator or an authorized representative of the National Transportation Safety Board (NTSB) or any federal, state, or local law enforcement officer. A sample certificate is shown in *Figure 1-1.*

Eligibility and Requirements

To be eligible for a Parachute Rigger Certificate issued by the FAA, individuals must be at least 18 years of age; be able to read, write, speak, and understand the English language; and comply with other requirements of 14 CFR, part 65, subpart F, which governs the certification of parachute riggers.

There are two levels of Parachute Rigger Certificate available in the United States: senior and master. The Senior Parachute Rigger candidate must pack a minimum of 20 parachutes of one type and be able to demonstrate the ability to maintain and make minor repairs. The Master Parachute Rigger candidate must have 3 years of experience as a parachute

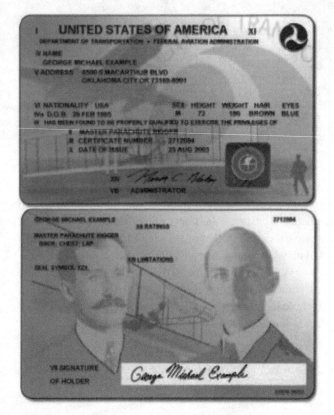

Figure 1-1. *Airman's Certificate—Master Parachute Rigger.*

rigger and have packed at least 100 parachutes of two types in common use (for a total of 200 pack jobs). There are four type ratings that may be placed on a Parachute Rigger Certificate: back, chest, seat, and lap. Of these, the first three are used today. The lap rating applies to parachutes that are basically obsolete. A Senior Parachute Rigger is considered a journeyman technician, and the Master Parachute Rigger is considered an expert.

The two types of certificates differ in the level of experience and responsibility. A Senior Parachute Rigger may pack, as well as maintain, a parachute by making minor repairs. A Master Parachute Rigger has all the privileges of the lesser certificate plus the ability to make major repairs and alter parachutes according to approved data. A major repair is one that, if improperly done, can appreciably affect the airworthiness of the parachute. An example of a major repair might be replacing a damaged canopy panel or altering a harness by changing the size of a main lift web. A minor repair is anything other than a major repair, such as a small patch on a canopy or the replacement of a defective or worn connector link.

Earning a Parachute Rigger Certificate

When an applicant meets the requirements and demonstrates sufficient knowledge and skills as outlined in 14 CFR part 65, subpart F, the supervising parachute rigger (either a senior or

Master Parachute Rigger) "signs off" on the trainee's logbook and provides a letter to the FAA that allows the applicant to take the necessary tests. *[Figure 1-2]*

To Whom It May Concern:

This is to certify that David D. Wolf has packed in excess of 20 back-type parachutes under my supervision in accordance with the manufacturer's instructions and all applicable FAA directives. In addition, he has demonstrated a sound knowledge of the parachute, its construction, packing, maintenance, and use, as well as subparts A & F of 14 CFR part 65.

Sincerely Yours,
Joe Smith
Master parachute rigger #123456789

Figure 1-2. *Certification letter signing off a parachute rigger candidate for FAA testing.*

Once the rigging candidate has successfully achieved a rigger's certificate, they can now begin to learn through experience. Rigging is best learned through apprenticeship; however, it takes a lot of time to become intimately familiar with materials, learn how to identify stains, and experience packing the myriad of sport parachute systems.

Testing

The applicant should take a letter similar to the one depicted in *Figure 1-2*, the applicant's logbook, and any other necessary identification to the nearest FAA Flight Standards District Office (FSDO) or International Field Office (IFO). An FAA Aviation Safety Inspector (ASI) (airworthiness) examines these documents for completeness and eligibility. The applicant is asked to fill out FAA Form 8610-2, Airman Certificate and/or Rating Application. When the inspector has determined that the applicant is eligible to take the test, he or she signs the FAA Form 8610-2. *[Figure 1-3]* Once this is done, the applicant may then go to any of the designated FAA airman knowledge testing centers to take the airman knowledge written test.

The knowledge test consists of 50 multiple-choice questions that are not designed to be tricky or misleading. They cover all basic rigging and packing subject areas in addition to 14 CFR part 65 regulations. A minimum score of 70 percent is required to pass the test. The test is scored immediately on conclusion of the test and a Certified Airman Knowledge Test report is issued to the applicant. *[Figure 1-4]* After

passing the test, the candidate may then make an appointment for taking the oral and practical portion of the test with a Designated Parachute Rigger Examiner (DPRE).

Under 14 CFR, part 183, DPREs are Master Parachute Riggers who have attended an FAA course and are authorized to conduct oral and practical tests for the Administrator. In many cases, these individuals are full-time professionals who work in the parachute industry. Upon the successful completion of the oral and practical tests, in most cases, the DPRE issues a Temporary Parachute Rigger Certificate and a seal symbol to the candidate. *[Figure 1-5]* In some FSDO jurisdictions, the district office may issue the temporary certificate and/or seal symbol. The seal symbol consists of three letters or numbers or a combination of both. *[Figure 1-6]* The seal symbol is very important; it serves as the identifying mark for that individual parachute rigger and is used to seal any parachute that he or she packs.

Alternate Means of Qualifying for a Parachute Rigger Certificate

Active duty military personnel and civilian personnel who work for the military as parachute riggers may qualify for a Senior Parachute Rigger Certificate under the provisions of 14 CFR part 65, section 65.117, Special Certification Rule. If they meet the practical requirements, they need only take a special 25-question test.

A Senior Parachute Rigger applying for a Master Parachute Rigger Certificate only needs to take the oral and practical test. A person with 3 years experience as a parachute rigger, but not holding a Senior Parachute Rigger Certificate, must take both the knowledge test and the oral and practical test. Any parachute rigger, senior or master, who wishes to add additional ratings to his or her certificate needs to take only a practical test for the type rating sought. No additional knowledge test is necessary.

Retesting

If the applicant fails the knowledge test, he or she may retake the test under the following conditions: An applicant may apply for retesting by presenting the failed test report:

- 30 days after the date the applicant failed the test; or

- before 30 days have expired if the applicant presents a signed statement from an airman holding the certificate and rating sought by the applicant certifying that the airman has given the applicant additional instruction in each of the subjects failed and that the airman considers the applicant ready for retesting.

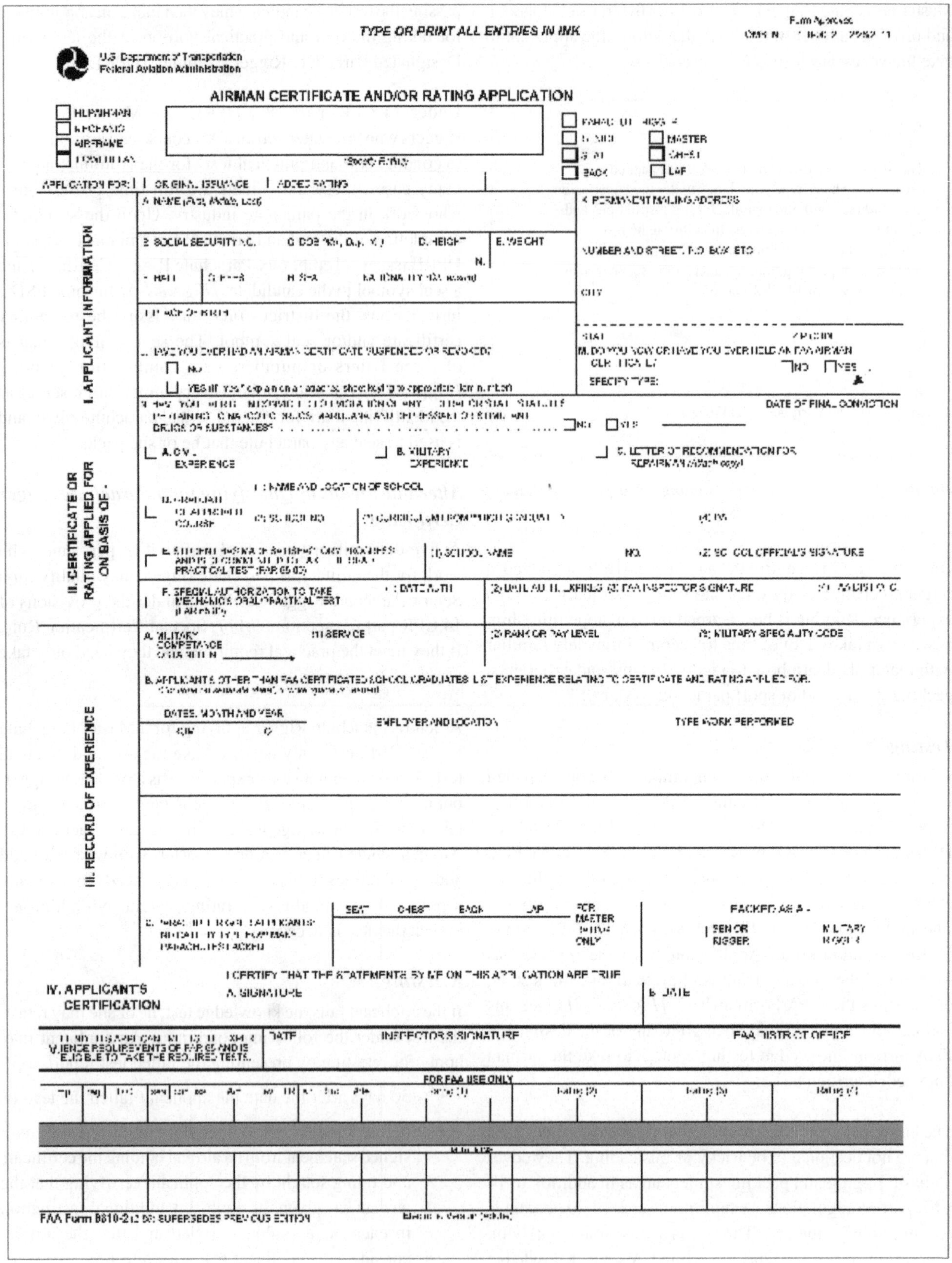

TYPE OR PRINT ALL ENTRIES IN INK

Form Approved

U.S. Department of Transportation
Federal Aviation Administration

AIRMAN CERTIFICATE AND/OR RATING APPLICATION

MECHANIC

AIRFRAME

(Specify Rating)

MASTER

SEAT

CHEST

BACK

LAP

APPLICATION FOR: ORIGINAL ISSUANCE ADDED RATING

I. APPLICANT INFORMATION

A. NAME (First, Middle, Last)

K. PERMANENT MAILING ADDRESS

B. SOCIAL SECURITY NO.

D. HEIGHT

E. WEIGHT

NUMBER AND STREET, P.O. BOX, ETC.

CITY

L. HAVE YOU EVER HAD AN AIRMAN CERTIFICATE SUSPENDED OR REVOKED?

M. DO YOU NOW OR HAVE YOU EVER HELD AN FAA AIRMAN CERTIFICATE?

NO

YES

SPECIFY TYPE:

DATE OF FINAL CONVICTION

DRUGS OR SUBSTANCES?

II. CERTIFICATE OR RATING APPLIED FOR ON BASIS OF:

A. CIVIL EXPERIENCE

B. MILITARY EXPERIENCE

C. LETTER OF RECOMMENDATION FOR REPAIRMAN (Attach copy)

NAME AND LOCATION OF SCHOOL

PRACTICAL TEST

F. SPECIAL AUTHORIZATION TO TAKE MECHANICS ORAL/PRACTICAL TEST

A. MILITARY COMPETENCE OBTAINED IN

SERVICE

(2) RANK OR PAY LEVEL

(3) MILITARY SPECIALTY CODE

III. RECORD OF EXPERIENCE

DATES, MONTH AND YEAR

EMPLOYER AND LOCATION

TYPE WORK PERFORMED

SEAT

CHEST

BACK

LAP

FOR MASTER RATING ONLY

PACKED AS A:

SENIOR RIGGER

MILITARY RIGGER

I CERTIFY THAT THE STATEMENTS BY ME ON THIS APPLICATION ARE TRUE

IV. APPLICANT'S CERTIFICATION

A. SIGNATURE

B. DATE

DATE

INSPECTOR'S SIGNATURE

FAA DISTRICT OFFICE

FOR FAA USE ONLY

Rating (1)

Rating (2)

Rating (3)

Rating (4)

FAA Form 8610-2

SUPERSEDES PREVIOUS EDITION

Figure 1-3. *FAA Form 8610-2, Airman Certificate and/or Rating Application.*

U.S. DEPARTMENT OF TRANSPORTATION
Federal Aviation Administration

Airman Knowledge Test Report

NAME:	APPLICANT ID:
EXAM: Parachute Rigger Senior (RIG)	EXAM ID:
EXAM DATE: 04/20/2004	EXAM SITE:
SCORE: 96 GRADE: PASS	TAKE: 1

Below are subject matter knowledge codes in which questions were answered incorrectly. For code descriptions see the latest version of AC 60-25 Reference Materials and Subject Matter Knowledge Codes for Airman Knowledge Testing, available via the internet: http://afs600.faa.gov
A single code may represent more than one incorrect response.

L90 P38

Expiration Date: 04/30/2006

DO NOT LOSE THIS REPORT

Authorized instructor's statement. (If applicable)

I have given Mr./Ms. ____________________ additional instruction in each subject area shown to be deficient and consider the applicant competent to pass the test.

Last __________ Initial _____ Cert. No. _____ Type _____
(Print clearly)

Signature ____________________

FRAUDULENT ALTERATION OF THIS FORM BY ANY PERSON IS A BASIS FOR SUSPENSION OR REVOCATION OF ANY CERTIFICATES OR RATINGS HELD BY THAT PERSON.

ISSUED BY: ADMINISTRATOR
FEDERAL AVIATION ADMINISTRATION

Figure 1-4. *Sample Airman Knowledge Test Report.*

It is also possible for candidates who pass the test but receive a marginal score to retake the test with the anticipation of getting a higher score. In this case, the candidate must wait a minimum of 30 days from the date the last test was taken to retake a passed test. Prior to retesting, the individual must give his or her current airman test report to the proctor. The most recent test taken reflects the official score.

Responsibilities of a Certificated Parachute Rigger

Parachute riggers have a broad range of responsibilities that include ensuring that proper facilities and equipment are available to him or her, adhering to certain performance standards, record keeping, and use of their seal. The following describes the responsibilities of a certificated parachute rigger.

Facilities and Tools

Issuance of a Parachute Rigger Certificate is just the first step toward becoming a professional parachute rigger. As the un-certificated apprentice gains experience packing, he or she should also begin to acquire an inventory of tools and manuals necessary to exercise the privileges of a certificate. In compliance with 14 CFR part 65, section 65.127, there are several items required. One of these requirements is a smooth tabletop that is at least 3 feet wide by 40 feet long. Note that there is no specification for height. A table is only desirable if the parachute rigger is going to pack round parachutes. With the predominance of square reserve parachutes in the skydiving community, some parachute riggers specialize in packing only square reserves. A table can be used for packing this type of parachute, but the manufacturer may specify any smooth, clean surface of a size that accommodates the canopy. In this case, a clean, carpeted floor does the job and a table may not be necessary. According to 14 CFR part 65, subsection 65.127(b), the parachute rigger needs suitable housing that is adequately heated, lighted, and ventilated for drying and airing parachutes. This is subject to interpretation by the parachute rigger and the Administrator since the standards fluctuate based on location and time of year.

A parachute rigger must have enough tools and equipment to pack and maintain the types of parachutes for which he or she is rated to service. This may include only the basic tools of a packing fid, temporary pin, and pull-up cord if this is all that the manufacturer says is necessary to pack its product. However, there is a broad selection of tools necessary for a well-equipped parachute rigger to possess. These are covered in detail in Chapter 6, Hand Tools, Sewing Machines, and the Parachute Loft.

Performance Standards

A number of performance standards are defined in 14 CFR part 65, section 65.129 to guide the parachute rigger's performance of the duties that fall under the certificate. The parachute rigger may not:

- Pack, maintain, or alter any parachute unless he or she is rated for that type.
- Pack a parachute that is not safe for emergency use.
- Pack a parachute that is not thoroughly dried and aired.
- Alter a parachute in a manner not specifically authorized by the Administrator or the manufacturer of the parachute.

The last item in this list is one that has been abused by many Master Parachute Riggers over the years. The Master Parachute Rigger must have Administrator or manufacturer approval, in writing, to be in compliance with this regulation.

Aside from the necessary tools, 14 CFR part 65, subsection 65.129(f) states that parachute riggers may exercise the privileges of the certificate only if they understand the current manufacturer's instructions for the operation involved. This means that the rigger must possess a copy of the instructions or have access to them during the operation. If they do not have a copy, but the owner of the parachute provides them, then the parachute rigger may pack or maintain the parachute.

I. UNITED STATES OF AMERICA DEPARTMENT OF TRANSPORTATION · FEDERAL AVIATION ADMINISTRATION ii. **TEMPORARY AIRMAN CERTIFICATE**		III. CERTIFICATE NO. Pending

THIS CERTIFIES THAT   IV. Frank Alvin Adams
     V. 2530 S.W. 57ᵗʰ street
        Oklahoma City, OK 73119-9999

DATE OF BIRTH	HEIGHT	WEIGHT	HAIR	EYES	SEX	NATIONALITY	VI.
09/13/1962	72 IN	180	Black	Blue	M	USA	

IX.   has been found to be properly qualified and is hereby authorized in accordance with the conditions of issuance on the reverse of this certificate to exercise the privileges of

    Senior Parachute Rigger

RATINGS AND LIMITATIONS

XII. Seat, Chest, and Back types

XIII. Seal Symbol—KRR

VII. AIRMAN'S SIGNATURE

THIS IS [X] AN ORIGINAL ISSUANCE [ ] A REISSUANCE OF THIS GRADE OF CERTIFICATE   DATE OF SUPERSEDED AIRMAN CERTIFICATE

BY DIRECTION OF THE ADMINISTRATOR

X. DATE OF ISSUANCE 06/02/2005	X. SIGNATURE OF EXAMINER OR INSPECTOR *Floyd E. Long* Floyd E. Long	EXAMINER'S DESIGNATION NO. OR INSPECTOR'S REG. NO. 1404108 DATE DESIGNATION EXPIRES 10/31/2005

FAA Form 8060-4 (8-79) USE PREVIOUS EDITION

Figure 1-5. *FAA Form 8060-4, Temporary Airman Certificate.*

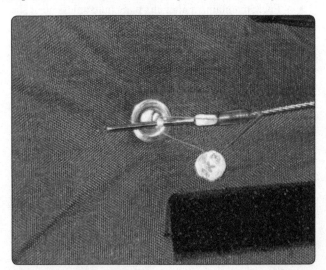

Figure 1-6. *Parachute Rigger's Seal.*

A variation on this theme is accessing the packing instruction via the Internet. Many manufacturers provide manuals via their websites. If the parachute rigger does not download the actual instruction, they must show that they had access during the packing of the parachute. For example, a laptop computer may not have a printer attached but could still meet this requirement.

Parachute riggers are not necessarily required to download the instructions to a hard drive or disk as long as they are able to access the manual in real time. However, if a problem is identified with the parachute rigger's pack job at a later date, the parachute rigger would need to prove to the Administrator that he or she had access to the instructions. Without a hardcopy or downloaded computer files, it would appear that the parachute rigger had not met the rule requirement.

Currency Requirements

Once an individual obtains a Parachute Rigger Certificate, it is valid for life unless surrendered, suspended, or revoked. If the individual intends to work as a parachute rigger and not just have the certificate, it is necessary that he or she maintain currency as a practicing parachute rigger. These currency requirements include at least one of the following.

- Performing parachute rigger duties for at least 90 days within the preceding 12 months.

- Demonstrating to the Administrator the ability to perform those duties.

Record Keeping

Maintaining proper records of parachute rigger activities is an important responsibility. This is necessary for the protection of the parachute rigger, the user of the parachute, and the satisfaction of the Administrator. Under 14 CFR part 65, section 65.131, certificated parachute riggers must document the packing, maintenance, and alteration of parachutes they have performed or supervised. These records normally are documented in a parachute rigger's logbook. The following information must be documented:

- Parachute type and make
- Serial number
- Name and address of the owner
- Description of the work performed
- Date and location of work performed
- Results of any drop tests

These records must be kept for a minimum of 2 years. *Figure 1-7* shows a sample of a logbook page. In addition, each parachute rigger must note on the parachute packing record or data card the following information: *[Figure 1-8]*

- Date and location of packing
- A notation of any defects found on inspection
- Parachute Rigger Certificate number
- Parachute rigger name and signature

While not required on the data card, it has become commonplace for the parachute rigger to note the work performed as well. This is usually noted as assemble and pack (A&P) or inspect and repack (I&R). Professional parachute riggers often use an ink stamp on the data card that indicates name, certificate number, seal symbol, and provides an area for signature. This allows the customer or other parachute riggers to read the name (some signatures are illegible) and to correlate the last entry with the seal on the parachute.

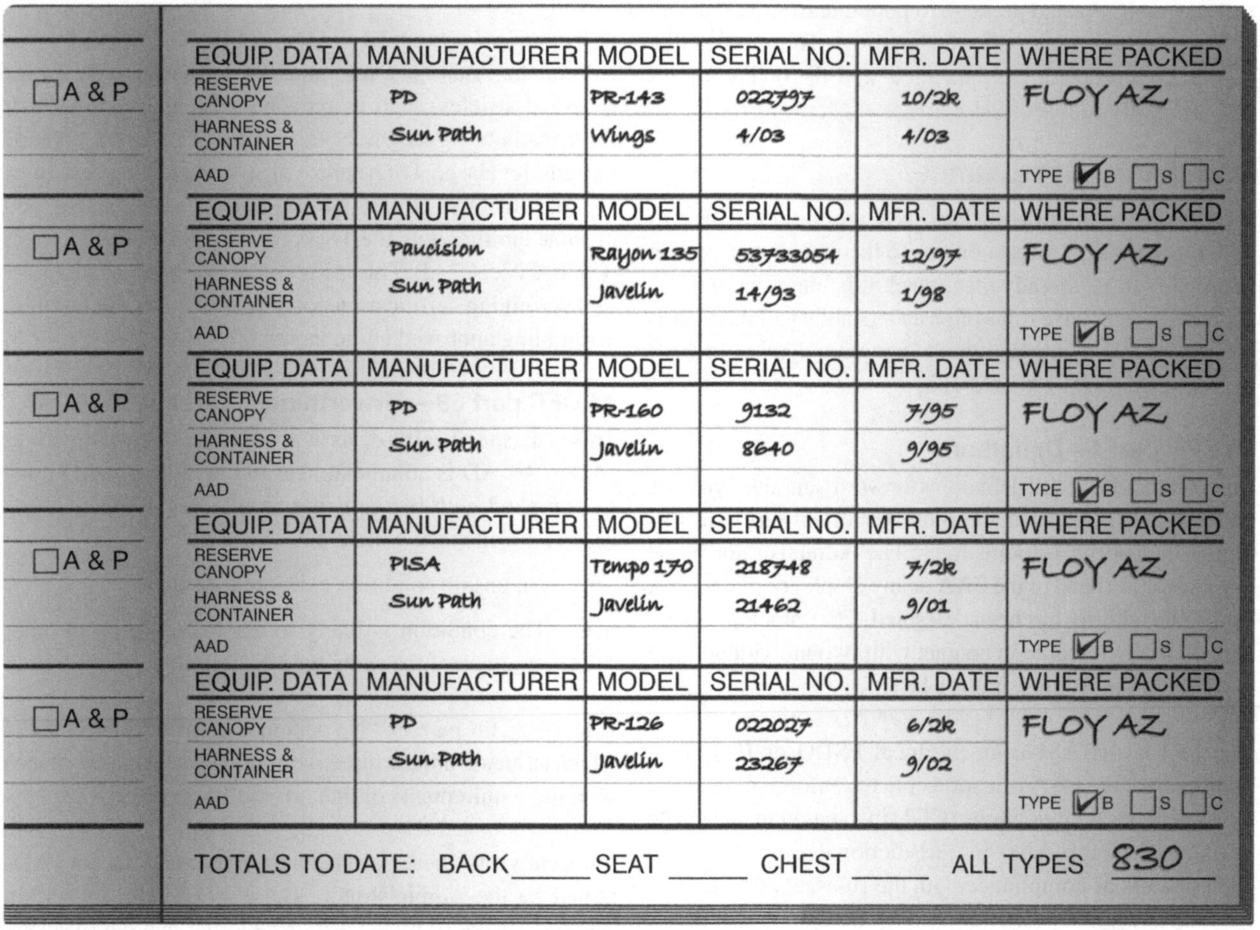

	EQUIP. DATA	MANUFACTURER	MODEL	SERIAL NO.	MFR. DATE	WHERE PACKED
☐ A & P	RESERVE CANOPY	PD	PR-143	022797	10/2k	FLOY AZ
	HARNESS & CONTAINER	Sun Path	Wings	4/03	4/03	
	AAD					TYPE ☑B ☐S ☐C
	EQUIP. DATA	MANUFACTURER	MODEL	SERIAL NO.	MFR. DATE	WHERE PACKED
☐ A & P	RESERVE CANOPY	Paucision	Rayon 135	53733054	12/97	FLOY AZ
	HARNESS & CONTAINER	Sun Path	Javelin	14/93	1/98	
	AAD					TYPE ☑B ☐S ☐C
	EQUIP. DATA	MANUFACTURER	MODEL	SERIAL NO.	MFR. DATE	WHERE PACKED
☐ A & P	RESERVE CANOPY	PD	PR-160	9132	7/95	FLOY AZ
	HARNESS & CONTAINER	Sun Path	Javelin	8640	9/95	
	AAD					TYPE ☑B ☐S ☐C
	EQUIP. DATA	MANUFACTURER	MODEL	SERIAL NO.	MFR. DATE	WHERE PACKED
☐ A & P	RESERVE CANOPY	PISA	Tempo 170	218748	7/2k	FLOY AZ
	HARNESS & CONTAINER	Sun Path	Javelin	21462	9/01	
	AAD					TYPE ☑B ☐S ☐C
	EQUIP. DATA	MANUFACTURER	MODEL	SERIAL NO.	MFR. DATE	WHERE PACKED
☐ A & P	RESERVE CANOPY	PD	PR-126	022027	6/2k	FLOY AZ
	HARNESS & CONTAINER	Sun Path	Javelin	23267	9/02	
	AAD					TYPE ☑B ☐S ☐C

TOTALS TO DATE: BACK_____ SEAT _____ CHEST _____ ALL TYPES *830*_____

Figure 1-7. *Parachute Rigger Logbook Page.*

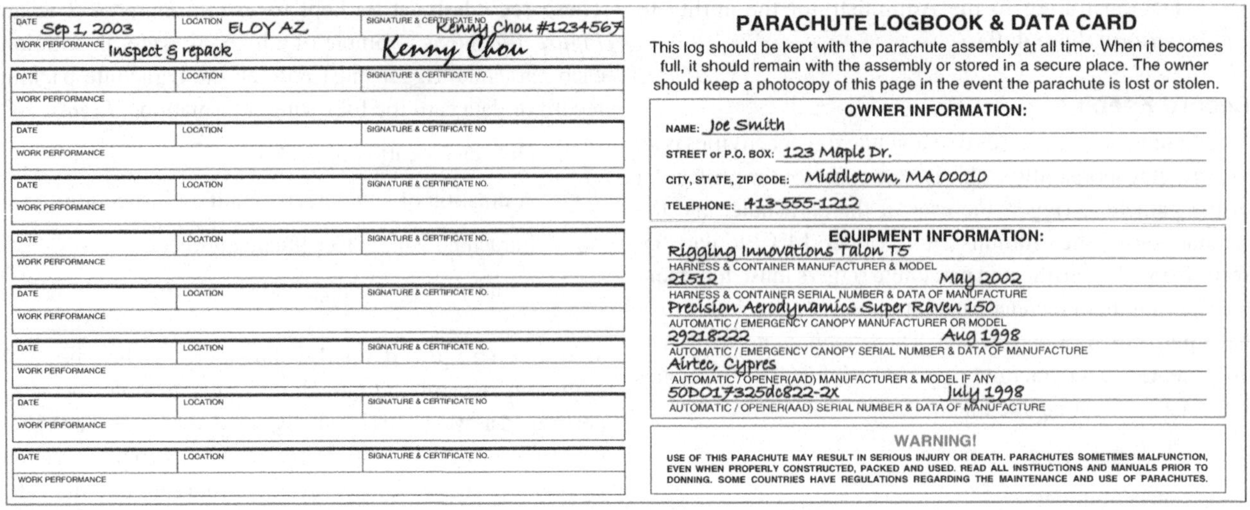

DATE Sep 1, 2003	LOCATION ELOY AZ	SIGNATURE & CERTIFICATE NO. Kenny Chou #1234567
WORK PERFORMANCE Inspect & repack		Kenny Chou

DATE	LOCATION	SIGNATURE & CERTIFICATE NO.
WORK PERFORMANCE		

DATE	LOCATION	SIGNATURE & CERTIFICATE NO
WORK PERFORMANCE		

DATE	LOCATION	SIGNATURE & CERTIFICATE NO.
WORK PERFORMANCE		

DATE	LOCATION	SIGNATURE & CERTIFICATE NO.
WORK PERFORMANCE		

DATE	LOCATION	SIGNATURE & CERTIFICATE NO.
WORK PERFORMANCE		

DATE	LOCATION	SIGNATURE & CERTIFICATE NO.
WORK PERFORMANCE		

DATE	LOCATION	SIGNATURE & CERTIFICATE NO.
WORK PERFORMANCE		

DATE	LOCATION	SIGNATURE & CERTIFICATE NO.
WORK PERFORMANCE		

PARACHUTE LOGBOOK & DATA CARD

This log should be kept with the parachute assembly at all time. When it becomes full, it should remain with the assembly or stored in a secure place. The owner should keep a photocopy of this page in the event the parachute is lost or stolen.

OWNER INFORMATION:

NAME: Joe Smith

STREET or P.O. BOX: 123 Maple Dr.

CITY, STATE, ZIP CODE: Middletown, MA 00010

TELEPHONE: 413-555-1212

EQUIPMENT INFORMATION:

Rigging Innovations Talon T5
HARNESS & CONTAINER MANUFACTURER & MODEL
21512   May 2002
HARNESS & CONTAINER SERIAL NUMBER & DATA OF MANUFACTURE
Precision Aerodynamics Super Raven 150
AUTOMATIC / EMERGENCY CANOPY MANUFACTURER OR MODEL
29218222   Aug 1998
AUTOMATIC / EMERGENCY CANOPY SERIAL NUMBER & DATA OF MANUFACTURE
Airtec, Cypres
AUTOMATIC / OPENER(AAD) MANUFACTURER & MODEL IF ANY
50D017325dc822-2x   July 1998
AUTOMATIC / OPENER(AAD) SERIAL NUMBER & DATA OF MANUFACTURE

WARNING!

USE OF THIS PARACHUTE MAY RESULT IN SERIOUS INJURY OR DEATH. PARACHUTES SOMETIMES MALFUNCTION, EVEN WHEN PROPERLY CONSTRUCTED, PACKED AND USED. READ ALL INSTRUCTIONS AND MANUALS PRIOR TO DONNING. SOME COUNTRIES HAVE REGULATIONS REGARDING THE MAINTENANCE AND USE OF PARACHUTES.

Figure 1-8. *Parachute Packing Record or Data Card.*

Sealing the Parachute

As noted previously, each certificated parachute rigger is issued a unique symbol with which to seal each parachute once he or she packs it in a manner prescribed by the manufacturer. A hand press, 4.75 pound tensile seal thread, and a lead blank are used for this purpose. This ensures that no one tampers with the parachute, and the owner knows that it is ready for use.

Regulatory Compliance

As with other airman certificates, there are additional parts of 14 CFR that are of direct concern to the parachute rigger in addition to those already mentioned. It is important that the parachute rigger have a thorough understanding of these parts in order to avoid any inadvertent non-compliance: 14 CFR parts 1, 21, 39, 91, 105, and 183.

14 CFR part 1—Definitions

This part provides legal definitions for words and abbreviations under this title. One of the more important terms in this part is that of the Administrator. The Administrator is the administrative head of the FAA or any employee of the FAA to whom authority has been delegated. The parachute rigger is most likely to come in contact with two individuals who may act on the Administrator's behalf.

The first is the ASI from the local FSDO or IFO. This employee of the FAA is responsible for enforcement of the Code of Federal Regulations (CFR) in aviation matters. The ASI (airworthiness type) has jurisdictional responsibility in such matters as compliance with the rules, approving data for major repairs or alterations, investigation of accidents, overseeing airshows and demo jumps, or any aviation-related matter.

The second is the local DPRE. This private person is empowered to conduct practical tests for the Administrator.

14 CFR part 21, subpart O—Technical Standard Orders (TSO)

A Technical Standard Order (TSO) is issued by the Administrator and is a minimum performance standard for specified articles, such as parachutes. It is important that the parachute rigger understand the TSO process and the various levels of TSO approval under which parachutes are manufactured. Every parachute rigger should read and become familiar with the TSOs for parachutes, the 23 series (C23b, C23c, C23d). This is important to the parachute rigger in determining certification compatibility when he or she is assembling approved components.

14 CFR part 39—Airworthiness Directives (ADs)

This part specifically deals with Airworthiness Directives (ADs). An AD is an amendment to the CFR. An AD must be complied with before using an affected product. In the case of a parachute, when:

- An unsafe condition exists in a product.

- The condition is likely to exist or develop in other products of the same type or design.

Under 14 CFR part 39, "No person may operate a product to which an airworthiness directive applies except in accordance with the requirements of that airworthiness directive."

In recent years, there have been a number of parachute ADs issued by the Administrator. These ADs prescribe certain actions to be taken by the parachute rigger in order to ensure the safety and function of parachutes that have been found in some manner to be defective. If the parachute rigger does not comply with the AD, the parachute rigger cannot pack, maintain, or alter the affected parachute. ADs are mailed to each certificated parachute rigger on the FAA listing. If the parachute rigger has moved and not complied with the requirements for an address change, the rigger may not receive the AD. This introduces an additional problem. Under 14 CFR, part 65, subpart A—General, section 65.21, airmen must register their change of address within 30 days of moving or they are not able to exercise the privileges of their certificate.

14 CFR part 91—General Operating and Flight Rules

14 CFR part 91, section 91.307 of 14 CFR deals with parachutes and parachuting. This section defines an "approved parachute" and states the repack time for parachutes. Both of these are of vital interest to the parachute rigger.

14 CFR part 105, subpart C—Parachute Equipment and Packing

14 CFR part 105 deals with the use of parachutes in the United States. The following areas are of interest to parachute riggers:

- Main parachutes used for intentional jumping must be packed by the person jumping or by a U.S. certificated parachute rigger.

- The auxiliary parachute must be packed by a certificated and appropriately-rated parachute rigger.

- If the parachute is made from synthetic materials, it must be packed within 180 days of its use. If it is made from materials subject to mold or mildew (natural fibers), then it must be packed within 60 days of use.

- If a main static line is used, it must meet certain requirements as to its use and configuration.

- An approved parachute is defined as a parachute manufactured under a type certificate or a TSO (C-23 series), or a personnel-carrying U.S. military parachute (other than a high altitude, high speed, or ejection type), identified by a Navy Air Facility, an Army Air Field, an Air Force-Navy drawing number, an Army Air Field order number, or any military designation or specification number.

Rigging Ethics

As parachute riggers gain additional experience, they are occasionally faced with situations that involve less than ideal circumstances. For example, they may be presented with a new jumper who has purchased old or damaged equipment that may or may not be airworthy; or it may be a pilot who purchased an acrobatic plane that came with a parachute that is far too small for his or her weight. These situations involve more than just the technical knowledge for a Parachute Rigger Certificate.

In the case of the pilot above, depending on which TSO the parachute is certified, there may be a weight and speed limitation for the system. For example, TSO C23c category B has a limitation of 254-pound exit weight and a speed limitation of 150 knots. Imagine a pilot who weighs 225 pounds and his airplane regularly exceeds the 150-knot envelope during maneuvering. If this pilot brings a parachute to a parachute rigger for repacking, the first thing the parachute rigger should notice is the size of the pilot. When the parachute rigger inspects the parachute, he notices that it has a 22-foot diameter round canopy. The parachute rigger finds that with the pilot at 225 pounds, his clothes at 5 pounds, and the parachute at 20 pounds, he is at 250 pounds or just under the limit. However, in looking at the owner's manual, the parachute rigger cannot find any information in the weight-carrying limit of the canopy. In addition, this particular parachute was made by a company that is no longer in business. The parachute appears to be in good condition visually but is 30 years old. In this situation, the parachute rigger is faced with a number of questionable areas that are detailed below.

Certification Specifications

The practical matter of the above pilot's use of the parachute is that he is at the maximum limits of the certification specifications of that parachute. If he does not eat a big breakfast or gain much weight before using the parachute, he might stay under the weight limit. The speed limitation is probably exceeded on a regular basis during acrobatic maneuvers. If he needs to use the parachute at some point, there should be enough of a safety margin built into the design and testing of the parachute to be sufficient.

Pilot Versus Parachute Size

With 250 pounds under a 22-foot diameter canopy, the pilot probably drops from the sky at an excessive rate of descent. A common assumption in this situation is that it is unlikely he needs to use the parachute, but if he does, will it save his life?

Parachute Service Life

There is no service life on the parachute; it may be considered airworthy as long as it meets its TSO. While the parachute appears to be in good condition, there are not many non-destructive tests available to the parachute rigger in the field to make this determination. It may be possible to drop test the parachute, but the cost would probably outweigh the value of the system. It is up to the parachute rigger to make the determination as to the airworthiness of the parachute system. When the parachute rigger seals the parachute and signs the data card, the rigger is saying it is ready, thereby putting the customer's life on the line.

What should the parachute rigger do? This is not just a theoretical situation—it is one that has been experienced many times by many parachute riggers. All of the above information plus economic factors complicate the parachute rigger's decision. If the rigger does not pack the parachute, the pilot may take it down the road to another parachute rigger for a second opinion who may not have the same standards. An added factor is liability exposure. If the parachute rigger signs off on a questionable parachute and an accident occurs later, the rigger may be exposed to disciplinary action from the Administrator in addition to civil action in the courts. There are no hard and fast rules in these situations, but instead the parachute rigger must exercise the best judgment he or she can summon based on experience and the information at hand.

Most professional parachute riggers would refuse to pack the parachute described in the scenario above due to the age of the parachute, the size of the individual, and the potential use parameters. The conscientious rigger should give the pilot all of the facts concerning permissible exit weights and speeds and probable system performance, or lack thereof. Perhaps the pilot can be convinced to purchase a more appropriate emergency parachute, one that is certified for higher weight and speeds.

Chapter Summary

This first chapter summarized the need-to-know areas of 14 CFR and familiarized the rigger candidate with the 8610-2 Rating Application and other pertinent documents. Become familiar with 14 CFR online at http://www.ecfr.gov/cgi-bin/text-idx?SID=ea18c91ab7072a02b2cefba39393ebfc&tpl=/ecfrbrowse/Title14/14tab_02.tpl. There is an overview of the rigger's responsibilities, limitations, and currency requirements. Becoming a well-rounded parachute rigger is a serious undertaking and requires independent study and determination to learn the history of parachutes, as well as current methods and materials.

The most important thought to keep in mind with regard to parachute rigging is that the purpose of the 180-day inspection and repack cycle is to inspect the parachute and all of its sub-assemblies, as well as the harness/container system and all of its sub-assemblies. Almost any parachute could theoretically remain packed for years and still open and function normally if stored in a perfect environment, as long as all the materials were chemically stable. History has shown however, that in rare instances fabrics can break down spontaneously and their chemical makeup can change, possibly compromising the integrity of the entire system. Therefore it is imperative that a thorough inspection is done on a frequent and regular basis by a competent rigger prior to repack. The conscientious rigger is the ultimate safety net between the jumper and the ground.

Chapter 2

Design and Construction

Introduction

It is important for the aspiring rigger to understand basic design parameters and construction techniques of modern parachute systems. The master rigger must have a thorough understanding of these areas to perform any desired or necessary alterations. An understanding of how the systems or components were originally designed, and why they were constructed as they were, is essential. Any proposed alteration may degrade the function and/or structural integrity of the assembly or component thereby causing it to fail.

TSO Documents			C23c		C23d	
			AS-8015a		AS-8015b	
			1984-1994		1994-Present	
...cifications	Low speed	3000 lb	Category A	Weight: 300 lb Speed: 150 knots	Variable- Maximum operating weight x 1.2	
	Standard categ...	5000 lb	Category B	Weight: 300 lb Speed: 175 knots	Maximum operating weight x 1.2	
			Category C	Weight: 300 lb Speed: 230 knots		
Placard limitations	Low speed	3000 lb	Category A	Weight: 198 lb Speed: 130 knots	Placard with average peak force measured during the strength drop.	
	Standard category	5000 lb	Category B	Weight: 254 lb Speed: 150 knots		
			Category C	Weight: 254 lb Speed: 175 knots		
Number of drop tests		28		68		68

Parachute Design and Construction

The design parameters for certificated parachutes are set forth in Federal Aviation Administration (FAA) documents, specifically within the Technical Standard Order (TSO) system. Parachute certification standards fall within the TSO C23 series. Currently, there are three TSO documents under which parachutes are manufactured: C23b, C23c, and C23d. Appendix A of this handbook explains these standards in detail. Military parachutes are manufactured and certified under a military drawing system; however, some manufacturers have certified them under the TSO system as well.

Advisory Circular (AC) 105-2D, Sport Parachuting explains that a parachute assembly normally, but not exclusively, consists of the following major components: a canopy, a deployment device, a pilot chute and/or drogue, risers, a stowage container, a harness, and an actuation device (ripcord).

Component Parts

Parachute assemblies and component parts are identified in the following discussion. The appropriate nomenclatures, as well as the commonly accepted names, are defined below.

Main Parachute Canopy

The main parachute canopy is used in conjunction with a reserve parachute assembly as the primary parachute canopy for a premeditated jump. The main canopy consists of everything from the main riser connector links to the bridle attachment point (excluding the steering toggles). The major parts are the suspension lines and the canopy. *[Figure 2-1]*

Reserve Parachute Canopy

The reserve parachute canopy is worn in conjunction with a main parachute used for premeditated jumps. The reserve parachute consists of everything from the reserve riser connector links to the bridle attachment point (excluding the steering toggles). The major parts are the canopy, suspension lines, and any type of deployment device that is sewn to the canopy or lines.

Emergency Parachute Canopy

The emergency parachute canopy is worn for emergency, unpremeditated use only. The canopy may be identical to the reserve parachute canopy.

Harness/Container

The harness and container assembly includes all the remaining parts necessary to complete an airworthy parachute system except for the canopies. The basic harness/

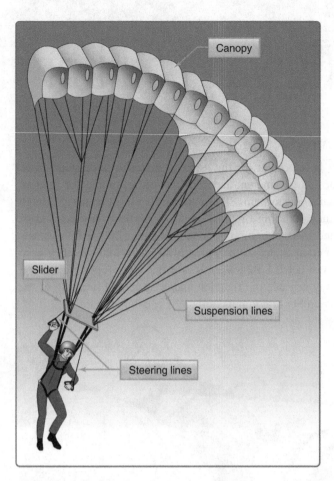

Figure 2-1. *Component parts of a ram-air parachute.*

container assembly is what remains when all items that can be removed without unstitching have been removed. Most sport parachute assemblies have the harness and containers integrated into one assembly, but many military assemblies may be disassembled into separate harness and container subassemblies. The following items are subcomponents of the harness/container assembly and are shown in *Figure 2-2*.

Pilot Chutes and Bridles for the Main and Reserve Parachutes

The pilot chute is a small parachute or similar device that enters the airstream when released to act as a drag device and withdraw the canopy from the container. As such, it maintains tension on the canopy and lines during the deployment process, except for reserve "Free Bags." Pilot chutes are either spring-loaded or manually thrown into the airstream as a "hand deployed" pilot chute. Some military or emergency pilot chutes are ballistically deployed. A bridle is a piece of line or webbing that connects the canopy or deployment device to the pilot chute.

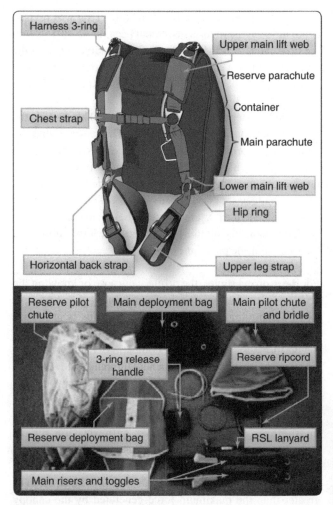

Figure 2-2. *Subcomponents of the harness/container assembly.*

Ripcords or Equivalent Devices for the Main and Reserve Parachutes

The ripcord is a device for securing the container closed prior to use. It usually consists of a handle, a flexible cable, one or more pins, and a device for securing the cable to the handle. Some ripcords use a stiffened cable instead of a pin. Similar to the ripcord is the main riser retain/release cable/handle assembly if the parachute is equipped with a main riser release system, such as the 3-ring release.

Deployment Devices for the Main and Reserve Parachutes

Deployment devices are designed to provide an orderly and controlled deployment of the parachute during use. Typical devices include bags, sleeves, pockets, straps, diapers, and sliders.

Main Parachute Release Mechanism and Associated Handles or Static Lines

The main parachute release mechanism has two parts. One part is attached to the harness and the other to the risers.

Typically such devices are the 3-ring release or Capewell releases. These types may utilize a separate release handle to provide release of both sides with one motion. This cable/handle assembly consists of a cable to each riser and a velcro-mounted handle. The cables must be kept lubricated to function properly. There are several types of cable coatings used by various manufacturers. Nylon coating, which is hydroscopic, includes the yellow (Lolon) coated cables and the clear coated cables. This type of cable should be oiled frequently as climate conditions dictate. When you pull the cable between your fingers, if it squeaks like clean hair, then it needs to be lubricated. The Red or (new) orange-coated cable is pure FEP Teflon coating and requires no maintenance. Typically when the cable is removed from its housing, it has black oil in spots along the cable. This black oil is the residue of the cutting oil used in the manufacture of the housings. It is not harmful. In fact, if this black oil is distributed evenly along the cable, it provides limited lubrication. There is no need to worry about sand or dirt being attracted to the oil on the cable as it is more important for the cable to be lubricated than it is to be clean. *[Figure 2-3]* The reserve may employ a static line (RSL) that is activated upon cutaway. This is covered in greater detail later in the chapter.

Figure 2-3. *Lolon cable is yellow. Teflon cable is red or orange.*

Risers and Associated Steering Toggles

Risers are part of the suspension system between the lines and the harness or load. Generally made of webbing, emergency parachutes usually have the risers integral to the harness. If they are detachable and not integral and are being used for an emergency parachute, they require a cross connector, as they are tested with only one side connected. Main risers used on sport or military systems used for intentional jumping have release mechanisms installed. Steering toggles are usually design specific to the riser for the type of canopy installed. Ram air canopies use the steering toggle to lock the deployment brake. Pulling on the toggle after opening releases the brake. Premature brake release is a major cause of malfunctions. *[Figure 2-4]*

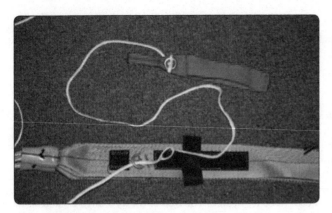

Figure 2-4. *Toggle through brake eye and stowed.*

Other Harness/Container Assembly Components

Other components designed to function as part of the harness/container assembly, such as closing loops, also may be used. Closing loops used with automatic activation devices (AADs) on reserve or emergency parachutes are usually design specific to ensure proper operation of the system.

TSO Standards

The original TSO C23b for parachutes came into existence in 1949. The specifications were revised in 1984 to C23c and again in 1994 to C23d. The TSO is a simple two-page document that specifies the requirements for certification. This document also references a performance standard that the parachute must meet. C23b parachutes were tested to standards under National Aircraft Standards Specifications NAS-804. When the TSO was revised in 1984, the specification document was drafted under the auspices of the Society of Automotive Engineers (SAE) S-17 committee as Aerospace Standard AS-8015. When the TSO was revised again in 1994, the revised document became AS-8015b with the original as AS-8015a. *Figure 2-5* is a table showing the pertinent points of each of the TSO certifications. For a more thorough study of the documents, refer to Appendix B.

The TSO system consists of two parts. The first is the performance standards listed above. This ensures that the parachute performs as specified. The second is the production approval, which ensures that the manufacturer is able to produce the parachute as designed and tested. While minor design changes are allowed, any major design change must be submitted to the FAA for approval before implementation. A major change is anything that affects the airworthiness of the system of the parachute.

For the aspiring rigger, the primary purpose of knowing the TSO system is determining the compatibility of components when assembling the parachute system. This is necessary in order to ensure that, besides fitting together properly, the performance standards are compatible. Under Advisory Circular (AC) 105-2, Sport Parachute Jumping, "the assembly or mating of separately approved components may be made by a certificated and appropriately rated parachute rigger or parachute loft in accordance with the manufacturer's instructions and without further authorization by the manufacturer or the FAA." Under these guidelines, there are certain parameters that must be met. One of them is to ensure that "the strength of the harness must always be equal to or greater than the maximum force generated by the canopy during the certification tests." Full knowledge of the TSO documents ensures that the above requirements are met.

TSO Documents					
TSO number	**C23b**		**C23c**		**C23d**
Performance standard	NAS-804		AS-8015a		AS-8015b
Effective dates	1949-1984		1984-1994		1994-Present
Performance specifications	Low speed	3000 lb	Category A	Weight: 300 lb Speed: 150 knots	Variable- Maximum operating weight x 1.2
	Standard category	5000 lb	Category B	Weight: 300 lb Speed: 175 knots	Maximum operating weight x 1.2
			Category C	Weight: 300 lb Speed: 230 knots	
Placard limitations	Low speed	3000 lb	Category A	Weight: 198 lb Speed: 130 knots	Placard with average peak force measured during the strength
	Standard category	5000 lb	Category B	Weight: 254 lb Speed: 150 knots	drop.
			Category C	Weight: 254 lb Speed: 175 knots	
Number of drop tests		28		68	68

Figure 2-5. *TSO comparisons.*

Canopy Design

Accomplished design skills are not necessary for the rigger to properly service parachutes. The skills involved to become a designer can take several years of training and practice. It is necessary, however, that the rigger understands some of the basic concepts to relate the performance characteristics to the design theory of the components involved. For the average rigger, these concepts are accepted as those proven and tested in the finished product. The following are specific areas that the rigger should understand to determine the identity, function, and assembly of parachute components and their interaction.

Understanding the sequence and method of deployment is necessary when assembling components to assure proper function. Most ram air parachutes are trimmed nose down, and as such the canopy tries to fly over its nose during deployment. This flight angle causes the top skin nose of the canopy to roll over the bottom skin leading edge closing off the cell preventing inflation. To counter this, the trailing edge of the canopy is deflected downward to apply brakes during inflation; this holds the nose up and open allowing air intake. These are called "deployment brakes" and are implemented by providing a "brake eye" in the steering line of the canopy located so as to apply the proper amount of brakes. The steering line is pulled down through the steering guide ring on the risers and locked with the nose of the steering toggle during the packing process. Loss of one or both brakes during opening will most likely cause a malfunction. Loss of one causes the canopy to turn into that side as the cells remain collapsed and the inflated side over-flies the collapsed side. In flight corrective action is to grab both toggles and apply both brakes evenly and quickly.

Nomenclature

All riggers should become familiar with Parachute Industry Association (PIA) Technical Standard 100 (TS-100), Standardized Nomenclature for Ram-Air Inflated Gliding Parachutes (See Appendix I). This document is the official language and terminology used for ram-air parachutes. It specifies the parts of the parachute, the various construction methods, and the seam configurations used. This is necessary for the rigger to understand the manuals and repair procedures provided by the manufacturers for their products.

Figure 2-6 identifies the components of a typical round emergency parachute. The nomenclature of this design has remained constant for several decades with a few exceptions. While some riggers who skydive think that the square parachute has replaced it, the round parachute still has many uses, and in certain instances, fulfills some

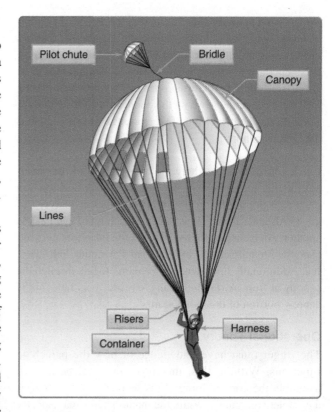

Figure 2-6. *Round parachute assembly.*

mission requirements better than the square parachute. Poynter's Parachute Manual, Volume 1, Chapter 8, provides an excellent discussion of the design parameters and characteristics of round parachutes for those needing more technical background.

Construction Concepts and Techniques

TS-100 describes the various ram-air construction methods such as half-cell chord wise, full-cell "I" beam chord wise, full-cell interlocking "T" chord wise, and span wise configurations. When learning the various construction methods, the beginning rigger can become confused as to how the seams are folded together. Seeing the schematic diagrams of the various configurations can help in the repair sequence. Additionally, there are two basic methods of construction for the main seam used on modern ram airs. One method is to roll the adjacent bottom skins with the attendant rib together and double needle 301 stitch to hold the joint. Line attachment tabs are then appliquéd over the rolled seam for subsequent line attachment. The other method is the foil method where the rib has the line attachment tab attached directly to it and is flat stitched to the bottom skins allowing the bottom edge of the rib to be exposed.

Round parachute construction is divided into two primary techniques: bias and block construction. Bias construction is most prevalent in the early parachutes and military designs. It is generally the stronger of the two techniques due to its ability to stretch more during opening. In bias construction, the fabric is cut and sewn so that the warp and filler threads are at 45° to the centerline of the gore. A typical example is the 28' C-9 canopy.

Block construction is where the warp threads of the panels are parallel to the hem of the canopy. Block construction gained in popularity in the lightweight sport reserves of the 1970s and 1980s. They were easier to build and packed smaller. An example of this design is the Phantom/Aerostar canopies, manufactured by National Parachute Industries, Inc. Additionally lines may run from link to link through the canopy or from skirt to link using reinforcement tape for the canopy portion of the radial seam.

Operational Theory

The rigger must have knowledge of how the parachute functions. Without this, the rigger may not be able to assemble the correct components so that they function as a complete assembly. While the manufacturer may specify what components are to be used with their particular design, with the vast numbers of products on the market today, there are an infinite number of combinations being used by the skydiving community. While seeming to be compatible with each other, many designs have subtle differences that affect their performance and operation. Such differences include pilot chute drag capability and bag extraction force requirements. Pilot chutes should not be interchanged unless the drag capability and container extraction force is known.

Materials

The materials used in construction have changed over the last several years. This has resulted in better performance and durability. The use of incorrect materials can have a detrimental effect on the opening, flying, and landing characteristics of the parachute. The growth in popularity of the ram-air canopies in the 1970s required new fabrics for the designs to function. Very low permeability fabric was necessary for the canopy to remain inflated and maintain the aerodynamic airfoil shape. To reduce the drag created by the suspension lines, newer lightweight and high-strength materials were used. First Dacron®, followed by Kevlar®, and now Spectra® and Vectran®. While reducing the line bulk and drag, these materials have introduced newer problems into the designs.

The ultra-low permeability fabrics inflate faster and have almost zero stretch. As a result, the opening forces increase considerably. These effects have contributed to newer packing and deployment methods to reduce the loads on the parachutist

and harness. These, in turn, affect the design of the container systems. Using this as an example, the rigger can see the chain of cause and effect in the design process. Complete coverage of materials is presented in Chapter 3 of this handbook.

Damage

Damage patterns identified during the inspection of canopies can highlight problems caused from packing or incorrect use. By being able to identify these patterns, the rigger can provide the user with correct technique and, thereby, prevent possible injury or death. In addition, the rigger can provide valuable feedback to the manufacturer of potentially serious problems with new designs once they have been subjected to real world conditions. While manufacturers conduct extensive testing programs before releasing new products to the market, very often, subtle problems do not arise until the parachute has been in the field for an extended period of time.

Containers

The container component assembly of the parachute system is that part which encloses the canopy(s) and lines, the deployment device (if used), and the pilot chute unless it is externally mounted as on a "pop top." It is held closed by the use of cones or loops, which are secured by ripcord pins or locking pins such as are used on hand deploy systems. Containers may consist of single units as are used on pilot emergency systems or multiple units such as are used on skydiving piggyback systems. The term "pack" is used interchangeably with container. The harness and container assembly may be called the pack and harness. The term "packtray" is used to refer to the bottom panel or section of the container where the lines may be stowed during packing.

Early containers were simply a bag-shaped unit that the canopy was stuffed into and then tied closed. The parachute was static line deployed and the parachutist simply fell away from the balloon or aircraft allowing the canopy to deploy. With the advent of manually deployed free fall systems, the need for a more secure and tailored design became evident.

Originally, the parachute systems were identified by the position at which they were located in relation to the body of the user. These were the back parachute, seat parachute, chest parachute, and lap parachute. The containers were usually rectangular in shape with four closing flaps. These configurations were primarily dictated by the need to fit the assembly into the flightdeck of the aircraft.

With the growth of skydiving, the container configurations and the associated terminology changed. The original location of the main parachute on the back and the reserve on the chest became known as the "conventional" configuration. *[Figure 2-7]* The original tandem configuration with both

Figure 2-7. *Conventional container.*

Figure 2-8. *Piggyback containers.*

the main and reserve on the back became known as a "piggyback," and the introduction of a two-person parachute system became the new "tandem." *[Figure 2-8 and 2-9]*

Configuration

When canopies were packed into early bag-type containers, they always wanted to assume a spherical or round shape. For the container to remain flat, it was necessary to tailor the fabric and then use frames or bow stiffeners to keep it flat and compress the pilot chute. Back designs utilized multiple cones and pins, usually three or four to maintain the length and width. Seat containers were usually more square and thicker since they were held in place by the seat pan. Most use two cones and pins for closing. The same was used for chest and lap parachutes. Many military systems still utilize these basic configurations today.

With the introduction of skydiving in the 1960s, most equipment was of modified military designs, and the first generation of commercial products was simply colored versions of these designs. In the 1970s, skydiving canopies had progressed to ram-air designs, which were smaller in volume and had different deployment requirements. Container designs evolved to meet these requirements. The introduction of the hand deploy pilot chute was probably the

Figure 2-9. *Tandem container system.*

most influential concept in the evolving container design. Cones were replaced by fabric closing loops, and main ripcords and pins were replaced by hand deploy bridles and locking pins. It was no longer necessary to compress the spring-loaded pilot chute inside the container. Thru closing loops were used to compress the pack and make it thinner to conform to the body shape. The use of deployment bags and other devices helped provide shaping to the container. This was true for both square and round canopies.

Today, most modern container designs have completely done away with frames and bow stiffeners. This has resulted in smaller, more flexible, more comfortable, and more efficient container designs. Instead of metal stiffeners, nylon plastic is used to reinforce the container flaps for backing the grommets. The nylon is lighter, easier to work with, and cheaper. Many of the modern military designs now follow the design concepts pioneered by the sport industry as they have proven better and more cost effective. *Figure 2-10* shows a modern military container.

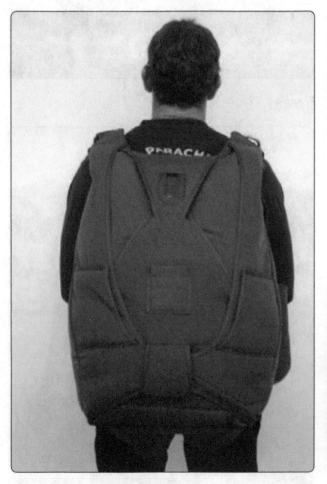

Figure 2-10. *Modern military container.*

Modern Design Concepts

The containers of today do more than simply enclose the canopy and deployment device. Sport containers in particular need to be designed so that they contribute to the deployment needs of the specific parachute. Piggyback designs have separate requirements for the main and reserve containers.

The reserve container is generally small, tight, and mostly wedge-shaped. Virtually all popular sport systems are designed around the use of a ram-air canopy. The deployment method of choice is a Type 5 deployment bag. In the early days of the ram-air reserve, there were certain container design requirements specified by the manufacturers which are listed below:

1. A hesitator loop configuration secures the bridle and holds the bag in until the reserve pilot chute is deployed and under drag. *[Figure 2-11]*

Figure 2-11. *Square reserve hesitator loop configuration.*

2. Nonrestrictive corners to allow the bag to be lifted off by the bridle in the event of a horseshoe-type malfunction. *[Figure 2-12]*

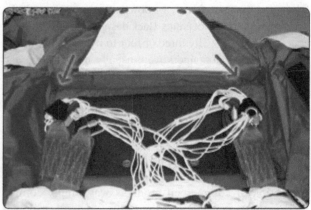

Figure 2-12. *Non-restrictive container corners.*

These requirements were adhered to for many years. Today, containers achieve the required holding and deployment needs through design tailoring. The bottom corners of the reserve container are designed so that the bag is held in place while the pilot chute and bridle deploy and then releases the bag, rotating it out of the container top to bottom into the airstream. At the same time, the bag can still deploy quickly in the event of a horseshoe-type malfunction.

The main container is less restrictive than the reserve in holding the main canopy in place during deployment. This is important so that there is no tendency for the bag to twist or be unstable on deployment. With many of the main canopies used today, if the bag is unstable, it results in the main canopy opening unevenly and causing spins and possible malfunctions. Along with the main bag, the main risers must be able to deploy evenly for the same reasons.

In the early days of skydiving, the primary body position was a stable, face-to-earth position. This resulted in the main container being behind the parachutist out of the airflow. One of the primary problems faced during those days was the high incidence of pilot chute hesitations. This was the result of poor training and lack of understanding of that air flow. Eventually skydivers learned to sit up during deployment causing the air to flow over their back sweeping the pilot chute into the main stream. Hand deployed pilot chutes were developed to make packing easier and eliminate the need for a metal ripcord.

In the face-to-earth position, the primary purpose of the container is to hold the canopy and pilot chute closed, and then allow it to open during deployment. Today, body positions experienced during free fall range from head-down to feet-to-earth and everything in between. Where speeds formerly experienced ranged from 110 miles per hour (mph) to maybe 140 mph, today speeds in a head-down position can exceed 200 mph. This has changed the container dynamics to ensure a more secure system and increased protection from the wind blast. These changes have resulted in more secure and streamlined configurations to accommodate these new requirements. *Figure 2-13* shows a modern container design shaped to meet the high-speed airflows of today.

An additional area that needs to be addressed when designing piggyback systems is the main riser covers. In the early days of sport piggyback designs, the main risers were held in position by webbing keepers. As the sport progressed, the use of fully enclosed main riser covers became the norm. In their attempt to protect the main risers during high-speed free fall, some designs tend to restrict the deployment of the reserve container in the event of a "total" main pack malfunction. When this happens and the main container remains closed, the main riser covers do not open. Because of this, there is additional restriction over the upper corners of the reserve

Figure 2-13. *Modern aerodynamic container design.*

container. This contributes to higher reserve bag release forces. In severe cases, this can result in a reserve pilot chute in tow with potential serious consequences. The balance between sufficient main riser protection and the requirement for unhindered reserve deployment is a critical design feature.

Most modern sport parachute containers have housings of some sort to accommodate ripcords and riser release cables. These flexible metal conduits come in 3 basic types in varying diameters: non-compressible, relaxed, and non-extendable. The housing type is critical to provide proper protection and function for the usage. Non-extendable is used for most ripcord housings, except on Navy seat packs. Relaxed refers to the ripcord housing that is not completely compressible. Non-compressible housing is the correct type to use for 3-ring cutaway systems so the compression does not cause the sides to release unevenly.

Harness Design

According to Poynter's Parachute Manual, "the harness is an arrangement of cotton, linen, nylon, or Dacron® webbing, which is designed to conform to the shape of the load (usually the body), to be carried in order to secure it properly so that the opening forces and the weight of the load are evenly distributed during opening and descent."

2-9

The earliest harness was nothing more than a swing seat that the parachutist sat on and then held onto the risers or suspension straps. It soon became apparent that if the openings were in any way uneven, it could be very precarious for the parachutist. While the sling seat worked for the ride down, it was necessary to add additional straps to secure the parachutist. These straps included the leg, back, and chest straps. The standard harness configuration is equipped to secure a torso, head, arms, and legs with straps. Others have been added over time for additional purposes, such as survival kits or cushions. *Figure 2-14* shows a basic military style harness. This harness configuration has seven points of adjustment to allow fitting of most military personnel.

Figure 2-14. *Military harness.*

Most of the early parachute systems had the harness detachable from the containers. This allowed interchangeability for various models. In the 1970s, skydiving systems began to integrate the harness into a true harness/container assembly. This was accomplished by sandwiching the harness between the container and backpad and sewing them together. *Figure 2-15* shows one of the earliest custom systems called the "super swooper." This harness was the precursor of today's sport harnesses.

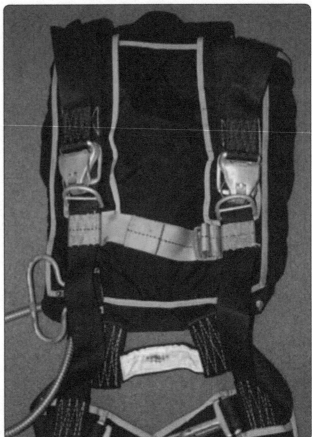

Figure 2-15. *Super swooper harness.*

As skydiving and the sport parachute industry has grown, most of the equipment is now custom-built for each individual. The standard piggyback harness configuration of today is a fixed main lift web with adjustments only at the chest and leg straps. *[Figure 2-16]* Elimination of the extra hardware and webbing has resulted in a dramatic reduction in weight of modern systems. Along with this has been an increase in comfort and flexibility. One of the most innovative designs adopted in recent years is the "articulated" harness. This design incorporates metal rings at the hip junction and the chest-strap attachment. *[Figure 2-17]* These rings allow a full range of motion both in the air and on the ground and increase the fit and comfort of the harness. Note however that hardware incorporated into the main lift web or junction of a harness should be equal in strength to the webbing or at least the certification of the harness. Type 7 harness webbing is 6,000 pounds tensile. Type 13 harness webbing is 7,000 pounds tensile. The stainless steel "RW-8" is certified to 3,500 pounds. The stainless steel 5010 Harness Ring is certified to 5,000 pounds.

The "stepped" harness is not as strong as the continuous horizontal harness *[Figure 2-18]*. If point loading occurs on a stepped harness, stitching may break, and the junction can

Figure 2-16. *Standard piggyback harness.*

fail with disastrous results. With a continuous horizontal, if all the stitching were to fail, the wearer would still be wrapped in webbing and restrained in the harness.

In recent years and with the increasing popularity of vertical skydiving or "free flying," greater speeds are experienced with corresponding higher loads on the harnesses. For many years, harnesses were overbuilt as they were basically copies of military designs. As the sport has progressed, equipment has been made lighter and smaller.

Bridles and Deployment Devices

In the early days of parachutes, the lines and canopy were stowed in the container. During the deployment process, the canopy was extracted first, followed by the lines. This was known as a "canopy first" deployment. If the canopy inflated before tension was applied to the lines, a malfunction was highly likely and a hard opening shock a certainty. Over the years, it was learned that the deployment process needed to be controlled to prevent malfunctions. Hence the introduction of deployment devices that changed the deployment sequence to "lines first" by preventing canopy skirt from spreading until the lines were fully extended.

At the start of the World War II, with the advent of airborne paratroops, the main canopy was deployed from a direct bag static line system. In this system, the main canopy was packed in a bag that was permanently attached to the static

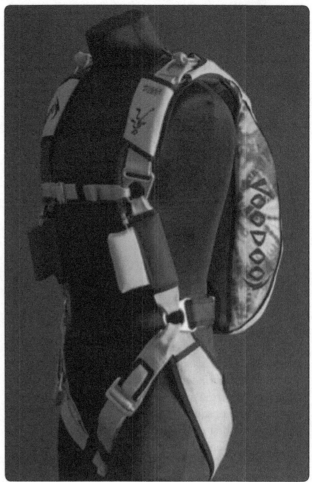

Figure 2-17. *Fully-articulated harness.*

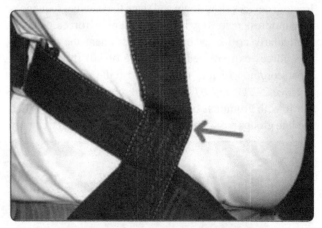

Figure 2-18. *Stair-stepped harness (aka stepped harness) junction warping.*

line. After deployment, the bag and static line remained with the aircraft. This system is still used today with some modifications. For emergency parachutes, the military adopted the "quarter bag" in the 1950s for use with high-speed emergency systems. *[Figure 2-19]* This was fairly complicated to pack but effective in controlling the parachute during opening. In the early 1960s, the sleeve was developed

Figure 2-19. *Quarter bag.*

and soon became popular for sport parachuting or skydiving. With the growth of skydiving and the increased use of the reserve parachute, it soon became obvious that the reserve parachute needed to be controlled more. In the mid 1970s, the two-stow diaper was developed for use with emergency and reserve parachutes. This design was soon followed by the three-stow diaper and the piglet-style diaper invented by Hank Ascuitto. During this time period, the deployment bag became the preferred method of deploying the increasingly popular ram-air or square canopies. In 1977, Para-Flite, Inc. introduced the first ram-air reserve canopy, which utilized the "free bag" deployment system. This design continues to this day virtually unchanged as the preferred method of deploying square reserve canopies.

Reefing devices slow down and stage the opening sequences of canopies, resulting in lower opening forces. This is particularly critical at higher speeds where the excessive "G" forces experienced may injure or kill the user. The most common reefing device used today is the "slider." *[Figure 2-20A and B]* This device consists of a piece of fabric with grommets or rings at the corners through which the line groups pass. This restricts the inflation of the canopy

and slows down the opening. While other methods have been developed for military or aerospace applications, the slider is the preferred method of reefing ram-air canopies. Without this device, skydiving would not be as developed as it is today.

Deployment Types
There are currently six different types of deployment methods, which are listed below.

Type 1: Canopy First Deployment
With this method, the lines are stowed vertically or horizontally in the container. Examples of this method are the T-7A chest pack or the B-12 back parachute. *[Figure 2-21]*

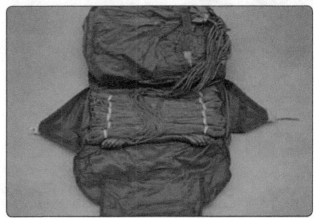

Figure 2-21. *Type 1 deployment—T-7A reserve.*

Type 2: Two-Stow Diaper or Half Diaper
This method utilizes split line groups. Two stows from one line group lock the diaper, compensated by offsetting stows of the other line group in the container with the remainder of the lines stowed in the container. Examples of this method are the early Strong 26' Lo-Po and the Pioneer "K" series reserves. *[Figure 2-22]*

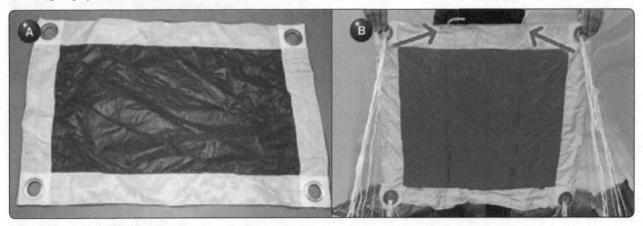

Figure 2-20. *A) Non-collapsible slider and B) collapsible slider.*

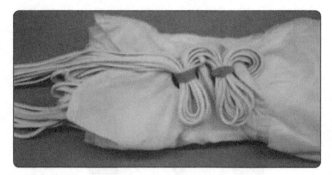

Figure 2-22. *Type 2 deployment—Lo-Po Reserve.*

Type 3: Ascuitto or Piglet-Style Flat Diaper

This deployment features a full diaper with all lines stowed left to right or perpendicular to the radial seam. Examples of this method are the Piglet, Phantom, and Security Aero Conical (SAC) canopies. *[Figure 2-23]*

Figure 2-23. *Type 3 deployment—Phantom canopy.*

Type 4: Handbury or Preserve Full Diaper

This features a choker-type diaper that wraps around the canopy skirt. It is locked with three stows and all lines are stowed on the diaper parallel to the radial seam. Examples of this method are the Preserve series canopies, Strong Lo-Po Lite, and the Hobbit square reserve. *[Figure 2-24]* The military quarter bag is basically a version of the Type 4 method.

Figure 2-24. *Type 4 deployment—Preserve diaper.*

Type 5: Free Bag

With a free bag, the canopy is stowed in the bag, and lines are either stowed on or in the bag. They were originally used on the Safety Flyer reserve. This is the dominant and preferred method for virtually all modern square reserves. *[Figure 2-25]*

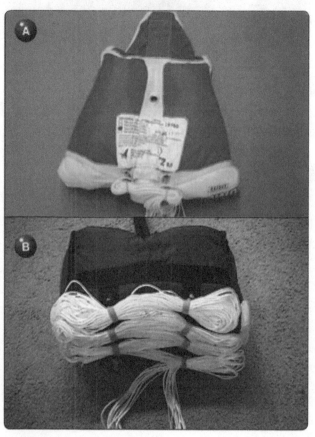

Figure 2-25. *A) Type 5 deployment—Freebag and B) Type 5 deployment—Speedbag.*

Type 6: Sleeves

The sleeve type includes a fabric tube that encloses the full length of the folded canopy. Lines are stowed on the sleeve. They were originally used on early sport canopies, particularly the Para-Commander. *[Figure 2-26]* A modern version, known as a "slag," is used on some ram-air canopies. An additional deployment method is the "tail pocket." This is a fabric pocket sewn on the tail of a ram-air canopy in which the lines are stowed. *[Figure 2-27]*

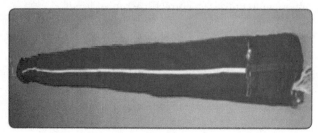

Figure 2-26. *Type 6 deployment—Sleeve.*

Figure 2-27. *Tail pocket.*

Securing the Deployment Device

With all deployment methods, it is necessary to properly fold or stow the canopy and secure the deployment device with the lines. The early parachutes utilized hesitator loops to secure the lines. *[Figure 2-28]* This method is still used today in many military systems.

Figure 2-28. *Hesitator loops.*

In modern designs that utilize types 1 through 4 and 6, the preferred method of locking the deployment device is rubber bands. The specification for standard rubber bands is MIL-R-1832. Type 1 are made of natural rubber and are ½" × 2". These were designed for use with the thicker Type III nylon lines such as on the 28' C-9 canopy. Many of the newer lightweight, round canopies use smaller diameter and fewer lines. Consequently, the standard rubber bands do not work well. Some manufacturers supply smaller, 1¼" diameter rubber bands to be used with their canopies. It is extremely important to utilize the correct size rubber bands.

With the introduction of the free bag system in 1977, Para-Flite, Inc., used a BUNA-N "O" ring to secure the locking stows. *[Figure 2-29]* During testing of the free bag system, they found inconsistent holding and breaking strengths of rubber bands. They wanted the locking stows to release at a consistent force to prevent bag lock. The "O" rings provided this. A couple of years later, the "O" rings were upgraded to a thicker diameter model. In 1983, Para-Flite, Inc. replaced

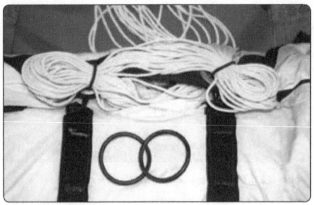

Figure 2-29. *Para-Flite O rings.*

the "O" rings with the Safety Stow®. The Safety Stow® is a continuous loop of elastic shock cord that runs through a webbing channel and through two grommets to secure the first two locking stows. *[Figure 2-30]* In the event of any restriction on the locking stow, as the loop stretches, it allows first one side to release and then the opposite side.

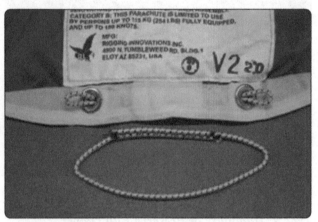

Figure 2-30. *Safety Stow®.*

It is important to maintain the rubber bands or Safety Stow®. Rubber bands are susceptible to heat degradation and may dry out. If they break prematurely during use, the parachute may malfunction. Non-mil. specification rubber bands may react to natural brass grommets and may become gummy and sticky, causing the lines to stick to the diaper or bag. Rubber bands should be replaced during routine Inspection and Repack. *[Figure 2-31A and B]* The BUNA-N "O" rings should be replaced with the Safety Stow®. The Safety Stow® should be inspected for broken stitching or internal rubber strands. *[Figure 2-32]*

In response to occasional violent openings on ram-air canopies, Parachute Labs (Jump Shack) in 2003 introduced the "speed bag" to eliminate "line dump" (line strip). The lines are retained in rubber bands 25 percent in from the edge of the bag. This balances the mass of the stows between the

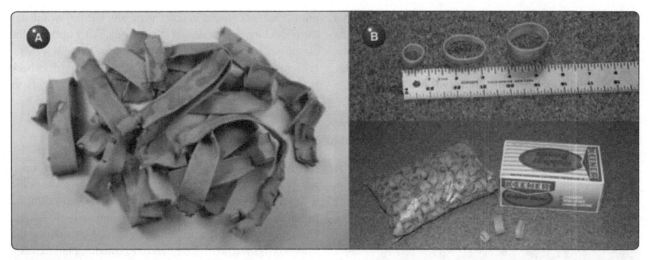

Figure 2-31. *A) Old rubber bands and B) new rubber bands. They come in 3 sizes: ⅜" wide × 1¼" diameter, ⅜" wide × 2" diameter and ¾" wide × 2" diameter.*

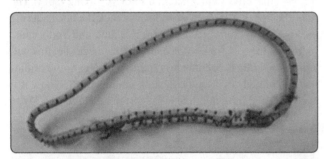

Figure 2-32. *Bad Safety Stow®.*

bights and center span of the stow. The bag has an additional flap on the top side that has slots for the rubber bands mounted on the bottom flap. These two flaps overlap closing the bag over the canopy. The design was used on main canopies only for the first three years. Its success led to the release as a reserve bag in 2006.

Bridles

The bridle is a cord or webbing strap that is used to connect the pilot chute to the canopy or deployment device. Main and reserve bridles, while sharing the same function, operate differently.

Early bridles were simply a length of suspension line tied off to the two components. It was soon learned that the length of the bridle affected the function of the pilot chute and the opening characteristics of the canopy. On most round emergency and reserve parachute assemblies, the length and type of the bridle is fixed for optimum performance. The rigger cannot change the configuration of the bridle without approval of the manufacturer.

There are two basic types of round canopy bridles. The first is a tubular nylon bridle that is tied on. The second is a pre-sewn bridle with loops at each end. The loop of one end is passed through the attach point on the pilot chute and then back through itself forming a lark's head knot. The other loop of the bridle is then similarly attached to the canopy apex. *[Figure 2-33]* With this type, it is essential for the loop to remain loose to ensure the bridle is free floating and self-centering around the apex lines. Hand tack the loop to ensure this. *[Figure 2-34]*

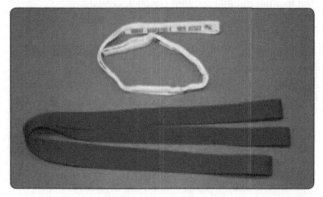

Figure 2-33. *Pre-sewn round bridles.*

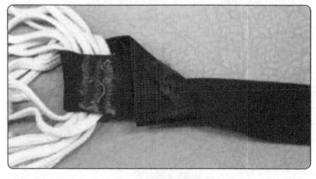

Figure 2-34. *Hand tack floating bridle loop.*

Square reserve bridles are generally built into the free bag. The bridle material is usually 2 feet wide or more for high drag. The original concept of the free bag is to allow the square reserve to deploy if the reserve pilot chute is captured resulting in a horseshoe-type malfunction. The high-drag bridle would then pull the reserve bag off the parachutist's back and allow the canopy to deploy free from the bag. In the late 1980s, assistor pockets were added to some bridles for additional drag as square reserves became bigger and heavier. *[Figure 2-35]*

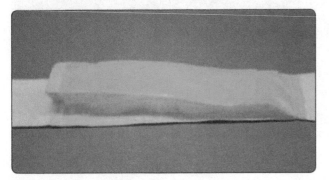

Figure 2-35. *Freebag assistor pocket.*

Early main bridles were simply longer versions of the reserve bridles. This was necessary to compensate for the "burble" created in free fall by the parachutist. In the mid 1970s and with the advent of the hand deploy pilot chute, the length of the bridle was critical in order to allow proper extraction of the locking pin that secured the pack closed.

In recent years and with the almost total use of ram-air parachutes, the need for collapsible main pilot chutes has become widespread. As the main canopies have become smaller and faster, the drag of the inflated main pilot chute after opening can have an adverse effect on canopy performance. This problem has been solved through the use of a collapsible pilot chute/bridle system. There are two primary designs used to accomplish this.

The first is the "bungee" collapsible configuration. This consists of a length of elastic shock cord inside a tape sheath on the bridle near the pilot chute end. *[Figure 2-36]* When relaxed, it holds the apex of the pilot chute collapsed. When the

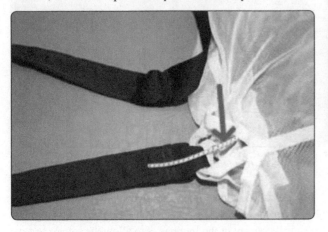

Figure 2-36. *Bungee collapsible bridle.*

pilot chute is deployed into the airstream, the airflow inflates the pilot chute, which deploys the canopy. After opening, the elastic pulls the apex down again and collapses the pilot chute, reducing the drag. While this system works, its main drawback is that certain airspeeds are needed to inflate the pilot chute. Remember, the primary function of the pilot chute is to initiate deployment. Collapsing the pilot chute is secondary.

The second type is the "kill-line collapsible" configuration. This consists of a bridle with a full length channel through which passes a line of Kevlar® or Spectra®. *[Figure 2-37]* The bridle is "cocked" and the lower end of the bridle is collapsed during packing. This allows the pilot chute to inflate immediately. During the deployment sequence, as the canopy inflates, the lower end is stretched to length and the centerline pulls the apex of the pilot chute down and collapses it. This configuration has become almost universal in use for skydiving today. The only drawback is if the user forgets to cock the bridle during packing. This results in a collapsed pilot chute and a pilot chute in tow. In the early days of use of the kill-line bridle, this was a problem but has become less frequent today. Some bridles have a colored "eye" at the locking pin location to show if it is cocked and the centerline is set correctly. *[Figure 2-38]*

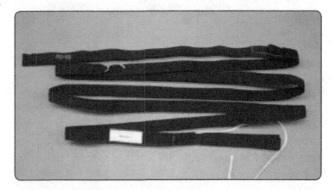

Figure 2-37. *Kill-line collapsible bridle.*

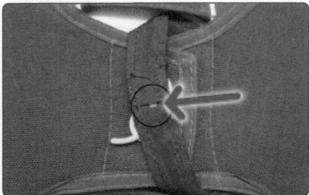

Figure 2-38. *Kill-line eye or window.*

The kill-line configuration is used almost exclusively on tandem systems due to the high speeds involved and the size of the drogue pilot chutes. Some bridles are made from 2"

Kevlar® tape and have tubular nylon centerlines. Others are made from Type 4 square weave with a Spectra centerline. The advantage of the latter is that it can be cut with a hook knife in the event of an on-person malfunction. *[Figure 2-39]*

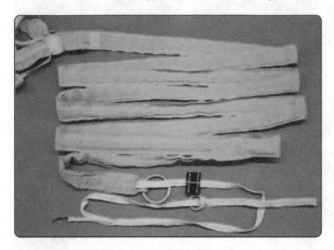

Figure 2-39. *Tandem main collapsible bridle.*

Another method of collapsing the pilot chute is to install a No. 8 grommet in the deployment bag and allow the bag to float on the bridle. After the canopy deploys, the bag slides up the bridle, inverts, and covers the pilot chute. This is commonly called the "poor man's collapsible pilot chute system." The drawback to this design is the high wear on the bridle and pilot chute mesh.

Pilot Chutes

A pilot chute is a small parachute that is used to deploy the main or reserve parachute. In the earliest uses of parachutes, the parachute was static line deployed. With the advent of manually operated or "free fall" parachutes, the need for a pilot chute was quickly recognized.

There are two basic types of pilot chutes. The first is the spring-loaded design. This uses a collapsible spring, which is compressed in the parachute container and held closed with the ripcord. When the ripcord is pulled, the pack opens and the pilot chute launches into the airstream. The pilot chute provides drag and pulls the canopy from the pack as the parachutist or load falls away. During this process, the pilot chute also provides tension on the lines of the deploying canopy and helps the opening sequence. Spring-loaded pilot chutes are used primarily for emergency and reserve parachutes. In addition, they are used in military free fall and training systems for the main parachute.

The second type of pilot chute is the "hand deploy" design. This type consists of the pilot chute canopy but does not have a spring to launch it. Instead, the parachutist extracts the folded pilot chute from a pouch or the container and launches

it into the airstream. The pack is held closed by a locking pin attached to the bridle of the pilot chute. As the pilot chute inflates, it extracts the pin from the locking loop and pulls the parachute from the pack. The rest of the opening process is similar to the spring-loaded pilot chute. This configuration came into popularity in the mid 1970s and is now the primary method of deployment in skydiving.

Spring-Loaded Pilot Chutes

Spring-loaded pilot chutes date from the 1920s. However, it was not until 1940 that the spiral vane pilot chute was invented. This design used a spiral spring that is easy to collapse and pack. The most common type of spiral vane pilot chute used today is the MA-1 model. *[Figure 2-40A and B]* This is used in several military parachute assemblies. In the early days of skydiving, military pilot chutes, such as the MA-1 and others were popular. Soon commercial designs were introduced that improved on the MA-1 with better launch and drag characteristics. These included the Grabber® and Hot Dog® pilot chutes. Both of these were primarily for use with main parachutes.

With the advent of the hand deploy pilot chute for the main, most of the improvement in spring-loaded pilot chute design has focused on its use in the reserve or emergency parachutes. This has paralleled the improvements in container design and the increased use of AADs. Both of these require better pilot chutes than in the past.

One example for reserve use is the Magnum® pilot chute designed by National Parachute Industries. *[Figure 2-41]* With its unique shape, it provides maximum drag at low speeds, such as are experienced during cutaways. Its design has been licensed by other manufacturers for use in their assemblies. Additional designs include the Vector II reserve pilot chute and the Stealth pilot chute. The Vector II design is a "ballute" configuration that eliminates the use of mesh. In the event of an unstable launch on its side, the mass of fabric is sufficient to lift the pilot chute and deploy the parachute. The Stealth pilot chute uses a conventional mesh design but has a unique spring/cap configuration that allows the pilot chute to virtually disappear when packed, hence the name. The MA-1 spring with mesh in place of the vanes, and a closed canopy instead of the scalloped canopy provides the best of both worlds: a spring that does not lock up on itself and high drag without the possibility of snag.

Hand Deploy Pilot Chutes

The hand deploy pilot chute was introduced in 1976. There are two types of hand deploy designs. One is the throw-out pilot chute (TOP) configuration. This is the type where the pilot chute pulls the locking pin located on the bridle. *[Figure 2-42]* The original design had the pilot chute pouch

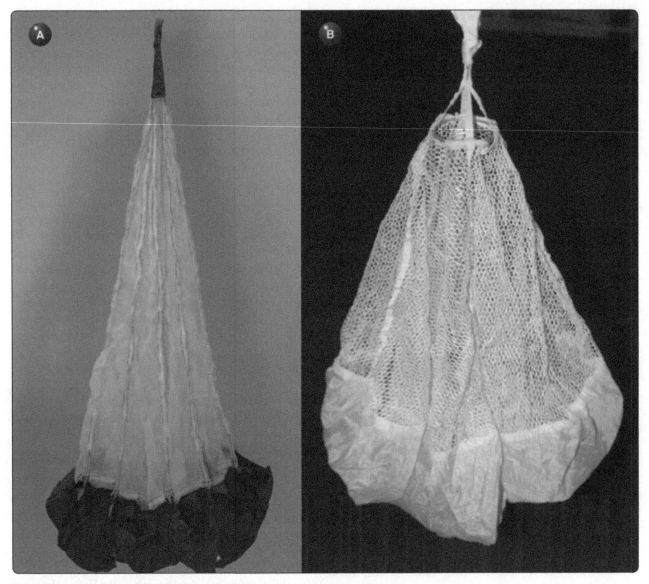

Figure 2-40. *A) MA-1 pilot chute and B) high-drag pilot chute with large hole mesh.*

mounted on the belly band. Today, the primary location is an elastic/Spandex® pocket mounted on the bottom of the main container (BOC). *[Figure 2-43]* Most of the difficulties of this design have to do with pilot chute in tow due to misrouting of the bridle or failure of the pin to extract.

The second type is the pull-out pilot chute (POP) configuration. This design has the pilot chute packed in the container, which is locked with a straight locking pin attached to a short lanyard and handle. *[Figure 2-44A and B]* This handle is usually mounted on the bottom corner of the main container. The parachutist grasps the handle and pulls the locking pin from the locking loop and puts the pilot chute into the airstream. The handle is usually attached to the bottom of the pilot chute and as the chute enters the airstream, the jumper loosens his grip on the handle allowing it to be pulled from his or her hand. This makes for a positive deployment. The main drawback to this system is losing the handle due to it being dislodged while

moving around in the aircraft or in the air. Fortunately, the handle does not go far and is easy to obtain because it is on a short lanyard that is tucked up under the side flap. .

Automatic Activation Devices (AADs) and Reserve Static Lines (RSLs)

Safety considerations have led to the development of AADs and reserve static line (RSL) systems. These devices allow for automatic deployment of the main or reserve parachutes in the event of an emergency.

Automatic Activation Devices

AADs are devices that activate the parachute automatically. Modern systems combine a barometric sensor with a rate of descent sensor so that the system is fully automatic once turned on and calibrated. The activation may be by either pulling the ripcord pin(s) or cutting the locking loop(s),

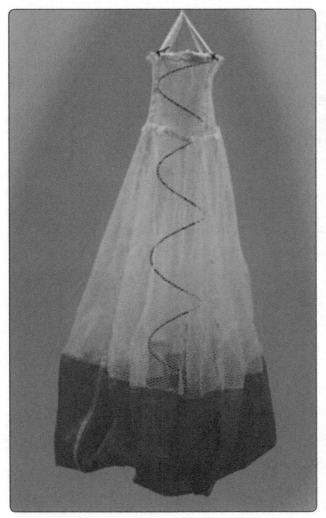

Figure 2-41. *Magnum pilot chute.*

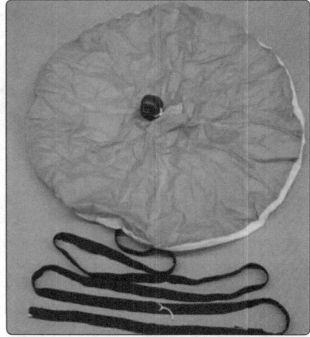

Figure 2-42. *TOP bridle/pin configuration.*

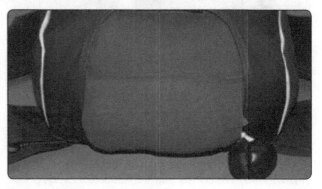

Figure 2-43. *BOC pocket location.*

causing the pilot chute to release. Most older models use a mechanical or pyrotechnic pin pulling technique. Newer models use a pyrotechnic loop cutting design.

For many years, AADs were primarily used by the military and student parachutists. The designs were bulky, expensive, and, to a degree, inconsistent. The installations themselves were cumbersome and awkward. In the early 1990s, a new generation of AADs became available. The CYbernetic Parachute RElease System (CYPRES®) uses modern parachute release technology. It is small, reliable, computer based, and uses a pyrotechnic loop cutter. It has an auto-off feature that turns the unit off after 14 hours of operation to conserve power. It also has the ability to calibrate the unit for operation at altitudes other than the calibrating ground level. Based on these concepts, other companies have developed similar systems and as a result, changed the approach to the design and use of AADs. Today, a good many sport parachutists use an AAD and some countries (rightly or wrongly), mandate their use by all parachutists.

The following describes the operation and installation requirements of the CYPRES® model AA. Other designs, such as the Vigil®, are compatible with these installation requirements.

Operation

The CYPRES® system is a barometrically controlled microprocessor that activates a pyrotechnic cutter that cuts the container locking loop. When calibrated to ground level, the barometric sensor activates the unit firing the cutter when the descending parachutist reaches an altitude of approximately 750 feet above ground level (AGL) and exceeds a rate of descent of 115 feet per second (fps).

The CYPRES® consists of three parts:

1. Battery and processing unit

2. Control unit

3. Cutter *[Figure 2-45]*

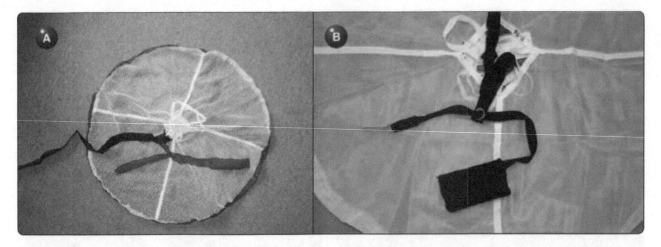

Figure 2-44. *A) POP handle with pilot chute and B) POP handle and lanyard.*

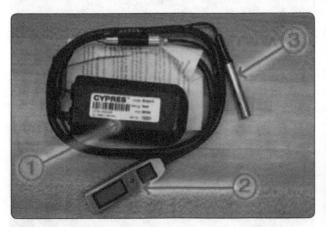

Figure 2-45. *CYPRES® AAD.*

The processing unit is generally located in a stowage pouch installed in the reserve container of the parachute system. *[Figure 2-46]* The control unit is contained in a vinyl pocket located either under the pin protector flap or in the upper back pad area. *[Figure 2-47]*

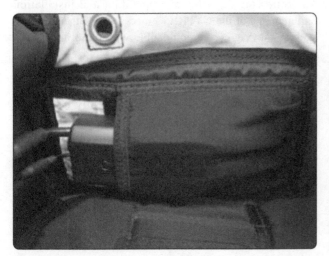

Figure 2-46. *CYPRES® container pouch.*

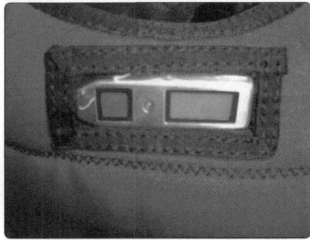

Figure 2-47. *CYPRES® control unit vinyl pocket.*

The cutter(s) may be located at the base of the pilot chute or on a flap over the pilot chute. *[Figure 2-48]* Each parachute system has its own particular requirements, and it is imperative that the rigger have the appropriate manuals for installation.

Figure 2-48. *CYPRES® cutter location.*

Reserve Static Line (RSL) Systems

A RSL system is a backup device for activating the reserve after a cutaway is performed. It usually consists of a line, webbing, or cable, which connects one or both main risers to the reserve handle, housing, or cable. The most common design used today has a ring through which the reserve ripcord cable is routed. The riser end attaches to a ring on the riser(s) with a snap shackle for quick release capability. When the risers are jettisoned, the lanyard pulls the cable, releasing the ripcord pin(s), and activates the reserve. This results in a minimum loss of altitude during the cutaway procedure. The use of an RSL has saved many lives over the years due to low cutaways.

Though originally developed in 1964, as the Stevens System, the RSL concept did not become popular until the advent of student piggyback systems and ram-air canopies. Through the use of an RSL system, the student parachutist need only pull the canopy release handle in the event of a partial malfunction, and the main canopy is cutaway and the reserve activates. In 1990, the PIA urged manufacturers to include RSLs as a standard feature on all harness/container systems. Many did and this resulted in an increase of RSL use for several years.

Conventional (chest mounted) parachute systems utilized a cross-connector at the junction of the riser to the lines of the canopy on each of the front and rear risers. This was so as to maintain drag if one side release before the other. The maximum amount of drag available is required to assure the reserve ripcord activation by the RSL and the release and separation of the off side riser. When applied to the piggy back, these cross connectors would hang up on the bottom of the reserve container preventing separation. Many manufacturers dismissed this need and elected to provide a reserve lanyard that was side sensitive (in that it would activate the reserve if the attached side released and the opposite side did not release). Others moved the lanyard to the base of the riser, which required only one cross connector. This location avoided the possibility of a hang up on the bottom of the reserve and retained the drag integrity.

In recent years and with the widespread acceptance of newer types of AADs, many parachutists feel that they no longer need an RSL. In reality, both systems complement each other. The AAD functions if the individual does not activate the main parachute. However, it is altitude and rate of descent (ROD) dependent. Below a certain altitude, if the ROD is not met, the AAD will not function. Consequently, if a cutaway is performed below the activation altitude, it may take some time for the descending parachutist to reach the ROD necessary to initiate activation, thereby necessitating rapid manual activation of the reserve. However, if an RSL is also installed, it would cause an immediate activation of the reserve as the main parachute disconnects and moves away from the parachutist.

In the last few years, as canopy design has resulted in smaller and more sensitive canopies, many parachutists have elected not to use an RSL. The rationale is that in a violently spinning malfunction, which some of these highly loaded canopies are prone to do, it is preferable to cutaway and regain stability prior to pulling the reserve. This reduces the chance of an entanglement with the deploying reserve. While this scenario has happened, it is a rare occurrence. Statistics show that many lives have been saved by using an RSL.

RSL Designs

There are four primary design configurations of RSLs in use today and are listed below:

1. A single-side RSL where the lanyard is attached to only one main riser, usually the left side. *[Figure 2-49]* Only the one side is required to release to activate the system. This is the most common design in use today due to its simplicity.

Figure 2-49. *Single side RSL configuration.*

2. A dual side RSL where both main risers are connected with a cross connector which is the RSL lanyard. *[Figure 2-50A and B]* Both risers need to release for the system to activate.

3. The LOR system developed by the French. This incorporates two lanyards, one from each riser, that are attached to individual curved pins that secure the reserve container with a dual locking loop. *[Figure 2-51]* Both risers must be released for the system to function.

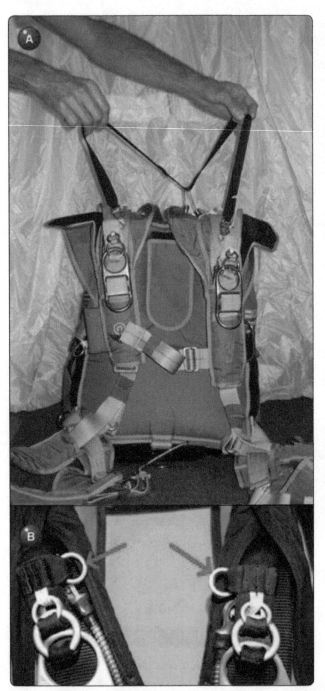

Figure 2-50. *A) Dual-side RSL configuration and B) dual-RSL routing diagram.*

4. The Collins Lanyard/Skyhook™ system. This design utilizes a special lanyard that is attached to the bridle of the reserve free bag. *[Figure 2-52]* Cutting away results in the free bag being pulled directly out of the container by the main risers and results in very little altitude loss.

Since the early 1990s, most (if not all) manufacturers have provided an RSL installation on their equipment either as standard or optional. If the rigger has a system without an RSL

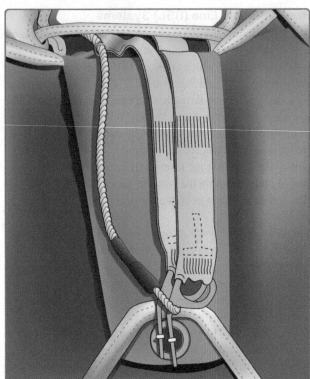

Figure 2-51. *LOR system.*

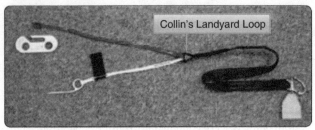

Figure 2-52. *Skyhook® system.*

and the owner wishes to have one installed, the rigger should check with the manufacturer as to the availability of a retrofit kit or return it to the manufacturer for installation. Because the installation of an RSL is an alteration to the original design, the rigger needs approval either from the manufacturer or the FAA.

Because of the nature of the RSL system, it is imperative that the rigger thoroughly understands the individual concepts. Unless he or she understands this and has the required manufacturer's instructions, the rigger should not attempt to assemble and pack a system with an RSL installation. The following describes the basic design and function of a single side RSL installation on a one-pin reserve container.

Main Riser Attachment

The main risers must have an attachment location for the lanyard. In this example, a small ring is installed near the lower hardware end of the riser on the inboard side. *[Figure 2-53]* It is

Figure 2-53. *Main riser RSL ring attachment.*

desirable to locate the ring as close to the lower end as possible so that the pivot arc of the rise does not load the lanyard. This allows the riser end of the lanyard end to be as short as possible. If there is excess lanyard, it is difficult to stow, and it is possible for the lanyard to become snagged and unseated. It is important that the correct risers with attachment ring be installed. While many risers have a ring installation, not all are installed at the correct location. Consequently, the lanyard length will not match the factory dimensions. This can result in premature reserve activation when the main is deployed.

Most RSL lanyard designs have a snap shackle or similar release device mounted at the riser end of the lanyard. *[Figure 2-54]* This allows the user to disconnect the lanyard under certain circumstances. The most common one involves landing in

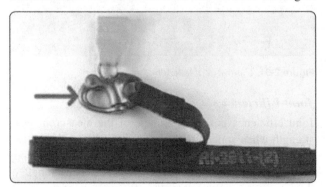

Figure 2-54. *Snap shackle on RSL lanyard.*

high winds where the parachutist may wish to cutaway the main canopy to prevent being dragged. If the lanyard were not released, the reserve would be deployed as the main is cutaway.

Ripcord Cable Routing

The routing of the ripcord cable from the handle to the pin determines where the lanyard connects to the cable. Most RSL attachments connect with the ripcord cable either at the yoke area or just above the ripcord pin. Generally, there is a double ring installation where the cable end of the lanyard is located. *[Figure 2-55]* On this particular installation, the connection is at the shoulder yoke area.

Figure 2-55. *Double-ring container installation.*

RSL Lanyard and Container Mount

These two components are interactive. That is, the design of the container directly affects the design of the lanyard. Once the two above locations are determined, then the routing of the lanyard can be completed. It was originally thought that the lanyard should have a long length to allow acceleration during activation to pull the ripcord cable. This has not proven to be true and most manufacturers keep their lanyards as short as possible to prevent snagging and easier stowing. The Racer cross-connector/lanyard is so sized as to not pull the reserve ripcord until both risers have separated

In the past, a Velcro® pathway was used for routing the lanyard. This was either on the shoulder yoke or the reserve riser. Experience has shown that the use of Velcro® generally results in high wear and eventual damage to the webbing. *[Figure 2-56]* On this design, the lanyard is stiffened with a short piece of coated cable and stowed in two pockets located on the yoke area. *[Figure 2-57]* It is secure and has no wear points. The ripcord end of the lanyard is routed to the dual guide ring attachment location and the ripcord cable routed through the rings. *[Figure 2-58]* The ripcord cable is then routed to the reserve closing loop. *Figure 2-59* shows the RSL lanyard and ripcord cable at the moment of riser extension and just as the cable is loaded. A point that the rigger should be

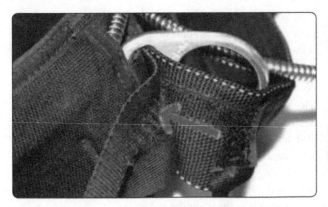

Figure 2-56. *RSL Velcro riser damage.*

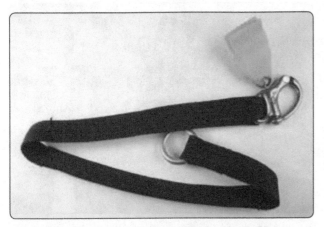

Figure 2-57. *One style of RSL lanyard without Velcro.*

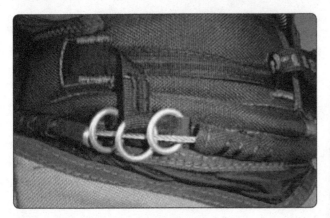

Figure 2-58. *Ripcord cable routing through rings.*

aware of is the "pigtail" configuration of the reserve ripcord that results from the use of the RSL. *[Figure 2-60]* Because of the sliding of the ring along the ripcord cable, a curling effect is imparted to the cable. This is a clear indication that the RSL lanyard activated the reserve. The rigger should carefully inspect the ripcord cable for any broken strands. If any are found, the ripcord should be replaced. If not, the cable can be straightened and returned to service.

With the single side RSL, it is imperative that the main riser with the RSL attachment leave after the opposite riser. If the opposite riser stays connected while the RSL

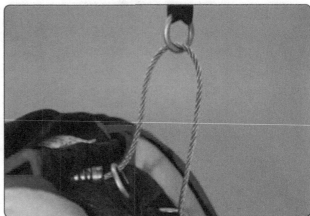

Figure 2-59. *RSL lanyard extension.*

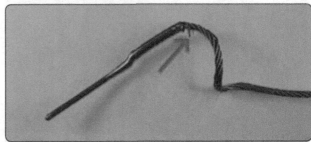

Figure 2-60. *Ripcord cable pigtail with broken strand.*

deploys the reserve, there is the possibility of a main/reserve entanglement. To ensure the correct staging of the cutaway, the release cable of the RSL side must be longer than the cable on the opposite riser. A minimum of 1 inch is the standard differential. *[Figure 2-61]* If non-compressible housings are not used, the staged separation is not reliable.

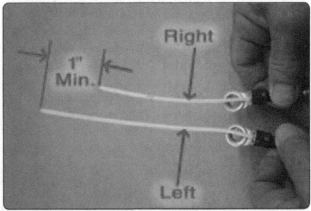

Figure 2-61. *Cutaway cable length differential.*

Joint Efficiency

Joint efficiency is the percentage of the measurement of strength when applied to the junction or fabrication of two or more materials. An example is the cross seam in a canopy gore where two panels of fabric are joined. The strength of the seam needs to be greater than the strength of the fabric.

To achieve this, there are several factors that need to be considered in the design. These include the following:

- Fabric—the weight and weave of the fabric affects the type of junction used.

- Thread type—this is affected by the weight of the fabric. Generally, the lighter the fabric, the smaller the thread used. Accordingly, a smaller needle is used in order not to damage the weave of the fabric.

- Stitch type—this is determined by the type of seam needed for the design. For the French fell seam normally used in joining the panels of a canopy, the 301 straight stitch is used.

- Stitches per inch—this has a direct correlation to the size of the thread used and the stitch type. There is a fine balance between the security of the seam and overstitching. Too many stitches per inch dramatically affects the strength of the seam by perforating the material. The number of rows of stitching also affects this. While more rows generally increase the strength of the seam, too many perforate the material as well.

- Thread tension—as lighter fabric and thread are used, the thread tension balance becomes more important.

- Reinforcing—the addition of reinforcing through the use of tapes, cords, etc., adds to the strength of the seam. However, their use may also reduce the elasticity of the seam at the same time.

Some of the previous factors also can affect heavier materials, such as tapes and webbings. In working with webbings in harness design, most construction methods have tended to overbuild the junctions. This has been done primarily because the materials have readily accepted heavier threads and stitch patterns.

An area that needs to be addressed is that of re-stitching webbing. Until recently, there was not much study done to determine how much strength is lost in this process. G.S. Dunker, a parachute engineer, conducted a study that evaluated the variables introduced when re-stitching webbing junctions. Some of these variables included the following:

- The treatment or conditioning of the webbing. Condition R webbing has a resin treatment to make it stiffer as opposed to condition U or untreated webbing.

- The size and condition of the needle used in the sewing. Larger needles make larger holes. A blunt needle or one whose point is damaged, will do more damage to the webbing and weaken it.

- The size of the thread used.

- The stitch pattern used and length. A W–W pattern is stronger than a box X pattern.

- The number of times the webbing is re-sewn.

All of these affect the ultimate strength of the webbing junction or stitch pattern.

Chapter Summary

It is important to know the history of parachute design in order to move forward technologically. The old saying, "Those who don't know history are destined to repeat it." Is especially applicable to parachute design and manufacture, where a relatively small, esoteric group of individuals who are loosely controlled and turn on a dime, churn out designs that some eager young test jumper is willing to try. This is not necessarily a bad thing. The civilian led sport parachute market is responsible for just about all the newest innovations in the industry over the past 45 years. But it should be kept in mind that a new design generally takes about ten years' wringing out in the field to discover it's failure modes and make it safe and reliable.

Chapter 3
Materials

Introduction

The correct identification and use of the various materials in parachute manufacturing and repair are of vital importance to all riggers. Just as important as acquiring knowledge of tools and machines, knowing and using the correct terminology for materials is essential to the rigger's job comprehension. In doing repairs or alterations, the rigger must be able to identify the types of materials used in order to duplicate the original manufacture and to ensure the correct level of safety necessary. Some materials may look similar, but there can be subtle differences between them that make a major difference in their strength or durability.

It is not the intent of this chapter to present information on every type of material or hardware ever used in parachutes. For very detailed specifications on a broader range of materials used in current production parachutes, as well as obsolete and military surplus parachutes, there are additional reference sources, such as "The Parachute Manual" by Dan Poynter. The purpose of this chapter is to present as much information on the essentials of modern materials seen in today's parachute systems.

Many riggers operate quite successfully with a basic level of material knowledge in their proverbial tool kit. There are certain materials that are commonly used on most parachute systems, and in dealing with these on a regular basis, the rigger becomes very familiar with their characteristics and proper application. It is fundamental that the rigger know their correct type, nomenclature, strength, and common use. In dealing with other riggers, manufacturers, and suppliers, the rigger is then able to identify the referenced material in order to obtain the appropriate repair part or describe the use of the material to others. All of this is part of the parachute rigger's lexicon, required to communicate their needs and accomplish the required tasks.

Specifications

All certificated parachute systems built under government approval programs require most, if not all, materials used in their construction to have some form of specification approval. The most common of these systems is the military specification (MIL-SPEC) system. In addition, there are other government specifications, such as Federal Standards, and commercial specifications in use. The MIL-SPEC system is the one with which most riggers are familiar. Contrary to popular perception, not all materials for use in parachute manufacturing must be MIL-SPEC. Any specification may be used, provided that the manufacturer can prove compliance with this specification, and that the specification is acceptable to the Federal Aviation Administration (FAA) for use in the parachute system. As a rule, the MIL-SPEC system has proven the most readily available and accepted method.

In recent years, the government has been accepting more commercial specifications in lieu of MIL-SPEC items. In 2002, the Parachute Industry Association (PIA) adopted approximately 270 parachute-related specifications, drawings, standards, and test methods. The PIA takes responsibility for the continued maintenance and revision of these specifications. As the specifications are revised, they keep their original identification number, but the PIA prefix precedes them. For instance, MIL-W-4088 webbing becomes PIA-W-4088. Through the involvement of the PIA Specifications Committee, the revised specifications, including new digital drawings, are made available to the industry.

The MIL-SPEC or PIA-SPEC system of identification consists of the initial letters MIL or PIA with a middle letter such as W for webbing or wire, then the identification or serial number of the specification. In addition, there may be a revision letter, such as A, B, C, D, etc. In the case of PIA-W-4088D, this is the fourth revision.

The materials and hardware listed herein are only a small part of those available, but the most commonly used in the majority of today's rigging profession. By learning the specifications and uses of these materials, the rigger establishes a sound basis for the repair and maintenance of modern parachutes.

To promote the latest specifications, the PIA nomenclature is called out unless otherwise noted. In the past, the common method to denote the various types of webbings, cords, etc., was to use the Roman numeral for the type (e.g., Type VIII for Ty-8, Type XVII for Ty-17). For this handbook, the standard is the Arabic numeral (e.g., Ty-7).

Many of the figures in this chapter use a neutral background with an XY grid for reference. The numbers are in one-inch increments for a proportional reference.

Fabrics

Nylon is the predominate fabric used in the manufacture of parachutes. Chemically speaking, nylon is made of repeating units linked by amide bonds and is frequently referred to as a polyamide (PA). It was invented in the late 1930s by Wallace Carothers while conducting research at DuPont. There are many different kinds of nylon and some of the major differences include the weave, weight, and finish. The various types of materials include canopy fabric, pack cloth, tapes, webbings, mesh, elastic fabrics, stiffener materials, and foams.

Canopy fabrics are primarily ripstop nylon. Ripstop weave is a plain weave with heavier threads woven into the material at right angles resulting in a boxlike pattern. The heavier thread and the unique weave results in ability of the threads to slide over one another inhibiting the tearing process and results in stronger fabrics. *[Figures 3-1 through 3-6]*

The composition of most containers is from either nylon duck (Para-pack) or Cordura®. Para-pack has a smooth somewhat shiny finish; Cordura has a matte, more rugged appearance. Both are sturdy and long lasting. Most sport containers also utilize a thin foam lining on the inside of the flaps to smooth out the fabric and absorb wear and tear. Other fabrics, such as mesh, Spandex®, and ballistic fabric, serve specialized purposes. *[Figures 3-7 through 3-16]*

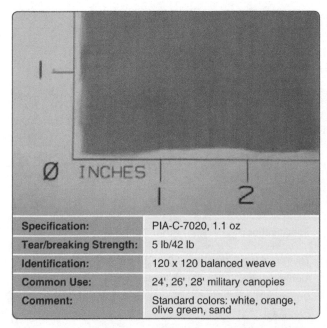

Specification:	PIA-C-7020, 1.1 oz
Tear/breaking Strength:	5 lb/42 lb
Identification:	120 x 120 balanced weave
Common Use:	24', 26', 28' military canopies
Comment:	Standard colors: white, orange, olive green, sand

Figure 3-1. *Cloth, parachute, nylon, Type-1.*

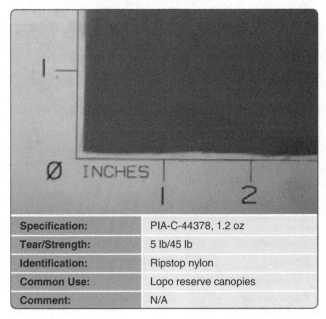

Specification:	PIA-C-44378, 1.2 oz
Tear/Strength:	5 lb/45 lb
Identification:	Ripstop nylon
Common Use:	Lopo reserve canopies
Comment:	N/A

Figure 3-2. *Cloth, parachute, nylon, Type-3, 30-50 CFM.*

Webbing and Tapes

While many webbings and tapes have the same specifications, they still have different designations. The difference is a common rule of thumb where anything 1 inch or wider and over 1000-lb strength is webbing. Anything less is a tape. There are, however, some examples that fall outside of this criterion.

The primary use for webbing is for load bearing purposes, such as harnesses and risers. Tapes are for use as support and reinforcing for canopies and containers. Most webbing and tapes, when manufactured, are left in their natural, untreated condition (condition U), or treated with a synthetic resin

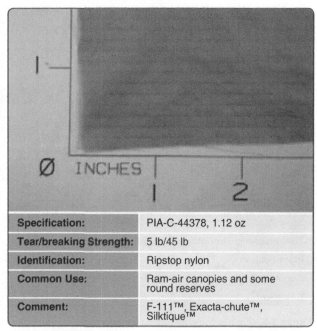

Specification:	PIA-C-44378, 1.12 oz
Tear/breaking Strength:	5 lb/45 lb
Identification:	Ripstop nylon
Common Use:	Ram-air canopies and some round reserves
Comment:	F-111™, Exacta-chute™, Silktique™

Figure 3-3. *Cloth, parachute, nylon, Type-1, Lo-Po, .5-3 CFM.*

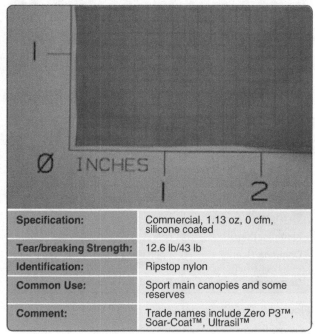

Specification:	Commercial, 1.13 oz, 0 cfm, silicone coated
Tear/breaking Strength:	12.6 lb/43 lb
Identification:	Ripstop nylon
Common Use:	Sport main canopies and some reserves
Comment:	Trade names include Zero P3™, Soar-Coat™, Ultrasil™

Figure 3-4. *Cloth, parachute, nylon, Type-1, zero porosity.*

named Merlon, for stiffness (condition R). A newer treatment, called "Ecco," is similar to a light condition R. This is a newer treatment that is ecologically friendlier than using Merlon. It also results in a medium stiffness that is easier to sew. This is for use primarily in the lighter weight tapes, such as ¾" Ty-3. Recently some harness/container manufacturers have begun to replace ¾" Ty-3 binding tape with ⅞" Ty-3 because modern container designs are getting thicker with the application of more stiffeners and more padding. There are pros and cons to this trend.

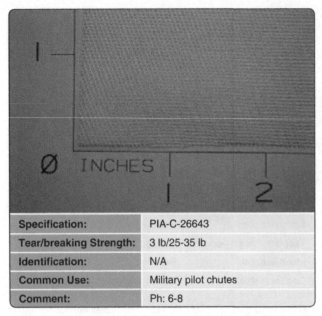

Specification:	PIA-C-26643
Tear/breaking Strength:	3 lb/25-35 lb
Identification:	N/A
Common Use:	Military pilot chutes
Comment:	Ph: 6-8

Figure 3-5. *Cloth, netting, nylon (marquisette).*

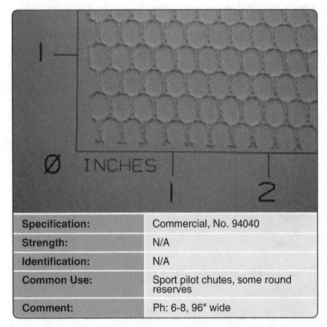

Specification:	Commercial, No. 94040
Strength:	N/A
Identification:	N/A
Common Use:	Sport pilot chutes, some round reserves
Comment:	Ph: 6-8, 96" wide

Figure 3-6. *Cloth, mesh, large hole, nylon.*

Webbing Selection

When a repair requires replacement of webbing and tapes, care must be taken to use the correct webbing or tape for the job. Generally, there are two types of webbings used in industry: needle weave and shuttle weave. Remember this: "Needle Never, Shuttle Sure." This is because needle weave webbing is rarely, if ever, used in personnel parachute assemblies.

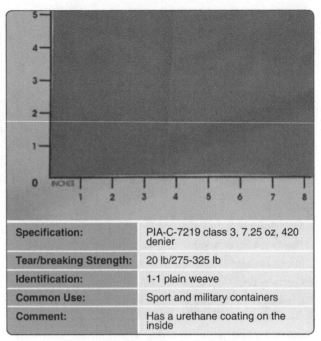

Specification:	PIA-C-7219 class 3, 7.25 oz, 420 denier
Tear/breaking Strength:	20 lb/275-325 lb
Identification:	1-1 plain weave
Common Use:	Sport and military containers
Comment:	Has a urethane coating on the inside

Figure 3-7. *Cloth, duck, nylon (Para-pak).*

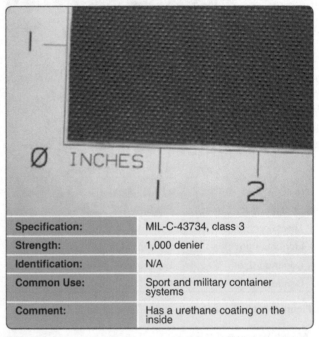

Specification:	MIL-C-43734, class 3
Strength:	1,000 denier
Identification:	N/A
Common Use:	Sport and military container systems
Comment:	Has a urethane coating on the inside

Figure 3-8. *Cloth, nylon, Cordura®.*

The reason for this limitation is because of the reaction of the webbing when "edge nicked" while under tension. In tests of the most advanced needle weave products several years ago, it was dramatically demonstrated, numerous times, that the webbing would fail catastrophically when the edge was nicked with sharp metal while under tension.

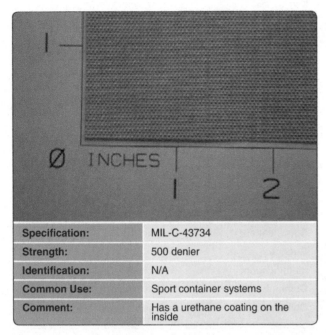

Specification:	MIL-C-43734
Strength:	500 denier
Identification:	N/A
Common Use:	Sport container systems
Comment:	Has a urethane coating on the inside

Figure 3-9. *Cloth, nylon, Cordura®.*

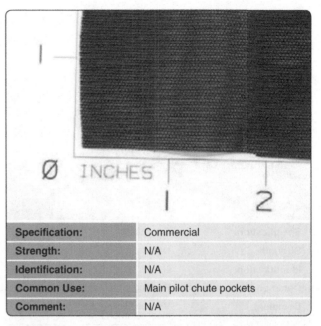

Specification:	Commercial
Strength:	N/A
Identification:	N/A
Common Use:	Main pilot chute pockets
Comment:	N/A

Figure 3-11. *Elastic fabric, Spandex®.*

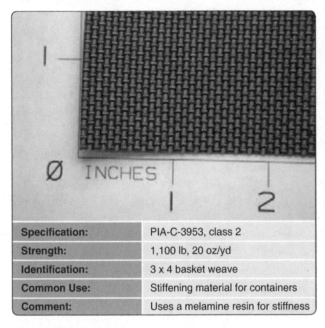

Specification:	PIA-C-3953, class 2
Strength:	1,100 lb, 20 oz/yd
Identification:	3 x 4 basket weave
Common Use:	Stiffening material for containers
Comment:	Uses a melamine resin for stiffness

Figure 3-10. *Cloth, duck, nylon, ballistic.*

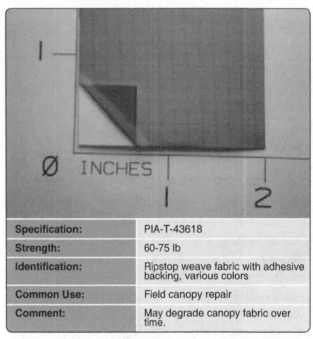

Specification:	PIA-T-43618
Strength:	60-75 lb
Identification:	Ripstop weave fabric with adhesive backing, various colors
Common Use:	Field canopy repair
Comment:	May degrade canopy fabric over time.

Figure 3-12. *Pressure sensitive adhesive tape—ripstop tape.*

The two types may be identified by comparing their edges. Fold the webbing in half and align the selvage edges. They should be identical in weave. If they are, then it is shuttle weave and acceptable for use. If they are not, then it is needle weave.

One should never be substituted for the other in a repair. The rigger should have material certification and lot tractability for any materials used in the repair. The material certification should additionally identify the type. *[Figures 3-17 through 3-32]*

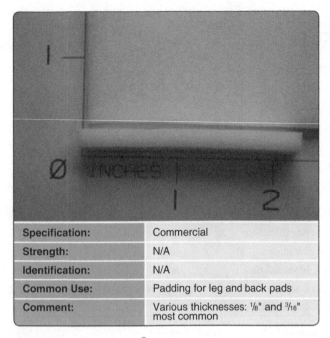

Specification:	Commercial
Strength:	N/A
Identification:	N/A
Common Use:	Padding for leg and back pads
Comment:	Various thicknesses: ⅛" and ³⁄₁₆" most common

Figure 3-13. *Foam, Volara®.*

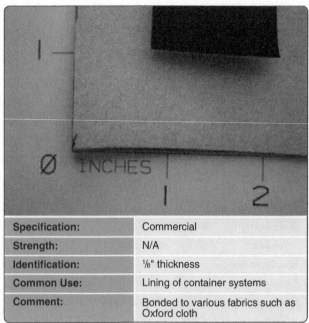

Specification:	Commercial
Strength:	N/A
Identification:	⅛" thickness
Common Use:	Lining of container systems
Comment:	Bonded to various fabrics such as Oxford cloth

Figure 3-15. *Foam, ester liner.*

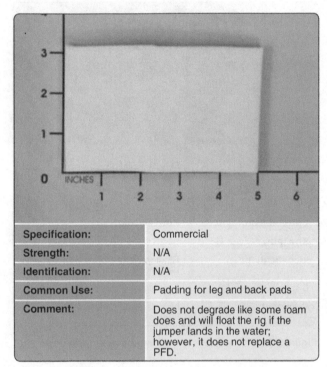

Specification:	Commercial
Strength:	N/A
Identification:	N/A
Common Use:	Padding for leg and back pads
Comment:	Does not degrade like some foam does and will float the rig if the jumper lands in the water; however, it does not replace a PFD.

Figure 3-14. *Foam, ¼" closed cell athletic foam.*

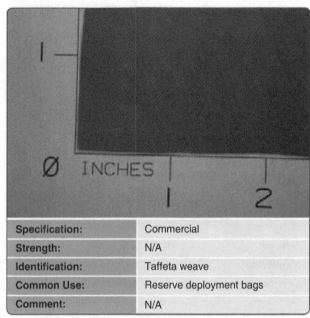

Specification:	Commercial
Strength:	N/A
Identification:	Taffeta weave
Common Use:	Reserve deployment bags
Comment:	N/A

Figure 3-16. *Oxford cloth, 200 denier.*

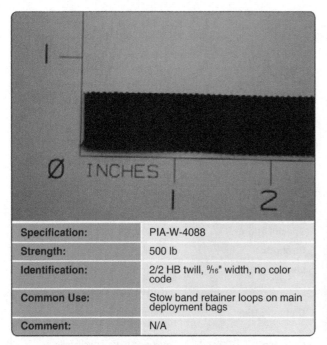

Specification:	PIA-W-4088
Strength:	500 lb
Identification:	2/2 HB twill, ⁹⁄₁₆" width, no color code
Common Use:	Stow band retainer loops on main deployment bags
Comment:	N/A

Figure 3-17. *⁹⁄₁₆" Type-1 Webbing.*

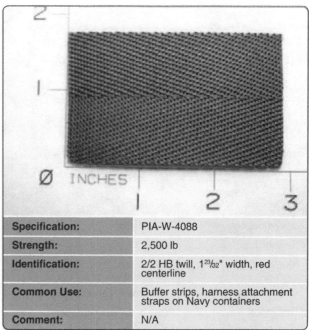

Specification:	PIA-W-4088
Strength:	2,500 lb
Identification:	2/2 HB twill, 1²³⁄₃₂" width, red centerline
Common Use:	Buffer strips, harness attachment straps on Navy containers
Comment:	N/A

Figure 3-19. *Type-6 Webbing.*

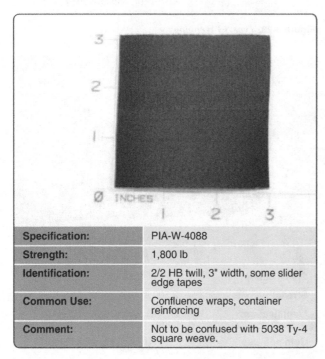

Specification:	PIA-W-4088
Strength:	1,800 lb
Identification:	2/2 HB twill, 3" width, some slider edge tapes
Common Use:	Confluence wraps, container reinforcing
Comment:	Not to be confused with 5038 Ty-4 square weave.

Figure 3-18. *3" Type-4 Webbing.*

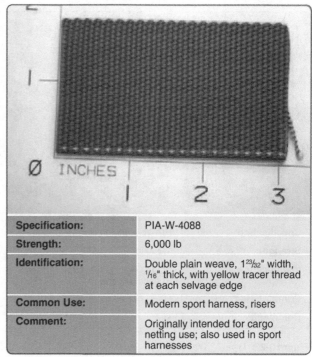

Specification:	PIA-W-4088
Strength:	6,000 lb
Identification:	Double plain weave, 1²³⁄₃₂" width, ¹⁄₁₆" thick, with yellow tracer thread at each selvage edge
Common Use:	Modern sport harness, risers
Comment:	Originally intended for cargo netting use; also used in sport harnesses

Figure 3-20. *Type-7 Webbing.*

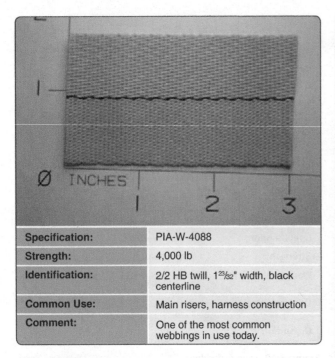

Specification:	PIA-W-4088
Strength:	4,000 lb
Identification:	2/2 HB twill, 1²³/₃₂" width, black centerline
Common Use:	Main risers, harness construction
Comment:	One of the most common webbings in use today.

Figure 3-21. *Type-8 Webbing.*

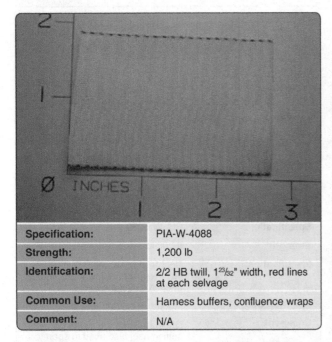

Specification:	PIA-W-4088
Strength:	1,200 lb
Identification:	2/2 HB twill, 1²³/₃₂" width, red lines at each selvage
Common Use:	Harness buffers, confluence wraps
Comment:	N/A

Figure 3-22. *Type-12 Webbing.*

Cords, Lines, and Threads

The most common uses of cord and lines are the suspension lines of the canopy. There are many different types in use. Today, the most common are nylon, Dacron, and Spectra®. The rigger needs to know the different types and their uses. Each may have special techniques to work with them.

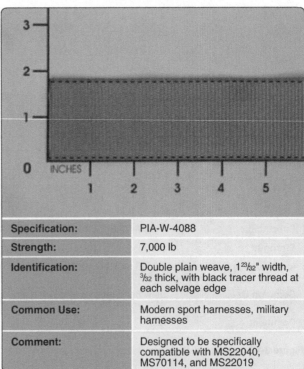

Specification:	PIA-W-4088
Strength:	7,000 lb
Identification:	Double plain weave, 1²³/₃₂" width, ³/₃₂ thick, with black tracer thread at each selvage edge
Common Use:	Modern sport harnesses, military harnesses
Comment:	Designed to be specifically compatible with MS22040, MS70114, and MS22019

Figure 3-23. *Type-13 Webbing.*

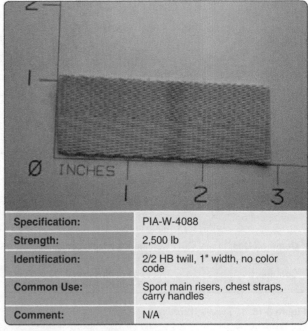

Specification:	PIA-W-4088
Strength:	2,500 lb
Identification:	2/2 HB twill, 1" width, no color code
Common Use:	Sport main risers, chest straps, carry handles
Comment:	N/A

Figure 3-24. *Type-17 Webbing.*

Almost all cords, lines, and threads are constructed of Nylon, again because of its inherent strength and relative elasticity. *[Figures 3-33 through 3-43]*

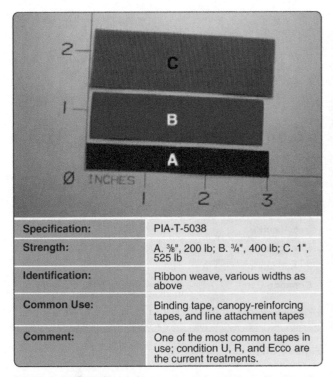

Specification:	PIA-T-5038
Strength:	A. ⅜", 200 lb; B. ¾", 400 lb; C. 1", 525 lb
Identification:	Ribbon weave, various widths as above
Common Use:	Binding tape, canopy-reinforcing tapes, and line attachment tapes
Comment:	One of the most common tapes in use; condition U, R, and Ecco are the current treatments.

Figure 3-25. *Type-3 Tape.*

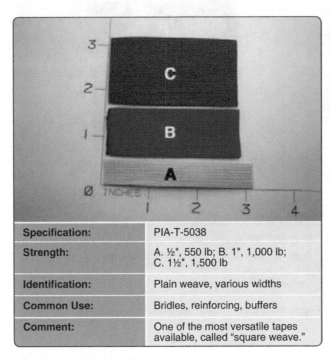

Specification:	PIA-T-5038
Strength:	A. ½", 550 lb; B. 1", 1,000 lb; C. 1½", 1,500 lb
Identification:	Plain weave, various widths
Common Use:	Bridles, reinforcing, buffers
Comment:	One of the most versatile tapes available, called "square weave."

Figure 3-26. *Type-4 Tape.*

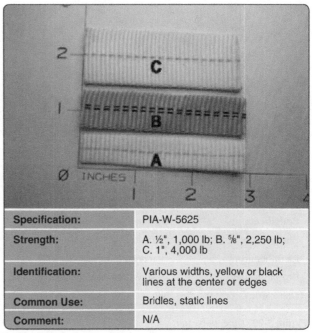

Specification:	PIA-W-5625
Strength:	A. ½", 1,000 lb; B. ⅝", 2,250 lb; C. 1", 4,000 lb
Identification:	Various widths, yellow or black lines at the center or edges
Common Use:	Bridles, static lines
Comment:	N/A

Figure 3-27. *Tubular webbing.*

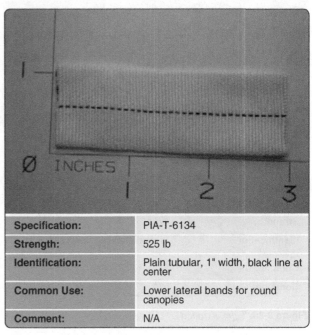

Specification:	PIA-T-6134
Strength:	525 lb
Identification:	Plain tubular, 1" width, black line at center
Common Use:	Lower lateral bands for round canopies
Comment:	N/A

Figure 3-28. *Type-1, 1" Parachute construction tape.*

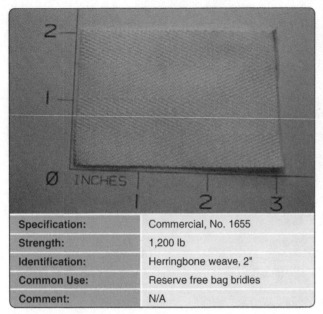

Specification:	Commercial, No. 1655
Strength:	1,200 lb
Identification:	Herringbone weave, 2"
Common Use:	Reserve free bag bridles
Comment:	N/A

Figure 3-29. *Tape, polyester, 2".*

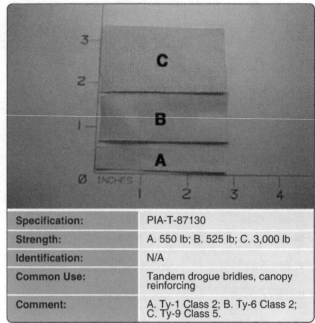

Specification:	PIA-T-87130
Strength:	A. 550 lb; B. 525 lb; C. 3,000 lb
Identification:	N/A
Common Use:	Tandem drogue bridles, canopy reinforcing
Comment:	A. Ty-1 Class 2; B. Ty-6 Class 2; C. Ty-9 Class 5.

Figure 3-31. *Kevlar® tape.*

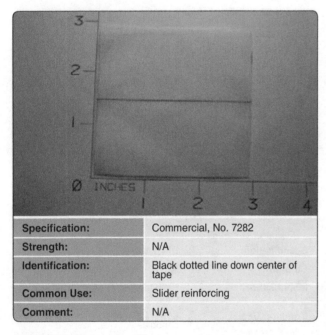

Specification:	Commercial, No. 7282
Strength:	N/A
Identification:	Black dotted line down center of tape
Common Use:	Slider reinforcing
Comment:	N/A

Figure 3-30. *Tape, nylon, 3".*

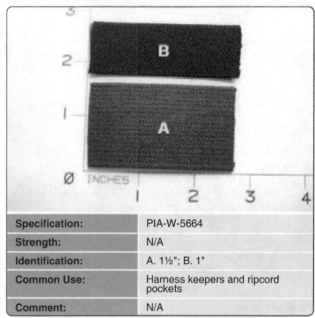

Specification:	PIA-W-5664
Strength:	N/A
Identification:	A. 1½"; B. 1"
Common Use:	Harness keepers and ripcord pockets
Comment:	N/A

Figure 3-32. *Cotton elastic webbing.*

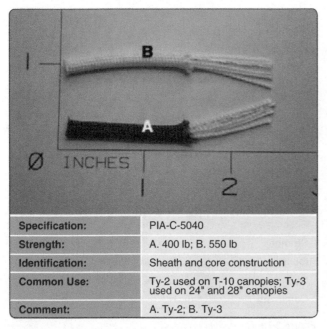

Specification:	PIA-C-5040
Strength:	A. 400 lb; B. 550 lb
Identification:	Sheath and core construction
Common Use:	Ty-2 used on T-10 canopies; Ty-3 used on 24" and 28" canopies
Comment:	A. Ty-2; B. Ty-3

Figure 3-33. *Cord, nylon, Type-2 and Ty-3.*

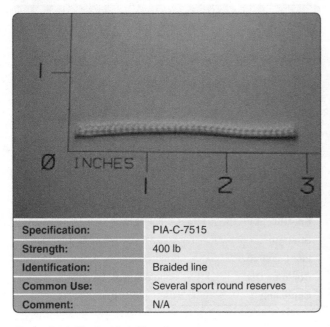

Specification:	PIA-C-7515
Strength:	400 lb
Identification:	Braided line
Common Use:	Several sport round reserves
Comment:	N/A

Figure 3-34. *Cord, nylon, Type-1a.*

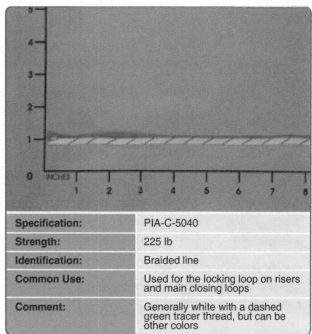

Specification:	PIA-C-5040
Strength:	225 lb
Identification:	Braided line
Common Use:	Used for the locking loop on risers and main closing loops
Comment:	Generally white with a dashed green tracer thread, but can be other colors

Figure 3-35. *Cord, nylon, Type-2a.*

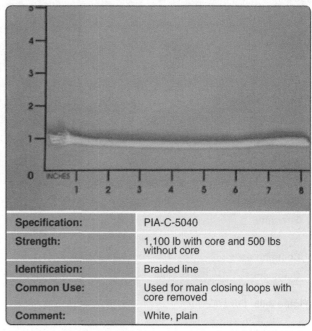

Specification:	PIA-C-5040
Strength:	1,100 lb with core and 500 lbs without core
Identification:	Braided line
Common Use:	Used for main closing loops with core removed
Comment:	White, plain

Figure 3-36. *Cord, Nylon, Type-5.*

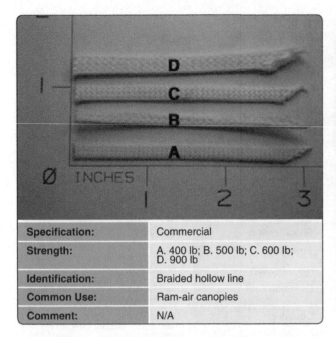

Specification:	Commercial
Strength:	A. 400 lb; B. 500 lb; C. 600 lb; D. 900 lb
Identification:	Braided hollow line
Common Use:	Ram-air canopies
Comment:	N/A

Figure 3-37. *Cord, Dacron.*

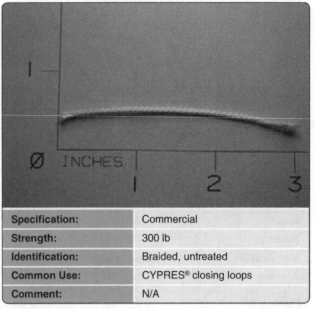

Specification:	Commercial
Strength:	300 lb
Identification:	Braided, untreated
Common Use:	CYPRES® closing loops
Comment:	N/A

Figure 3-39. *Cord, Spectra®.*

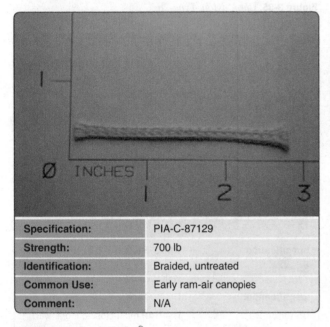

Specification:	PIA-C-87129
Strength:	700 lb
Identification:	Braided, untreated
Common Use:	Early ram-air canopies
Comment:	N/A

Figure 3-38. *Cord, Kevlar®.*

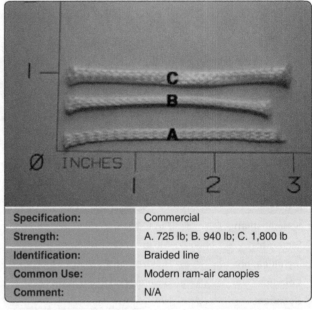

Specification:	Commercial
Strength:	A. 725 lb; B. 940 lb; C. 1,800 lb
Identification:	Braided line
Common Use:	Modern ram-air canopies
Comment:	N/A

Figure 3-40. *Cord, Spectra®.*

Hardware

Hardware, as defined in the context of parachutes, is "all metal parts associated with parachutes, their systems, and their suspended loads." Most riggers identify hardware as the snaps, adapters, rings, links, and releases commonly used on harnesses. In addition to these components, other hardware includes items such as lightweight links and snaps, ripcords and handles, stiffeners, grommets, springs, and snap fasteners. *[Figures 3-44 through 3-79]*

Most load bearing hardware consists of drop-forged alloy steel, sheet alloy steel, or forged aluminum alloy. Lightweight hardware may be stamped from the sheet alloy steel, or in rare instances, cast. Ripcord pins are cold forged. The majority of the load bearing hardware is forged carbon steel with either cadmium or zinc plating.

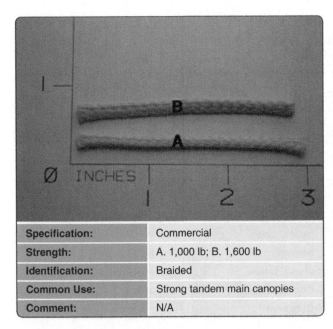

Specification:	Commercial
Strength:	A. 1,000 lb; B. 1,600 lb
Identification:	Braided
Common Use:	Strong tandem main canopies
Comment:	N/A

Figure 3-41. *Cord, Vectran® LCP.*

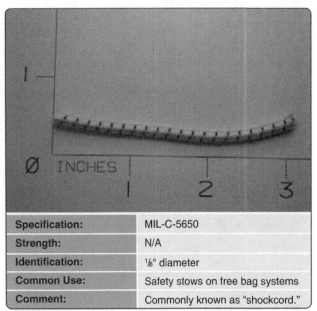

Specification:	MIL-C-5650
Strength:	N/A
Identification:	⅛" diameter
Common Use:	Safety stows on free bag systems
Comment:	Commonly known as "shockcord."

Figure 3-43. *Cord, elastic.*

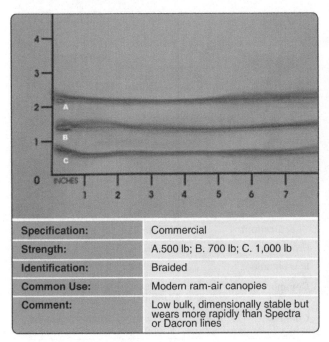

Specification:	Commercial
Strength:	A.500 lb; B. 700 lb; C. 1,000 lb
Identification:	Braided
Common Use:	Modern ram-air canopies
Comment:	Low bulk, dimensionally stable but wears more rapidly than Spectra or Dacron lines

Figure 3-42. *Cord, HMA.*

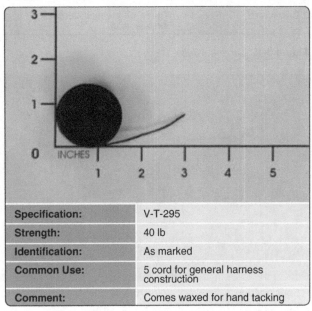

Specification:	V-T-295
Strength:	40 lb
Identification:	As marked
Common Use:	5 cord for general harness construction
Comment:	Comes waxed for hand tacking

Figure 3-44. *Cord, nylon, 5 cord Belbob.*

In recent years, there has been a movement to produce newer design hardware of stainless steel. This removes the problem of plating and the environmental problems associated with it. However, stainless is harder on the forging dies and the finishing processes take longer. Consequently, stainless hardware is generally more expensive than carbon steel.

All specification hardware has the appropriate number stamped or marked on it. The MS prefix is on those with the MIL-SPEC certification. All with the newer PIA certification have the mark with the PS (Parachute Standards) prefix. *[Figure 3-64]* Most of the current hardware has the mark with the MS prefix. As current stocks deplete, the mark on new production is with the PS prefix.

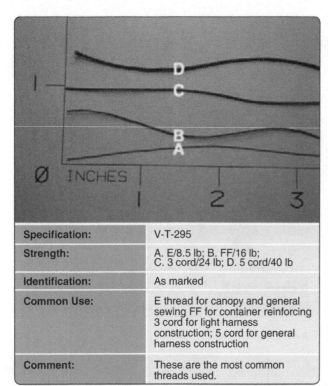

Specification:	V-T-295
Strength:	A. E/8.5 lb; B. FF/16 lb; C. 3 cord/24 lb; D. 5 cord/40 lb
Identification:	As marked
Common Use:	E thread for canopy and general sewing FF for container reinforcing 3 cord for light harness construction; 5 cord for general harness construction
Comment:	These are the most common threads used.

Figure 3-45. *Thread, nylon.*

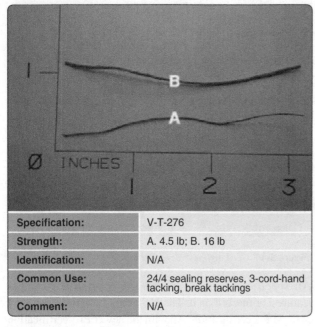

Specification:	V-T-276
Strength:	A. 4.5 lb; B. 16 lb
Identification:	N/A
Common Use:	24/4 sealing reserves, 3-cord-hand tacking, break tackings
Comment:	N/A

Figure 3-46. *A. Thread, cotton, 24/4; B. Thread, cotton, 3-cord.*

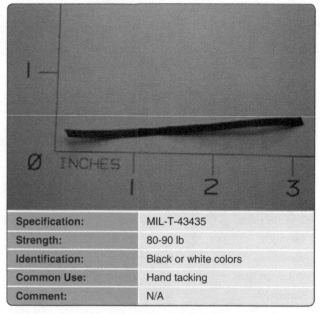

Specification:	MIL-T-43435
Strength:	80-90 lb
Identification:	Black or white colors
Common Use:	Hand tacking
Comment:	N/A

Figure 3-47. *Thread, nylon, flat braided (supertack).*

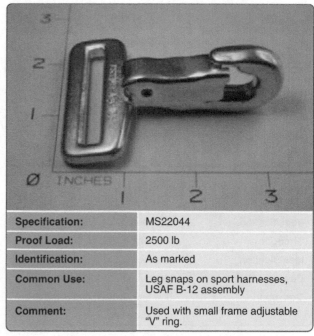

Specification:	MS22044
Proof Load:	2500 lb
Identification:	As marked
Common Use:	Leg snaps on sport harnesses, USAF B-12 assembly
Comment:	Used with small frame adjustable "V" ring.

Figure 3-48. *Snap, B 12.*

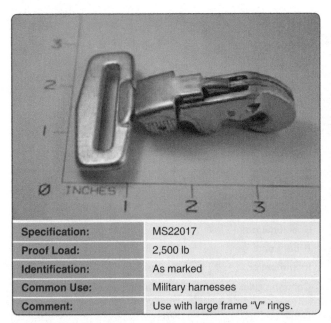

Specification:	MS22017
Proof Load:	2,500 lb
Identification:	As marked
Common Use:	Military harnesses
Comment:	Use with large frame "V" rings.

Figure 3-49. *Ejector snap, non-adjustable.*

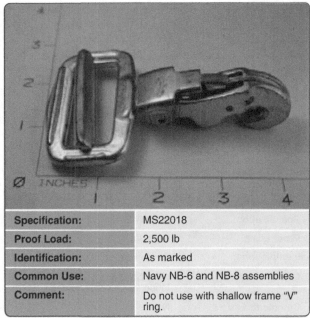

Specification:	MS22018
Proof Load:	2,500 lb
Identification:	As marked
Common Use:	Navy NB-6 and NB-8 assemblies
Comment:	Do not use with shallow frame "V" ring.

Figure 3-51. *Snap, quick fit ejector.*

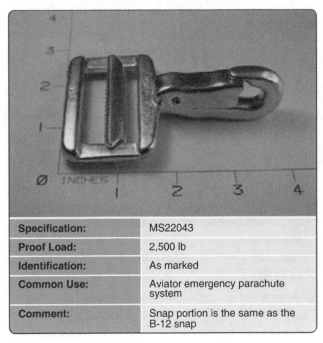

Specification:	MS22043
Proof Load:	2,500 lb
Identification:	As marked
Common Use:	Aviator emergency parachute system
Comment:	Snap portion is the same as the B-12 snap

Figure 3-50. *Snap, quick fit.*

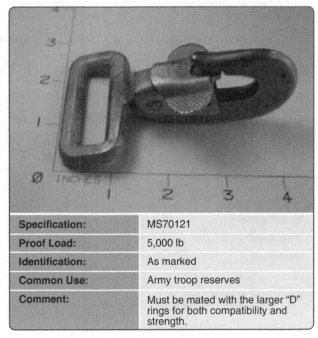

Specification:	MS70121
Proof Load:	5,000 lb
Identification:	As marked
Common Use:	Army troop reserves
Comment:	Must be mated with the larger "D" rings for both compatibility and strength.

Figure 3-52. *Snap, parachute chest-type pack.*

Specification:	MS22042
Proof Load:	5,000 lb
Identification:	As marked
Common Use:	Navy chest assemblies, strong tandem passenger harness
Comment:	N/A

Figure 3-53. *Snap, quick connector, parachute harness.*

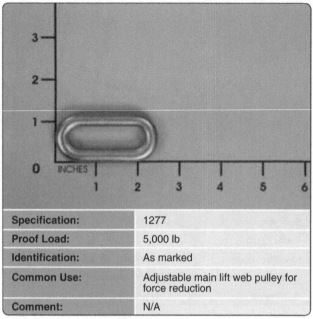

Specification:	1277
Proof Load:	5,000 lb
Identification:	As marked
Common Use:	Adjustable main lift web pulley for force reduction
Comment:	N/A

Figure 3-55. *Adjuster, oval ring.*

Specification:	MS22046-1
Proof Load:	5,000 lb
Identification:	As marked
Common Use:	Army T-10 harness
Comment:	N/A

Figure 3-54. *"D" ring harness, old style.*

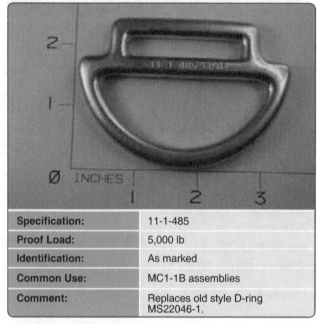

Specification:	11-1-485
Proof Load:	5,000 lb
Identification:	As marked
Common Use:	MC1-1B assemblies
Comment:	Replaces old style D-ring MS22046-1.

Figure 3-56. *"D" ring harness, new style.*

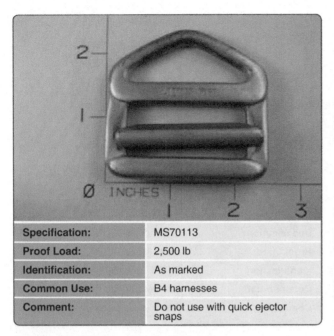

Specification:	MS70113
Proof Load:	2,500 lb
Identification:	As marked
Common Use:	B4 harnesses
Comment:	Do not use with quick ejector snaps

Figure 3-57. *"V" ring, quick fit, shallow frame.*

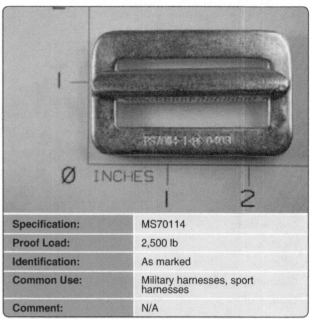

Specification:	MS70114
Proof Load:	2,500 lb
Identification:	As marked
Common Use:	Military harnesses, sport harnesses
Comment:	N/A

Figure 3-59. *Adapter, quick fit, small frame.*

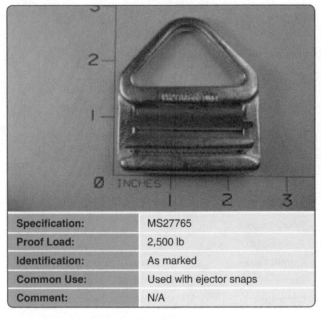

Specification:	MS27765
Proof Load:	2,500 lb
Identification:	As marked
Common Use:	Used with ejector snaps
Comment:	N/A

Figure 3-58. *"V" ring, quick fit, large frame.*

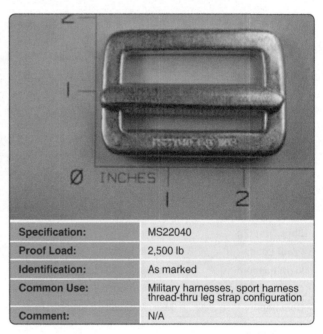

Specification:	MS22040
Proof Load:	2,500 lb
Identification:	As marked
Common Use:	Military harnesses, sport harness thread-thru leg strap configuration
Comment:	N/A

Figure 3-60. *Adapter, quick fit, large frame.*

Specification:	MS22019
Proof Load:	2,500 lb
Identification:	As marked
Common Use:	Navy harnesses
Comment:	Does not grip as well as MS70114 and MS22040

Figure 3-61. *Adapter, quick fit, reversible.*

Specification:	Commercial
Proof Load:	2,500 lb
Identification:	DJ-SSA, stainless steel
Common Use:	Harness and leg strap adapters
Comment:	A smaller version of the MS70114 adapter

Figure 3-63. *Adapter, quick fit.*

Specification:	Commercial
Proof Load:	2,500 lb, stainless steel
Identification:	SP-888
Common Use:	Sport harness leg strap adapters
Comment:	Manufactured by Wichard in France

Figure 3-62. *Adapter, 2 piece.*

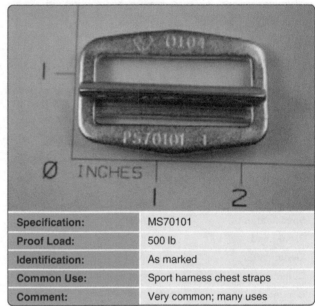

Specification:	MS70101
Proof Load:	500 lb
Identification:	As marked
Common Use:	Sport harness chest straps
Comment:	Very common; many uses

Figure 3-64. *Adapter, quick fit, lightweight.*

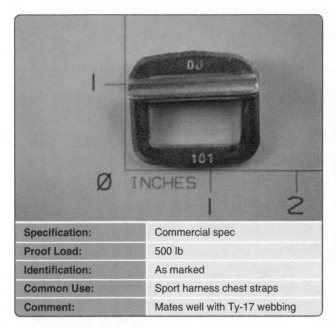

Specification:	Commercial spec
Proof Load:	500 lb
Identification:	As marked
Common Use:	Sport harness chest straps
Comment:	Mates well with Ty-17 webbing

Figure 3-65. *Adapter, quick fit, 1".*

Specification:	MS22002
Proof Load:	3,000 lb
Identification:	As marked
Common Use:	C-9 canopies
Comment:	N/A

Figure 3-67. *Link, removable connector.*

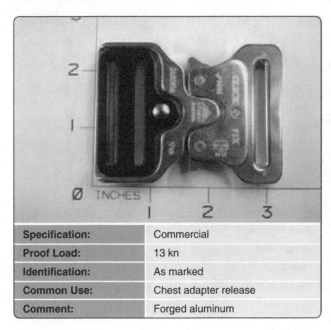

Specification:	Commercial
Proof Load:	13 kn
Identification:	As marked
Common Use:	Chest adapter release
Comment:	Forged aluminum

Figure 3-66. *Adapter, quick fit release.*

Specification:	MS22021
Proof Load:	3,000 lb
Identification:	As marked
Common Use:	Navy and Air Force canopies
Comment:	N/A

Figure 3-68. *Link, removable connector, speed.*

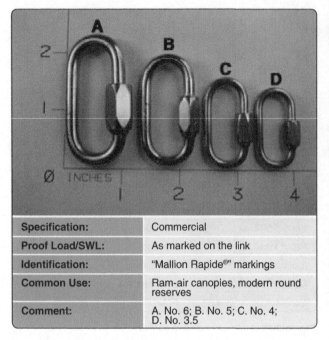

Specification:	Commercial
Proof Load/SWL:	As marked on the link
Identification:	"Mallion Rapide®" markings
Common Use:	Ram-air canopies, modern round reserves
Comment:	A. No. 6; B. No. 5; C. No. 4; D. No. 3.5

Figure 3-69. *Link, Rapide®.*

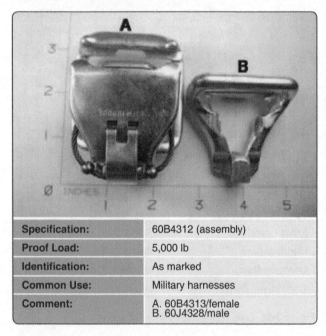

Specification:	60B4312 (assembly)
Proof Load:	5,000 lb
Identification:	As marked
Common Use:	Military harnesses
Comment:	A. 60B4313/female B. 60J4328/male

Figure 3-70. *Release, parachute canopy quick disconnect, Capewell.*

Plastics and Synthetics

The term "plastic" used here is a generic term for synthetic materials. The use of these materials is primarily for stiffeners in containers. They replace the metal stiffeners used in military systems. High-density polyethylene (HDPE) was the first material used followed by Lexan®. Time has

Specification:	Commercial
Proof Load:	2,500 lb
Identification:	RW-1, 445
Common Use:	3-ring release systems
Comment:	No. 445 shown

Figure 3-71. *Ring, harness, 3-ring.*

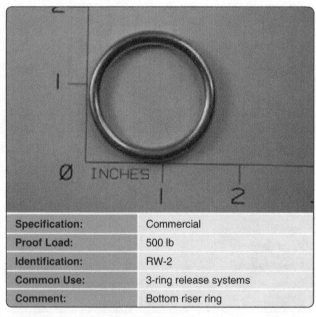

Specification:	Commercial
Proof Load:	500 lb
Identification:	RW-2
Common Use:	3-ring release systems
Comment:	Bottom riser ring

Figure 3-72. *Ring, riser, middle, 3-ring.*

proven that moly disulfide (MDS) filled nylon is superior to the other materials and has become the most commonly used stiffener material. Today, the use of Lexan® is primarily in clear windows in pin protector flaps. Stiffeners should have rounded edges to prevent wear points and to minimize the ability of lines to half hitch around them. *[Figures 3-80 through 3-84]*

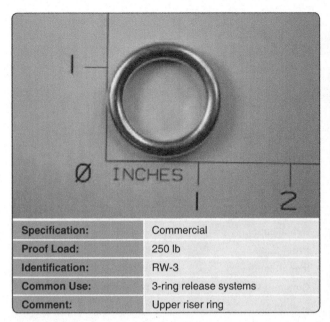

Specification:	Commercial
Proof Load:	250 lb
Identification:	RW-3
Common Use:	3-ring release systems
Comment:	Upper riser ring

Figure 3-73. *Ring, riser, small, 3-ring.*

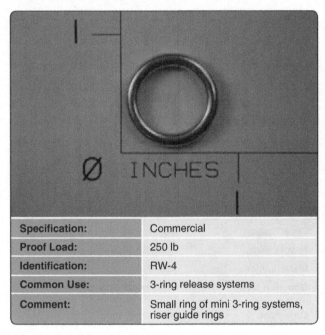

Specification:	Commercial
Proof Load:	250 lb
Identification:	RW-4
Common Use:	3-ring release systems
Comment:	Small ring of mini 3-ring systems, riser guide rings

Figure 3-74. *Ring, riser, mini, 3-ring.*

Fasteners

Fasteners are various types of devices designed to hold parts or components together or allow them to be held open or closed. The most common designs are hook and loop fasteners (Velcro®), snaps, grommets, and slide fasteners (zippers).

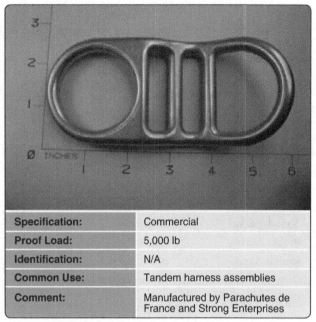

Specification:	Commercial
Proof Load:	5,000 lb
Identification:	N/A
Common Use:	Tandem harness assemblies
Comment:	Manufactured by Parachutes de France and Strong Enterprises

Figure 3-75. *Ring, harness, tandem.*

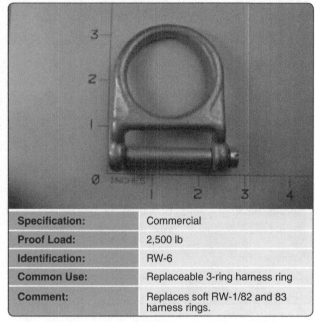

Specification:	Commercial
Proof Load:	2,500 lb
Identification:	RW-6
Common Use:	Replaceable 3-ring harness ring
Comment:	Replaces soft RW-1/82 and 83 harness rings.

Figure 3-76. *Ring, harness, replaceable, 3 ring.*

Specification:	Commercial
Proof Load:	2,500 lb
Identification:	2058
Common Use:	Tandem drogue release
Comment:	N/A

Figure 3-77. *Ring, harness, "O" 2058 Cadmium Ring.*

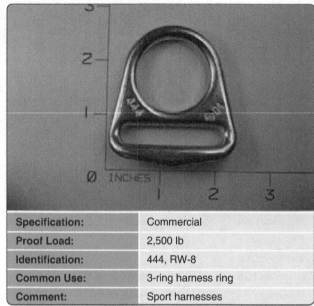

Specification:	Commercial
Proof Load:	2,500 lb
Identification:	444, RW-8
Common Use:	3-ring harness ring
Comment:	Sport harnesses

Figure 3-79. *Ring, harness, mini.*

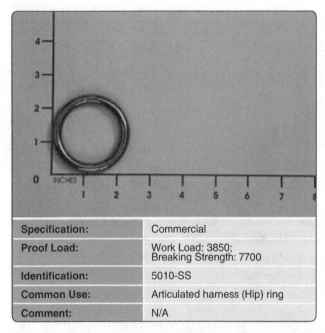

Specification:	Commercial
Proof Load:	Work Load: 3850; Breaking Strength: 7700
Identification:	5010-SS
Common Use:	Articulated harness (Hip) ring
Comment:	N/A

Figure 3-78. *Ring, harness, 5010-SS Ring.*

Specification:	Commercial
Proof Load:	2,500 lb
Identification:	555, RI-1
Common Use:	Sport student harness, pilot emergency harness
Comment:	N/A

Figure 3-80. *Ring, quick fit.*

Of all these, Velcro® and grommets play a major part in parachute manufacture. The use of Velcro® is primarily for protector flap closure designs, while grommets are for use in pack closing systems. Both fasteners are subject to extreme wear and tear in their normal use. Consequently, routine maintenance involves the repair and replacement of these items. *[Figures 3-85 through 3-89]*

Housings

Housings are spiral-wound flexible tubing. Almost all are stainless steel. Their design is to route, house, and protect the ripcord cable. They are anchored to the container at one end and the ripcord pocket or mount at the other end. Most ripcord housings are compressible only, but some military

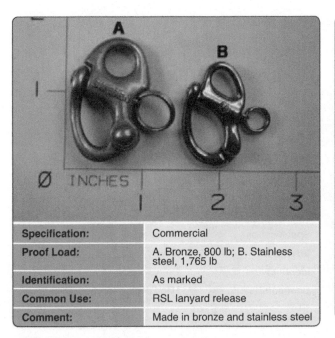

Specification:	Commercial
Proof Load:	A. Bronze, 800 lb; B. Stainless steel, 1,765 lb
Identification:	As marked
Common Use:	RSL lanyard release
Comment:	Made in bronze and stainless steel

Figure 3-81. *Snap shackle.*

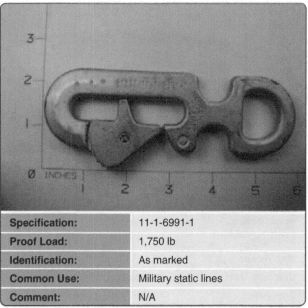

Specification:	11-1-6991-1
Proof Load:	1,750 lb
Identification:	As marked
Common Use:	Military static lines
Comment:	N/A

Figure 3-83. *Snap, static line, new style.*

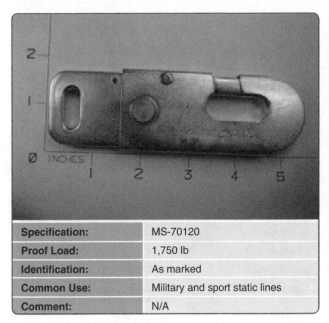

Specification:	MS-70120
Proof Load:	1,750 lb
Identification:	As marked
Common Use:	Military and sport static lines
Comment:	N/A

Figure 3-82. *Snap, static line, old style.*

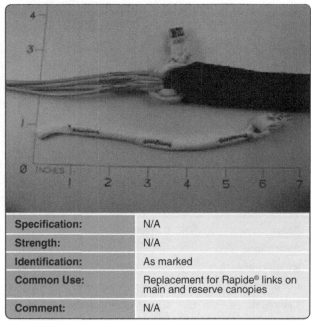

Specification:	N/A
Strength:	N/A
Identification:	As marked
Common Use:	Replacement for Rapide® links on main and reserve canopies
Comment:	N/A

Figure 3-84. *Soft link.*

housings used with seat parachutes are expandable as well. The reason that ripcord housings are compressible and non-expandable is to prevent premature loading of the cable and pin as the rig is donned and the user moves around. One-pin sport container systems generally use a .26" inside diameter housing. Two-pin and most military containers use a .375" inside diameter housing. Ripcord housings are measured under slight tension.

The 3-ring release system employs the smaller .20" or .18" housing for use with Lolon (yellow), or Teflon (orange or red), coated release cables. These "cutaway" housings must be expandable and non-compressible. The reason for this is, in the case where the loop load is excessive, the non-compressible housing will resist the loop or "push" against it allowing an effective "pull" of the cable from the loop.

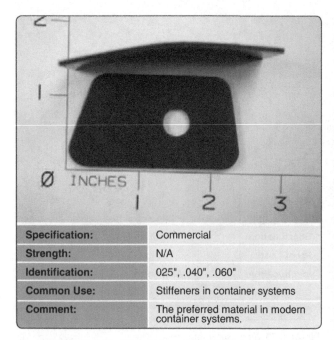

Specification:	Commercial
Strength:	N/A
Identification:	025", .040", .060"
Common Use:	Stiffeners in container systems
Comment:	The preferred material in modern container systems.

Figure 3-85. *Molydisulfide Nylon—MDS (Nylatron®).*

Specification:	Commercial
Strength:	N/A
Identification:	Orange color
Common Use:	Hand deploy handles, pinless student ripcords
Comment:	N/A

Figure 3-87. *HDPE tubing, 1 ½".*

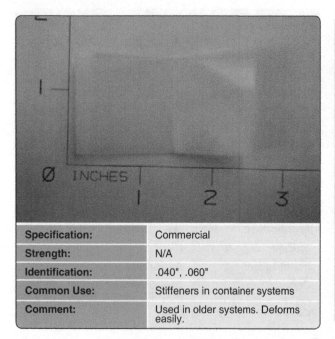

Specification:	Commercial
Strength:	N/A
Identification:	.040", .060"
Common Use:	Stiffeners in container systems
Comment:	Used in older systems. Deforms easily.

Figure 3-86. *Poylethylene, high density (HDPE).*

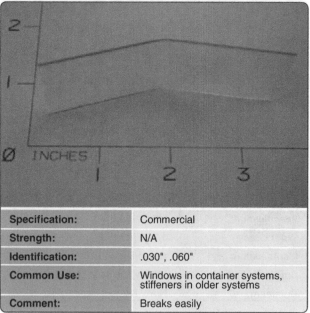

Specification:	Commercial
Strength:	N/A
Identification:	.030", .060"
Common Use:	Windows in container systems, stiffeners in older systems
Comment:	Breaks easily

Figure 3-88. *Polycarbonate—Lexan®.*

Thus the term "push-pull system." A compressible housing compresses until it reaches its limit of compression, which could be as much as 20 percent of the total length. In a two-cable scenario, such as the 3-ring, the differential could be as much as to allow the short side to release without releasing the long side. Cutaway housings should be measured in a relaxed state and then compressed to ensure that it remains within the manufacturer's allowable tolerance. [*Figures 3-90A* through *3-92C*]

Ripcords, Cables, and Swages

The standard ripcord used today on most parachute systems consists of a stainless steel handle, $\frac{3}{32}$" 7 × 7 corrosion resistant steel cable, a stainless steel terminal ball, and one or more stainless steel pins swaged onto the cable. The handles come in various shapes and sizes in order to be compatible with main lift web lengths and pocket sizes and particulars, such as whether the ripcord grip is inboard or outboard. The terminal ball may be of several configurations, such as a

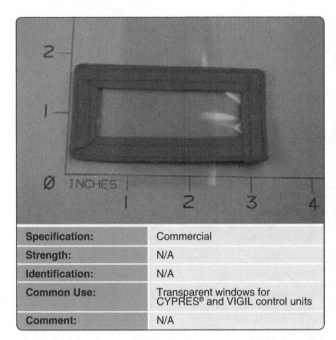

Specification:	Commercial
Strength:	N/A
Identification:	N/A
Common Use:	Transparent windows for CYPRES® and VIGIL control units
Comment:	N/A

Figure 3-89. *Vinyl.*

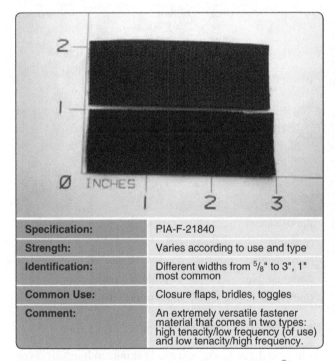

Specification:	PIA-F-21840
Strength:	Varies according to use and type
Identification:	Different widths from ⅝" to 3", 1" most common
Common Use:	Closure flaps, bridles, toggles
Comment:	An extremely versatile fastener material that comes in two types: high tenacity/low frequency (of use) and low tenacity/high frequency.

Figure 3-90. *Fastener tape, hook and pile, nylon (Velcro®).*

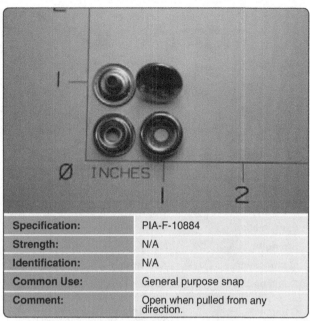

Specification:	PIA-F-10884
Strength:	N/A
Identification:	N/A
Common Use:	General purpose snap
Comment:	Open when pulled from any direction.

Figure 3-91. *DOT Fasteners, Durable.*

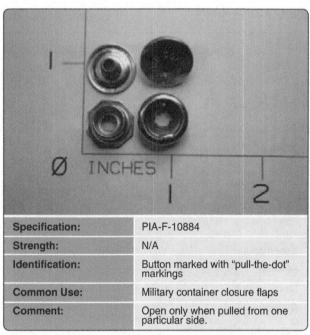

Specification:	PIA-F-10884
Strength:	N/A
Identification:	Button marked with "pull-the-dot" markings
Common Use:	Military container closure flaps
Comment:	Open only when pulled from one particular side.

Figure 3-92. *DOT Fasteners, Pull-the-dot.*

ball and shank design. The pins usually are one of two basic designs: intermediate pin or terminal pin. The advantage of the intermediate pin is that it can be visually inspected easily by the rigger in the field. The end of the 7 × 7 cable can actually be seen where it is ground off at the bend in the shank of the pin. Metal ripcord assemblies are used on reserve and emergency parachute systems and military mains. Main ripcords may also consist of plastic handles and nylon coated cable without pins.

On modern sport parachutes, the hand deploy pilot chute replaced the conventional ripcord, by either throw-out or pull-out. These configurations use the curved or straight locking pins attached to the pilot chute bridle. *[Figures 3-93 through 3-101]*

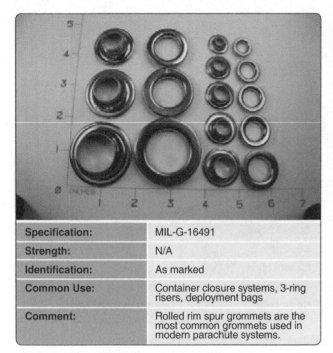

Specification:	MIL-G-16491
Strength:	N/A
Identification:	As marked
Common Use:	Container closure systems, 3-ring risers, deployment bags
Comment:	Rolled rim spur grommets are the most common grommets used in modern parachute systems.

Figure 3-93. *Grommets.*

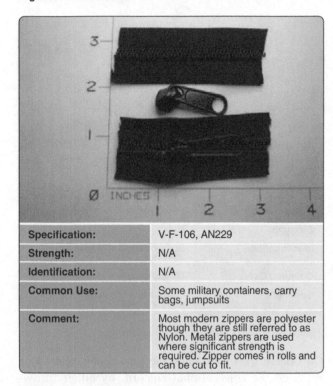

Specification:	V-F-106, AN229
Strength:	N/A
Identification:	N/A
Common Use:	Some military containers, carry bags, jumpsuits
Comment:	Most modern zippers are polyester though they are still referred to as Nylon. Metal zippers are used where significant strength is required. Zipper comes in rolls and can be cut to fit.

Figure 3-94. *Interlocking slide fasteners (zippers).*

Miscellaneous

The miscellaneous category includes remaining items that do not fit in any of the other categories. They fall somewhat under the category of hardware, but are not load-bearing type hardware like legstrap friction adaptors or hip rings. Most of the these items are made of stamped metal rather

Specification:	PIA-H-7750
Strength:	N/A
Identification:	ID approximately .375"
Common Use:	Military parachute assemblies
Comment:	Brass or steel ferrules

Figure 3-95. *Housing, flexible, ripcord.*

Specification:	Commercial
Strength:	N/A
Identification:	ID approximately .26"
Common Use:	Most modern sport systems
Comment:	Brass or steel ferrules

Figure 3-96. *Housing, flexible, ripcord.*

than forged steel. The plastic-looking, nylon "SR-Type Snaps" are used on gear bags, helmets, and as temporary holds for things such as tandem passenger drogue release handles. *[Figures 3-102 through 3-118]*

Chapter Summary

Material identification and understanding of its functional application is one of the most important aspects of becoming a parachute rigger. In order to properly inspect and recertify equipment—which is the rigger's primary task—one has to be able to recognize when a material is worn beyond its

Specification:	Commercial
Strength:	N/A
Identification:	.18" – .20" ID
Common Use:	3-ring release systems
Comment:	Brass ferrules

Figure 3-97. *Housing, flexible, 3-ring.*

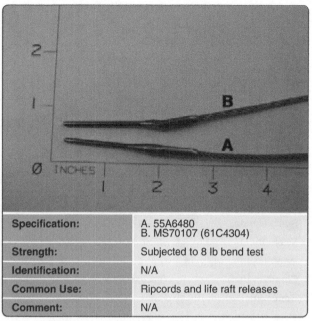

Specification:	A. 55A6480 B. MS70107 (61C4304)
Strength:	Subjected to 8 lb bend test
Identification:	N/A
Common Use:	Ripcords and life raft releases
Comment:	N/A

Figure 3-99. *A. Pin, ripcord, terminal; B. Pin, ripcord, intermediate.*

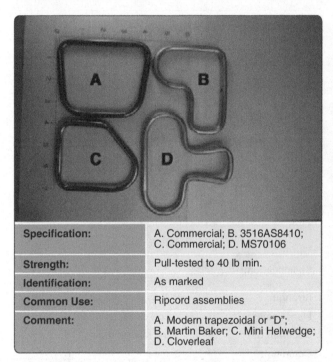

Specification:	A. Commercial; B. 3516AS8410; C. Commercial; D. MS70106
Strength:	Pull-tested to 40 lb min.
Identification:	As marked
Common Use:	Ripcord assemblies
Comment:	A. Modern trapezoidal or "D"; B. Martin Baker; C. Mini Helwedge; D. Cloverleaf

Figure 3-98. *Handle, steel, ripcord.*

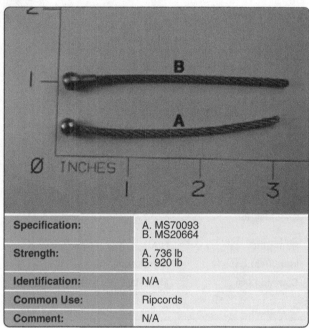

Specification:	A. MS70093 B. MS20664
Strength:	A. 736 lb B. 920 lb
Identification:	N/A
Common Use:	Ripcords
Comment:	N/A

Figure 3-100. *A. Ball, terminal; B. Ball and shank.*

required strength or if the wrong material has been selected to make a repair.

New high-tech fabrics are continually being explored, especially in the area of canopy connector lines and canopy cloth. Great improvements have been made in the reduction of permeability of canopy fabrics. Permeability is a measure of the ease with which a fluid (air in this case) can move through the fabric. Various forms of silicone and polyurethane coatings are used to create what we call in the vernacular, "Zero-P." Generally, coated canopy cloth is referred to as 0 cfm (cubic foot per minute), and uncoated canopy cloth is referred to as 0-3 cfm. When we speak of porosity, we are referring to a measure of the tiny open spaces in the weave of the fabric. As canopy fabric wears, it becomes more porous and the permeability increases.

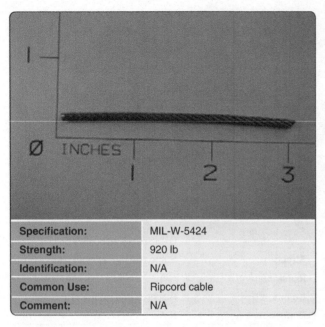

Specification:	MIL-W-5424
Strength:	920 lb
Identification:	N/A
Common Use:	Ripcord cable
Comment:	N/A

Figure 3-101. *7×7 stainless steel corrosion resistant cable.*

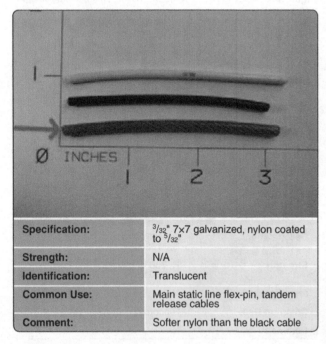

Specification:	$^{3}/_{32}$" 7×7 galvanized, nylon coated to $^{5}/_{32}$"
Strength:	N/A
Identification:	Translucent
Common Use:	Main static line flex-pin, tandem release cables
Comment:	Softer nylon than the black cable

Figure 3-102A. *Static line cable.*

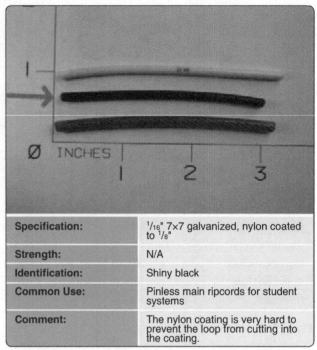

Specification:	$^{1}/_{16}$" 7×7 galvanized, nylon coated to $^{1}/_{8}$"
Strength:	N/A
Identification:	Shiny black
Common Use:	Pinless main ripcords for student systems
Comment:	The nylon coating is very hard to prevent the loop from cutting into the coating.

Figure 3-102B. *Black pinless r/c cable.*

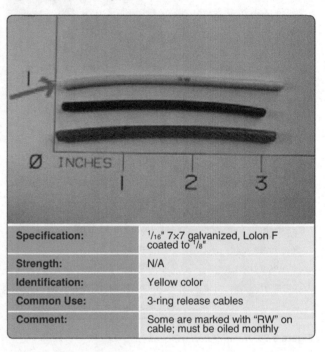

Specification:	$^{1}/_{16}$" 7×7 galvanized, Lolon F coated to $^{1}/_{8}$"
Strength:	N/A
Identification:	Yellow color
Common Use:	3-ring release cables
Comment:	Some are marked with "RW" on cable; must be oiled monthly

Figure 3-102C. *Lolon 3-ring cable.*

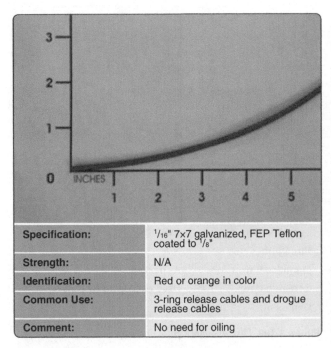

Specification:	¹/₁₆" 7×7 galvanized, FEP Teflon coated to ¹/₈"
Strength:	N/A
Identification:	Red or orange in color
Common Use:	3-ring release cables and drogue release cables
Comment:	No need for oiling

Figure 3-103. *Teflon 3-ring cable.*

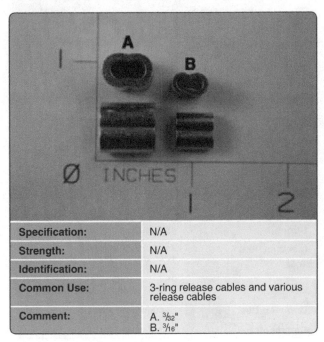

Specification:	N/A
Strength:	N/A
Identification:	N/A
Common Use:	3-ring release cables and various release cables
Comment:	A. ³/₃₂" B. ³/₁₆"

Figure 3-104. *Nicopress swage, ³/₃₂" and ³/₁₆".*

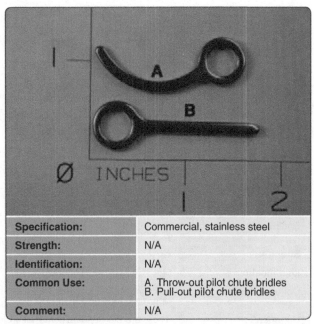

Specification:	Commercial, stainless steel
Strength:	N/A
Identification:	N/A
Common Use:	A. Throw-out pilot chute bridles B. Pull-out pilot chute bridles
Comment:	N/A

Figure 3-105. *A. Release pin, curved; B. Release pin, straight.*

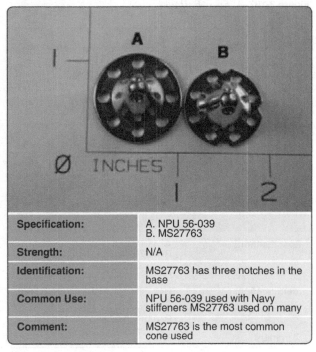

Specification:	A. NPU 56-039 B. MS27763
Strength:	N/A
Identification:	MS27763 has three notches in the base
Common Use:	NPU 56-039 used with Navy stiffeners MS27763 used on many
Comment:	MS27763 is the most common cone used

Figure 3-106. *Cones.*

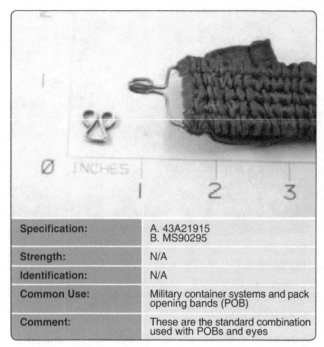

Specification:	A. 43A21915 B. MS90295
Strength:	N/A
Identification:	N/A
Common Use:	Military container systems and pack opening bands (POB)
Comment:	These are the standard combination used with POBs and eyes

Figure 3-107. *A. Eyes; B. Hooks.*

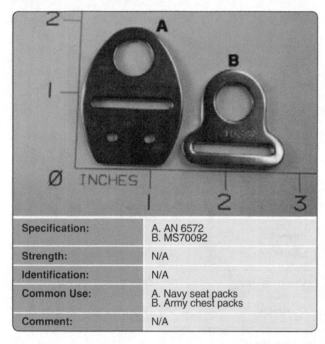

Specification:	A. AN 6572 B. MS70092
Strength:	N/A
Identification:	N/A
Common Use:	A. Navy seat packs B. Army chest packs
Comment:	N/A

Figure 3-108. *End tabs.*

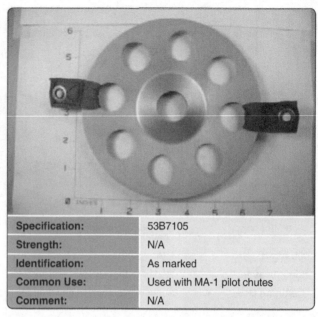

Specification:	53B7105
Strength:	N/A
Identification:	As marked
Common Use:	Used with MA-1 pilot chutes
Comment:	N/A

Figure 3-109. *Disc assembly, pilot chute ejector.*

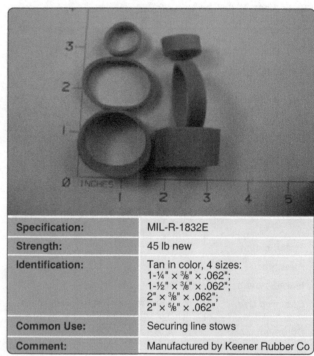

Specification:	MIL-R-1832E
Strength:	45 lb new
Identification:	Tan in color, 4 sizes: 1-¼" × ⅜" × .062"; 1-½" × ⅜" × .062"; 2" × ⅜" × .062"; 2" × ⅝" × .062"
Common Use:	Securing line stows
Comment:	Manufactured by Keener Rubber Co

Figure 3-110. *Rubber bands, parachute suspension line.*

Specification:	Commercial
Strength:	N/A
Identification:	11.0R
Common Use:	Securing ripcord housings
Comment:	N/A

Figure 3-111. *Clamp, housing, single.*

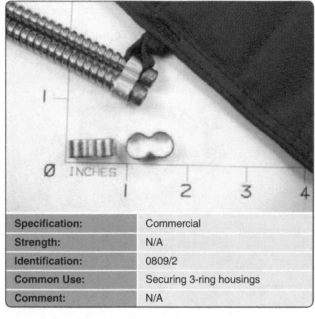

Specification:	Commercial
Strength:	N/A
Identification:	0809/2
Common Use:	Securing 3-ring housings
Comment:	N/A

Figure 3-112. *Clamp, housing, double.*

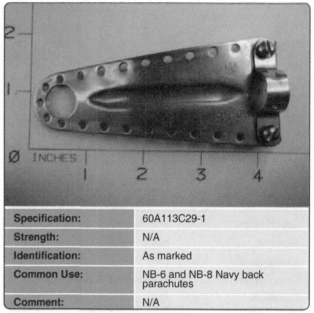

Specification:	60A113C29-1
Strength:	N/A
Identification:	As marked
Common Use:	NB-6 and NB-8 Navy back parachutes
Comment:	N/A

Figure 3-113. *Stiffener, housing, Navy.*

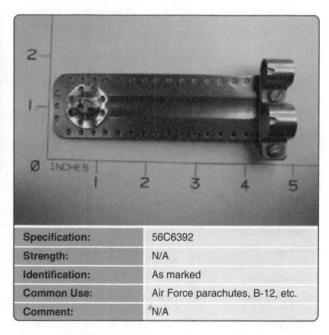

Specification:	56C6392
Strength:	N/A
Identification:	As marked
Common Use:	Air Force parachutes, B-12, etc.
Comment:	N/A

Figure 3-114. *Stiffener, housing, Air Force.*

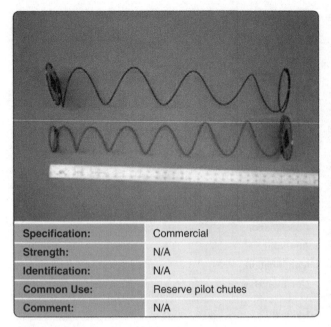

Specification:	Commercial
Strength:	N/A
Identification:	N/A
Common Use:	Reserve pilot chutes
Comment:	N/A

Figure 3-115. *Cylindrical spring, pilot chute.*

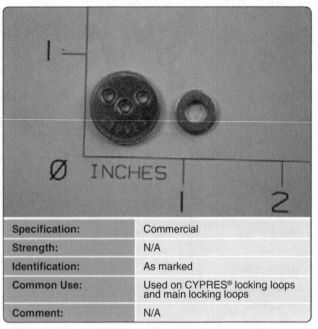

Specification:	Commercial
Strength:	N/A
Identification:	As marked
Common Use:	Used on CYPRES® locking loops and main locking loops
Comment:	N/A

Figure 3-117. *Washers, locking, loop.*

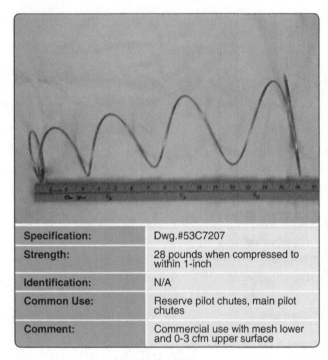

Specification:	Dwg.#53C7207
Strength:	28 pounds when compressed to within 1-inch
Identification:	N/A
Common Use:	Reserve pilot chutes, main pilot chutes
Comment:	Commercial use with mesh lower and 0-3 cfm upper surface

Figure 3-116. *MA-1 Spring, pilot chute.*

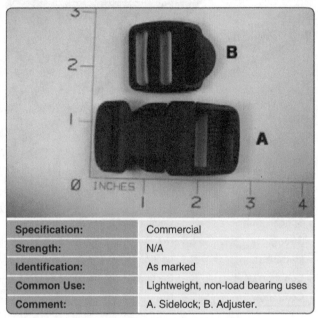

Specification:	Commercial
Strength:	N/A
Identification:	As marked
Common Use:	Lightweight, non-load bearing uses
Comment:	A. Sidelock; B. Adjuster.

Figure 3-118. *Nylon hardware.*

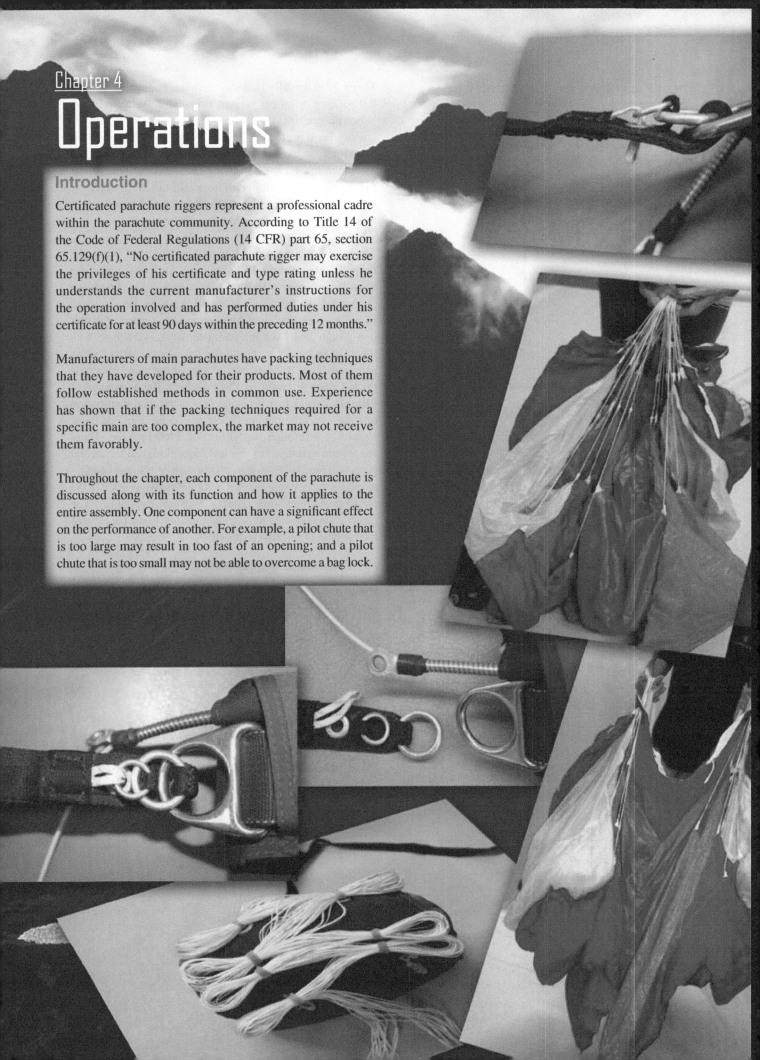

Chapter 4

Operations

Introduction

Certificated parachute riggers represent a professional cadre within the parachute community. According to Title 14 of the Code of Federal Regulations (14 CFR) part 65, section 65.129(f)(1), "No certificated parachute rigger may exercise the privileges of his certificate and type rating unless he understands the current manufacturer's instructions for the operation involved and has performed duties under his certificate for at least 90 days within the preceding 12 months."

Manufacturers of main parachutes have packing techniques that they have developed for their products. Most of them follow established methods in common use. Experience has shown that if the packing techniques required for a specific main are too complex, the market may not receive them favorably.

Throughout the chapter, each component of the parachute is discussed along with its function and how it applies to the entire assembly. One component can have a significant effect on the performance of another. For example, a pilot chute that is too large may result in too fast of an opening; and a pilot chute that is too small may not be able to overcome a bag lock.

Sport Parachute Main Packing Techniques

When we talk about "square" parachutes, what we really mean is rectangular plan form, semi-elliptical, or elliptical plan form. *[Figures 4-1* through *4-3]* Plan form refers to the shape of the canopy from a "birds eye view."

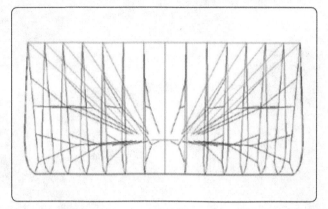

Figure 4-1. *Rectangular plan form canopy.*

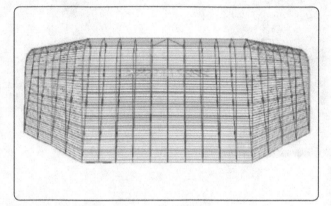

Figure 4-2. *Tapered tip plan form canopy.*

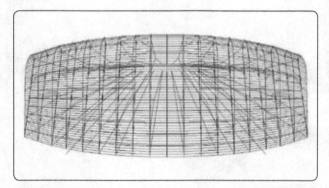

Figure 4-3. *Elliptical plan form canopy.*

There are essentially two ways to pack a square parachute: flat packing or proper ram-air orientation (PRO) packing. When flat packing, the canopy is laid on its side so that you are viewing it in profile. The canopy is S-folded stacking the line groups on top of one another. Variations to this method include rolling the nose from the leading edge to the A line, toward the tail, or splitting the nose cells in half, rolling them inward, and tucking them into the center cell. The tail is then split and cocooned around the rest of the canopy.

The most common method of packing "square" mains and reserves, however, is PRO packing. Developed by John Sherman in the early 1970s when "squares" were first being introduced, the premise was to pack them the same way one would pack a round parachute—that is, to separate the four line groups and flake the perimeter of the parachute with the nose facing forward and the tail of the canopy facing rearward. If one were tall enough to raise the round parachute off the floor, it could be PRO packed. The advantage of PRO packing is that it results in a more even distribution of forces during opening shock and on-heading openings. *Figures 4-4* through *4-35* illustrate PRO packing. There are several variations to this technique designed for special purposes. Free fall cameramen may require a slower opening to reduce the opening shock. Canopy Relative Work (CRW) parachutists may want faster sub-terminal openings. The rigger should be able to provide guidance to the parachutist for the type of opening required.

Figure 4-4. *Check line continuity and separate line groups. Cock the slider.*

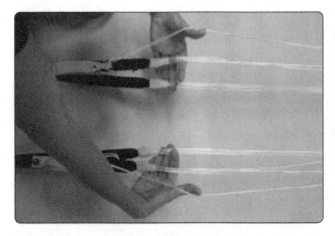

Figure 4-5. *Set the brakes and walk up the lines pushing the slider ahead of you. This is also known as "Doing a 4-line."*

Figure 4-7. *Flake out the cells of the canopy at the nose, pressing them against your thigh.*

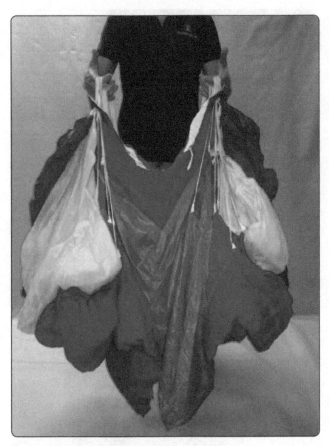

Figure 4-6. *The nose of the canopy is facing the packer. The tail of the canopy is facing outward.*

Figure 4-8. *Tuck the nose of the canopy between your legs.*

Figure 4-9. *Flake the canopy fabric between the A-B, B-C, C-D line groups following the perimeter of the canopy.*

Figure 4-10. *Separate and clear the material between the line groups.*

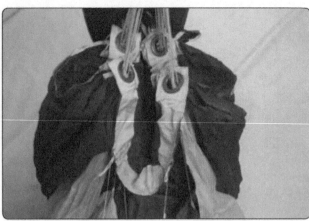

Figure 4-12. *The slider can be quartered or simply halved with the slider grommets resting up against the slider stops at the stabilizers.*

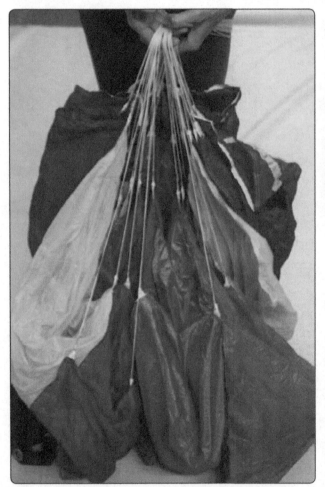

Figure 4-11. *Note the staggered order of the line groups. The As are the highest; the Ds are the lowest except for the upper control lines at the very bottom of the picture.*

Figure 4-13. *Pull the tail up over the canopy and hold it under your thumb.*

Figure 4-14. *Roll the tail to prevent the canopy from splaying out when it is laid down on the ground. Be sure to prevent the upper control lines from coming around to the nose of the canopy. Keep them centered and back.*

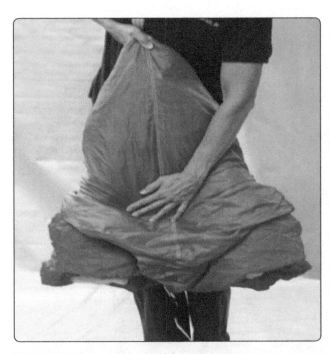

Figure 4-15. *Press the air out of the canopy.*

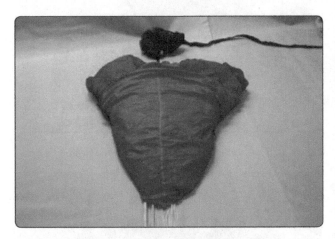

Figure 4-16. *Lay the canopy down on the ground.*

Figure 4-17. *Cocoon the canopy making it a uniform width.*

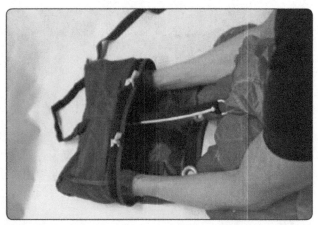

Figure 4-18. *The "cocoon" should be slightly wider than the deployment bag.*

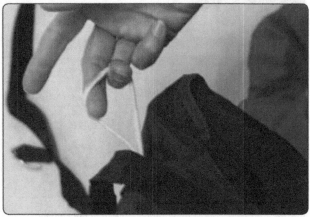

Figure 4-19. *Pull the kill line out of the bag at this time.*

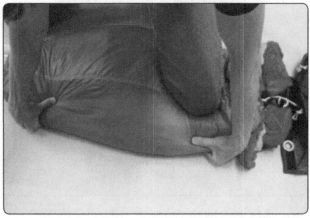

Figure 4-20. *Use a knee to keep control of the top of the canopy.*

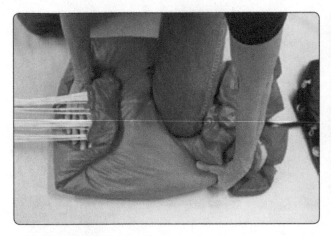

Figure 4-21. *Make the first "S" fold.*

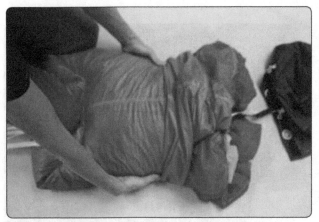

Figure 4-22. *Use a knee to maintain control of the canopy.*

Figure 4-23. *Make an additional "S" fold.*

Figure 4-24. *Most canopies take two S folds. Pull PCA ring outward so that it is up against the grommet inside the bag.*

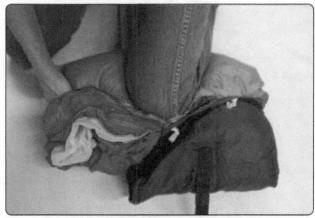

Figure 4-25. *Insert the canopy into the bag one side at a time.*

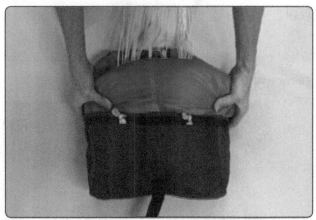

Figure 4-26. *The objective is to fill the corners of the bag and keep the center of the pack job soft.*

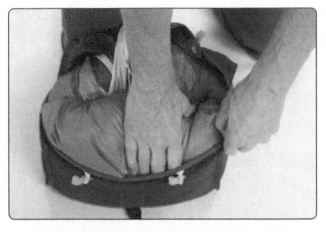

Figure 4-27. *Shove the canopy down into the bag filling the corners.*

Figure 4-28. *Use the flap of the bag to help control the canopy.*

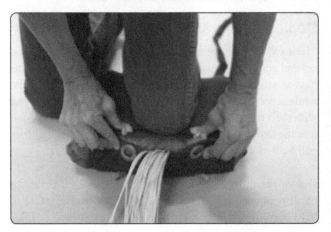

Figure 4-29. *The closing flap of the bag is pulled so that the grommets meet the rubber bands. You should not have to stretch the rubber bands very far.*

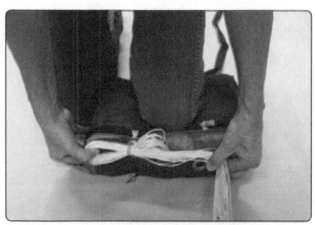

Figure 4-30. *Make a locking stow.*

Figure 4-31. *The second locking stow. Note the generous size of the bight.*

Figure 4-32. *Keep the stows neat and separate. Here, the weight and mass of the lines is balanced to prevent line strip.*

Figure 4-33. *Pull pilot chute kill line from bottom of bag.*

Figure 4-34. *Pull the kill line through the bridle.*

Figure 4-35. *Drop the excess line into the pilotchute.*

Deployment and Inflation Characteristics

Main canopies have changed dramatically over the last several years and, consequently, different opening problems have emerged. Some canopies are inherently hard openers, while others are inherently slow openers. Accuracy canopies, with their thick airfoils and large overhanging topskins, fall into the first category, while thinner airfoils, with flatter trim and baffled leading edges, tend to fall into the latter.

One of the most common problems encountered is that of hard openings. Line strip or line dump is the leading cause of hard openings. This occurs when inadequately-stowed lines come off of the bag all at once instead of releasing one line bight at a time in an orderly fashion, and subsequently the canopy is allowed to inflate prior to line stretch resulting in sometimes an explosive opening. Securing the lines so that it takes approximately 12 pounds of force to release each bight is accomplished with a proper stow band and balancing the weight and mass of the lines by placing 50 percent of the line weight and mass on the mid-section of the bag and 25 percent of the weight and mass on each side of the bag. This alleviates the problem of line strip.

There are other methods employed to reduce hard openings, such as rolling the nose of the canopy to delay the initial inflation process as the leading edge unfurls. This rolling technique varies from a single roll to several rolls. *[Figure 4-36]* If this does not solve the opening problem, riggers should contact the manufacturer for advice. Most manufacturers are very cooperative and have considerable expertise in working with their products.

Figure 4-36. *Rolling the nose of the canopy.*

The manufacturer may recommend modifying the slider size or deployment brake settings. Of these options, the easiest to do is to change the brake setting. Reducing the brake setting results in less pressure on the canopy during opening, thereby reducing the opening force. The negative effect of reducing the brake setting is an increase in opening surge. The new brake setting must find the balance of these results that best fit the user. If changing the brake setting does not work, then the rigger may wish to increase the size of the slider to slow the openings. This usually means replacing the slider with a larger one. This has the effect of increasing the drag on the slider and restricting the canopy inflation. Another effective method of preventing hard openings is to install a 2-inch diameter rubber band on the center B or C line attachment tab and stowing the apex of the slider in a single wrap of that band. *[Figure 4-37]* The jumpers' airspeed also has a significant effect on opening shock. Jumpers should make a conscious effort to slow down before putting out their pilot chute, and then assume a slightly head high attitude in preparation for opening.

As canopies age and accumulate substantial jumps on them, many begin to develop slow openings, commonly known as "sniveling." If the canopy was originally packed with the nose rolled, reducing the number of rolls may speed up the openings. However, many times the slow openings are due to other causes. Probably the main reason for canopies developing slow openings is increased porosity that occurs with frequent use. It is especially noticeable on canopies that have a "lip" or a baffled nose. These particular design features cause a canopy to open slower for softer openings, which

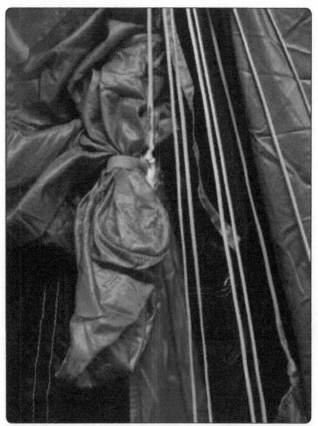

Figure 4-37. *Rubber band on center C-Line attachment tab holding apex of slider.*

is a desirable characteristic, but as the canopy fabric wears and permeability increases, the openings may get too slow.

The effect on fabric that originally had a permeability of 0–3 cubic feet per minute (CFM) or 0–5 CFM, such as PIA-C-44378, may not be as dramatic. With these canopies, pulling down the tail by deepening the brake setting speeds up the inflation of the canopy. The rigger must be careful not to set the brakes so deeply as to place the canopy in a stall during opening. If this does not work, then decreasing the size of the slider or the fabric type of the slider may help speed up the openings. The size and condition of the pilot chute may also contribute to the perceived speed of opening.

Another cause is when the canopy gets out of trim due to the stretch of the suspension lines or shrinkage of steering/ brake lines. The rigger should check the trim of the canopy against the manufacturer's specifications and either re-trim the canopy or re-line it. This may have a pronounced effect of improving the openings, as well as the flying characteristics.

Main Pilot Chute

Hand deploy pilot chutes are made from either the PIA-C-44378 (0–3 CFM) (formerly known as F-111 which is a proprietary brand name that is no longer manufactured.

Currently 0-3 CFM is commonly referred to as Silktique and Exazta-Chute) fabric or zero porosity (0 CFM) fabric. The PIA-C-44378 fabric begins as a very low-porosity fabric but, as it is used, the permeability increases. When this happens, the drag of the pilot chute decreases. Consequently, the ability of the pilot chute to "lift" the weight of the canopy decreases and the speed of the opening is affected. Experience has shown that pilot chutes made from this type of fabric exhibit a decrease in performance at around 500 jumps under normal use. Pilot chutes made from the ZP fabric last considerably longer than those made from 0–3 CFM fabric. However, there has been some disagreement concerning the use of the two different fabrics in pilot chutes. One canopy manufacturer advocates the use of F-111-type fabric only. They believe the ZP fabric contributes to hard openings. Most parachutists like ZP pilot chutes because they last longer. The size of the pilot chute has a direct correlation to the type of opening experienced. In the early days of hand deploy chutes, a 36-inch 0–3 CFM pilot chute was standard on most systems. As the canopies became smaller and lighter, pilot chutes became smaller as well. Today, 24-, 26-, 28-, and 30-inch pilot chutes are all common.

Several factors dictate the size of the pilot chute used. The first is the weight of the canopy. Another factor is the main container closing configuration. Some systems are designed to hold the deployment bag so securely that it requires more drag to extract it from the container. This type may require a larger pilot chute than the type of container that allows unrestricted extraction of the bag. This same problem can develop when an individual packs an oversized main canopy into the main container. If a larger deployment bag is used to hold the additional volume and the bag is forcibly stuffed into the container, the bag can be restricted from being pulled smoothly from the container. If the pilot chute is too small, a pilot chute in tow can result. If the parachutist puts a larger pilot chute on the system, the bag can be extracted from the container, but the increased size of the pilot chute contributes to increased snatch force during the opening sequence. This results in perceived hard openings.

It should be noted that deployment bags are matched dimensionally to containers—not to canopies. If the tray of your container is 12 inches wide, 7 inches long, and 5 inches thick, the bag should also be those dimensions. Forcing a larger bag into the container overstresses the flaps, grommets, stiffeners, and some loop anchors. Conversely, if you put a smaller canopy than was originally intended into the container, you should use the same bag and pack the canopy as wide and "fluffy" as possible. In other words, do not squish all of the air out of the pack job as you normally would. The main closing loop should be appropriately shortened.

Using a smaller bag than the container was built for can result in unsafe conditions as well. In the event of a premature container opening, the bag may float out before the jumper has an opportunity to deploy the pilot chute. Some friction is desirable so that the bag rotates out of the container in the proper sequence—bridle up, lines down. There is an exception to this tenet for wingsuiters, who essentially open in a track. So, the size of the pilot chute and, to some extent, the deployment bag can have considerable effect on the opening of the main parachute.

Bridle Length

The length of the bridle has an effect primarily on the deployment of the main pilot chute itself. In the case of a throw-out pilot chute, the bridle must be long enough to get the deployed pilot chute out of the turbulence in the wake of the jumper's back. If the bridle is too short, the pilot chute stays in the parachutist's burble. The length of the bridle from the locking pin to the pilot chute averages around 7 feet.

Recent years have seen the growth of the use of the "birdman" flying suits or wingsuits. Because of the increased surface area and the decreased free fall speeds, the use of a longer bridle has become common, with a 9-foot length working well. Along with the longer bridle, containers have been modified to allow the bottom to open fully and the main bag to be extracted rearward towards the feet due to the more horizontal trajectory of the parachutist. Some manufacturers have also reoriented the mouth of the main deployment bag for wingsuiters so that the lines are sitting on the floor of the container tray rather than the bottom flap. This way the bag rotates 90° out of the container rather than 180°.

In the case of a pull-out pilot chute, where the jumper actually pulls the pin, the pilot chute is placed with an arc motion of the arm in the fast air near his or her head so as to avoid the burble. The jumper's grip on the pull-out handle is gradually released as they rotate into a head-high position, reducing the size of the burble, and in preparation for opening.

Rubber Bands

The rubber stow bands play an important part in the deployment sequence and serve two important functions. First, they hold the mouth of the deployment bag closed and prevent premature deployment of the main canopy. Secondly, they hold the line stows securely to allow a clean, orderly deployment of the lines. With the advent of smaller diameter lines, such as 550 or 725 Spectra® and HMA®, smaller diameter rubber bands have been developed to properly secure these lines. If the smaller rubber bands are not available, many parachutists double stow the larger rubber bands around the small lines.

There are other products, which are designed to replace rubber bands and last longer, but they have downsides. Rubber bands other than military standard (Mil Spec) rubber bands may not break at the desired 40–45 pounds and can lead to bag locks. Other products may not have enough retention ability and allow the lines to "dump." *Figure 4-38* shows the various rubber bands and Tube Stoes®. In addition to the correct rubber bands, the length of the line stows is important as well. In the past, 1-inch stows were common, but today 3-inch stows are recommended by several manufacturers. *Figure 4-39* shows the comparison between the two lengths. The main point to remember is that the lines must be stowed neatly and securely.

Figure 4-38. *Rubber bands and Tube Stows®.*

Figure 4-39. *Line stow length comparison.*

Assembly of the Main Canopy To The Harness and Container

The rigger should be familiar with the various types of canopy releases currently in use. In skydiving, the most common release is the 3-ring release system. It was originally developed in 1976 for skydiving, but has since become the dominant release system for intentional jumping, both civilian and military.

Riggers must be familiar with the assembly of the 3-ring release since they may have to connect new canopies to the harness and container or have to disconnect the main canopy to untangle it after landing. Shown in *Figures 4-40* through *4-47* is the correct assembly sequence. The rigger must also be able to inspect the 3-ring release to determine any wear. In particular, the following areas need to be inspected:

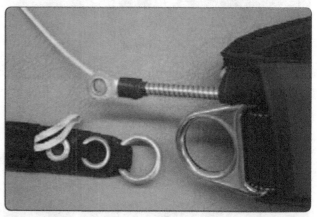

Figure 4-40. *3-ring layout.*

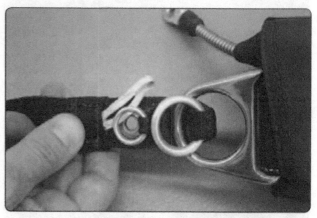

Figure 4-41. *3-ring middle through large ring.*

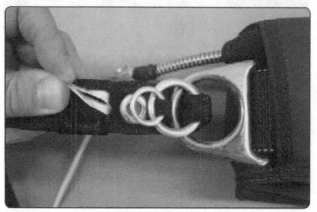

Figure 4-42. *3-ring small through middle ring.*

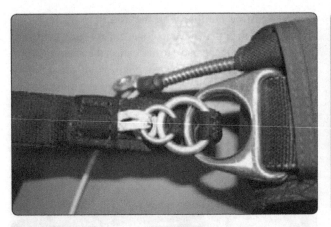

Figure 4-43. *3-ring loop over the top ring.*

Figure 4-44. *3-ring loop profile view.*

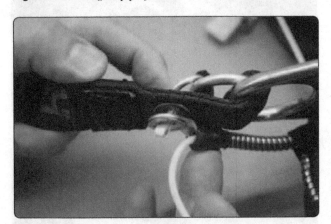

Figure 4-45. *3-ring housing terminal over loop (rear).*

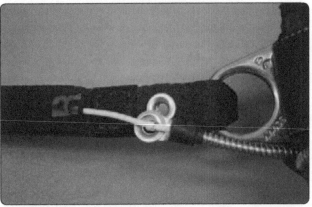

Figure 4-46. *3-ring cable through loop.*

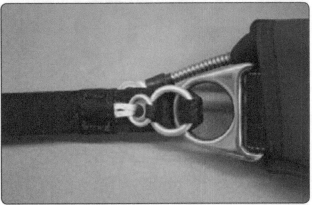

Figure 4-47. *3-ring assembled (from front).*

- Harness 3-ring attachment—check for wear on the webbing and any damage to the ring or chipping of the plating. *[Figure 4-48]*

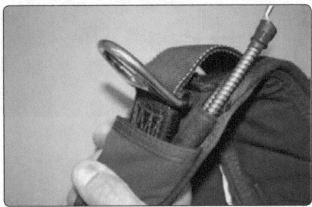

Figure 4-48. *Harness 3-ring inspection.*

- Main riser rings—check for webbing wear, hardware plating, grommet wear, and locking loop wear/damage. *[Figure 4-49]*

Figure 4-49. *Riser release end.*

- Release housings—check for damage to terminal endings and grommet, obstructions or dirt in housing, and check security of the housing tacking to the harness. *[Figure 4-50]*

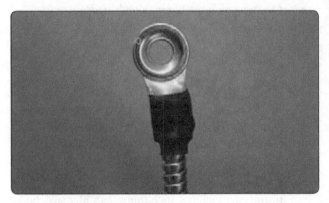

Figure 4-50. *Release housing and terminal.*

- 3-ring release handle—check the cable for cleanliness and cracks, and ensure that the cable ends are sealed. Yellow Lolon cables must be oiled monthly to ensure release-ability. *[Figure 4-51]* Red or orange Teflon cables do not require oil but should still be inspected every 180 days; inspect the Velcro® on the handle. *[Figure 4-52]*

Any questions concerning the particular harness 3-ring installation should be directed to the harness and container manufacturer.

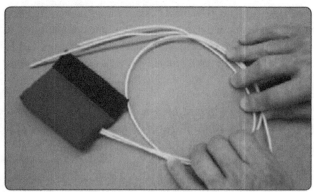

Figure 4-51. *A 3-ring release handle with yellow Lolon cable needs oiling.*

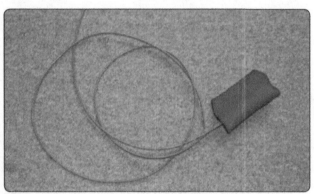

Figure 4-52. *A 3-ring release handle with orange Teflon cable does not need oiling.*

Assembly of Components and Compatibility

Advisory Circular (AC) 105-2D, Sport Parachuting states that "the assembly or mating of approved parachute components from different manufacturers may be made by a certificated, appropriately rated parachute rigger in accordance with the parachute manufacturer's instructions and without further authorization by the manufacturer's or the FAA." This allows the rigger to assemble different canopies to different harness and container systems. This is an important authorization for any rigger in that there are dozens of possible combinations.

When various parachute components are interchanged, the parachute rigger should follow the canopy manufacturer's instructions, as well as the parachute container manufacturer's instructions. However, the container manufacturer's instructions take precedence when there is a conflict between the two. The logic behind this is that the container is the active component and the canopy is the passive component with regard to deployment. Determining compatibility is more than simply determining the volume compatibility of a canopy to a container size. Other factors, that need to be considered are the deployment type, technical standard order (TSO) certification, and placard limitations.

Reserve Bag Extraction Force

When we ask the question, "How do you determine compatibility between approved parachute components," the answer is, "Rig functionality must not be compromised." Some say if a reserve canopy is too bulky, the reserve deployment bag is not easily extracted. If you can get the bagged canopy in the container, it should take no more than 18 pounds of pull force to extract it.

TSO Certification and Placard Limitations

This area is one where many riggers have some confusion. According to AC 105-2, Sport Parachute Jumping, "the strength of the harness must always be equal to or greater than the maximum force generated by the canopy during certification tests." In the case where the harness is certificated under TSO-C23b and the canopy under TSO-C23c, the maximum generated force of the canopy must not exceed the certificated category force of the harness and container (i.e., Low Speed Category (3,000 pounds) and Standard Category (5,000 pounds)). In this instance, no additional marking on the container is necessary.

In the case where the canopy is certificated under TSO-C23b and the harness under TSO-C23c, the strength of the harness must be equal to or greater than the certificated category force of the canopy.

For the current TSO-C23d, the peak force measured during the strength drops must be placarded on the outside of the harness. In this case, the strength of the canopy must not exceed that of the harness.

The rigger, when making the determination as to whether a particular canopy and rig combination is compatible, must consider all of the above areas. If there is any doubt, the rigger should contact the rig manufacturer for guidance.

Harness Strength

TSO-C23b was originally written back in the 1940s before the advent of square parachutes. It had two categories under which a parachute system could be certified. The "Low Speed" category was limited to use in aircraft under 150 miles per hour (MPH) and certified to 3,000 pounds. This category required large block letters decrying "limited to use in aircraft under 150 MPH." It also had a "Standard Category." This category required no warning labels and had neither weight nor speed limitations and was tested and certified to 5,000

pounds. It is important to note that neither category had a weight limitation.

Weight has only a minimum effect on parachute opening forces. To be exact, if you were to increase a given weight by 50 percent, you would only see a 5 percent increase in opening force; likewise if you double that given weight, you would only see a 10 percent increase in opening force.

This seems counter intuitive until you think about it. Speed is the critical factor that hurts us and our equipment when we have the occasional hard opening. But because speed is often derived from mass or weight, we associate the hard opening with primarily weight. Let us look at the calculations.

The math model for opening forces is described in the "Recovery Systems Design Guide" by Theodore Knacke. The definitions and formula is as follows:

- Force—total opening forces
- C_d—drag coefficient of canopy
- S_o—square footage of canopy
- Q—dynamic pressure in pounds per/square foot ($\frac{1}{2} \rho v^2$)
- X_1—decreasing load factor

  NOTE: There are 2 methods for deriving this factor. The Pflanze method and a lookup of the chart included in the reference manual. The chart is the simplest for personnel parachutes and effectively results in being one tenth of the pound per square foot loading.

- C_x = shock load coefficient which is derived from testing and includes such things as slider size, brake setting, angle of nose cut, etc. For this exercise we will use a value of 1 as this number ranges from .5 to 1.5 or so. Without a slider it can go as high as 10.

  Therefore: Force = $C_d \times S_o \times Q \times X_1 \times C_x$

If we group the $C_d \times S_o \times Q$ and calculate them, at first we get a big number ie:

C_d = .8 S_o = 200 square feet Q = 33 PSF @ 117MPH together = .8 × 200 × 33 = 5,280 pounds. This number is then ameliorated by the X_1 decreasing load factor and the C_x shock load factor. If the C_x is 1 (and we will assume this for this example), then it has no effect on the outcome.

The X_1 factor is the key because it is based on pounds per square foot loading multiplied by 1. If you try different weight values and reiterate the formula, you can see it only changes the X_1 factor by fractional amounts and only affects the outcome minimally as described earlier.

National Aerospace Standards (NAS) 804 has the best requirements for structural integrity of any standard written to date. This is because it has a strength requirement: 3,000 pounds for the Low Speed Category and 5,000 pounds for the Standard Category. Other standards (AS8015) use a performance requirement (weight versus speed) for structural integrity verification. This would be acceptable except for one small problem. AC 105-2, Sport Parachute Jumping, allows for mixing and matching of approved components. This is a problem because different canopies open with different opening characteristics at the same weights and speeds. This is defined and accounted for by the C_x value. Therefore, if a harness is built and tested using a canopy with a low C_x and matched with a canopy (under the provisions of AC 105-2) with a high C_x, the results could be disastrous.

NAS 804 systems need no further consideration other than originally called for. The Low Speed designation is limited to use in aircraft under 150 MPH at any weight. Likewise, the Standard Category of 5,000 pounds has no weight or speed limitations. This is an unlimited category. One reason for this is because of the limited effect of weight on opening forces. Speed is what kills. If a human body were to reach a 5,000 pound shock load, it would come apart before the harness or canopy. At less than 150 MPH, even at a high weight, it will not exceed 3,000 pounds.

It may be evident now that there is a flaw in our structural requirements due to the mixing and matching of approved components under the performance standard versus a structural standard. This came about as a result of the change from a Structural Standard (NAS-804) to a Performance Standard (AS 8015b). Now we have no way to determine compatibility for TSO-C23c (AS8015b).

It may not be possible to have compatibility using performance standards alone. That is why we added placards for the "weight tested to" for harnesses and the "force generated" for canopies to TSO-C23d. There is no way to determine compatibility from one parachute system to another within the same category of the same standard if they are judged using a performance standard. Just because they were tested at the same weight and speed does not mean they saw the same opening forces. Different canopies open with different characteristics. Listed below is a hypothetical comparison of the opening characteristics of two different systems tested to the same performance standard. The math is the same as previously discussed. The two canopies have very different opening characteristics, and they produce very different results when tested at the same levels. When a mix

of the two systems is applied and subjected to a high-stress sport jump, the capability of the harness may be exceeded.

Both systems were tested using a 300-pound test dummy at 180 knots (207 MPH) Cat "B" TSO-C23c.

System 1: 200 square foot canopy W/.8 C_d produces a 1,304 pounds force on opening at test speeds.

System 2: 100 square foot canopy W/.9 C_d produces a 3,668 pounds force on opening at test speeds.

The ratio of opening force differential is 2.8 to one or System 2 opens with 2.8 times greater force than System 1.

Let's say a harness is built for System 1 using 1,500 pounds capable hardware. It passes the structural drops, as it only sees 1,304 pounds.

Another harness is built for System 2 that has a canopy with desirable flight characteristics but that tends to open hard.

The jumper wants the canopy with desirable flight characteristics in his new System 1 rig. If compatibility is derived from performance standards, then these are compatible since they were both tested using a 300-pound drop test dummy at 180 knots. It is entirely possible that a sport opening under extreme conditions could produce an opening of 1,600 pounds, which exceeds the capability of the 1,500 pound hardware. *[Figure 4-53]*

Canopy Characteristics			
Variable	System 1	System 2	System 2 with 100-foot canopy
C_d	0.8	0.9	0.9
S_o	200	100	100
Q	108.7	108.7	50
Subtotal	17,392	9,783	4,500
X_1	0.15	0.25	0.20
C_x	0.5	1.5	1.5
Force =	1,304.4	3,668.625 (Ratio 2.8125)	1,620 pounds

Figure 4-53. *Canopy characteristics.*

TSO-C23b does not really have any limitations except for speeds below 150 for "Low Speed" category with no weight limit. That standard is good for all skydiving scenarios. The 3,000 pounds test load is strong enough for anything and force is a good base line for compatibility.

The current regulation for placarding (AS8015c/TSO C-23d) calls for "Average Peak Force." Under AS8015b/TSO-C23c (the previous version), there is no way for a rigger to make the necessary determinations without help from the manufacturer doing some kind of retro placcarding as the requirement did not include force measurement. Fortunately, there are only a small number of systems/components certified under this rendition. Any component so certified would not be able to be used as there are no guidelines for compatibility.

Volume

An important criterion in determining compatibility is the volume of the canopy. The canopy has to fit into the container in such a manner as to not place undue stress on the system when packing and to be extracted by the pilot chute during deployment. The container manufacturer usually provides a volume chart of their systems stating what the volumes are for the various model sizes. Container volumes are somewhat nonsequitur; however, as container manufacturers derive their numbers in different ways. Some container manufacturers do not publish numbers per se; rather, they indicate a model designation that fits a size range of canopies.

The canopy manufacturer should provide the volumes of the canopy models. Measuring canopy volumes has proven to be an imprecise science as there are various methods that can be used. The most common method involves placing the canopy in a tubular chamber and compressing it with a standard amount of weight for a set time. The displaced volume is then measured. *Figure 4-54* shows one such volume chamber. Slight differences in volume can be seen from chamber to chamber and canopy to canopy. These variances occur due to humidity at the time the test is conducted and due to variation in the bulk of the fabric that the canopy was built with. For example, sometimes a 150 square foot reserve is 312 cubic inch and sometimes that very same model, built using a different dye lot of fabric is 363 cubic inch. Canopy volume charts can be found on the Parachute Industry Association (PIA) website at www.pia.com and the Parachute Labs website at www.jumpshack.com. While some canopy manufacturers disagree with the resultant numbers, most container manufacturers and riggers agree that these independent test methods are useful in determining volume compatibility.

Deployment Type

In Chapter 2 of this handbook, Design and Construction, the different types of canopy deployment devices were described. In some instances, the container system needs to be of a specific configuration to accommodate a certain deployment device. An example of this would be where a round canopy utilizing a Type 1 configuration is packed into a pilot emergency parachute system. In this case, the pilot chute is compressed directly onto the floor of the container system. *[Figure 4-55]* This same canopy can be packed into

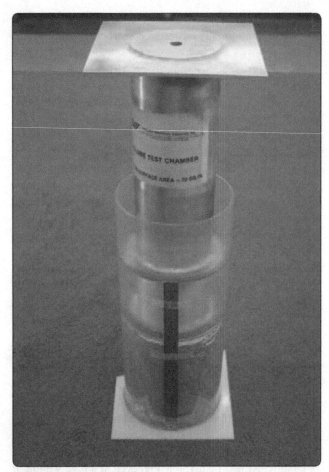

Figure 4-54. *Volume chamber.*

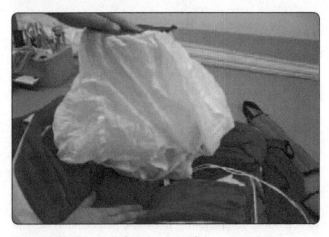

Figure 4-55. *Type 1 deployment in a pilot emergency rig.*

a sport reserve container, but the sport rig has two internal or staging flaps that compress and hold the canopy in place and are locked together by the bridle. *[Figure 4-56]* The pilot chute is then packed on top of the internal flaps. The rigger needs to know and understand these differences to determine how the two components interface for compatibility.

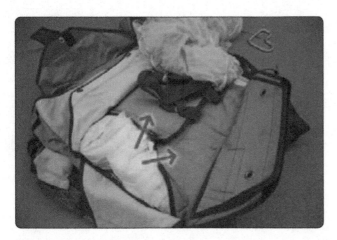

Figure 4-56. *Type 1 deployment in a sport piggyback.*

Chapter Summary

This chapter focuses on main parachute packing techniques. The first rule is that the lines must be straight (no tangles, also known as "step throughs"). If the lines are straight and the slider is up (in square parachutes), the parachute will most likely open. The speed of the opening directly impacts the comfort or discomfort perceived by the jumper. Opening speed and orderliness is controlled by attenuation devices such as the slider, deployment bag, stow bands, or the diaper on a round parachute. Accoutrements, such as pilot chutes and bridles, must be checked frequently for wear that could affect their performance.

Rubber bands should be changed when they begin to exhibit small holes or ragged edges. Minor maintenance now prevents hard openings and major failures later. Learn to be observant of small details about the parachute system even when packing the main. Virtually every pack job should be an inspection. It does not have to be as thorough an inspection as you would perform at the 180-day inspection and recertification, but the packer should be vigilant for damage or things that do not look quite right.

Compatibility can be complex. When in doubt about which TSO a component was certified in, and whether it is compatible with another component in terms of opening force generated by the canopy versus strength of the harness, do not hesitate to call the manufacturer for guidance.

One of the most critical things the rigger must observe when servicing their customers rigs is reserve bag extraction force. When a customer brings his or her container for inspection and repack, reserve bag extraction force should be tested with the container closed. A good rule of thumb is that the extraction force should be the same as the weight of the bagged canopy. If excessive forces are encountered, call the manufacturer.

Chapter 5
Inspection and Packing

Introduction

There are a dozen or more commonly seen harness container systems being actively used in the field today. The differences between them can be subtle or, in some cases, polar opposite. Most packing manuals can be found on-line or can be purchased from the container manufacturer. Canopy folding methods are fairly universal from rig to rig. It is the closing of the container that is proprietary. The single-pin rig shown in the following illustrations is somewhat representative of other single-pin reserves. Reserve Static Line (RSL) and Main Activated Reserve Deployment (MARD) configurations differ from rig to rig, and so individual manuals should be consulted for exact routing and setup. Rigs that use a pop-top or externally-mounted reserve pilot chute differ significantly from the single-pin rigs. There are sport and pilot emergency rigs that utilize this design.

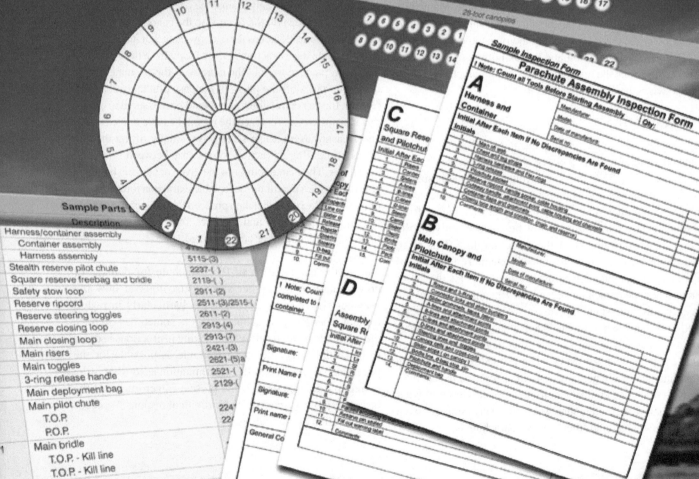

For most people, parachute rigging is all about packing parachutes. Rigging and packing may be synonymous, but there is a distinct difference. In its truest form, parachute rigging is the practice of assembling a parachute system with its various components into an operative assembly. Packing is the practice of folding the parachute canopy in an organized manner such that it fits into the container system and allows the canopy to open when the user activates the system.

There are five distinct stages involved in packing the parachute. They are:

1. Identification
2. Inspection
3. Rigging and/or repairs
4. Packing
5. Documentation

Identification

The first thing the rigger should do when a customer brings a parachute in for packing or repair is to confirm that the owner's information is correct on the packing data card. This ensures that the rigger's logbook entry is accurate. In a commercial loft, a work order is filled out with all the correct information about the customer and the parachute. Many lofts that do a high volume of business input this information into a computer database for tracking their customers. This data is then used to send automatic repack notices to customers. This ensures that the reserve or emergency parachute is legal to use when the customer needs it.

Inspection

The owner should bring the parachute to the rigger in its packed condition. This practice should be encouraged for several reasons. The canopy is a fragile item and is subject to damage or contamination if left exposed to the elements, and the container is designed to protect the canopy from damage. The parachute should be opened only in the controlled environment of the parachute loft. This is so the entire system can be examined externally for signs of damage or contamination before it is opened. Next, the owner should don the parachute and pull the ripcord as in a real life scenario to understand how to activate the system properly and experience what it feels like to actually pull the reserve ripcord. This gives the owner a great degree of confidence that the parachute will work when needed. It is something that jumpers rarely get to do, and their reaction is generally one of curiosity and satisfaction. Doing so also lets the owner see what is in there. It is surprising how many jumpers do not even know what color their reserve parachute is.

Generally, customers leave the parachute to be repacked; however, riggers should invite their customers to stay and observe the repack. Many riggers encourage this behavior since it results in a more educated individual. In a busy loft environment, however, a scheduled appointment might be needed to allow for the increased time necessary to explain the process. If the customer decides to watch the inspection and repack, the rigger should allow at least twice the usual time for the project so the customer can ask questions. Another benefit of this is that the customer gets to see the effort it takes to service a parachute. *Figure 5-1* shows a packing flow chart that details the sequence of events the rigger should follow from receiving the parachute to collecting the money from the customer.

Upon completion of the visual inspection, there are two options for continuing. If there are no visual indications of damage or contamination, move on to the next step of opening the parachute. If something suspicious is found, or if there is a hole in the container or discoloration to the container fabric, the rigger needs to see if the damage penetrated into the canopy. To do so, note the location and check internally after opening the parachute.

If the owner is participating in the inspection, it is a good idea to have them backed against the packing table or similar surface when they pull the ripcord so the canopy does not fall out on the floor. This keeps the canopy clean, but it also lets the rigger control the extraction of the canopy from the container. It is good practice to hold the canopy in the container while the owner takes off the pack. In the case of a bagged square reserve, the bag extraction force should be measured to ensure that it is not excessive. Place the rig on the table or clean floor and measure using a fish scale or by simply lifting the bag by its bridle. Bag extraction forces vary between brands of containers. The manufacturer of the given container should be able to provide a maximum acceptable extraction force in terms of pounds. The rigger can then proceed to thoroughly examine the previous pack job and to check those areas previously identified as damaged or contaminated.

During the examination of the parachute for damage or contamination, the rigger should also look at how the previous rigger packed the canopy. Particularly in regard to pilot emergency parachutes, riggers sometimes exercise great latitude in interpreting the packing instructions in order to make the parachute as comfortable as possible for the pilot. Each rigger makes the determination as to what is the correct packing method. If the present rigger finds that the last pack job was in error, the individual responsible needs to be notified of the findings.

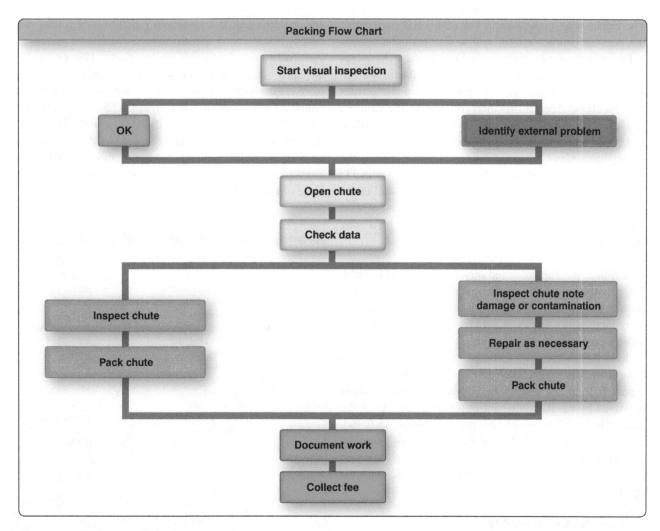

Figure 5-1. *Packing flow chart.*

The rigger should then verify the make, model, and serial number of the parachute. Sometimes the canopy may have been changed in an assembly, particularly in a sport rig. For sport rigs and some emergency rigs, be sure to check the Automatic Activation Device (AAD). The newest data cards provide space for information on the AAD to include service cycle and date of last battery replacement. With the recent widespread acceptance of AADs, this is one area the rigger cannot overlook.

The battery life cycle, the unit service life cycle, and how they interface with the inspection and repack cycle of the parachute are very important things to consider. The major question the rigger must ask is: If the battery or unit service life expires during the upcoming inspection cycle, should the rigger pack the parachute and seal it, thereby certifying it for the next 180-day inspection cycle? A comparable situation would be if an airframe and powerplant mechanic signs off an annual inspection on an aircraft. The mechanic is saying that the aircraft is airworthy at that time. However, the mechanic is not responsible for the future status of the aircraft if the

emergency locator transmitter (ELT) is due for battery service during the next year that the annual is valid; that responsibility lies with the aircraft owner. This scenario can be reasonably extended to the AAD and parachute. Generally, however, most riggers refuse to pack the parachute if the battery or unit life cycle expires during the 180-day inspection cycle.

Some AAD manufacturers have specific rules regarding battery and repack expiration dates. For example, the manufacturer might mandate that if the battery life expires during the 180-day inspection cycle, then the rigger is not to pack it unless the batteries are replaced or the unit is removed from the assembly. Regarding the 4-year service cycle required for some AADs, there is a 90-day grace period for servicing. If the 180-day inspection cycle expires within that 90-day period, then the rigger may inspect, repack, and recertify the assembly. If the inspection cycle extends past the 90-day period, then the rigger should not pack the assembly with the AAD. In any case, the rigger should follow the directions of the AAD manufacturer for that particular make and model of AAD.

The rigger must make sure to have the latest revision of the packing instructions, as well as any pertinent service bulletins from the manufacturer or Airworthiness Directives (AD) issued by the Federal Aviation Administration (FAA). The rigger may have a set of packing instructions that specifies a certain method for folding the canopy. However, the manufacturer may have changed the method and issued a revision to the manual or a complete new one. If the rigger is not completely sure that he or she has the latest information, then it is time to use the most valuable tool in their inventory—the telephone. A quick call to the manufacturer is all it takes to get the latest information. Most manufacturers publish their service bulletins in hard copy format and on their website.

In addition, the Parachute Industry Association (PIA) also has a listing of service bulletins at www.pia.com. It is most important that all riggers make an effort to maintain a comprehensive library of packing instructions and their associated service bulletins. Under Title 14 of the Code of Federal Regulations (14 CFR) part 65, section 65.129(e), the certificated rigger may not "pack, maintain, or alter a parachute in any manner that deviates from procedures approved by the Administrator or the manufacturer of the parachute." In addition, 14 CFR part 65, section 65.129(f), also states that the certificated rigger may not "exercise the privileges of his certificate and type rating unless he understands the current manufacturer's instructions for the operation involved."

Component Compatibility

Once the rigger has all of the current manuals and information, the inspection can continue. This covers not just the canopy but also the entire assembly. In addition to looking for damage or contamination to the system, the rigger must make sure that all of the component parts are compatible and approved by the manufacturer. *Figure 5-2* shows a sample parts list for a typical sport parachute, having dual parachutes in a single-harness system (a piggyback). This parts list delineates exactly what parts are used in the assembly of the system. The rigger should check each component part and its identifying label or stamp against the parts list. Mismatched component parts are among the most frequent problems found in the field. Many riggers are under the impression they can freely interchange component parts, but this may be done only within certain limits. Paragraph 11(a) of Advisory Circular (AC) 105-2, Sport Parachute Jumping, states: "The assembly or mating of approved parachute components from different manufacturers may be made by a certificated and appropriately-rated parachute rigger or parachute loft in accordance with the parachute manufacturer's instructions and without further authorization by the manufacturer or the FAA. Specifically, when various parachute components

are interchanged, the parachute rigger should follow the canopy manufacturer's instructions, as well as the parachute container manufacturer's instructions. However, the container manufacturer's instructions take precedence when there is a conflict between the two." In *Figure 5-2*, note the bold print at the bottom of the page: "NO SUBSTITUTION OF COMPONENT PARTS IS AUTHORIZED!" This manufacturer specifically states that you cannot use anything other than Original Equipment Manufacturer (OEM) parts. Substituting other parts places the rigger in violation of the Code of Federal Regulations (CFR).

Sample Parts List		
Quantity	Description	Part number
1	Harness/container assembly	6111-(4)
	Container assembly	4111-(4)
	Harness assembly	5115-(3)
1	Stealth reserve pilot chute	2237-( )
1	Square reserve freebag and bridle	2119-( )
1	Safety stow loop	2911-(2)
1	Reserve ripcord	2511-(3)/2515-( )
2	Reserve steering toggles	2611-(2)
1	Reserve closing loop	2913-(4)
1	Main closing loop	2913-(7)
2	Main risers	2421-(3)
2	Main toggles	2621-(5)a
1	3-ring release handle	2521-( )
1	Main deployment bag	2129-( )
1	Main pilot chute	
	T.O.P.	2241-( )
	P.O.P.	2242-( )
1	Main bridle	
	T.O.P. - Kill line	2323-(1)
	T.O.P. - Kill line	2323-(2)
1	RSL lanyard	2811-(8)
1	Owner's manual and registration card	1311-(4)
NO SUBSTITUTION OF COMPONENT PARTS IS AUTHORIZED!		

Figure 5-2. *Sample parts list.*

A common problem found in the field concerns reserve ripcords. Several manufacturers of sport rigs use a one-pin ripcord with a mini trapezoidal handle and a cable length 27–29 inches long. Depending on the actual container it goes into, it is possible to use one manufacturer's ripcord in another container as long as the rigger feels there is sufficient excess cable for safety reasons.

However, imagine one ripcord is 27 inches overall and is used in a system that is approved under Technical Standard Order (TSO) C-23b and is rated at 300 pounds. Another ripcord is 28 inches overall and is used in a system approved under TSO C-23c and is rated at 600 pounds for use with a Reserve Static Line (RSL) installation. The problem here is the mating of different TSO standard components. Installing the first ripcord in the second container with an RSL lanyard may be degrading the safety aspect of the system. So how does the rigger tell which is which? The ripcord approved under TSO C-23b has minimal markings, perhaps only a manufacturer's part number. The ripcord approved under TSO C-23c has several markings on the handle as required by the TSO. It should have the manufacturer's part number, manufacturer's identification, TSO-C23c, and the batch or serial number or date of manufacture. *[Figure 5-3]* In reality, as long as the cable lengths are compatible, the function of the ripcord will probably work. The problem surfaces in the event of a problem or incident involving the system. At this point, the FAA could find the mismatched component and take action against the rigger who packed the parachute.

Figure 5-3. *Reserve ripcord with TSO markings.*

A bigger problem surfaces when the rigger substitutes a reserve deployment bag made by another manufacturer. Most reserve deployment bags are compatible with the appropriate container based on dimensions and volume. If the deployment bag does not fit correctly, there can be a problem with proper functioning of the system. These are two examples of the more common compatibility issues that are regularly found in the field. There are others that the rigger may encounter and need to address as well. The best solution is for the rigger to follow the manufacturer's parts list strictly to ensure the safety of the parachute system.

After the rigger has determined that all of the component parts are compatible, he or she can now commence the actual inspection of the parachute assembly. *Figure 5-4* shows a typical pilot emergency parachute assembly with a round canopy laid out on the packing table. Make sure the canopy is straight and the apex lines are even. Then apply firm tension to the canopy and lines using a tension board. The standard is to start at the top of the assembly.

The assembly shown in *Figure 5-4* can be broken down into the following six separate areas:

1. Pilot chute and bridle
2. Canopy and deployment device
3. Suspension lines and connector links
4. Container
5. Harness including risers
6. Ripcord

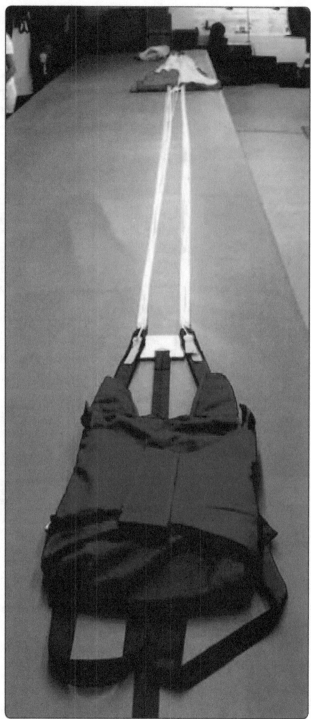

Figure 5-4. *Round canopy pilot emergency parachute assembly.*

Inspection/packing checklists allow riggers to track their progress as they do their inspection. *[Figure 5-5]* It is desirable for riggers to complete their inspection uninterrupted, which ensures that the inspection process is followed and nothing gets overlooked. This rarely happens, however, due to normal interruptions, such as phone calls or customer

Parachute Assembly Inspection Form

! Note: Count all Tools Before Starting Assembly	Qty:

A

Harness and Container

	Manufacturer:
	Model:
	Date of manufacture:
	Serial no:

Initial After Each Item If No Discrepancies Are Found

Initials

1.	Main lift web	
2.	Chest and leg straps	
3.	Harness hardware and Flex-rings	
4.	3-ring release	
5.	Pilotchute pocket	
6.	Reserve ripcord, handle pocket, cable housing	
7.	Cutaway handle, attachment point, cable housing and channels	
8.	Container flaps and grommets	
9.	Closing loop length and condition (main and reserve)	
10.	Comments:	

B

Main Canopy and Pilotchute

	Manufacturer:
	Model:
	Date of manufacture:
	Serial no.:

Initial After Each Item If No Discrepancies Are Found

Initials

1.	Risers and 3-Ring	
2.	Connector links and slider bumpers	
3.	Slider grommets, tapes, fabric	
4.	A-lines and attachment points	
5.	B-lines and attachment points	
6.	C-lines and attachment points	
7.	D-lines and attachment points	
8.	Steering lines and toggles	
9.	Canopy cells and cross-ports	
10.	Slider stops (on canopy)	
11.	Bridle line, d-bag stop, pin	
12.	Pilotchute and handle	
13.	Deployment bag	
14.	Comments:	

C

**Square Rese...
and Pilotchut...**

Initial After Eac...

1.	Risers
2.	Connec...
3.	Sliders...
4.	A-lines...
5.	B-lines...
6.	C-lines...
7.	D-lines...
8.	Steeri...
9.	Canop...
10.	Slider...
11.	Deplo...
12.	Bridle...
13.	Pilotc...
14.	Pack...
15.	Com...

D

**Assembly...
Square Re...**

Initial After...

1.	In...
2.	Li...
3.	Sl...
4.	R...
5.	S...
6.	S...
7.	S...
8.	P...
9.	Packed according to manufacturer...
10.	Reserve pin sealed
11.	Fill out warning label
12.	Comments:

E

**Assembly of...
Main Canopy...**

Initial After Each...

1.	Inspecti...
2.	Line co...
3.	Slider o...
4.	Release...
5.	Rapide...
6.	Steering...
7.	Steering...
8.	D-bag...
9.	Fill out...
10.	Comm...

! Note: Coun...
completed to...
container.

Signature:

Print Name...

Signature:

Print name...

General Co...

Figure 5-5. *Inspection form.*

questions. Using the inspection checklist ensures that after an interruption, the rigger is able to continue at the proper spot without missing anything. This checklist is divided into seven sections that make it usable for all types of parachute assemblies. It includes an area for counting the tools at the beginning and end of the inspection and packing procedure. This ensures that no tools are overlooked or left in the parachute. While this may sound implausible to some, it has happened over the years, sometimes with fatal consequences.

Round Canopies and Pilot Emergency Systems

The first thing the rigger should check is the continuity of the canopy to make sure it is straight. Do so by laying the system on the table as if the wearer were laying face down, head toward the canopy. (On some models, such as military seat parachutes, it may be face down with the feet towards the canopy.) Make sure to follow the manufacturer's instructions. Ensure that the canopy is right side out (i.e., the data panel faces out) and the gore numbers are readable on the outside. Attach the required tension devices and apply light tension. Standing at the canopy, split the riser line groups and grasp the two gores that separate them. The top panel should have line number 1 and the last line of the sequence depending on the number of lines on the canopy. Starting with number 1, the lines will run in sequence counterclockwise around the canopy. *[Figure 5-6]* The four lines attached to these two gores comprise the standard "four-line check" for a round canopy. By running these four lines from the canopy to the connector links, the rigger can make a quick check of straightness. If the rigger was the last person to pack the parachute, he or she may feel this is sufficient to ensure continuity. However, most riggers do a full check of all the lines, even on their own pack jobs.

Straightening the Canopy

If a rigger finds lines out of sequence or the canopy is inside out, it becomes necessary to remove any twists, tangles, or turns. There are two things to remember when encountering this situation. First, if the parachute was originally straight and the entanglement occurred from handling, it is possible to untangle the parachute without disconnecting anything. Second, if the parachute was assembled incorrectly in the first place, it is virtually impossible to straighten it without disassembling it. These two scenarios become particularly acute when the rigger is brought a parachute for repacking and it was assembled incorrectly. At first, the rigger assumes it to be correct, but when a correct continuity cannot be done, it becomes very frustrating, and the rigger may spend an excessive amount of time trying to straighten the canopy.

The rigger should always start at the top or apex end of the canopy. Make sure that the top gore with the data panel is facing up. Follow the gore to the apex so that the upper lateral band is on the outside. Attach the apex to the upper tension

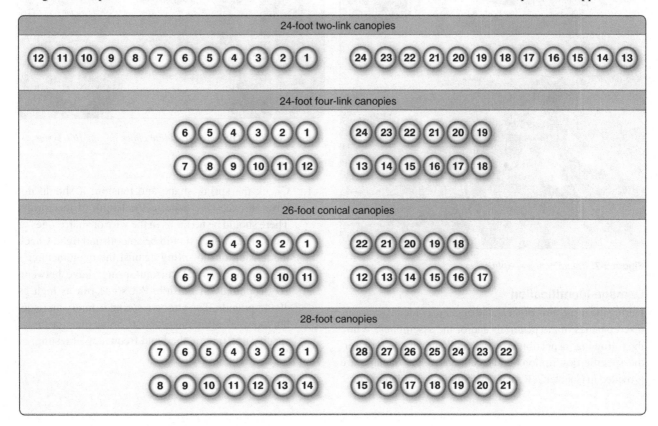

Figure 5-6. *Line continuity chart.*

device. Next, flake the gores in sequence to see if the canopy is straight. Split the canopy so the left and right line groups are separate at the skirt of the canopy. *[Figure 5-7]* Pick up the two center gores and grasp the four lines. *[Figure 5-8]* These are line number 1 and the last line of the sequence. Run these lines down toward the risers and/or container. On most canopies, these lines run to the inside, top connector link of a four-link system or to the inside of a two-link system. *[Figure 5-9]* If these lines are correct, continue the checking of the line continuity. If the lines are not straight, release the risers from the harness, if possible. If not, take one of the two top lines and untangle it until the line runs straight back to the canopy without going around any of the other lines. Untangle the risers and harness/container until the rest of the lines are straight. Repeat with the other riser, if applicable. Attach the rest of the connector links to the tension device and do a thorough continuity check from the canopy to the connector links. If the lines were incorrectly assembled, disconnect the link from the riser, remove the lines, and reinstall them onto the connector link in the correct order. Reinstall the connector link to the riser. Check the entire canopy for correct continuity. Make sure the connector link is tightened properly.

Figure 5-7. *Round canopy—split gores.*

Damage Identification

During the inspection process, the rigger may identify various discrepancies in the materials and/or the assemblies. While the following inspection processes call out what to look for, the specific descriptions and treatment of the damage are provided in Chapter 7, Repairs, Alterations, and Manufacture.

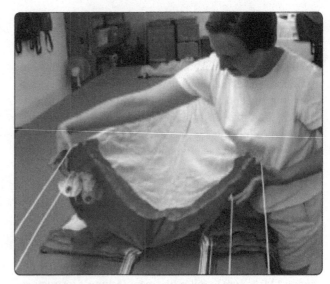

Figure 5-8. *Round canopy—four line check at canopy.*

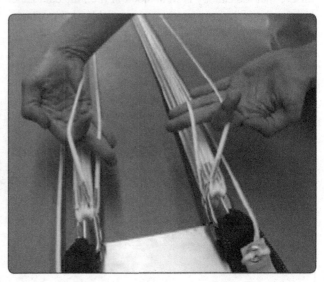

Figure 5-9. *Round canopy—four-line check at four-link system.*

Pilot Chute and Bridle

1. Check the spring shape and tension; it should not have an excessive bend to the length of the spring. There should be no kinks in the wire or sharp edges or burrs. The swages should be smooth and tight. Check the tension of the spring against the manufacturer's specifications. Most current springs have between 20–30 pounds of tension, but some run as high as 40–45 pounds. Too strong a spring is rarely an issue, but too weak often is a problem. Some manufacturers specify a testing method and frequency of testing.

2. Check the canopy cap for security to the canopy portion along the stitching and seams. If it has a grommet in the cap or an alignment strap, check the grommets for tightness and smooth edges on the inside. Sharp edges can cut the locking loop. Check the alignment strap for centering and tacking.

3. Check the canopy fabric for any holes, burns, stains, or other damage. Check the seams for loose stitching and look over the mesh portion, if used. Small holes may be allowed, but consult the manufacturer's manual. Check the attachment loop at the base of the pilot chute for security. Check any hand tacking, if used, to secure the spring to the base of the pilot chute.

4. If the parachute uses a sewn-on bridle, check the stitching. If it is a tied-on model, check the knots and any hand tacking called out in the instructions. Be sure to check the length against the parts list. Make sure the canopy end of the bridle is looped around the apex lines and not around a tension loop. If a floating loop is called out, make sure the locator tacking is secure.

Reserve Canopy

If available, use a canopy damage chart appropriate to the canopy for documenting your inspection for repair of any damage found. *Figure 5-10* shows a typical chart for round canopies.

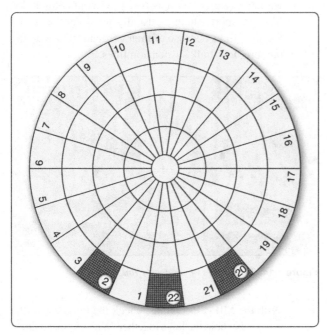

Figure 5-10. *Round canopy damage chart.*

1. Check the apex lines for damage and continuity, as well as the upper lateral band. If there is a tension loop, make sure it is secure. If there is a vent collar ring, check the elasticity of the material.

2. Inspect gores and panel fabrics by starting at the top center gore of the canopy, working your way up one gore while inspecting the fabric, seams, tapes, and lines. When you reach the apex, pull the next radial seam toward you, stretching out the fabric, and work your way down the gore to the lower lateral band. *[Figure 5-11]* This method is the most efficient use of your time and physical efforts. Work your way around the canopy, inspecting each gore from top to bottom.

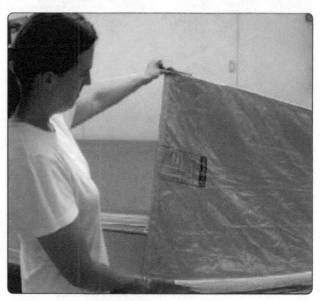

Figure 5-11. *Round canopy gore inspection.*

3. The manufacturer may call for the tensile testing of the fabric after inspection of the canopy for obvious visual damage. This is very important because there was a fabric deterioration problem with certain parachutes several years ago. An AD was issued, and while the exact cause was never determined, a side benefit was the development and adoption of a non-destructive fabric pull test method. This method was adopted by the PIA as Technical Standard (TS)-108, Parachute Canopy Fabric Pull Test, Non-Destructive Method. This method of testing canopy fabric for strength has been adopted by several canopy manufacturers as suitable for testing their canopies. However, the rigger must be careful in using this test method. The proper equipment is essential for accurate testing and the type of material must be known in order to test to the correct strength. The testing equipment is shown in *Figure 5-12.* The full standard can be found in Appendix I of this handbook.

4. Along with the pull test, the AD also requires testing the canopy mesh with a solution of Bromo Cresol Green indicator to determine the presence of an acid condition. The Bromo Cresol Green indicator is a dark blue liquid in its standard state. It turns yellow when

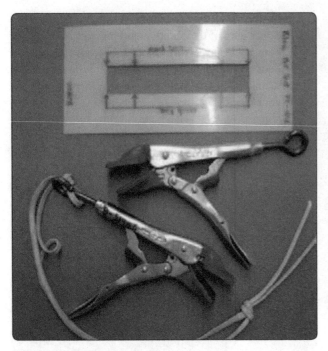

Figure 5-12. *TS-108 test equipment.*

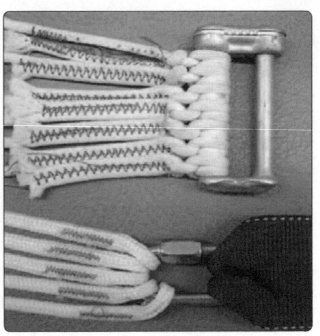

Figure 5-13. *Connector link line attachment methods.*

it contacts acid—the stronger the acid, the brighter the yellow. If the test is positive, the canopy needs to be treated to neutralize the condition. The AD highlights the manufacturer's service bulletin as to how to comply with this test and procedure.

5. If the canopy has a deployment device, such as a diaper, check that it is securely attached, particularly after use. Check the grommets, line stow bands, elastics, or other line stow devices. Pay particular attention to where the stitching attaches to the canopy fabric. This area can be particularly prone to damage during opening.

Suspension Lines and Connector Links

1. The lines, their attachment points, and the associated stitching should be checked for damage or missing stitches. With the older sheath and core nylon lines, such as Type-III found on military surplus canopies, the zigzag stitching at the links are prone to raveling. The more modern non-continuous line canopies use Dacron® or nylon braided lines. The common attachment at the links for these lines uses the "finger-trap" method to secure the lines to the link with a bar tack securing the lines. Most manufacturers now use a contrasting color thread for the bar tack in order to make inspection easier. Make sure all bar tacks are in place. *Figure 5-13* shows both methods of line attachment to the links.

2. There are three basic types of separable connector links in common use today for round canopies: the standard "L" bar type, MS-22002; the Navy speed link, MS-22021, and the Quick link, commonly called the Maillon Rapide® link (named after the French company that first manufactured them). *[Figure 5-14]* The older military surplus canopies are usually found with the two types of MIL-SPEC connector links. Modern sport canopies usually are found with the Rapide® links because of their compatibility with the modern, low-bulk suspension lines.

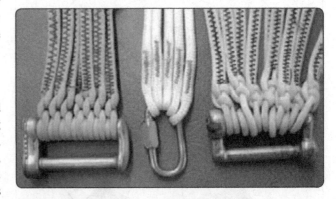

Figure 5-14. *Three types of connector links.*

3. With the MIL-SPEC links, check the tightness of the screws that hold the links together. With the speed links, make sure the knurled side of the end cap is facing up and the plates face outboard on the riser. The screw should be checked for tightness at each repack.

4. If the canopy is equipped with Rapide® links, they should be oriented on the riser with the barrel inboard and to the bottom so it tightens upward. The link

should be tightened hand tight, then approximately one quarter turn further. The actual force recommended for a number 5 link is approximately 30 inch-pounds. Most riggers do not possess the force gauge to measure this, so they use the quarter turn guide. After tightening the links, a "telltale" should be applied to the barrel. *[Figure 5-15]* A telltale is a marker, usually nail polish, that provides a breakable seal to show if the barrel has moved. If the seal is broken, the rigger knows the link may be loose. In doing a repack, if the telltale is intact, the rigger should not loosen the link and retighten it because continual tightening can strip the threads, causing the link to fail.

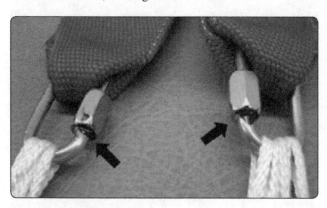

Figure 5-15. *Telltale marker.*

Harness

1. Starting at the riser end, check the webbing for any wear or damage and inspect the stitching at the riser ends. If the canopy has steering lines and a guide ring on the riser, make sure the ring is secure and the steering line is attached to the steering toggle correctly. With a round canopy, make sure the steering line has sufficient slack in it when under tension. If the line is too tight, it can fail at opening because of too much stretch.

2. Continue down the risers. If canopy releases are installed, check their operation. With the Capewell cable release, open the release and make sure there is no dirt or sand in the mechanism. Also, check for wear, particularly on the cable ring.

3. Check all of the harness webbing for wear from chafing, abrasion, and sunlight degradation. Pay particular attention to the buffer and chafing strips where used to prevent wear from the hardware. These buffers are there to provide early warning before the load-bearing webbing starts to wear. Check the elastic keepers so the running ends of the straps can be properly stowed.

4. Check all of the hardware, paying particular attention to the leg snaps. Quick ejectors are particularly prone

to failure of the springs. Obviously, those with broken springs should be replaced. B-12 snaps are prone to having the gate sides bent to the point they do not close properly. This gate may be repaired with a screwdriver and pliers. *[Figure 5-16]* Straightening the side of the gate allows the snap to close properly.

Figure 5-16. *B-12 snap gate repair.*

5. An area of concern for many riggers, one for which there is not much guidance, is how much plating wear and associated corrosion of the hardware is allowable. This depends on the location of the damage. If it is a solid ring or buckle, and the damage has occurred from dragging or abrasion in an area that is not in contact with webbing, one solution is to clean the rust with a fine emery cloth and cover it with clear nail polish. This keeps the area from continued rusting. It does not, however, prevent further damage caused by the original rusting. If the rusting is caused by two pieces of hardware interacting with each other, the problem is more serious. If allowed to continue, the rust pattern may cause the two pieces to fuse together under the most severe conditions. In this case, the hardware must be removed and replaced. If the hardware in contact with webbing, such as a leg strap adapter, and becomes corroded, it must be replaced. This problem frequently arises when the parachute is exposed to salt water and not properly rinsed. The hardware rusts inside the leg strap webbing causing accelerated wear and must definitely be replaced. *[Figure 5-17]*

6. The ripcord housing and pocket should be checked for wear and fit of the ripcord. On the housing, check the ends and the ferrules. On more modern assemblies, these ferrules are brass and more susceptible to wear than the MILSPEC types. Look inside to make sure there are no obstructions to interfere with the ripcord.

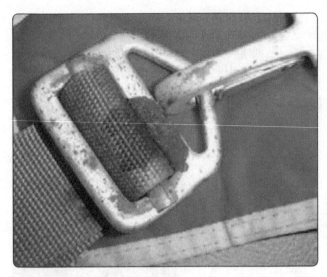

Figure 5-17. *Rusty leg snap hardware.*

The ripcord pocket may be elastic, Velcro®, or a military style with a spring to hold in the ripcord. Whichever type, make sure the ripcord is held securely, yet at the same time make sure it is not too tight so the ripcord can be removed easily. Also, check the tackings that hold the housing and pocket.

Container

1. As stated in the beginning of this chapter, the initial external inspection of the container should alert the rigger to any damage inside. Note any holes, abrasion, or fraying of the pack material.

2. Check the grommets for sharp edges and pulling out of the material from under the grommet. Cones should have the stitching secure. Check the plating on the cones in the area of the eye. Sharp edges can cause a cone lock. Eyelets should have the tacking secure. Snap fasteners should be securely set in the material. Check for wear and security of the opposing parts. Make sure that "pull-the-dot" types are set correctly for direction. Stiffeners, both metal and plastic, should not be bent or cracked. There should be no sharp edges. Pack opening bands (POBs), if used, should be in good shape and not stretched out. Make sure the hooks are in good shape, too. On the military style POBs, it may be necessary to retack the pull tabs at the end. Metal frames, if used, should be straight. Buffers at the corners should be in good condition. Tackings, if used, should be secure.

3. The container-closing loop is an extremely important part of the container system. A worn loop may fail, which would cause a premature opening of the container. With the parachute still in a packed condition, check for the correct length. If the loop is made too

long or stretched during use, the pilot chute can extend and move off center. This may result in a poor launch or a pack job that is uncomfortable for the user. After determining that the loop is of the correct material and length, check the eye(s) of the loop on the inside for wear. It is not uncommon for the loop to appear to be in good condition when viewed from the outside but worn partially through when examined from the inside. *[Figure 5-18]* Many riggers simply replace the loops at each repack, regardless of the condition.

Figure 5-18. *Worn closing loop.*

Ripcord

There are a number of things that need to be inspected to approve the ripcord:

1. Check the pin(s) for straightness, smoothness, cracks, or other damage.

2. Check the cable for fraying, kinks, or severe bends.

3. Check the swage for wear and security. Look for signs of movement on the cable.

4. Check the handle for wear, damage, rust, or abuse.

Any damage or discrepancies found during the inspection should be noted and the appropriate repair performed by a certificated and appropriately-rated rigger according to the manufacturer's instructions or approved manuals.

Airing and Drying

During the inspection process, the rigger must determine the condition of the canopy and system regarding dryness and moisture. In the past, it was necessary for the parachute to be aired and dried for 24 hours prior to packing it. According to 14 CFR part 65, section 65.129(c), "No certificated parachute rigger may pack a parachute that has not been thoroughly dried and aired." This determination is at the discretion of the rigger.

Ram-Air Reserves and Sport Piggyback Systems

The following inspection procedures share much with the previous section on round canopies. The differences between ram-air reserves and sport piggyback systems are identified in the following section. Inspect as follows:

Pilot Chute and Free Bag/Bridle

1. The rigger should inspect the pilot chute in the same manner as in the section on round canopies.

2. The free bag should be checked to include all grommets, especially those bags that have a through loop configuration. Any sharpness in this area can result in a damaged closing loop. For those free bags that utilize a Safety-Stow® locking system, make sure the elastic loop is of the correct size, the elastic is in good shape, and the zigzag stitching is secure. Many riggers fabricate these loops in the field, which in most cases, is an unauthorized procedure. The Safety-Stow® loop is an integral part of the approved reserve deployment system and is manufactured under an approved quality control system from approved materials. The rigger should use only OEM-approved parts for this.

3. Check the bridle for any damage or wear. For those bridles that have assistor pockets, make sure the stitching is secure and the pockets are not damaged. Check the Velcro® on the line stow pocket for wear and security. If the Velcro® does not hold securely, the parachute can experience "line dump" during deployment, possibly causing a malfunction or out of sequence deployment. Some deployment bags use rubber bands to stow the lines. If this is the case, check their condition and replace them if necessary.

4. There are still older ram-air canopies in the field that did not use a free bag but a diaper deployment system. If this is the case, the diaper should be inspected the same as that on a round canopy. Be sure to use the correct type and length of bridle, since it is generally not the same as a round bridle.

Ram-Air Reserve Canopy

Shown in *Figure 5-19* is a typical ram-air reserve and harness and container system layout. The terminology used in describing the parts of the ram-air canopy is called out in PIA Technical Standard TS-100, Standardized Nomenclature for Ram-air Inflated Gliding Parachutes, which can be found in Appendix I of this handbook.

Figure 5-19. *Ram-air/piggyback layout.*

1. When inspecting and assembling ram-air canopies, begin with the upper surface of the canopy. *[Figure 5-20]* Work your way up and down the top panel of the cells looking for any damage or contamination. Check the seams for loose stitching and packing tabs if used, for security.

2. Check the trailing edge seam for secure stitching, paying particular attention to the line attachment

Figure 5-20. *Ram-air canopy hanger—top skin inspection.*

tapes and their associated bar tacks. Next, look at the interior of the cells, carefully checking the crossports for damage or fraying of the edges of the fabric.

3. Now proceed to the lower surface of the canopy. Carefully check all the seams and the line attachment tapes and bar tacks.

4. Some manufacturers require the use of PIA Technical Standard TS-108, Canopy Fabric Pull Test, at certain intervals. In addition, the manufacturer's warning/ TSO label may require that the rigger mark the label to signify each time it is repacked and after each use. *[Figure 5-21]* This label is found on the upper surface trailing edge of the canopy. It is important to comply with this requirement, not only because the manufacturer requires it, but also it establishes the trail of use for the canopy, which allows future riggers (and the manufacturer) to track its use and condition over time. Some riggers feel that they are doing their customers a favor by not marking the boxes in order to show it has little use when it comes to selling it. Since most individuals have a specific rigger pack their parachute on a regular basis, it does not take a lot of detective work to inspect the rigger's logbook to see how many times they have packed any particular parachute.

Canopy Assembly and Line Continuity

The first task is to check the line continuity of the canopy. The following method may be used by riggers who do not have access to a canopy hanger. *Figure 5-22* shows examples of a seven-cell and nine-cell canopy when viewed from the bottom as by the jumper when in flight. The examples show the line attachment nomenclature referred to in the continuity check. *Figure 5-23* shows the standard canopy nomenclature as referred to in the continuity check.

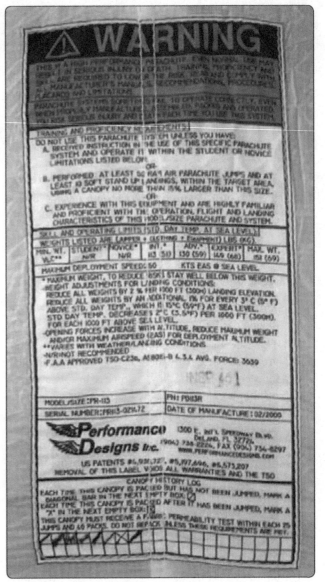

Figure 5-21. *PIA warning label.*

1. First, lay out the canopy on its left side, the slider spanwise with its tape down, and lay out the container with the harness up.

2. If slider bumpers are used, thread one bumper over each riser and down a few inches.

3. Place the slider on the risers spanwise with its tape facing the canopy.

4. Locate the leading edge and A line attachment. Follow the line 8A (10A) to the outboard side of its link and attach the link to the right riser, finger tight.

5. Pick up line 1A at the canopy attach point. Follow it down to the outboard side of its link and attach the link to the left front riser, finger tight.

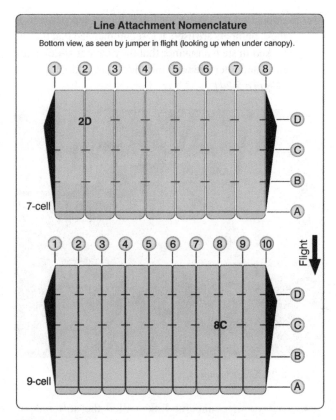

Figure 5-22. *Line attachment nomenclature drawing.*

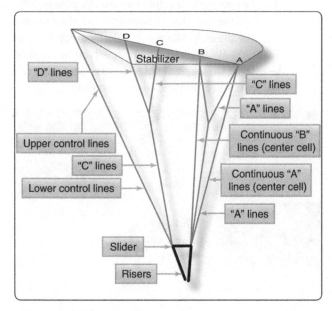

Figure 5-23. *Ram-air canopy layout and nomenclature.*

6. Turn the container over, harness down, and orient the rear risers to receive their respective links. This simplifies C/D link attachment.

7. Rotate the leading edge under the rest of the canopy. Split the aft section along with its associated control line groups to make the C/D links easily accessible for routing and installation.

8. Locate the data panel at the center cell's upper surface trailing edge. From this center reference point, follow the trailing edge to the left stabilizer and pick up line 1D.

9. Route this line to the outboard side of its link and attach the link to the left rear riser, finger tight.

10. Again from the center reference, follow the trailing edge to the right stabilizer and pick up line 8D (10D).

11. Route this line to the outboard side of its link and attach the link to the right rear riser, finger tight.

12. Return to the center reference point of the trailing edge. Locate and pick up the left side upper control lines consecutively. Verify their continuity to the junction with the lower control line.

13. Removing twists as you go, follow the left lower control line to its running end. Route it through the appropriate slider grommet and then through the guide ring.

14. Remove the toggle from the riser and route the running end of the lower control line through the toggle attachment loop or grommet.

15. Slide the toggle up to the mark on the control line. Secure it with an overhand knot tied closely to the toggle.

16. The control line attachment for the right side is done in a similar manner.

17. When the control line installation is complete, compare the two toggle settings under equal tension to ensure their uniformity.

18. At this time, verify the continuity of the control line system. Begin at the trailing edge on each side, ensuring that all twists have been removed from the upper and lower control lines. Check that the lower control lines have been properly routed through their appropriate slider grommets and that the toggles have been properly secured equidistant from the trailing edge.

19. Separate the aft section and control line groups to their respective sides and locate the center reference point at the trailing edge.

20. Following the trailing edge control surface outboard leads the rigger to the left stabilizer's bottom seam and the attachment point of line 1D.

21. Holding D lines 1,2,3, and 4 (1,2,3,4,5) in your right hand and D lines 5,6,7, and 8 (6,7,8,9,10) in your left hand, verify the continuity of the C and D lines through the cascades to their respective rear risers.

22. Gather in the control lines and flip the canopy over so the leading edge faces up. Verify this orientation by locating the attachment points of A lines 1 and 8 (10).

23. In the same direction you flipped the canopy, rotate the container system harness up.

24. Pick up the front riser groups, follow them to the canopy, and separate.

25. Pick up A lines 8,7,6, and 5 (10, 9,8,7,6). If you have continuous center cell lines, follow the bottom seam down and pick up line 5B (6B). Verify continuity of the A and B lines, through the cascades, to the right front riser.

26. Pick up A lines 1,2,3, and 4 (and 5). If you have continuous center cell lines, follow the bottom seam down and pick up line 4B (5B). Verify continuity through the cascades to the left front riser. The continuity check is now complete.

27. Tighten the connector links with an appropriate size wrench. Do not over tighten. Inspect the links for any marks or damage possibly done during the tightening process. Mark the barrel of the connector links with a telltale mark.

28. Move the slider upward from the risers onto the suspension lines.

29. Move the slider bumpers upwards and into position over the connector links. Hand tack the bumpers in place according to the type used.

Inspection

1. Starting at the lower surface of the canopy, check the line attachment loops and their associated bar tacks. Follow the line downward to the cascade junction, if applicable, and check the bar tack at this location. Continue down the line to the connector links and check the bottom loop and bar tack.

2. Starting at the top and working your way downward, inspect the steering lines. Check all junctions and bar tacks, paying particular attention to the brake loops. Check the security of the steering toggles to ensure the correct attachment method is followed. If the toggles are improperly tied, they may come off when the jumper deploys the brakes. Make sure the toggle matches the size of the brake loops. If they are too large, they may hang up and not release when needed. For compatibility, the toggles should be those supplied with the harness and container.

3. If Rapide® links are used on the canopy, check them as set forth in the section on round canopies. The link orientation and tightness is the same. Some canopy manufacturers provide and prescribe the use of "slider bumpers" with their canopies. These are made from either webbing or from vinyl or rubber tubing and are designed to protect the grommets of the slider from impacting the connector links during deployment. If these bumpers are used, it is recommended that they be tacked in such a manner that they cannot slide up the lines and interfere with the slider during deployment. [Figure 5-24]

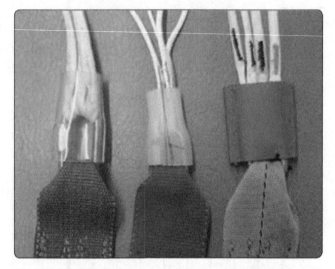

Figure 5-24. *Slider bumpers.*

4. A type of connector link, called the soft link, is used with certain reserve canopies. [Figure 5-25] Manufactured from Spectra® line, they loop through the bottom of the suspension line and the end of the reserve riser. The strength of these soft links far exceeds that of the metal links when installed properly. If installed on the reserve, the rigger should have the manufacturer's instructions to ensure the correct installation.

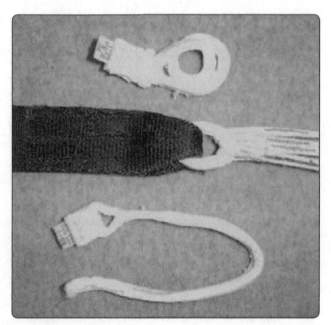

Figure 5-25. *Soft links.*

Harness

1. When inspecting the harness, start at the riser end, checking the condition of the webbing and stitching. Pay particular attention to the security of the steering line guide rings and the method of stowing the excess steering line. If these guide rings fail, it can result in fatal consequences to the user.

2. Check all of the hardware on the harness in the same manner detailed in the Pilot Emergency Parachute Section in this chapter.

3. Check the canopy release system for wear and operation. The release in almost universal use today is the 3-Ring® release system. *[Figure 5-26]* With this system, it is imperative that the rigger also checks the release cable housings for security and cleanliness. Without proper maintenance, this system can be subject to hard pull forces and the inability to release properly. Since the successful operation of the reserve deployment is somewhat dependent on cleanly releasing the main, a properly operating release system is necessary. The primary areas for inspection are the release locator Velcro® on the harness and the cable housings. Check the housing ends for sharp edges on the inside of the grommets. If the housings are tacked to the harness, make sure these are secure. If the customer did not bring the main canopy with the reserve, the rigger should encourage the customer to at least bring the 3-Ring® release handle in for inspection and service.

Container

In addition to those container areas referenced under the pilot emergency system, the sport piggyback container has features unique to this configuration.

1. Check the installation of the AAD, if one is installed, making sure the stowage pockets, cutter mounts, and control unit are secure. Check that the cables are routed correctly. If they are exposed, they may get snagged during packing and damaged or disconnected. Upon completion, inspect the condition of the closing loop.

2. Check the RSL. The RSL is not considered part of the certified reserve system, but if it is installed, the rigger is responsible for the entire RSL assembly since it is attached to the ripcord handle, cable, or housing. This includes the cable housings for tacking and security, any guide rings used, and the RSL lanyard itself. Check the release or snap shackle, if used, and any Velcro® or other positioning or locating methods. An area frequently overlooked is the RSL attachment ring on the main risers, which are frequently replaced. *[Figure 5-27]* In many cases, the attachment ring does not match up to the original design. The rigger should inspect the release handle for proper cable lengths. If the design has only one riser attached to the RSL, it is imperative that the cables be trimmed to release the side opposite the lanyard first so that the reserve is not deployed before the risers are separated from the harness.

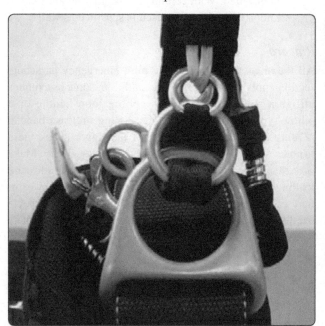

Figure 5-26. *3-Ring® release system.*

Figure 5-27. *RSL/riser attachment.*

3. Check the main deployment system, of which there are three basic types in use today. The first is a ripcord similar to the pilot emergency system. The second type is the throw-out pilot chute (TOP). The third is the pull-out pilot chute (POP).

a. Next, inspect the main ripcord system. Check the ripcord and main pilot chute the same as with the pilot emergency system. Inspect the ripcord pocket for proper holding of the ripcord handle.

b. For throw-out pilot chutes, inspect the pilot chute fabric and mesh for holes. Check the TOP handle at the top of the pilot chute for security, paying special attention to the tape holding the handle, which is particularly prone to wear. Check the bridle attachment to the pilot chute. If it is of a centerline collapsible design, check the centerline for wear and stretch and make sure the length of the bridle is correct. Check the curved locking pin for wear or damage as well as the tape, which attaches it to the bridle. *[Figure 5-28]* Check the pilot chute pocket for fit and wear. Most of today's installations are what is known as a "bottom of container" (BOC) configuration. It is particularly important that the elastic material from which the pocket is made is in good condition. A loose pocket can result in a premature deployment of the main parachute.

c. If repacking a pull-out parachute, check the pilot chute and bridle in the same manner of the throw-out parachute inspection. Check the lanyard and handle for wear.

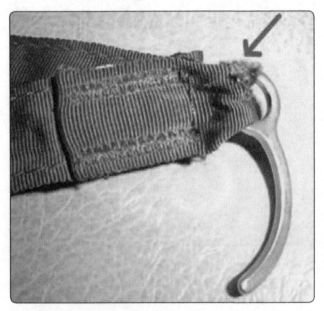

Figure 5-28. *TOP bridle with worn pin tape.*

4. If Velcro® is used on the main pin protector flap, be sure to inspect its condition. If a plastic closing flap or tongue is used, check for deformation or breakage. *[Figure 5-29]*

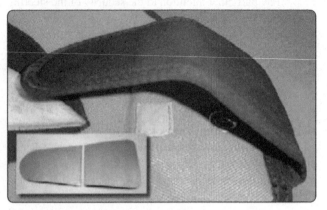

Figure 5-29. *Main pin protector flap plastic breakage.*

5. If Velcro® is used on the main riser covers, be sure to check its condition. If plastic, check for breakage and deformation. If the plastic is excessively deformed, it is a sign that the covers do not fit properly and may open prematurely causing problems.

6. For the container-closing loop, the same criteria applies as in the pilot emergency parachute. In addition, make sure the loop material is the same as specified in the owner's manual, especially if an AAD is installed. With certain AADs, a particular type of knot and washer to be used is specified as well.

Ripcord

All the areas mentioned in the pilot emergency parachute section apply to the sport rig. In addition, some assemblies utilize a ripcord that has a webbing loop handle or a pillow-type handle similar to the 3-Ring® release handle. *[Figure 5-30]* It is important that the rigger check these handles for proper markings and fit to the assembly. Make sure that there is sufficient slack in the cable to allow no loading of the pin in any attitude or position that the wearer may conceivably get into. Most, if not all of these style handles, utilize Velcro® to secure them to the harness. Make sure the Velcro® is in good condition for holding ability but not so much as to inhibit the pull force.

Remember, while both the pilot emergency parachute and sport piggyback assemblies share many areas in common, each has peculiar requirements for its use. It is important for the rigger to recognize these and handle each system accordingly.

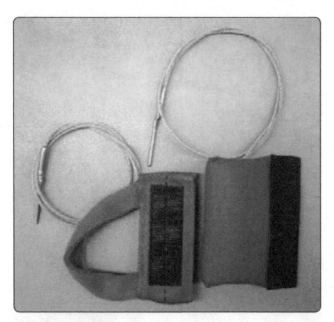

Figure 5-30. *Loop and pillow ripcords.*

Rigging and Repairs

When the entire assembly inspection is complete, the rigger has a list of the discrepancies found during the procedure. At this point, a determination must be made on how to remedy these defects. For senior riggers, certain remedial action may be outside the scope of their certificate. If so, those riggers need to find an appropriately certificated and rated rigger to do the work or return the parachute to the manufacturer for repair. In the case of major canopy or harness work, this may be the best solution regardless.

Aside from the qualification limitations of the rigger, the manufacturer may be better equipped to perform major repair or overhaul. They have the original patterns, templates, and design data, as well as the certified materials. In addition, their labor rate is probably less than what the rigger may charge the customer, particularly if he or she has not done this repair before. The factory has the experience and practice that results in the repair looking just like new. While some riggers may look at any given project with anticipation, they also need to look at what is best for the customer.

Many times, the master rigger has a repair facility and stocks it with the necessary materials. In most cases, these materials come from sources with no traceability as to their origin. The manufacturer is required to use only those materials that have been tested, certified, and approved to meet the standards of their quality control system under the TSO system. During one recent routine inspection and repack, the rigger found severe failure of the harness stitching at the main lift web/leg strap junction. Upon further examination, it was determined that the thread used to sew the harness was not nylon. The harness was returned to the manufacturer, who

then determined that the thread was indeed cotton and not the required nylon. The thread broke at approximately 10 pounds versus 45 pounds for 5-cord nylon. Further investigation revealed that the harness was originally manufactured with a harness size three inches shorter. There were telltale marks left from where the original harness was stitched. This modification was evidently performed by someone who either was not qualified to perform the work or had gotten a batch of the wrong thread by mistake and did not recognize the difference. Attempts to find out who did the alteration were unsuccessful. The manufacturer repaired the harness at no charge and returned it to the customer. To preclude this type of problem, many professional riggers and lofts establish good working relationships with the manufacturers and procure certain materials from them. They keep these marked and in a separate area and use them only on the appropriate projects.

Another area of concern is a master rigger who does major alterations without proper approval of the manufacturer. The rigger may do major repairs to return the assembly to its original condition without further authorization of the Administrator or manufacturer, but alterations are another story. Title 14 CFR part 65, section 65.129(e), states that "No certificated parachute rigger may pack, maintain, or alter a parachute in any manner that deviates from the procedures approved by the Administrator or the manufacturer of the parachute." There are a number of common alterations seen in the field. Among them are: harness re-sizing, AAD installations, RSL retrofits, chest strap relocation, and others. The manufacturer's approval can vary from a verbal message over the phone to a formal engineering procedure complete with drawings and specifications. If the work is done correctly, the truth probably lies somewhere in the middle. If riggers want to ensure they are following code, they should obtain some form of written approval from the manufacturer in whatever form they provide.

The bottom line is that the purpose of the system is to provide an infrastructure that ensures the safety of the public. Professional riggers strive to do the right thing both morally and legally.

Packing

Packing is the heart of the rigging profession. Once riggers satisfy all the necessary inspection requirements, they may then proceed with the packing process. This section describes a generic round parachute packing method into a modern back-type pilot emergency system. The steps for doing this are common to most parachutes of similar types. Once the basics are mastered, it is a simple matter of following the manufacturer's instructions for other makes and models.

Round Canopy into a Pilot Emergency Parachute System

The steps for packing this type of parachute are broken down into the following sections:

1. Layout

2. Flaking and pleating the canopy

3. Folding the skirt and the long fold

4. Closing the diaper and stowing the lines

5. Skirt or diaper placement

6. Accordion fold of the canopy into the container

7. Closing the container

Before beginning, the rigger must have the necessary tools to pack the parachute. The packing manual includes a list of tools necessary for the procedure. *Figure 5-31* shows the recommended tools needed to pack the parachute described in this section. Do not forget to count your tools before beginning.

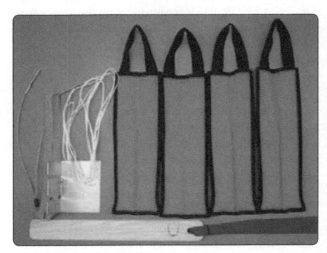

Figure 5-31. *Round parachute packing tools.*

Layout

1. The parachute must be positioned on the table face down with the wearer's head toward the canopy. The rear of the canopy faces up. Normally the data panel is on the middle gore that faces up. *[Figure 5-32]*

2. Attach the canopy tension loop to the upper table tension device, then attach the connector links or risers to a tension board or similar device at the bottom of the table. *[Figure 5-33]* Be sure to apply light tension.

3. Straighten the apex of the canopy making sure the lower lateral band or skirt is somewhat even. *[Figure 5-34]* Apply additional tension to the canopy and lines.

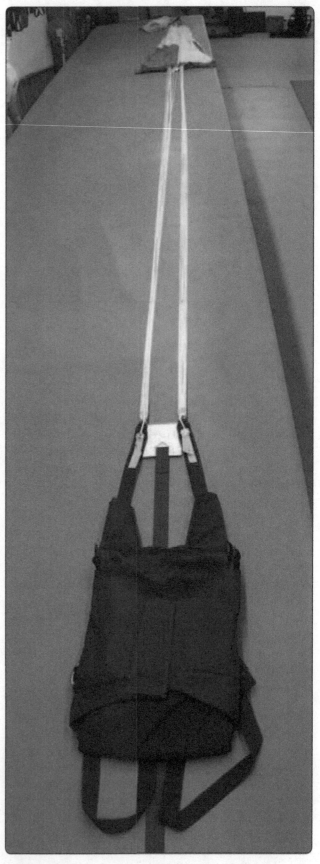

Figure 5-32. *Round parachute assembly on packing table.*

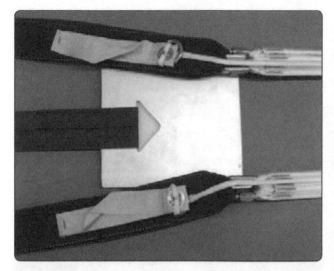

Figure 5-33. *Riser and connector links attached to the tension board.*

Figure 5-34. *Straightening the canopy apex.*

Pleating the Canopy

1.   Flake the canopy in the normal manner with an equal number of gores to each side. *Figures 5-35* through *5-41* show the proper technique.

Figure 5-35. *Flaking 1.*

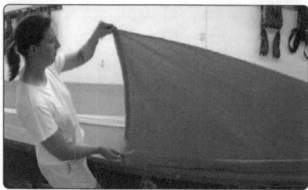

Figure 5-36. *Flaking 2.*

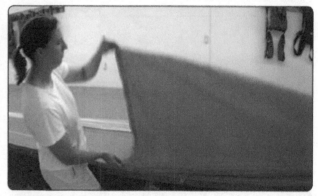

Figure 5-37. *Flaking 3.*

Figure 5-38. *Flaking 4.*

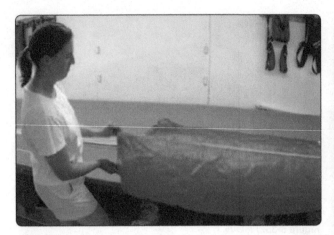

Figure 5-39. *Flaking 5.*

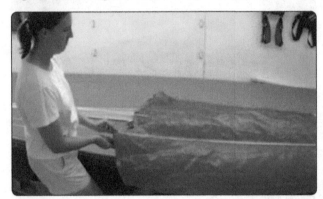

Figure 5-40. *Flaking 6.*

Figure 5-41. *Flaking 7.*

2. Pleat the canopy with an equal number of gores to each side. Make sure the canopy skirt is even. *[Figures 5-42 through 5-44]*

Fold the Skirt

1. Fold the skirt so it is parallel to the radial seams. *[Figure 5-45]*

Figure 5-42. *Pleating 1.*

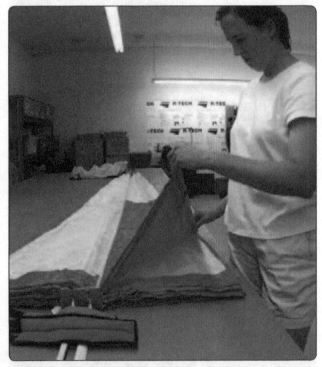

Figure 5-43. *Pleating 2.*

Figure 5-44. *Pleating 3.*

Figure 5-45. *Folding.*

2. Fold the canopy lengthwise in thirds, and then fold once more to the center in what is commonly called fifths. *[Figures 5-46 through 5-48]* Place packing weights on the canopy to hold it in place.

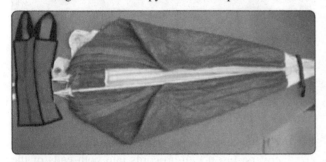

Figure 5-46. *Fifths 1.*

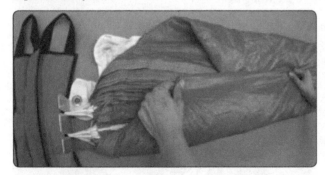

Figure 5-47. *Fifths 2.*

Closing the Diaper and Stowing the Lines

1. Pull the container towards the canopy and form a loop of suspension lines above the top of the diaper. *[Figure 5-49]* Be sure to leave enough room to close the diaper.

2. Close the diaper starting with the top grommet. Lock the grommet with a bight of line no more that 1.5 inches long. *[Figure 5-50]* Close the middle grommet in the same manner. *[Figure 5-51]*

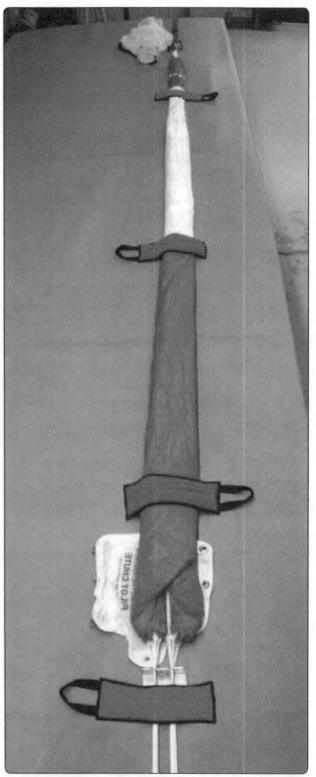

Figure 5-48. *Fifths 3.*

3. Close the bottom grommet over the bottom rubber band and then the end flap grommet over the side grommet. *[Figure 5-52]* Close with a bight of line no longer than 1.5 inches long.

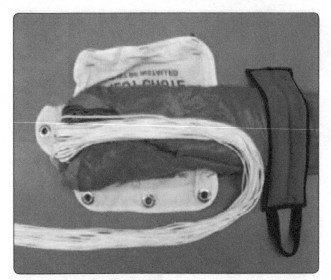

Figure 5-49. *Locking stow 1.*

Figure 5-50. *Locking stow 2.*

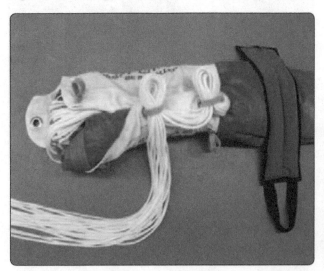

Figure 5-51. *Locking stow 3.*

4. Finish stowing the remainder of the suspension lines using bights no more than 1.5 inches long. *[Figure 5-53]*

Figure 5-52. *Locking stow 4.*

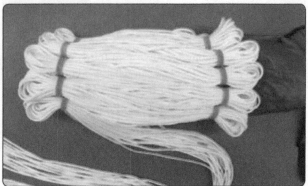

Figure 5-53. *Line stows.*

Skirt or Diaper Placement

1. Lay the risers in the container and close the riser covers. Insert pull-up cords into both ends of the closing loop.

2. Turn the skirt of the canopy 90 degrees and lay one edge of the diaper even with the top edge and inside the pack tray. *[Figure 5-54]*

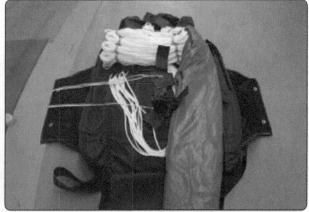

Figure 5-54. *Diaper stow.*

Accordion Folding the Canopy

1. Fold the canopy toward the bottom of the container leaving enough to fill the upper corner of the container.

2. Fold the canopy toward the bottom of the container and leave approximately 4 inches of canopy past the bottom. *[Figure 5-55]*

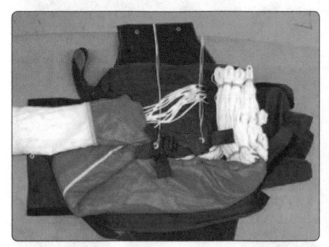

Figure 5-55. *S fold 1.*

3. Fold the canopy back towards the top of the container and spread the canopy sideways to fill out the width of the container. *[Figure 5-56]* Make two folds between the lower edge of the diaper and the lower end of the closing loop. *[Figure 5-57]*

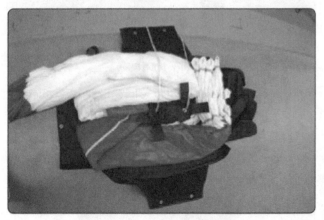

Figure 5-56. *S fold 2.*

4. Lay the remainder of the canopy and apex across the middle of the container and fold in an appropriate manner to fill the empty area of the container on the pack tray stiffener below the diaper. *[Figure 5-58]*

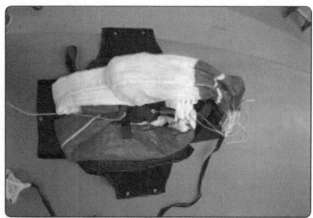

Figure 5-57. *S fold 3.*

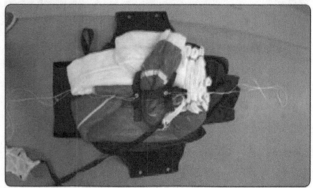

Figure 5-58. *Apex location 1.*

Closing the Container

1. Close the bottom flap of the container first, threading the pull-up cord through the grommet at the upper end of the bottom flap. Place the canopy protector flaps into position as shown in *Figure 5-59.*

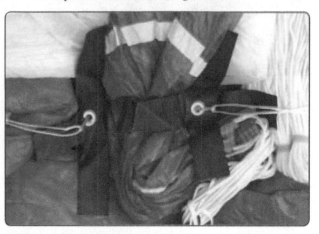

Figure 5-59. *Apex location 2.*

2. Close the top flap, being sure to push the canopy and diaper into the corners of the container while closing. Thread the upper pull-up cord through the upper grommet on the top flap.

3. Thread the lower pull-up cord through the lower grommet on the top flap making sure the canopy protector flaps are in position. *[Figure 5-60]* Pull the lower pull-up cord through both grommets until the closing loop appears and install a temporary pin.

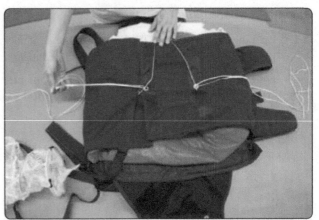

Figure 5-61. *Upper temp pin seated.*

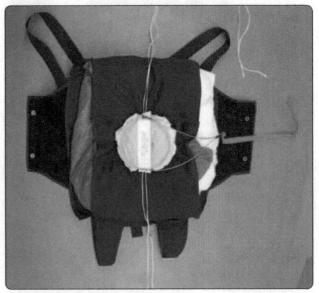

Figure 5-62. *Pilot chute seated in position.*

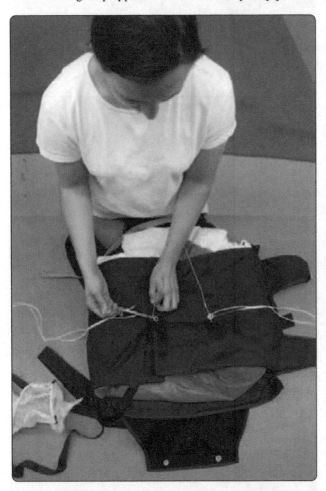

Figure 5-60. *Closing bottom flap.*

4. Pull the upper pull-up cord through the grommet until the upper closing loop appears and install a temporary pin. *[Figure 5-61]*

5. Compress the pilot chute between the rubber bumpers and make sure the pilot chute canopy fabric is tucked into the coils of the spring. Thread the pull-up cords through the grommets in the grommet strap. Removing one temporary pin at a time, pull up the closing loops and secure the pilot chute in place with two temporary pins. *[Figure 5-62]* Close the Velcro® on the top and bottom flaps.

6. Close the right side flap. Close the left side flap and install the ripcord pins. *[Figure 5-63]*

Figure 5-63. *Ripcord pins in place.*

7. Seal the last pin according to the manufacturer's instructions or in an approved manner.

Ripcord Pull Force

The correct packing is the most important aspect of repacking a parachute, but the cosmetic appearance of the container is important as well. This is true both for a pilot emergency and a sport piggyback system. Pilots want their parachute as snug and as flat as possible to keep the parachute comfortable when in use. Skydivers want theirs as snug and streamlined as possible so it stays closed during free fall. The key to these requirements is to make sure the pilot chute is held down securely. To do that, the closing loop needs to be as short as the rigger can make it and still meet the requirements for the maximum pull force. Under the TSO system, the maximum allowable pull force for the ripcord is 22 pounds. Most riggers develop a feel for the closing of the container and the resultant force. However, new riggers need to check their packing technique to measure the pull force, which is done without a seal or thread.

Start by having someone put on the parachute to replicate the real shape and conformity of the parachute system. To pull the ripcord while the parachute is lying on the table is not realistic. The rigger then takes the ripcord handle from the pocket and attaches a calibrated scale to it. *[Figure 5-64]* Ideally, a recording scale should be used to register the

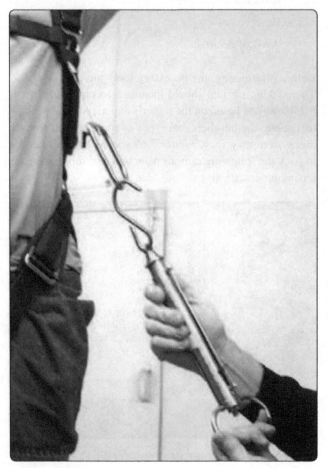

Figure 5-64. *Ripcord pull test.*

maximum force during the pull. Next, the rigger needs to pull the ripcord in a smooth, quick motion, duplicating the motion of the user and the test requirements of the TSO. Take note of the force required to pull the ripcord pin(s) clear of the locking loop(s) and activate the system. If the force is less than 22 pounds, the rigger can then re-close the container and seal the ripcord. If the force is over 22 pounds, the rigger must make whatever adjustments are needed, such as lengthening the locking loop or re-stowing the canopy, to achieve a pull force below 22 pounds.

Sealing the Parachute

As stated in 14 CFR part 65, section 65.133, "Each certificated parachute rigger must have a seal with an identifying mark prescribed by the Administrator, and a seal press. After packing a parachute, he shall seal the pack with his seal in accordance with the manufacturer's recommendation for that type of parachute." Most manuals simply say to "seal the parachute." The following describes a commonly approved method.

Take a length of seal thread approximately 20 inches long. Fold in half and make two lark's head knots around the ripcord cable adjacent to the shank of the ripcord pin. *[Figure 5-65]* Pass one end of the thread through the seal and then under the pin on the opposite side of the locking loop or cone. *[Figure 5-66]* Bring the end back through the second hole in the seal and tie a knot with the other end of the thread. *[Figure 5-67]* Leave enough slack in the thread to allow for movement of the pin without breaking the thread. However, make sure the pin cannot be extracted from the locking loop without breaking the thread. Slide the seal over the knot and compress the seal with the seal press. *[Figure 5-68]* Trim the excess thread.

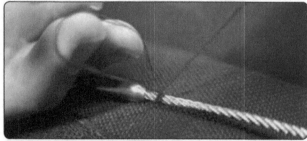

Figure 5-65. *Lark's head the thread on the cable.*

Count all of your tools. Fill in the appropriate information on the packing data card and the rigger's logbook. Place the data card in the packing data card pocket.

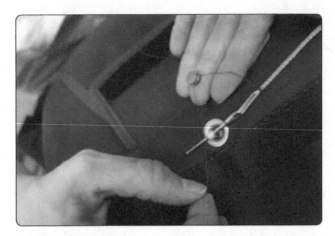

Figure 5-66. *Threading the seal thread.*

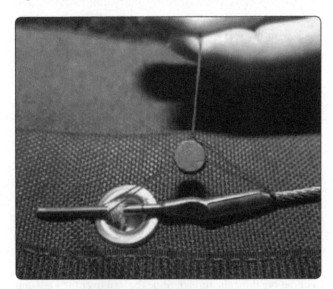

Figure 5-67. *Positioning the seal.*

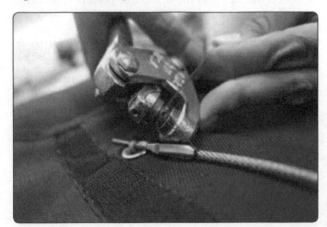

Figure 5-68. *Compressing the seal.*

Ram-Air Reserve into a Sport Piggyback System

In the preceding text, the discussion is centered on a parachute system that was already assembled. This next section focuses on the assembly of a ram-air parachute system, the component parts, and the process from the assembly stage

through to packing. While this section provides guidance and an overview of packing a ram-air canopy into a sport piggyback system, it is imperative that the rigger receive proper training from a certificated and properly rated rigger who has been trained to pack ram-air reserves. Title 14 CFR part 65, section 65.129(f) states, "No certificated parachute rigger may exercise the privileges of his certificate and type rating unless he understands the current manufacturer's instructions for the operation involved..."

The following procedure is typical of many current 1-pin container systems. While this configuration comprises the majority of those manufactured today, there are other designs still in use that require different techniques. The rigger must become thoroughly familiar with the other configurations before attempting to assemble and pack these systems.

Assembling the Reserve System

The following components are necessary to assemble the harness and container to the ram-air reserve:

1. The harness, container, and associated parts to include the reserve pilot chute and free bag, reserve ripcord, reserve steering toggles, reserve closing loop, and RSL, if desired.

2. Reserve canopy.

3. AAD, if desired.

Before progressing, the necessary tools must be available. The packing manual should include a recommended tools list. However, based on the rigger's experience and packing technique, the numbers and types of tools needed to pack this system may vary. *Figure 5-69* shows the tools needed to pack the following ram-air parachute assembly using the technique described.

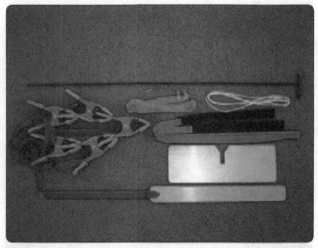

Figure 5-69. *Ram-air canopy packing tools.*

Before starting, always count your tools and then follow the assembly procedures listed below:

1. Connect the canopy to the risers of the harness, ensuring line continuity is correct.

2. Tighten the connector links and seal with a telltale mark.

3. If used, install and secure the connector link bumpers per the canopy manufacturer's instructions.

4. Route the control lines through the slider grommets and guide rings on the rear of the riser. Fasten the steering toggles in the required manner. [*Figure 5-70*]

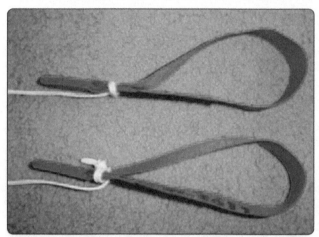

Figure 5-70. *Tying toggles.*

5. Install the AAD, if desired, according to the manufacturer's instructions.

6. Install a closing loop of the correct type and length.

7. Attach the reserve free bag to the reserve pilot chute.

The following steps should be used for packing this type of parachute:

1. Layout and setting up packing clamps.

2. Stacking and pleating the reserve canopy.

3. Setting the deployment brakes.

4. Folding the canopy.

5. Placing the canopy into the deployment bag and stowing the lines.

6. Placing the bag into the container and closing the container.

Step 1. Layout and Setting Up Packing Clamps

1. Anchor the risers at the connector links including the steering lines. [*Figure 5-71*]

2. Place packing weight on top of it.

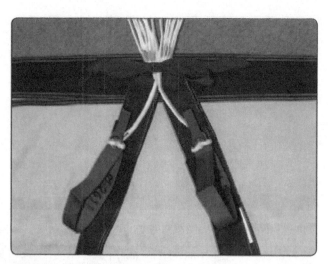

Figure 5-71. *Anchor risers.*

3. Pull the slider down to the connector links. Make sure the tapes face upward toward the canopy. [*Figure 5-72*]

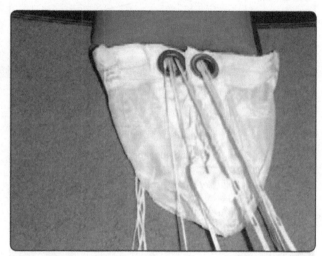

Figure 5-72. *Pull slider down.*

4. Lay the canopy on its right side. (**NOTE:** A mirror image of the layout is permissible).

5. Flake the canopy so the top seams are even. Place a clamp on the top of the canopy in line with each line attachment point as in *Figure 5-73*.

Step 2. Stacking and Pleating the Reserve Canopy
NOTE: The canopy stack should look like *Figure 5-74*.

It is imperative that the rigger maintains control over the packing process at all times. In particular, it is important to keep the lines taut and straight and to keep the center wind channel of the canopy stack clear and the line attachment tabs stacked neatly.

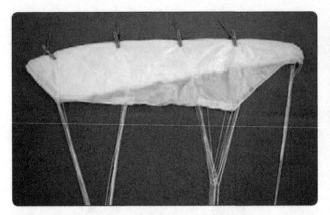

Figure 5-73. *Clamps on top of canopy.*

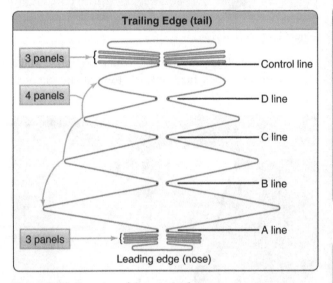

Figure 5-74. *Drawing of canopy stack.*

Trailing Edge (tail)

3 panels

4 panels

3 panels

Control line

D line

C line

B line

A line

Leading edge (nose)

1. Pull tension on the "A" lines. Split the leading edge in half. *[Figure 5-75]*

Figure 5-75. *Split the leading edge.*

2. Fold half under "A" lines. *[Figures 5-76 and 5-77]*

3. Pick up the "B" lines by the clamp and hold vertically over the "A" clamp. *[Figure 5-78]* Note the spread of the leading edge panels.

4. Lower the "B" clamp and material down to the "A" clamp. *[Figure 5-79]* Spread the cells equally to both sides. Keep the center cell in the middle.

Figure 5-76. *Fold half under "A" lines.*

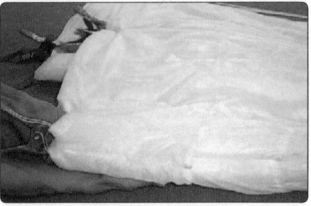

Figure 5-77. *Smooth panels under "A" lines.*

Figure 5-78. *Hold "B" clamp vertically over "A" clamp.*

5. Repeat this step with the "C" and the "D" line groups. *[Figures 5-80 and 5-81]*

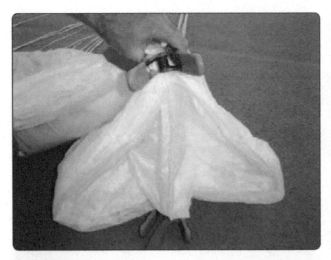

Figure 5-79. *Lower "B" clamp to "A" clamp, spreading the cells.*

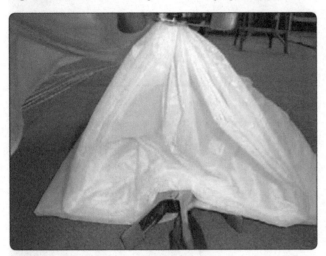

Figure 5-80. *Repeat with "C" lines.*

Figure 5-81. *Repeat with "D" lines.*

6. Split the trailing edge and separate the control lines into right and left groups. *[Figure 5-82]*

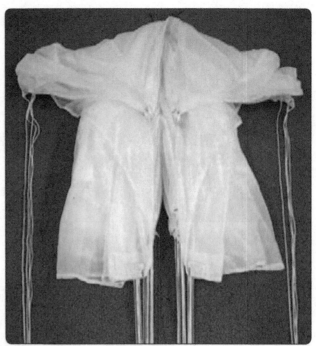

Figure 5-82. *Split the trailing edge.*

7. Remove the "D" clamp. Hold down the "D" lines at the line attachment point and pull down the control lines. *[Figure 5-83]* Do not disturb the center of the canopy stack.

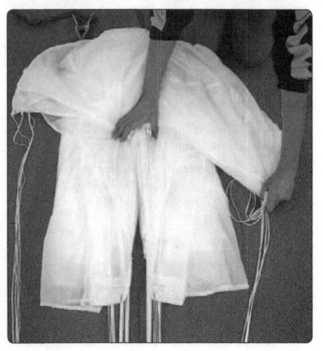

Figure 5-83. *Pull down the trailing edge.*

Step 3. Setting the Brakes

1. Set the deployment brakes and stow the excess line in the Velcro® keepers. *[Figure 5-84]*

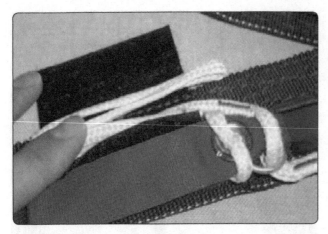

Figure 5-84. *Set the deployment brakes.*

2. The finished toggles should look like *Figure 5-85*.

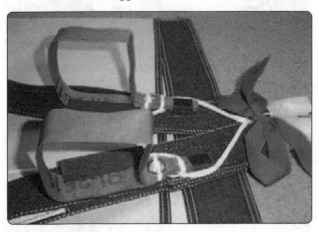

Figure 5-85. *Completed brakes.*

Step 4. Folding the Canopy

1. Fold all the trailing edge to one side, then pull the stabilizer panel taut. *[Figure 5-86]*

2. Flake the trailing edge of the canopy starting with the outboard control lines. Fold each cell in half on top of the "D" line group until you get to the center. *[Figure 5-87]*

3. Repeat with the opposite side.

4. Pull the slider up to the slider stops.

5. Remove remaining clamps from top of canopy. Make sure all suspension lines are in the center of the canopy stack. *[Figure 5-88]*

6. Fold the center of the trailing edge back to expose the center of the wind channel. *[Figure 5-89]*

7. Create an "S" fold in the stack. *[Figure 5-90]*

8. Position a packing paddle a third of the way up from the bottom of the canopy length on top of the stack. *[Figure 5-91]*

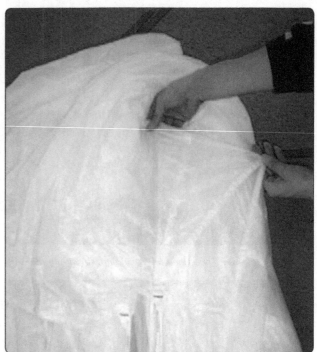

Figure 5-86. *Pull stabilizer taut.*

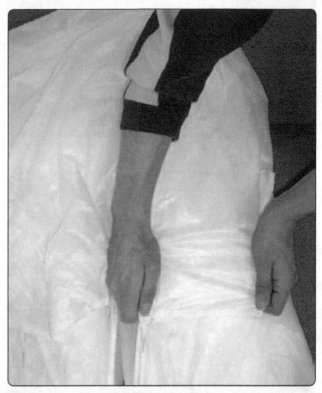

Figure 5-87. *Flake the tail.*

9. Place a gun cleaning rod at half the distance between the bottom and the packing paddle under the stack.

10. Pull the rod up and move the canopy with paddle towards container. *[Figure 5-92]*

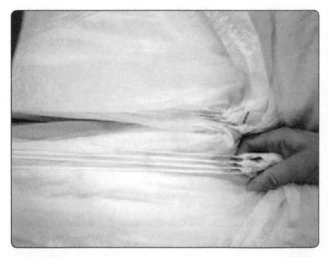

Figure 5-88. *Lines are taut in the center.*

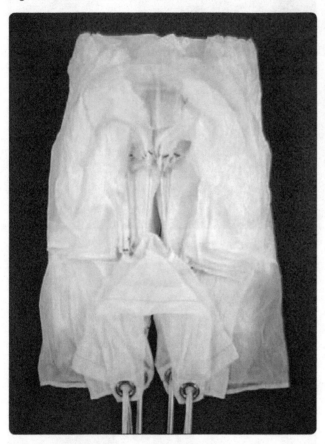

Figure 5-89. *Fold tail back for wind channel.*

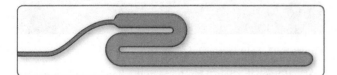

Figure 5-90. *"S" fold drawing.*

11. Pull the top center cell panel down to the bottom of the stack.

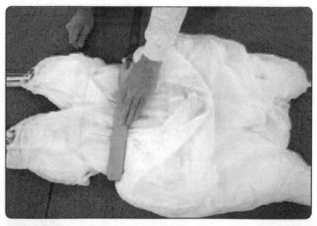

Figure 5-91. *Packing paddle at ⅓rd location.*

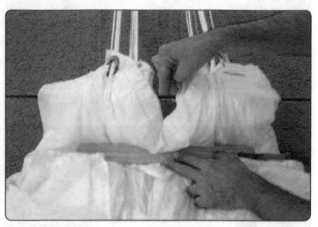

Figure 5-92. *Creating the "S" fold.*

12. Wrap the center cell around the folded canopy with the left and right about halfway to the center, then secure with clamps starting at the bottom. *[Figure 5-93]* The width of the folded canopy should be the width of the D-bag plus 2 inches (5cm).

13. Continue to wrap the center cell around the canopy stack and secure with additional clamps. *[Figure 5-94]*

Step 5. Placing the Canopy into the Deployment Bag and Stowing the Lines

1. Lift the base of the folded canopy and slide the reserve bag underneath. The grommets in the tongue of the bag should be even with the bottom of the stack. *[Figure 5-95]*

2. Make a second "S" fold to match *Figure 5-96.*

3. Split the loose fabric at the top to form two "ears." *[Figure 5-97]*

4. Gather the center cell material along the middle seam until you reach the bottom. Roll the material under, but do not cover the center cell. *[Figure 5-98]*

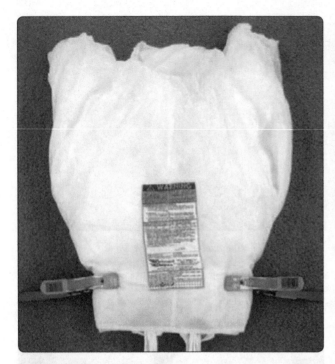

Figure 5-93. *Wrap tail, two clamps.*

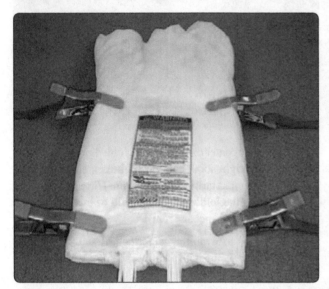

Figure 5-94. *Finish wrapping tail, four clamps.*

5. Hold down the center cell material and then shape the molar folds. *[Figure 5-99]*

6. Fold the ends of the molar folds under to create the bulk necessary to fill the top of the reserve bag. *[Figure 5-100]*

7. When placing the canopy in the bag, allow the folded canopy to stick out 2–3 inches at the mouth of the bag to fill the corners of the reserve container. *[Figure 5-101]*

8. Close bag and secure with the locking stows. *[Figure 5-102]*

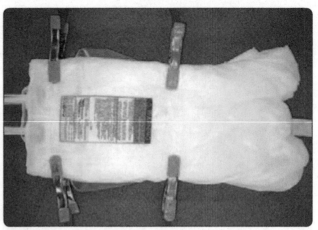

Figure 5-95. *Bag positioned under canopy.*

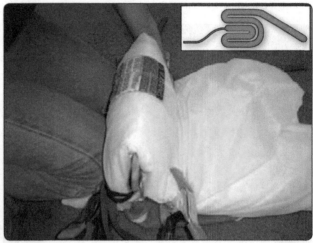

Figure 5-96. *Second "S" fold.*

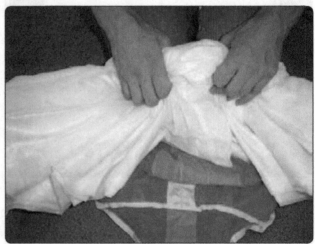

Figure 5-97. *Split fabric and form "ears."*

9. Shape the bag. The shape of the bag should reflect the desired shape of the reserve container.

10. Cover any exposed hook Velcro® to avoid contact with the lines.

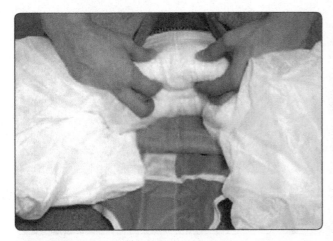

Figure 5-98. *Gather and roll center seam fabric.*

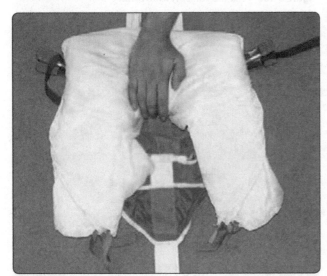

Figure 5-99. *Shape molar folds.*

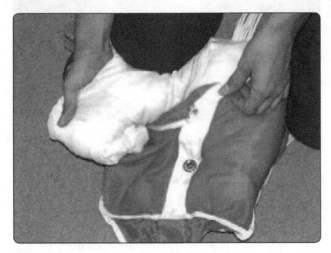

Figure 5-100. *Fold molar ends under.*

11. Stow the lines neatly leaving sufficient line between the bag and riser ends. *[Figure 5-103]*

12. Thread the pull-up cord through the closing loop.

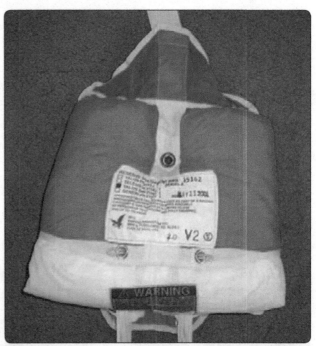

Figure 5-101. *Place canopy in bag.*

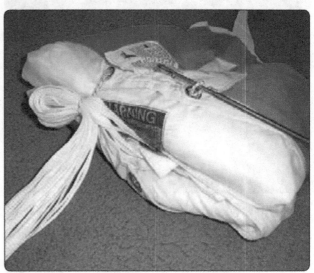

Figure 5-102. *Close bag and secure locking stows.*

Step 6. Placing the Bag into the Container and Closing the Container

1. Place reserve risers into the pack tray. Spread the risers with the rear riser to the outside to minimize the bulk against the back pad. *[Figure 5-104]*

2. Place the reserve bag into the container and S-fold the bridle in the center of the bag. *[Figure 5-105]*

3. Fold the top yoke portion of the bag over the bridle. *[Figure 5-106]*

4. Secure in place with a clamp. *[Figure 5-107]*

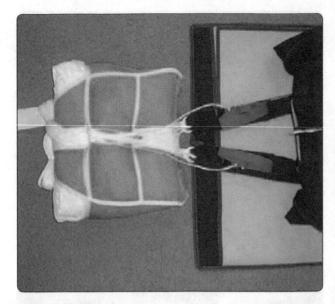

Figure 5-103. *Stow lines.*

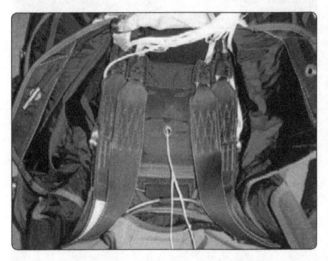

Figure 5-104. *Place risers in the pack tray and spread.*

Figure 5-105. *"S" fold the bridle on bag.*

5. Use the gun cleaning rod to thread the pull-up cord through the pilot chute. *[Figure 5-108]*

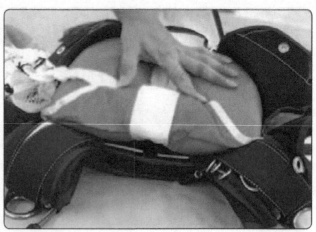

Figure 5-106. *Fold the yoke over the bridle.*

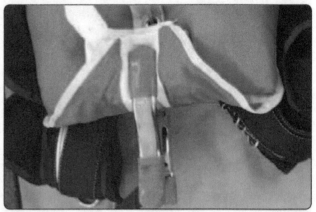

Figure 5-107. *Secure yoke/bridle with clamp.*

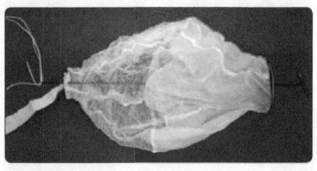

Figure 5-108. *Gun rod through the pilot chute.*

6. Center the base of the pilot chute on the center grommet of the deployment bag.

7. Compress the pilot chute while stuffing fabric and mesh between the spring coils.

8. Position the cap of the pilot chute with the arrow facing toward the top or bottom of the container. *[Figure 5-109]* Secure with a temporary pin.

9. If an AAD, such as a CYPRES®, is installed, route the pull-up cord through the cutter first, then through the right (#1) side flap grommet. *[Figure 5-110]*

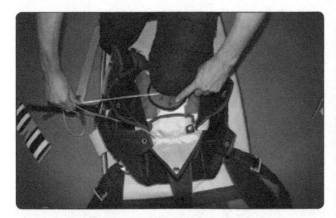

Figure 5-109. *Position pilot chute.*

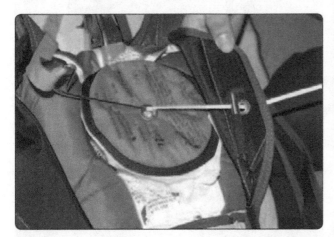

Figure 5-110. *Route pull-up cord through cutter and right flap.*

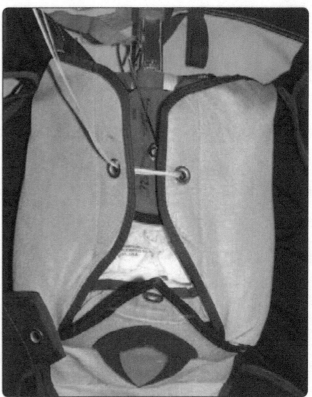

Figure 5-111. *Close right and left flaps simultaneously.*

10. Next thread the left (#2) side flap grommet. At the same time, close the side flaps. *[Figure 5-111]* Secure with a temporary pin.

11. Close the bottom flap (#3) and secure with a temporary pin. *[Figure 5-112]* **NOTE:** At this point, you should only be able to pull ¼–½ inch of loop through the first three flaps. If you can pull more, the loop is too long. Open container and shorten loop.

12. Close flap #4 and insert the ripcord pin. *[Figure 5-113]* CAUTION: Place the closing plate on the bottom edge of the inner top flap. This protects the plastic stiffener if you are kneeling on the pin protector flap. The rigger should determine how tight the closing loop is and decide whether to perform a pull test.

    Warning: Maximum allowable pull force on the reserve ripcord is 22 pounds (10 kg).

13. Once you are satisfied that the pull force is less than 22 pounds (10 kg), seal the ripcord and log the pack job.

14. Place the data card in the data card pocket. *[Figure 5-114]*

15. Count your tools.

16. Complete the placard data on the orange warning label. Failure to do so voids the TSO.

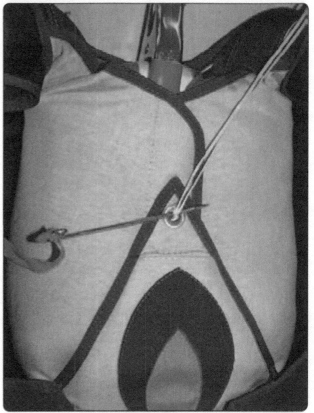

Figure 5-112. *Close #3 bottom flap.*

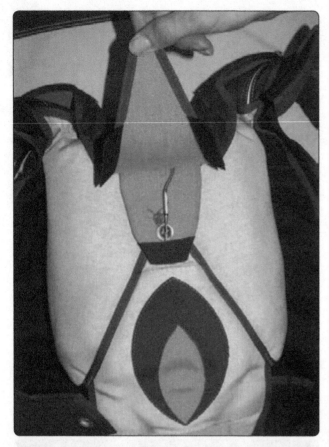

Figure 5-113. *Close flap #4 and insert ripcord pin.*

Figure 5-114. *Place data card in pocket.*

Ram-Air Reserve into a Two-Pin Piggyback

Many sport, military, and pilot emergency rigs feature the two pin, externally-mounted reserve pilot chute or Pop-Top. The Pop-Top closes use adjustable closing loops that are tightened after the pins are inserted. The following instructions demonstrate the PRO pack method without the use of clamps. *[Figures 5-115 through 5-165]*

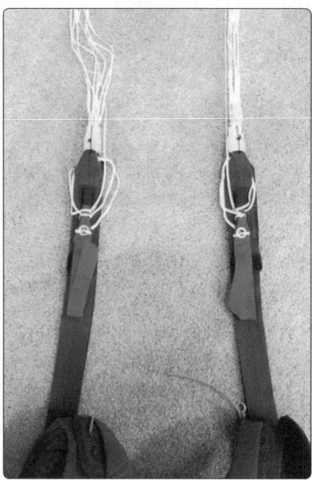

Figure 5-115. *Set brakes. Excess lower control line is inserted through top of riser, around nose of toggle, and toggle placed in nose keeper.*

Figure 5-116. *Four-line (separate the line groups).*

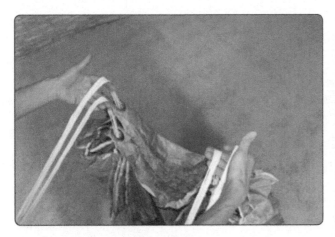

Figure 5-117. *Push the slider up to the slider stops.*

Figure 5-118. *Flake the nose cells of the canopy.*

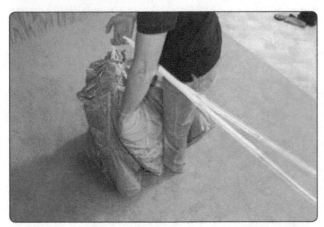

Figure 5-119. *Hold all flaked nose cells between the knees. Reach down and flake out material between A/B, B/C, and C/D lines.*

Documentation

One of the most important parts of the packing process is the requirement to keep proper records. 14 CFR part 65, section 65.131, specifies the information the rigger is required to document. There are two forms of required records. The first is the rigger's logbook. While the exact format is up to the rigger, there are commercially-produced logbooks

Figure 5-120. *Split nose of canopy; three cells to each side, exposing center cell.*

Figure 5-121. *Sweep arm underneath flaked canopy and gently lay it on the floor.*

Figure 5-122. *Pull up and smooth out the top skins of the canopy, cleaning up between the folds.*

Figure 5-123. *Pull the lines taught and to the center.*

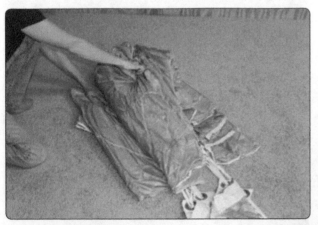

Figure 5-124. *If the PRO packed canopy was laid down carefully, it will be essentially flaked. Only minor straightening is necessary.*

available that provide space for the required notations. The second required record is the parachute data card. Both of these items have been addressed in Chapter 1, Introduction to Parachute Rigging.

Figure 5-125. *It is important to equally divide the canopy and maintain that division throughout the pack job.*

Figure 5-126. *Tuck the slider up between A/B and C/D line groups. Some manufacturers recommend stowing the apex of the slider with a rubber band to the center B or C line attachment tab (whichever one it best aligns with).*

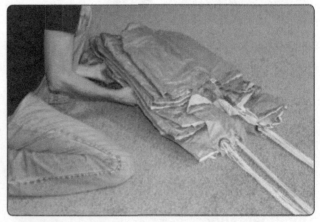

Figure 5-127. *Narrow the pack job by folding the divided sections in half. The sections can be folded under or up.*

Figure 5-128. *Without disturbing the rest of the folds, pull the center tail section down to the slider grommets.*

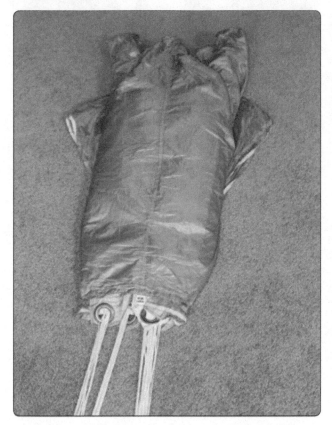

Figure 5-129. *Cocoon the canopy by wrapping the tail around and under. The nose is splayed out with three cells to the right, three cells to the left, and the center cell in the middle.*

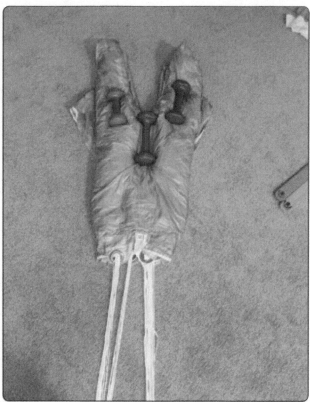

Figure 5-130. *Accordion the center cell, dividing the canopy in half. Weights can be used to control the pack job.*

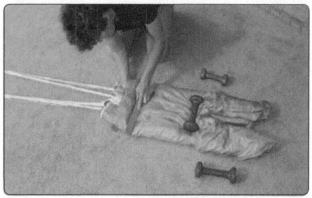

Figure 5-131. *Two packing paddles can be used to make a neat S-fold.*

There are several items of interest regarding the parachute data card. In the past, the data cards usually had information only for the identity of the parachute canopy, which is the primary component of the assembly. In recent years, with the growth of sport parachuting, this configuration is no longer standard. With the proliferation of many makes and models of canopies, harness, and containers, and the ability to interchange components, it is necessary to document the harness and container as well. The data card shown in Chapter 1, *Figure 1-8* has multiple identification spaces. With the widespread use of AADs, it has now become necessary to document the information required by the manufacturer such as the service cycle and battery life. The newest cards have provisions for this information.

With the ability to interchange components, what does the rigger do when a reserve canopy is removed from an assembly? Where does the data card go? This is a somewhat gray area, but the common practice is for the card to remain with the canopy. If the harness and container have had work

Figure 5-132. *The length and width of the S-fold is determined by the width of the container and the distance between the main/reserve vertical partition and the bottom flap grommet.*

Figure 5-133. *Make a second S-fold with the upper part of the canopy on top of the lower part.*

Figure 5-134. *Prepare the Reserve Deployment Speed Bag by using a hemostat to pinch the inner buffer tabs together as shown.*

done that requires documentation, it may be necessary for the rigger to fill out a duplicate card with the appropriate notations as to the work done on the harness. Riggers should make sure that they note that this card is a copy of the original.

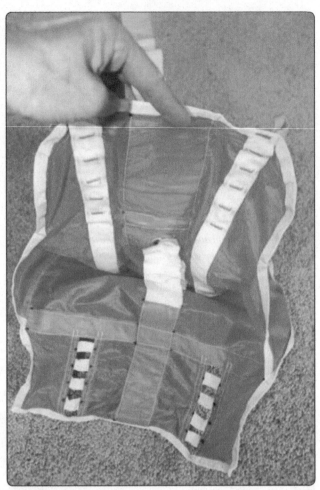

Figure 5-135. *Inside the Reserve Speed Bag the buffer tabs form a clear channel for the bottom closing loop.*

Finally, riggers are tasked with noting their name and certificate number on the data card. In many cases, this information is illegible. Riggers who take pride and responsibility in their profession and the work they do have no hesitation in letting the public know who did the work. Accordingly, many riggers have a permanent ink stamp with their name, certificate number, and seal symbol that they use to stamp the card and then countersign it. This is the mark of a truly professional rigger. While the seal symbol is not required on the data card, it allows anyone to check the signature against the seal on the parachute.

Chapter Summary

It is the responsibility of the attending rigger to ensure that the components of the approved parachute system are compatible in terms of shock load capability. This may be as simple as reading and comparing the TSO/Data Label that is permanently attached to the reserve canopy and the harness. This information may also be found in the respective

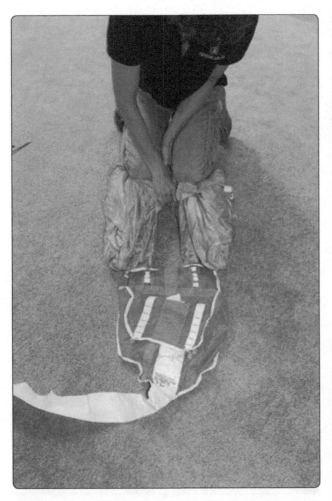

Figure 5-136. *The S-folds go below the buffer tabs when the canopy is in the bag.*

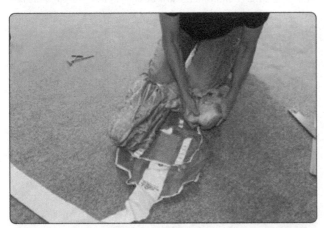

Figure 5-137. *Fold the ears under and pull the bag over the canopy.*

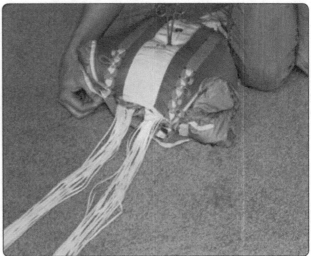

Figure 5-138. *Use the flaps of the bag to control the canopy and help push it into the bag.*

Figure 5-139. *The top flap closes first so that the rubber bands come through the slots in the bottom flap.*

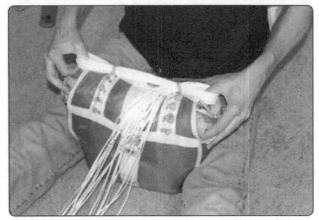

Figure 5-140. *Stow the lines from top to bottom. Each stow is a locking stow.*

Owners Manuals. If in doubt, call the manufacturer(s). Size compatibility, which may affect reserve bag extraction force, is of the utmost importance. In their zeal to make rigs more windproof, some manufacturers have created containers that

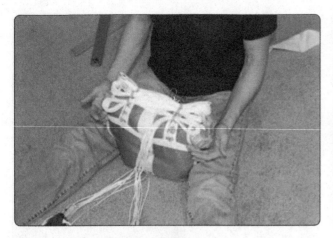

Figure 5-141. *Depending on the length of the lines and the width of the bag, all of the rubber bands may or may not be used.*

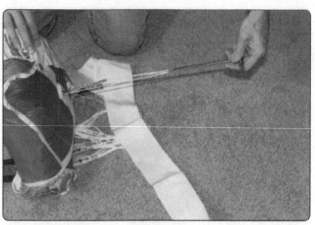

Figure 5-144. *The second bodkin is now threaded through the bag in the opposite direction.*

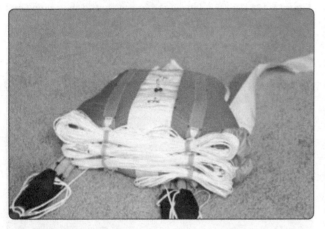

Figure 5-142. *Insert a bodkin through the channel in the bag where the hemostats were.*

Figure 5-145. *A bodkin that has been pre-loaded through the backpad of the container can now be easily pulled through the bag using this second bodkin.*

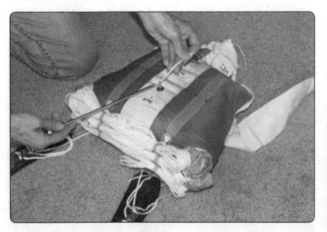

Figure 5-143. *Pull a second bodkin through the bag using a pull up cord.*

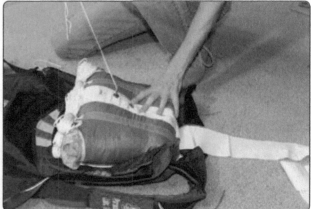

Figure 5-146. *The bottom bodkin shown in place.*

require more force to pull the bag from the container, due to stiffer riser covers, boxing at the top of the container, and longer cantilever pin protector flaps. Such rigs should not be overstuffed. Reserve pilot chutes should be in new condition to provide maximum drag.

Again, it should be emphasized that the reason for opening the container every 180 days is to inspect and recertify the canopy and container system for another 180 days. Recent language published by the FAA clarifies what the service life of a parachute is by stating that the rigger may extend

Figure 5-147. *Carefully tuck the corners of the bag into the bottom of the container.*

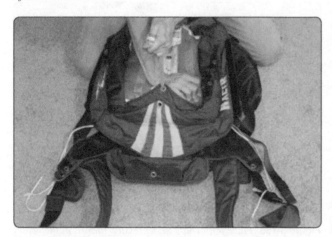

Figure 5-148. *Close bottom sub flap.*

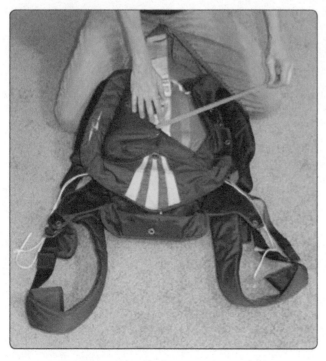

Figure 5-149. *Close either side flap (not side-sensitive).*

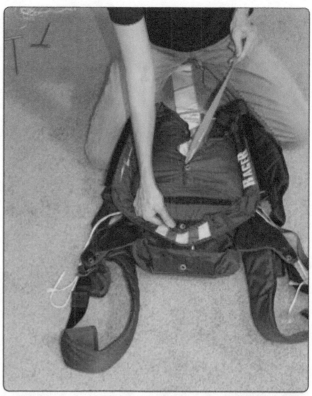

Figure 5-150. *Close opposite side flap.*

Figure 5-151. *Maintain the division of the canopy by pushing the ears down and outward. This is where the pilot chute spring will nest.*

the life of the system 180 days at a time, so effectively the service life of any parachute TSO'd under C23b, C23c, and C23d is 180 days.

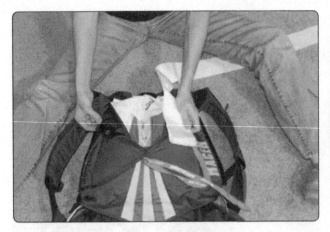

Figure 5-152. *S-fold bridle and evenly distribute on both sides of container.*

Figure 5-155. *Close top (yoke) flap.*

Figure 5-153. *Insert bodkin through the top grommets of the backpad and bag and close upper side flap. There should be little or no canopy fabric in this upper area if good division of the ears has been maintained.*

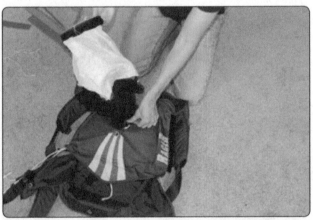

Figure 5-156. *Place pilot chute in depression formed in the center of the pack.*

Figure 5-154. *Close other side flap leaving a short section of bridle below the pilot chute.*

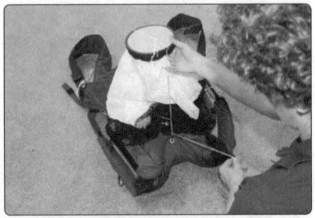

Figure 5-157. *Thread pull-up cords through each closing loop and through bodkin eyes.*

5-46

Figure 5-158. *Compress pilot chute tucking fabric and mesh between the coils of the spring.*

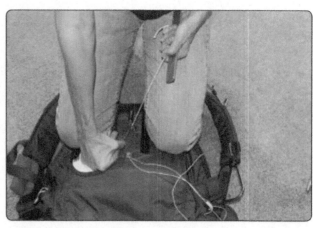

Figure 5-161. *Pull top closing loop through the grommet and insert pin.*

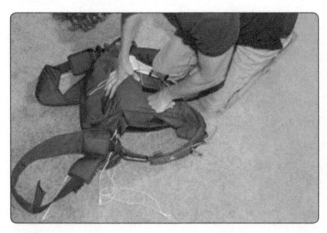

Figure 5-159. *Flip the container over and kneel on it to control the spring.*

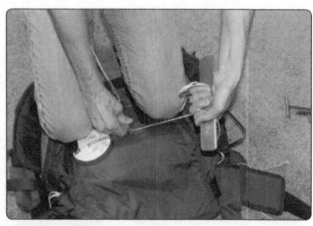

Figure 5-162. *Pull bottom closing loop through the grommet and insert pin.*

Figure 5-160. *Pull the bodkins with their respective pull up cords through the pack.*

Figure 5-163. *Pull on running ends of adjustable closing loop to shorten the opposite loop until pilot chute is sufficiently seated.*

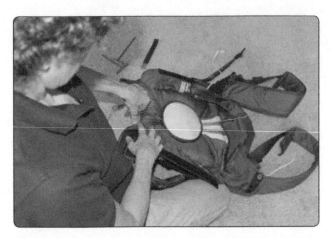

Figure 5-164. *Insert running ends into the isolated space between pilot chute "Hat" and top of the spring, using a hemostat or tweezers.*

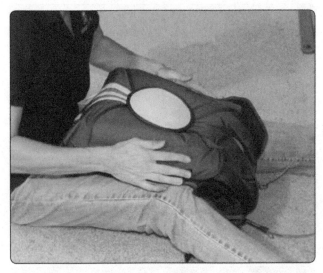

Figure 5-165. *Dress per manufacturer's instructions and attach seal to the last pin.*

Chapter 6

Hand Tools, Sewing Machines, and the Parachute Loft

Introduction

Riggers are taught that there are three things necessary to do a proper job: knowledge to do the work, the correct materials, and the right tools. The job cannot be done correctly without all three of these essentials. The right tools include various types of sewing machines, as well as a wide variety of specialized hand tools.

The importance of learning the names and nomenclature of rigging tools and equipment cannot be overemphasized. Just as learning the language of a foreign country allows an individual to live and operate efficiently within a society, learning the language of the rigger allows new riggers to operate and interact within their profession. Without the necessary vocabulary, a rigger is not able to work with other riggers and, more importantly, does not present a professional image to customers. For example, when shopping for tools or sewing machines for rigging, the same tool may have a different name when used by some other trade. Knowing the language of the rigger helps avoid confusion.

Sewing Machine Model Comparison

Make	Single needle light duty drop feed	Single needle medium duty needle feed	Single needle compound feed	Two needle feed	Zigzag medium duty	Bar tack	Harness machine heavy duty	Harness machine extra heavy duty
Singer	31-15	111W151	111W155	112W116	17W15	68 or 69 class	7-33	97-10
Consew	292R	N/A	206RB-4	333RB-1	199R-2A	N/A	733-R2	N/A
Juki	DLN-415		LU-563	LH-515				
Brother		B-791						
Mitsubishi	DB-130	DY-340-12	LU2-400	LT2-220	LZ-780-11			
					138	3334		

Hand Tools

A new senior rigger must acquire enough tools to pack and maintain the types of parachutes for which he or she is rated. In the course of training, the rigger candidate is exposed to various tools and individual rigging techniques. Some riggers adhere to a minimalist philosophy and use as few tools as necessary. This may initially consist of a packing paddle, a pull-up cord, and a temporary locking pin, or just a pull-up cord, when packing main parachutes at the drop zone (DZ). With some types of parachutes, these may be all the tools needed to pack them. Other riggers develop techniques that utilize an array of tools designed to make the job easier or the end result neater. Some manufacturers have designed specialized tools to make their particular parachute easier to pack and maintain. Each rigger develops a suitable technique and then obtains the tools to support it.

In the past, the list of tools needed to pack and maintain military surplus parachutes was limited. Since most military parachutes were simply variants of the same canopy designs, common tools could be used across the board. In today's high-tech world, some of these original tools are still used along with a number of newer designs. Many riggers and manufacturers design and build tools to fit a need, whether it is a new rig design or to make a job more productive.

All riggers need to create a tool kit tailored for their particular situation. *Figure 6-1* shows a commercially-available field rigger kitbag with tools. Although commercially-made kitbags are nice, they are expensive. Many riggers are "weekend" riggers, meaning they have a regular job during the week and work as a rigger on the weekend. This is typical of many skydiving riggers. Other riggers work full time in a loft or manufacturing environment.

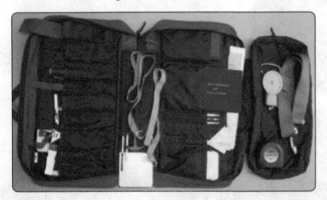

Figure 6-1. *Field rigger kitbag with tools.*

Depending on their needs, riggers have different approaches toward their tools. The weekend rigger may travel to a DZ where the primary job is packing. Therefore, the tool kit is more basic as the purpose of this kit is not to take the whole loft to the DZ. The rigger who works in a full-time loft may have a more comprehensive tool kit, since it does not have to be hauled around. For the weekend rigger, there are several field rigger kitbags available commercially that hold a full assortment of tools. Many riggers design and build custom kitbags tailored around their individual requirements. Doing this is an excellent way to show off sewing skills, while at the same time creating a needed tool kit. There are also contractor tool bags made of a strong fabric with many pockets and compartments that work well with the type of tools a rigger uses. These bags are inexpensive and are available at hardware and home improvement stores.

To stock the tool kit, the rigger must determine what tools he needs. This depends on where the tools are used: in the field, DZ, or in the loft. *Figure 6-2* shows a list of necessary tools that have been proven useful for today's rigger. The list of tools is broken down into two different categories: Category 1, items 6-3 through 6-49 are mandatory tools; Category 2, items 6-50 through 6-56 are optional tools as most of them are for use in the loft.

Hand Tools Description

The tool belt is one of the most useful items the rigger can have. *[Figure 6-3]* Most tool belts are custom built by the riggers themselves and include a selection of tools that are frequently used around the loft. It always seems that the tool the rigger needs at a particular moment is at the other end of the packing table or on another sewing machine. The use of a tool belt makes riggers more efficient as they are not always looking for and having to retrieve their tools. A well-designed tool belt holds the following tools as a minimum: scissors, thread snips, 6-inch ruler, marking pencils and pens, butane cigarette lighter, seam ripper, Exacto® knife or scalpel, short packing fid, and finger-trapping needles. Other tools can be added according to the needs of the individual rigger. The following is a list of common tools and a brief description of how they are used.

Seam ripper—used in the sewing industry for "picking" stitches and ripping out seams. It has a pointed sharp end and an inside cutting edge for slicing through thread. *[Figure 6-4]*

Hemostats or clamp—used by riggers for many clamping or retrieving operations. Two or three sizes should be obtained, as well as both straight and curved models. These tools can be found at hardware or auto parts stores. *[Figure 6-5]*

Scalpel or Exacto® knife—used for delicate cutting of materials or thread. The Exacto® knife is preferred as the handles come in various sizes and with a wide selection of blades. *[Figure 6-6]*

Rigger's Tool List	
Figure #	**Description**
6-3	Rigger's tool belt
6-4	Seam rippers
6-5	Hemostats or clamp
6-6	Scalpel or Exacto® knife
6-7	Thread snips
6-8	Butane cigarette lighter
6-9	6-inch stainless steel rule
6-10	Fabric marking pencils & felt tip markers
6-11	Scissors
6-12	Finger-trapping needle
6-13	Finger-trapping wire
6-14	Packing paddles and packing fid
6-15	Pull-up cords
6-16	Locking pull-up cord
6-17	Molar strap
6-18	Temporary locking pins (temp pins)
6-19	Velcro® line protectors
6-20	Closing plate
6-21	T-bar positive leverage device
6-22	T-handle bodkin
6-23	Pilot chute threading tool
6-24	Pilot chute locking rod
6-25	Line separator (suspension line holder)
6-26	Connector link separator tool
6-27	Shot bags
6-28	Seal press
6-29	Lead seals and seal thread
6-30	Rigger's logbook
6-31	Packing data card
6-32	Note pad
6-33	Rubber bands
6-34	Hand tacking needles
6-35	Straight & T pins
6-36	Navy end tab
6-37	Waxed nylon "supertack"
6-38	3-cord cotton thread—waxed
6-39	Tape measure
6-40	Shoulder strap hook
6-41	Pony clamps
6-42	6-inch adjustable wrench
6-43	Screwdriver—multi-tip
6-44	Needle-nose pliers
6-45	Cable cutters
6-46	Ripstop roller
6-47	Beeswax
6-48	Spring scale and fabric testing clamps
6-49	Hot knife element w/cutting tip, basting tip, and stand
6-50	Hot glue gun
6-51	Tension board assembly w/apex tiedown
6-52	Size "O" rolled rim spur grommet handset
6-53	Hole punches
6-54	Cutting pad
6-55	Rawhide mallet
6-56	Binding tool

Figure 6-2. *Rigger's tool list.*

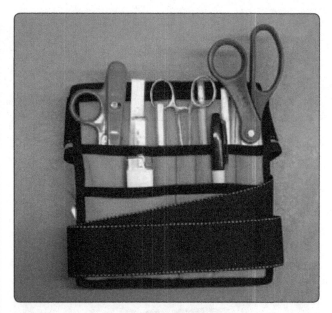

Figure 6-3. *Rigger's tool belt.*

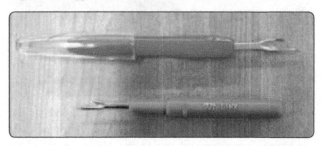

Figure 6-4. *Seam rippers.*

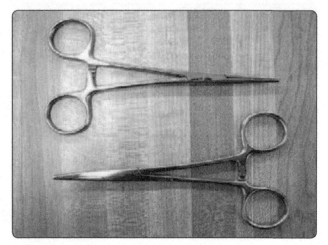

Figure 6-5. *Hemostats or clamps.*

Thread snips—used in the sewing industry for trimming or "snipping" thread when sewing. Handier and easier to use than scissors as the point is finer and allows more precise cutting of the thread. The ergonomic design takes some getting used to but proves superior in the long term. The stainless steel models are best, but some riggers prefer the plastic ones that have replaceable blades. *[Figure 6-7]*

Figure 6-6. *Scalpel or Exacto® knife.*

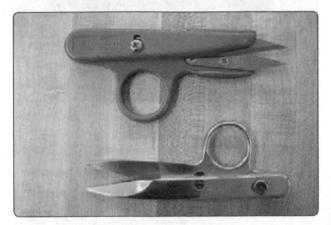

Figure 6-7. *Thread snips.*

Butane cigarette lighter—used for burning thread ends to seal the thread and keep stitches from raveling. It is also used for searing tapes, lines, and light webbing. One of these should be at each sewing machine or work site so the rigger does not have to leave the work to find one. *[Figure 6-8]*

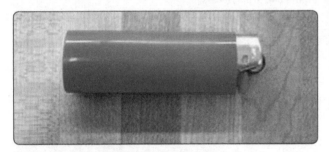

Figure 6-8. *Butane cigarette lighter.*

6-inch stainless steel rule—used for making fine measurements during work. At a minimum, the scale should read to ¹⁄₁₆ inch and have a dual (English/metric) readout. Certain models have one rounded end. This model can be used for removing cut stitches from work by rubbing the rounded end against the thread thereby lifting it and making it easier to remove. *[Figure 6-9]*

Fabric marking pencils and felt tip markers—used for marking webbing, tapes, and fabric. The Dixon #134s was used in the parachute industry for decades but is no longer available. The Dixon China Marker is now used by many riggers, as it contains no acid, and they come in 12 colors. Other types have been found to contain abrasives and

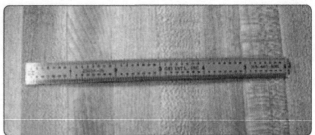

Figure 6-9. *6-inch stainless steel rule.*

compounds that, when used on canopy fabric, weaken the material. This particular brand of pencil has been found to have minimal effect on the fabric. Various colors, such as white, yellow, and red, are useful. Fine point felt tip markers are used for marking certain materials, such as Dacron® or Spectra® line. Black, red, and blue are most common. Felt tip pens, such as Sharpie® and Pilot® ultra- fine point permanent type, are used by many riggers. *[Figure 6-10]*

Figure 6-10. *Pencils and felt markers.*

Scissors—used for cutting all types of materials used in the parachute industry. A high-quality scissor is lightweight, ergonomic, and comes in right-hand and left-hand models. Also, a short 5-inch barber shear is very sharp even when "used" and works very well in cutting Cypres loop cord and other line material commonly used in parachute rigging. *[Figure 6-11]*

Finger-trapping needle—used for inserting suspension line into a "finger-trap" configuration. It is a heavy-duty threaded needle commonly called a "fid," not to be confused with a "packing fid" or "paddle." Plastic ones are available commercially, but the best ones are custom made from stainless steel or aluminum knitting needles. Cut to length, they are then drilled and tapped with screw threads in the flat end. The size 2, 6, and 8 needles are the most popular for the current line sizes. A blunt end needle is also used to finger trap Cypres loop cord. *[Figure 6-12]*

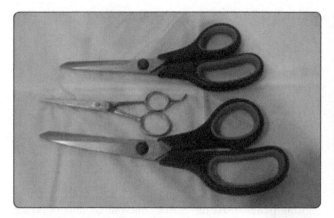

Figure 6-11. *Scissors and barber shears.*

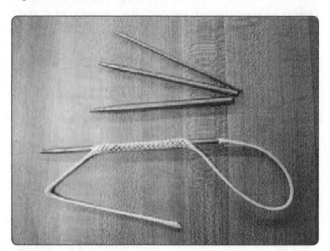

Figure 6-12. *Finger-trapping needle.*

Finger-trapping wire—used to finger trap line too small to use a needle on. It is made from a wooden or plastic dowel with a wire loop made from safety wire. *[Figure 6-13]*

Figure 6-13. *Finger trapping wire.*

Packing paddle—used for dressing the pack of the parachute when packing. This tool is made from either wood or aluminum. The MIL-SPEC paddle has rounded ends and is 1 ⁹⁄₁₆" × 12" long and tapers in thickness from ¼" to ³⁄₁₆". The wooden commercial paddle is 1¾" × 15" long. *[Figure 6-14A]*

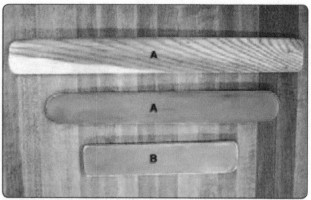

Figure 6-14. *Packing paddles and packing fid.*

Packing fid—similar to the packing paddle, used also for dressing the parachute pack and tucking in flaps. The fid is approximately 1⁹⁄₁₆" × 8" long and tapers from ¼" to ⅛". It is made from aluminum and was originally a United States Navy tool. Many riggers have both the fid and the paddle, but usually develop a preference for one or the other. *[Figure 6-14B]*

Pull-up cords—used to "pull-up" the locking loop of parachute containers when closing and pinning them. They are made from lengths of suspension line: Cypres loop cord or Type-3 tape. *[Figure 6-15]*

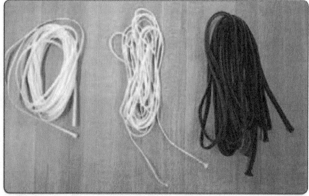

Figure 6-15. *Pull-up cords.*

Locking pull-up cord—used to lock the thickness of a two-grommet reserve deployment bag when packing the reserve canopy. It is made from 72 inches of red Type-3 suspension line and a size 94 Cordlok nylon fastener. It may be used on one-pin or two-pin reserve bags. *[Figure 6-16]*

Molar strap—used to control the folded reserve canopy prior to inserting it in the reserve free bag made from Type-8 webbing and a Camlok nylon buckle. The webbing should be at least 48" long and brightly colored to serve as a flag against leaving it on the canopy. *[Figure 6-17]*

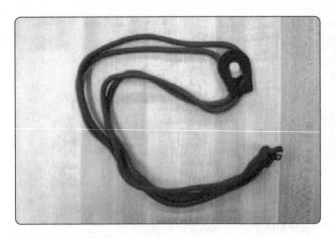

Figure 6-16. *Locking pull-up cord.*

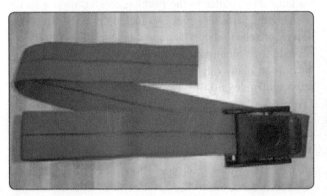

Figure 6-17. *Molar strap.*

Temporary locking pins (temp pins)—used to secure the pack in the temporarily closed condition prior to inserting the ripcord pins. All pins should have long, brightly-colored flags attached for recognition. *[Figure 6-18]*

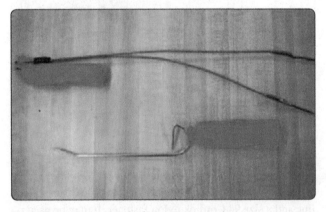

Figure 6-18. *Temporary locking pins (temp pins).*

Velcro® line protectors—used to cover the hook Velcro® on the line stow pocket of reserve free bags during the line stow process. They are made from pieces of 1" loop Velcro® with Type-3 tape flags attached. *[Figure 6-19]*

Figure 6-19. *Velcro® line protectors.*

Closing plate—used for closing one-pin containers. Made from ¼" aluminum with a "V" shaped notch for pulling the closing loop up through the pack flaps while compressing the container. *[Figures 6-20]*

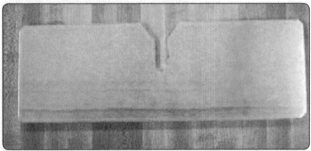

Figure 6-20. *Closing plate.*

T-bar positive leverage device—used to produce a "cranking" action to wind up the pull-up cord, thereby increasing leverage when closing the container. It must be used carefully as it is possible that too much force can be applied, damaging the container or creating too much force on the pin. *[Figure 6-21 A and B]*

T-handle bodkin—used primarily for closing container systems that have external pilot chutes, such as the Jump Shack Racer. A minimum of two is needed for the tool kit. *[Figure 6-22]*

Pilot chute threading tool—used for threading the pull-up cord through a one-pin pilot chute. A .22 caliber gun-cleaning rod works well. The best is a United States military surplus M-16 cleaning rod. It is made from steel, as opposed to aluminum, and breaks down into sections and a package that is 8" long. *[Figure 6-23]*

Pilot chute locking rod and strap-locking rod and strap used to compress pilot chutes and used to hold the reserve pilot chute, such as an MA-1 compressed on the pilot chute launching disc. It is a tempered steel rod approximately 18" × ³⁄₁₆". *[Figure 6-24]*

Figure 6-21. *(A) T-bar positive leverage device and (B) positive leverage closing device with plate.*

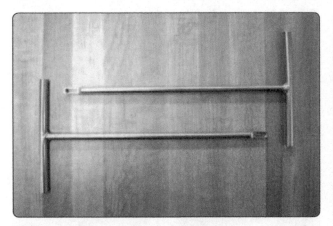

Figure 6-22. *T-handle bodkin.*

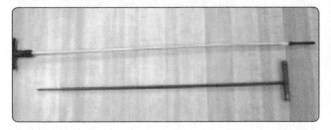

Figure 6-23. *Pilot chute threading tool.*

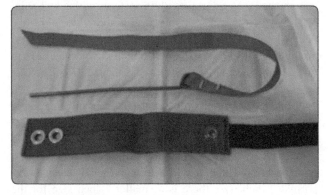

Figure 6-24. *Pilot chute rod and strap.*

Line separator (suspension line holder)—used to keep the suspension lines of the canopy in order while pleating. It is made from aluminum with three "fingers" and two slots. *[Figure 6-25]*

Figure 6-25. *Line separator (suspension line holder).*

Connector link separator tool—used to separate military style connector links, such as MS-22002 and MS-70118. The tool is Mil Spec PN 11-1-176. *[Figure 6-26]*

Shot bags—used to hold the canopy and suspension lines in place while folding. Packing weight made from nylon fabric and filled with lead shot for weight. These should be brightly colored or have a flag attached to prevent leaving in the parachute. Weight varies from 2–5 pounds according to needs. A minimum of four is needed. Making shot bags provides an excellent sewing project for the rigger candidate. *[Figure 6-27]*

Seal press—used for compressing lead seals when sealing the parachute under Title 14 of the Code of Federal Regulations 14 (CFR) part 65, section 65.133. The die of the press has the rigger's seal symbol engraved in the face for identifying the seal. *[Figure 6-28]*

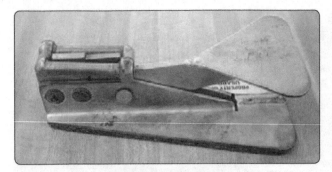

Figure 6-26. *Connector link separator tool.*

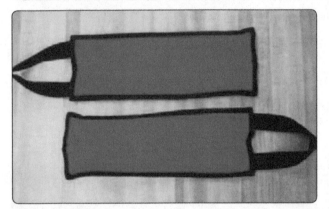

Figure 6-27. *Shot bags.*

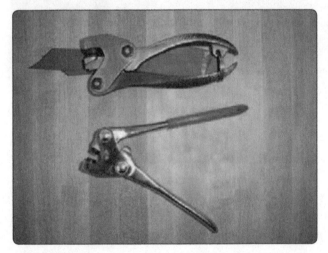

Figure 6-28. *Seal press.*

Figure 6-29. *Lead seals and seal thread.*

Figure 6-30. *Rigger's logbook.*

Lead seals and seal thread— used with the seal press to seal the parachute, usually ⅜" diameter. The thread is used to seal the parachute in accordance with 14 CFR part 65, section 65.133. A cotton thread, usually ticket 20/4 with a tensile strength of 4.7 pounds; also used as safety tie where required. Due to the fact that seal thread is only available in 100-pound lots, some manufacturers buy it and then put it up on smaller spools and make it available to riggers. *[Figure 6-29]*

Rigger's logbook—used by riggers to meet the recordkeeping requirements of 14 CFR part 65, section 65.131. *[Figure 6-30]*

Packing data card—used to fulfill the recordkeeping requirements of 14 CFR part 65, section 65.131(c) that is normally made of Ty-Vek® material and is kept with the parachute. Ty-Vek® is difficult to write on with a ball point pen. One pen that works very well is the "Pilot ultra-fine point NO XYLENE - permanent type SCA-UF." This pen can be found at office supply stores, although you may have to order them. They come in black, red, and blue. *[Figure 6-31]*

Note pad—used for recording miscellaneous information or making sketches when working on parachutes. *[Figure 6-32]*

Rubber bands—used for stowing suspension lines, bridles, or static lines. Three sizes are common today. Besides the normal 2-inch size, there is a smaller 1-inch size for the newer microline and a larger one used for tandem parachutes. Tube Stoes® used in place of rubber bands are required by some manufacturers, such as Butler Parachute Systems, Inc. *[Figure 6-33]*

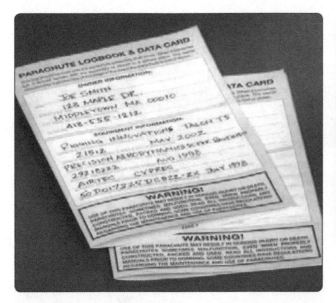

Figure 6-31. *Packing data cards.*

Figure 6-32. *Note pad.*

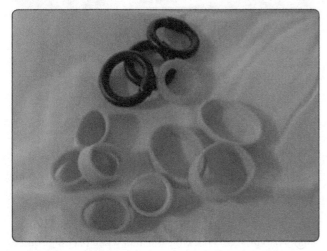

Figure 6-33. *Rubber bands with Tube Stoes®.*

Hand tacking needles—variety of sizes of straight and curved needles used for general sewing are necessary for every tool kit. *[Figure 6-34]*

Figure 6-34. *Hand tacking needles.*

Straight and T pins—used when doing canopy patches to pin the fabric together. The T pins are used for heavier duty work, such as container repair. *[Figure 6-35]*

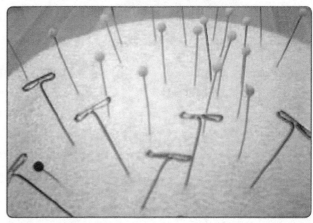

Figure 6-35. *Straight and T pins.*

Navy end tab—used for assisting in hand tacking thick materials. This is a container end tab from a United States Navy seat pack modified with a "dimple." The dimple allows the needle to be pushed through the material, and the holes in the tab allow gripping the needle to pull it through. *[Figure 6-36]*

Waxed nylon "supertack"—used for hand tacking requirements because it has superior knot holding properties. It is a waxed, flat, braided nylon cord that serves as a modern replacement for 6-cord nylon. Typically 80 – 90 pounds tensile strength, a 50-pound version is also available. This cord is available in black and white. *[Figure 6-37]*

Figure 6-36. *Navy end tab.*

Figure 6-37. *Waxed nylon "supertack."*

3-cord cotton thread–waxed—used for hand tacking and break tacking on the risers and connector links of emergency parachutes. Its tensile strength is 16 pounds. The color is usually natural. *[Figure 6-38]*

Tape measure—used for general measurement of items such as suspension lines and bridles. A good quality tape measure at least 25 feet long is necessary. A quality fabric tape measure is also necessary. If possible, get one with dual measurements (English/metric). *[Figure 6-39]*

Shoulder strap hook—packing assist device used to apply tension to the pull-up cord using upper-body strength thereby

Figure 6-38. *3-cord cotton thread–waxed.*

Figure 6-39. *Tape measure.*

freeing both hands to pin the container. This strap can be built by the rigger. *[Figure 6-40]*

Pony clamps—used for clamping material to hold it as a third hand. Also used as a packing assistant when packing square reserves. These do come in handy, although not used by all riggers. *[Figure 6-41]*

6-inch adjustable wrench—used for tightening Rapide® links and other jobs. A good adjustable wrench serves in place of

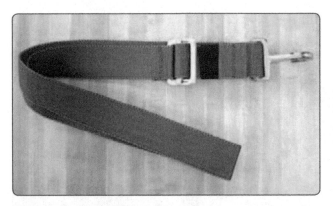

Figure 6-40. *Shoulder strap hook.*

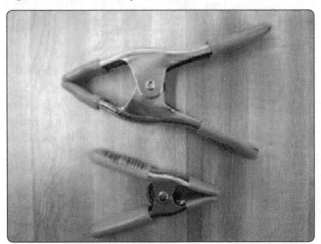

Figure 6-41. *Pony clamps.*

several different sized wrenches. A 4-inch adjustable wrench is very handy as it takes up less room in the rigger kit bag. *[Figure 6-42]*

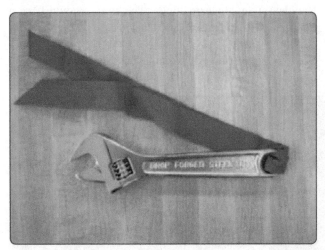

Figure 6-42. *6-inch adjustable wrench.*

Screwdriver–multi-tip—used for L-bar connector links and general use. A good quality screwdriver with interchangeable tips is the most versatile model. Good quality cannot be

stressed enough. If the tip of the screwdriver does not fit the slot in the screw of a L-bar connector properly, it can slip out and can cause damage to the screw head or injury to the rigger. *[Figure 6-43]*

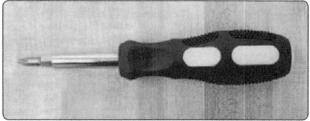

Figure 6-43. *Screwdriver–multi-tip.*

Needle-nose pliers—used for heavy-duty gripping and pulling, such as for needles in webbing. A small needle-nose plier is also handy for pulling thread after a seam ripper has been used. *[Figure 6-44]*

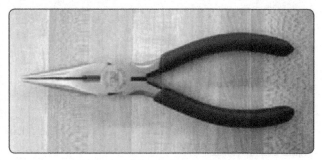

Figure 6-44. *Needle-nose pliers.*

Cable cutters—used for cutting stainless steel cable and trimming the 3-ring release cable to length. A good quality cable cutter, such as the Felco™ model C7, cuts the cable cleanly. Electrician's pliers or diagonal cutters flatten the ends of the wire unless they are of high quality and sharp. *[Figure 6-45]*

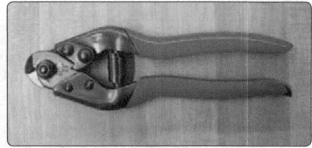

Figure 6-45. *Cable cutters.*

Ripstop roller—used for applying ripstop tape for canopy repairs. It removes air bubbles and wrinkles. A standard wallpaper roller works well. *[Figure 6-46]*

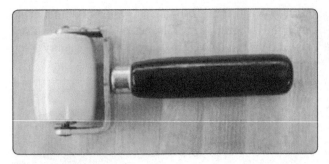

Figure 6-46. *Ripstop roller.*

Beeswax—used for waxing 6-cord nylon or any regular thread for hand tacking. *[Figure 6-47]*

Figure 6-47. *Beeswax.*

Spring scale and fabric testing clamps—used for measuring the ripcord pull force on reserve and emergency parachutes. With a minimum rating of 50 pounds, it is also used in conjunction with the fabric testing clamps to measure fabric strength on reserve canopies in accordance with Parachute Industry Association (PIA) TS-108. Some riggers do not use testing clamps as they can cause damage to good fabric, if not used properly. *[Figure 6-48]*

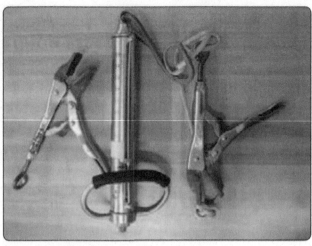

Figure 6-48. *Spring scale and fabric testing clamps.*

Hot knife element with cutting tip, basting tip, and stand—used for cutting and searing synthetic materials, such as nylon, Dacron®, and Spectra®. The basting tip is used for fusing canopy material in place prior to sewing during canopy repairs. The stand is necessary to keep the hot elements from causing a fire. A heavy-duty hot knife, although expensive, is a must have for any serious rigger. *[Figure 6-49 A and B]*

Hot glue gun—used to replace staples and hand basting in harness work. This modern tool has changed harness repair and construction techniques. *[Figure 6-50]*

Tension board assembly with apex tiedown—used on the round packing table to apply tension to the canopy when packing. There are two models available. One is for military style L-bar connector links and another, smaller one for Rapide® style connector links. The straps should have a quick release feature to release tension easily. *[Figure 6-51]*

Size "O" rolled rim spur grommet handset—used for doing container repairs. The "O" stainless steel model from

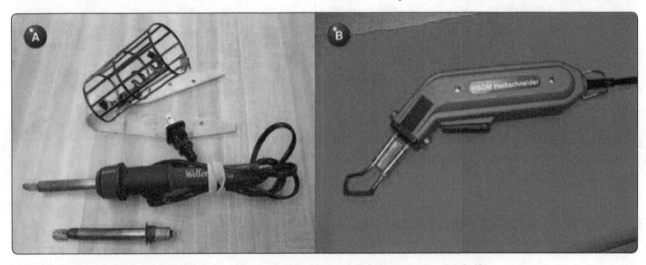

Figure 6-49. *(A) Hot knife element with cutting tip, basting tip, and stand and (B) heavy duty hot knife.*

Figure 6-50. *Hot glue gun.*

Figure 6-51. *Tension board assembly with apex tiedown.*

Figure 6-52. *Size "O" rolled rim spur grommet handset.*

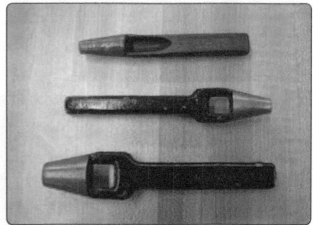

Figure 6-53. *Hole punches.*

Stimpson Co., Inc. is the most useful grommet set because it has a replaceable die insert section, that wears out in time and can be replaced. It is also the highest quality. The stainless steel set works for both brass and stainless steel grommets. For the rigger who does not replace as many stainless grommets, the hand set from Lord and Hodge size "0" will also set stainless steel spur grommets, but does not last as long as the commercial handset. The other sizes most often used are "3" and "5" to set brass or nickel plated. *[Figure 6-52]*

Hole punches—used for punching holes for grommets that come in various-sizes. Most often sizes used would be 0, 3, and 5. *[Figure 6-53]*

Cutting pad—used with hole punches. The best are plastic as these do not damage the punch. *[Figure 6-54]*

Rawhide mallet—used when punching holes and using grommet handsets. This is a preferred tool to use as the rawhide does not damage the other tools, and the weight makes the job easier and more consistent. The number 2 size

Figure 6-54. *Cutting pad.*

at 4 pounds is the most common. A quality rubber dead blow hammer works well also. *[Figure 6-55]*

Binding tool—used for turning corners when binding material, such as para-pak or Cordura®. The model shown in *Figure 6-56* is a soldering tool from an electronics repair

Figure 6-55. *Rawhide mallet.*

Figure 6-56. *Binding tool.*

store. The plastic handle has been replaced with a metal one. This is almost the perfect configuration for its use.

The above tools provide the rigger with the means to pack and maintain most of the common parachutes in use today. There are numerous other tools, both old and new, that individuals may wish to acquire for specialized parachutes shown in *Figure 6-57*. In particular, there are older style parachutes and military parachutes that cannot be packed without specialized tools designed specifically for them. At the same time, the profession is constantly developing new tools to make the job easier.

Sewing Machines

After the senior rigger has put together a personal tool kit, the next step is to acquire a selection of sewing machines in order to do minor repairs of defects found during inspection prior to packing. For example, if you find a small hole in the canopy, a sewing machine is necessary to make the correct repair. For this, a lightweight single needle machine is the perfect beginning. As your sewing skills progress, additional specialized machines can be added as space and finances allow. Always remember, only those repairs allowed under your certificate may be performed.

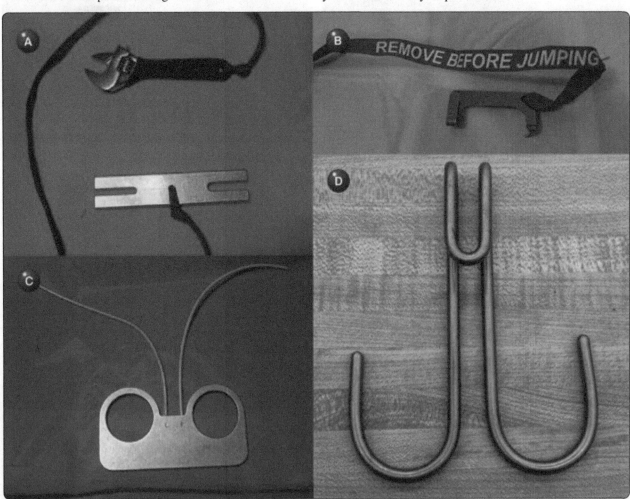

Figure 6-57. *(A) link fork, (B) pull check tool, (C) tool used to maintain continuity of risers when removing main parachute from harness, and (D) Pro Pack hook.*

When purchasing a new sewing machine, if money allows, buy the best and newest machines affordable. Do not avoid old machines because if they are not worn out and parts are available, they can be a good buy. If worn out, they are counterproductive. Buy self-lubricating machines as opposed to ones you need to oil manually. It is preferable to get machines with a reverse mechanism. Get an adjustable "K leg" stand and table. This allows you to set the height of the table to best fit your physical needs. Large people bending over a short table for any length of time understand the need for this feature. If the rigger is buying a new machine, it is possible to order an oversize table top in place of the standard 20" × 48" size. This allows better control over harness and containers so they do not overlap the table.

When buying any machine, particularly from a sewing machine dealer, get the operator's manual and the parts manual for the machine. The operator's manual tells you how to set up and operate the machine and is indispensable when the need to order parts arises. Manuals for older machines can be found online, along with parts manuals. When shopping for used or older machines, seek out reputable companies or individuals that used the machine for business, such as retiring parachute riggers, or upholstery shops, leather shops, etc. Whenever possible, it is always best to try the machine before you buy it.

Experience has shown that the average rigger who wishes to set up a loft needs three initial machines: a lightweight single needle, such as a Singer 31-15 or Mitsubishi DB-130, for canopy repair and lightweight maintenance; a double needle, such as a Singer 212W140 or Mitsubishi LT2-220, with a binder or taping attachment for binding material and light manufacture; and a medium-duty double throw (308) zigzag machine, such as a Bernina Model 217, for suspension line repair and replacement. *[Figures 6-58, 6-59, and 6-60]*

Figure 6-58. *Mitsubishi DB-130.*

For individuals on a tight budget or with space constraints, a good idea is to buy a double-needle machine first. By removing one needle and bobbin, the machine performs excellently as a single-needle machine. Replace the needle

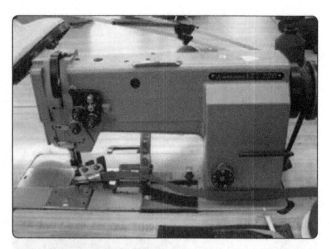

Figure 6-59. *Mitsubishi LT2-220.*

Figure 6-60. *Bernina Model 217.*

and bobbin, and the machine again is a double needle. This gives the rigger two machines for the price and space of one. A good zigzag machine also does multiple-duty. Its primary purpose is for zigzag sewing. However, adjusting the stitch regulator allows the rigger to do an acceptable job sewing bar tacks. By changing the stitch length and adjusting the width to the narrowest setting, some machines do good straight stitching, such as the Pfaff model 138.

An excellent machine for canopy patch work is an old Singer model 201-2 made in the 1950s. Because this machine was made for home use, they can be often be found in good working condition. The Singer model 201-2 is unique in that it takes up to a size 21 needle and is all gear driven with no belts. Another portable machine, which is very handy, is the Consew CP-146R Mini Walking Foot. *[Figure 6-61]* It sews a 301 straight or 304 zigzag stitch and sews through thicker material. Both sewing machines are good choices for traveling to the DZ.

Any machine used in parachute rigging must be capable of using at least a size 18 needle to handle size E (69) thread. E thread is used in most sewing done by a senior rigger.

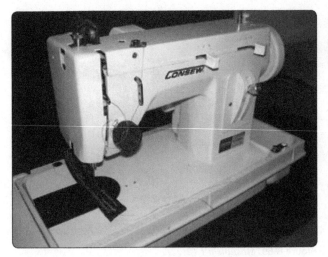

Figure 6-61. *Consew model CP-146R Mini Walking Foot.*

The double needle machine is preferable for binding tape repair, although with experience a rigger can install TY-3 tape with a single needle machine making two passes. When using this method, a tape folder must be used, and the inner stitch must be done first.

Advancing to master rigger requires additional specialized machines, such as a medium-duty, single needle, and compound feed machine, like a Consew 226R or a Juki LU-563. *[Figure 6-62]* The Consew 206RB is also a good choice for those on a budget. This type of machine is used for doing container repairs and light harness work. *[Figure 6-63]* The next machine should be a heavy-duty harness machine, such as a Singer 7-33, 7-34, or Consew 733R. *[Figure 6-64]* These machines specialize in sewing 5-cord nylon or heavier thread used in the manufacture and repair of parachute harnesses.

Lastly, a bar tack machine, such as a Pfaff 3334 or Singer 69 class, allows fast, strong, professional repairs and is invaluable in line replacement and manufacturing. *[Figure 6-65]* This selection of machines provides the rigger with the ability to undertake virtually any repair or modification needed on today's parachutes. Remember, all

Figure 6-62. *Juki LU-563.*

Figure 6-63. *Consew model 206RB.*

sewing machine manufacturers build models that fit within the various duty types. Those models mentioned are only representative for that category. *[Figure 6-66]*

Identification and Nomenclature

The purpose of the following information is not to make you an accomplished sewing machine expert and repairman. You should learn the basics about what makes your sewing machines work and how to perform routine maintenance

Figure 6-64. *On the left is a Singer 7-34 heavy duty harness sewing machine and on the right is a Consew 733R.*

Figure 6-65. *Pfaff 3334.*

and service. By doing so, simple problems can be fixed with little to no downtime or repair bills. The information on troubleshooting provides you with the basic knowledge needed to keep your machines running. *[Figure 6-67]*

Figure 6-68 shows a close-up of the head only. Only those parts, which the rigger must deal with on a regular basis in order to operate and maintain the machine, are shown. For those individuals who wish to become more involved in the machine, a thorough study of the operator's manual and parts manual is encouraged. The following numbers correspond with the part descriptions in *Figure 6-68*.

1. Bed—base of the machine.

2. Arm—upper casing of the machine.

3. Uprise—upright part of the machine that joins the base and the arm.

4. Faceplate—cover that protects the needle bar and presser bar mechanisms.

5. Balance wheel—pulley assembly that drives the machine via the motor and belt.

6. Reverse lever—mechanism that, when depressed, reverses the sewing operation of the machine.

7. Stitch regulator—adjustor that controls the length of the stitch. The larger the number, the longer the stitch; the smaller the number, the shorter the stitch.

8. Pre-tension thread guide—assembly that provides initial thread tension and thread straightening before the thread reaches the main upper thread tension assembly.

9. Thread retainer—provides direct guidance for the thread to the upper tension assembly.

10. Thread take-up cover—covers the thread take-up lever and protects the operator.

11. Right arm thread guide—provides thread guidance from the upper tension assembly to the thread take-up lever.

12. Upper tension regulating thumbscrew—regulates pressure of the tension discs on the thread.

13. Thread controller spring—provides for the correct amount of slack in the needle thread when the needle is descending so that the needle does not cut the thread.

14. Tension discs—provide tension on the upper thread.

15. Presser bar tension nut—regulates the pressure of the presser foot on the material.

16. Thread take-up lever—provides for slack in the needle thread after the stitch is formed and pulls the correct amount of thread from the spool for the next stitch.

17. Needle bar—holds the needle and carries the upper thread downward through the material to where the stitch is formed.

18. Presser foot bar—holds the presser foot in place to hold pressure on the material.

19. Presser foot—holds the material in place while the feed dog moves the material forward for the next stitch.

20. Needle plate—surrounds the feed dog and protects the material during the movement process.

21. Slide plate—covers the area of the bed to the left of the feed dog and provides access to the bobbin assembly.

22. Feed dog—feeds the material through the machine from the underside.

Sewing Machine Model Comparison								
Make	Single needle light duty drop feed	Single needle medium duty needle feed	Single needle compound feed	Two needle feed	Zigzag medium duty	Bar tack	Harness machine heavy duty	Harness machine extra heavy duty
Singer	31-15	111W151	111W155	112W116	17W15	68 or 69 class	7-33	97-10
Consew	292R	N/A	206RB-4	333RB-1	199R-2A	N/A	733-R2	N/A
Juki	DLN-415		LU-563	LH-515				
Brother		B-791						
Mitsubishi	DB-130	DY-340-12	LU2-400	LT2-220	LZ-780-11			
Pfaff					138	3334		
Bernina	—	—	—	—	217	—	—	—

Figure 6-66. *Sewing machine model comparison.*

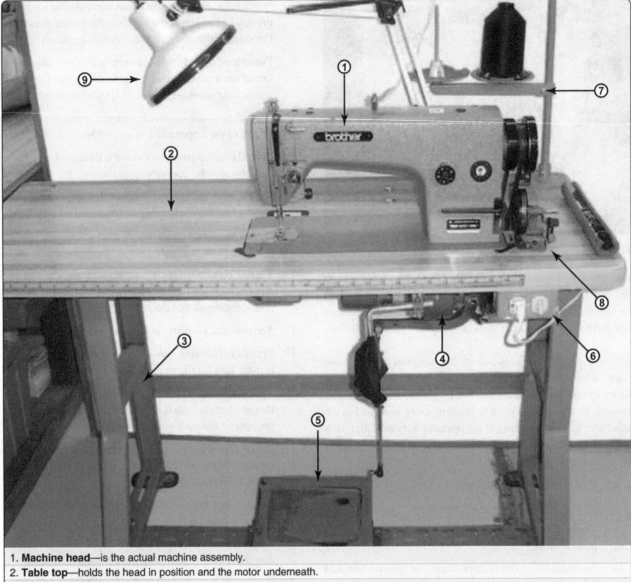

1. **Machine head**—is the actual machine assembly.
2. **Table top**—holds the head in position and the motor underneath.
3. **Stand**—supports the table top.
4. **Motor**—powers the sewing machine.
5. **Treadle**—the "gas pedal" that operates the motor. Pushing forward makes motor start and pushing backward stops the motor.
6. **On/off switch**—controls power to the motor.
7. **Thread stand**—holds the spools of thread for both the sewing machine and the bobbin winder.
8. **Bobbin winder**—feeds the thread to the bobbin during the winding process.
9. **Light**—necessary to observe the sewing operation.

Figure 6-67. *Front view of a modern, light-duty, single-needle machine.*

Sewing Theory

Once the rigger has become familiar with the parts of the machine, it is time to begin to understand the operation and theory of how the machines sew. The primary form of stitch pattern is called a 301 lockstitch. It is formed by two threads, one from the top and one from the bottom. The needle carries the thread from the top through the material, and the bobbin holds the thread on the bottom. The hook catches a small loop in the upper thread and carries it around the bobbin, and the two threads interlock between themselves to form

the stitch. *Figures 6-69* through *6-73* show the sequence in forming the stitch.

There are two types of principles of operation in sewing machines: the "oscillating" hook and the "rotary" hook. With the oscillating type, the bobbin and hook are positioned in a vertical plane to the bed of the machine. The hook rocks back and forth in a half revolution to complete the stitch. With the rotary type, the bobbin and hook may be either vertical or horizontal, and the hook makes two

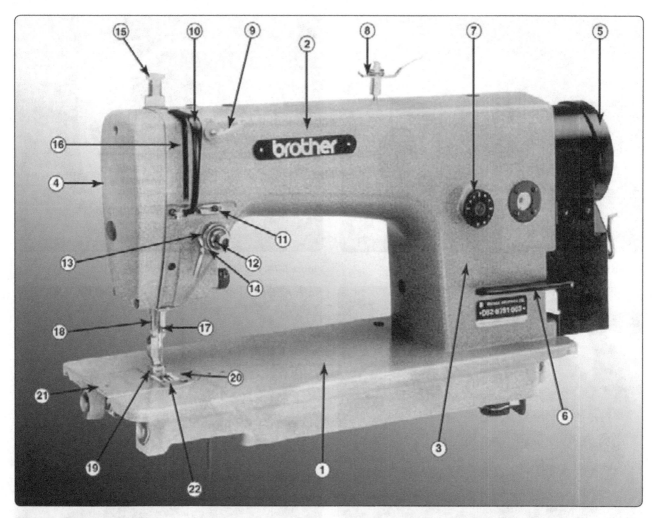

Figure 6-68. *Closeup of head.*

Figure 6-69. *First step in forming a stitch.*

Figure 6-70. *Second step in forming a stitch.*

complete revolutions to complete one stitch. The oscillating models are generally slower in operation while the rotary is the high-speed model. Aside from the larger, heavy-duty machines, most new machines are rotary in operation. *[Figures 6-74 and 6-75]*

There are three types of feed mechanisms to move material through the machines. The first and simplest is called a "drop feed" machine. With this type of feed, a feed dog on the bottom rises up to press the material against the presser foot from the top and moves it along while the needle bar

Figure 6-71. *Third step in forming a stitch.*

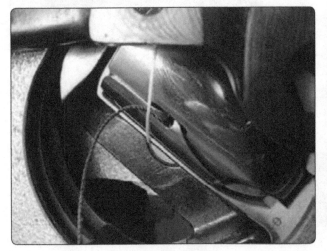

Figure 6-72. *Fourth step in forming a stitch.*

Figure 6-73. *Fifth step in forming a stitch.*

and needle move up and down penetrating the material and forming the stitch. This is generally the lightest duty of machines. The Singer 31-15 and Mitsubishi DB-130 are two examples of a drop feed.

Figure 6-74. *Oscillating hook.*

Figure 6-75. *Rotary hook.*

The second type of machine is the "needle feed" machine. With this type, the needle bar moves in addition to the feed dog and helps move the material. This is a medium-duty machine. The Brother B-791 is an example of a "needle feed" machine.

The third type of machine is a "compound feed" machine. This is a combination of the drop feed and needle feed along with an alternating presser foot. This is a more positive feed machine and is generally a medium-duty to heavy-duty machine. The Juki LU-563 and Consew 733R are good examples of "compound feed" machines.

Needles

The needle is one of the smallest parts of the machine but is probably the most important. It is the source of the perfect stitch and also the most aggravation. The use of the correct type and size of needle is most important in proper operation of a sewing machine. Improper needles cause a machine to produce poor stitching and may damage the material, or the machine might not sew at all. Using the wrong needle can also damage the machine. *[Figure 6-76]* Without getting into the advanced aspects of needle technology, there are a few simple things for the rigger to know.

1. There are three types of points—round, diamond, and twist. Round is used for cloth as it separates the fibers of the cloth as it passes through. The diamond is used for leather as it cuts the material.

2. Each type of needle has a number to identify its size. A typical description would be "16 × 95, size 20." The 16 is the size or diameter of the shank. The 95 is the length and also describes the type of point. Odd numbers denote round points and even denotes diamond points. The size 20 is the diameter of the shaft.

3. The rigger should always follow the instructions in the operator's manual for the proper needle, installation, and threading.

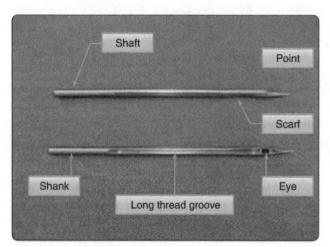

Figure 6-76. *Parts of a needle.*

Operation

Each sewing machine is unique and comes with a detailed operator's manual that explains step-by-step the procedures for sewing. Listed below are some common steps that can be used and are applicable to most machines.

*   Before you first sit down in front of the machine, check to see that the power cord is plugged in.

*   Many of the modern machines are self-lubricating and have an oil reservoir in a pan below the head. Make sure there is oil of the correct type and to the correct level.

*   Next, remove the bobbin case and bobbin from the machine and the upper thread from the needle. This allows you to check to see if the bobbin case is clear and free in operation.

*   Without turning the power on, depress the treadle lightly to release the clutch. Turn the balance wheel or drive pulley toward you, and cycle the needle up and

down several times to see if the machine turns freely. Listen for any sounds that seem abnormal and notice any feeling of tightness or binding of the machine.

*   If everything seems normal, re-thread the needle. Take a full bobbin, place it in the bobbin case, and install it in the shuttle of the machine. *[Figures 6-77 and 6-78]*

*   Cycle the needle down and pick up the bobbin thread. A correctly threaded and timed machine picks up the bobbin thread on the first cycle.

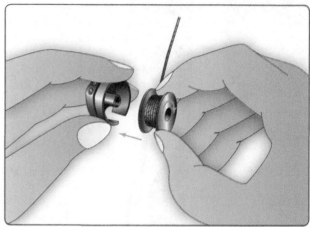

Figure 6-77. *Bobbin case.*

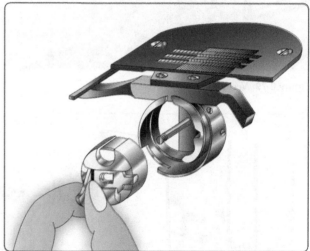

Figure 6-78. *Shuttle of the machine.*

Installing the Needle and Threading the Machine

Most single-needle-type machines have the needle positioned in the needle bar with the long thread groove facing to the left. It is important to always check the threading diagram to make sure the needle is installed correctly and ensure that the needle is installed all the way up to the stop in the needle groove of the needle bar. Check that the long thread groove faces in the direction for that type of machine and that the needle clamp screw is tight. *[Figure 6-79]*

Figure 6-79. *Needle with left orientation.*

Examples of single-needle machines where the thread groove does not face left are Singer 17W15 308-stitch or Singer 69 bar tack. The thread groove most often faces the bobbin, but not always in the case of a Horizontal Rotary Hook, such as Singer 201-2. Read the manual, if the needle does not pick up the bobbin thread, it may not be installed correctly.

Take a cone of thread and place it on the thread stand. Route the thread upward through the guide at the top of the stand and then to the pre-tension thread guide on top of the arm of the machine. *[Figure 6-80]* Most modern machines use a similar method of threading. However, there may be additional thread guides of different shapes to route the thread through. This is why the rigger should have a copy of the operator's manual for proper threading of each machine.

Once the machine is threaded correctly, take a sample of material suitable for the type of machine, thread, and needle. Form several layers and place it under the presser foot. Lower the presser foot while holding the upper and lower threads securely to the rear of the presser foot. Turn the balance wheel again and run a few stitches by hand to see if the machine sews properly. If everything works as expected, turn the power on and begin sewing. If you are unfamiliar with this particular machine, begin slowly until you get the feel of the clutch and speed of the machine. The harder you push, the faster the machine runs. Some industrial machines are able to run very fast. This can intimidate many. If you need to slow the machine down, you can replace the pulley on the motor with one smaller pulley. A parts and repair shop will have or be able to order the pulley you need. Order the smallest

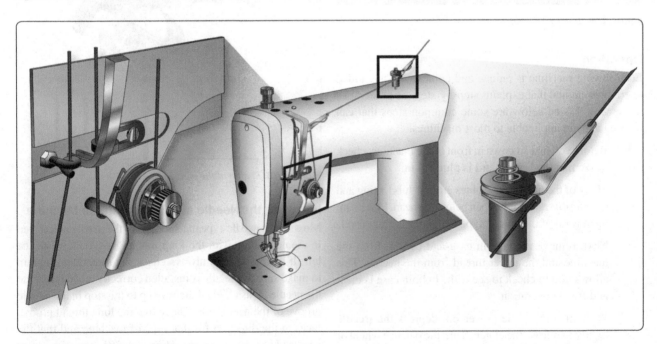

Figure 6-80. *Thread the machine.*

pulley that fits the shaft on your motor. You do have to know the make and model of the machine.

Another way to slow a machine is to replace the clutch motor with a rheostat motor. They operate the same way as a dimmer switch for a lamp. The operator sets the speed of the motor, and it does not run faster than what it is set at. When finished sewing, always place a piece of fabric under the presser foot in order to keep the feed dogs from causing damage to the presser foot.

If the machine does not sew correctly, consult the troubleshooting guide to determine what the problem is and how to remedy it. *[Figure 6-81]* If the machine jams, it is very important to not force it, as you can cause damage to the machine.

Machine Maintenance

The most important part of maintaining your sewing machines is to keep them clean and lubricated. Each machine should be wiped down daily with a clean rag to remove oil and dirt. The amount of use each machine gets dictates the cleaning required. However, on at least a weekly schedule, the moving parts should be cleaned with a small brush to remove dust, lint, dirt, and threads. An air hose or bottle is useful in blowing dirt out of places the brush cannot reach. Be careful

when doing this as small particles can be propelled through the air and can get into the eyes. At the very least, the dirt can be blown onto other machines and work.

After cleaning, each machine should be lubricated to ensure smooth operation. For those machines that are self-lubricating, check the level and condition of the oil in the reservoir. For these machines, a number 1 white oil that has a higher viscosity should be used. Depending on the amount of use, the oil should be changed every 6 months to a year. In no case should the oil be changed less than once a year. For machines that require manual lubrication, a number 2 white oil should be used as it has a lower viscosity to better adhere to the moving parts. This should be done daily at the end of the workday. Oiling the machine at this time allows the oil to seep downward through the mechanisms and collect on the bottom.

In the morning before use, take a clean rag and wipe off the excess oil so it does not stain the parachute materials. Pay particular attention to the shuttle race. Keeping this well lubricated ensures smooth operation and a quieter machine. One item that tends to get overlooked is the bobbin winder. The shaft of the winder has a small hole in the top and a drop of oil should be added at least once a week to keep it free.

Trouble	Probable Cause	Remedy
Needle breakage	Incorrect class and variety of needle being used	Use correct class and variety needle
	Needle loose in clamp	Tighten needle clamp screw
	Needle too small for fabric	Use larger needle
	Operator pulling on fabric	Allow machine to feed material
Needle thread breakage	Thread too heavy for needle	Use larger needle or smaller thread
	Right twist thread being used	Use left twist thread
	Machine incorrectly threaded	Check machine for proper threading
	Needle thread tension too tight	Loosen needle thread tension
	Thread take-up spring out of adjustment	Adjust thread take-up spring
	Burr on bobbin case, shuttle point, or tension discs	Smooth with emery cloth
	Thread rubbing against presser foot	Adjust presser foot
	Needle is bent or has blunt point	Replace needle
Bobbin thread breakage	Bobbin tension too tight	Adjust bobbin tension
	Bobbin incorrectly threaded	Thread bobbin to revolve clockwise
	Bobbin wound too fully to revolve freely	Remove some of the bobbin thread
	Rounds of bobbin thread lapped over one another bobbin	Ensure bobbin thread is straight when winding
	Bobbin case is dirty	Clean and lubricate bobbin case
Skipped stitches	Machine out of time	Time needle to shuttle
	Thread controller spring out of adjustment	Adjust thread controller spring
Drawing of seam	Both needle and bobbin tension too tight	Loosen needle and bobbin tension
Stitches piled up	Stitch regulator out of adjustment	Adjust stitch regulator
	Pressure on presser foot too tight	Loosen presser foot adjustment screw
Feed dog striking throat plate	Feed dog set too high	Lower feed dog to correct height

Figure 6-81. *Troubleshooting chart for light-duty, drop-feed sewing machines.*

Sewing Machine Attachments

The most common attachment that the rigger uses is a tape folder or "binder." This attachment folds tape, typically ¾-inch Type-3, used for binding the edges of container, bags, or any material needing an edge binder. Used in conjunction with a double-needle machine, it folds the tape in half for a professional appearance and greatly speeds up the work. [Figure 6-82]

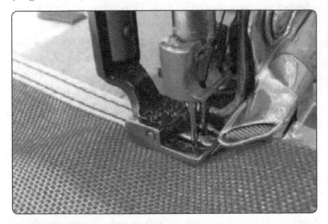

Figure 6-82. *Material with binding tape.*

There are two types of folders. One is a straight folder where the tape is fed straight into the machine under the presser foot. [Figure 6-83] This folder is used for most straight binding, has minimal adjustments, and is the least expensive usually costing around 35 dollars. The second type of folder is a right angle folder. [Figure 6-84] The best models of these are custom built by companies that specialize in attachments. They utilize special feed dogs, throat plates, and presser feet in addition to the folder. This type of folder is hinged to swing out of the way for changing bobbins. Most machines have several adjustments that allow for fine tuning the folder for optimum performance depending on the tape used. Folders can cost several hundred dollars.

Figure 6-83. *Straight binder.*

Figure 6-84. *Right angle binder.*

Another type of attachment is used to feed reinforcing tape such as ⅜-inch Type-3 onto a canopy seam. This is a simple guide that is attached to the presser foot and feeds the tape evenly to the needles. Yet another attachment is a seam folder used to make a French fell seam in canopy construction. *Figure 6-85* shows both of the above attachments used in conjunction with each other. Over the years, the sewing industry has developed literally hundreds of different attachments to speed up and improve the sewing process.

Figure 6-85. *Tape feeder and French seam folder.*

The Parachute Loft

The term "loft" comes from earlier times when the area used to pack and maintain parachutes was usually situated in the aircraft hangar above the aircraft. Hence, the term "loft." The name has continued to this day and is synonymous with the parachute workshop.

Under, 14 CFR part 65, section 65.127(b), a rigger must have: "Suitable housing that is adequately heated, lighted, and ventilated for drying and airing parachutes." Under 14 CFR part 65, section 65.127(d), the rigger must have: "Adequate housing facilities to perform his duties and to protect his tools and equipment." All of this only makes sense in that the properties stipulated are those that are best suited for storing and maintaining parachutes. Although these regulations have been in effect for over 40 years and were originally intended to apply to parachutes with organic fibers in them, they still apply today. From the practical side, keeping yourself and the parachute warm promotes efficient work habits. Good lighting means that you can properly inspect the parachute. Good ventilation allows the parachute to properly dry before packing.

Most individuals have been to automotive garages where there was oil on the floor and parts strewn everywhere. Yet when the mechanic is finished with your car, the cost is fair and your car runs like new. In contrast, modern professional garages sometimes look like hospital facilities in their cleanliness and organization, the cost is high, and your car does not start after you pay the bill. Where would you take your car? The loft, as depicted in *Figure 6-86*, is a dream for most riggers who do there rigging in there basement as a hobby. For the rigger who lives in a climate that is conducive to year round work and plans to make rigging a full time job, they may invest in a full-time loft. In colder climates, it is busy in the summer, and in winter, well cold. A clean, organized, and well-designed loft can inspire customer confidence, but the rigger's ability to work on the parachute is all that matters when you need that canopy over your head. The loft facility houses the sewing machines and other equipment over and above the hand tools that all riggers should have. A full-service loft has the following areas:

Packing and Inspection Area

A main part of the loft layout is a suitable packing area. According to 14 CFR part 65, section 65.127(a), the rigger must have: "A smooth top table at least 3 feet wide by 40 feet long." Technically, this is still required and is used primarily for round canopies. However, with today's square parachutes, the accepted practice is to pack on the floor on a suitable covering, such as carpet. Squares can be packed on a table, but there must be access to the canopy from both sides of the table in order to inspect and fold it properly. *[Figure 6-87]* Even when packed on a table, the parachute may have to be moved to the floor to aid in closing the container. If the rigger is packing a round parachute, a packing table is preferable as it makes the rigger's job easier and more comfortable. If there is no packing table, then there needs to be an open area big enough to lay out the round or square parachute. While not expressly required, most lofts have a canopy hanger for inspection, airing, and assembling square canopies. *[Figure 6-88]* Many riggers who do not have the room to hang a canopy at home take the canopy to the DZ where space is available. A square canopy can also be aired by S folding and hanging it from a simple hook. This way a square canopy can be aired in a small space, but it is important to note that this technique is to air the canopy out, not inspect it. *[Figure 6-89]*

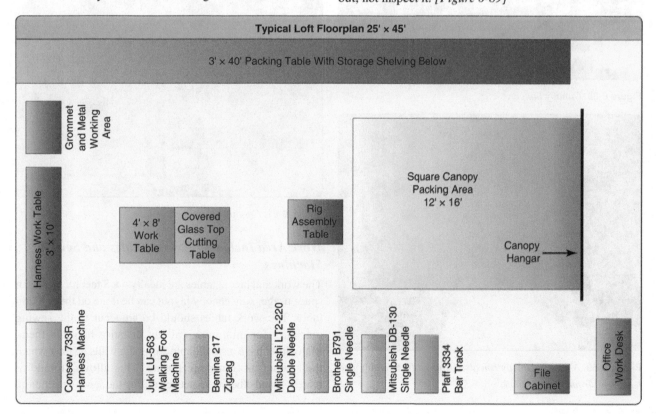

Figure 6-86. *Loft drawing.*

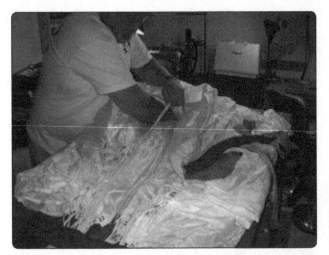

Figure 6-87. *A square canopy being packed on a table, which must be accessible from both sides of the table in order to inspect and fold it properly.*

Figure 6-88. *Canopy hanger.*

Figure 6-89. *A square canopy can also be aired by S folding and hanging it from a simple hook.*

Along with the canopy hanger, an assembly and inspection table is extremely useful. *[Figure 6-90]* It allows the harness and container to be assembled to the canopy without laying it on the floor. The assembly table allows the correct distance from the floor to mate with the canopy and provides an ideal storage area for the packing tools, wrenches, other equipment, and materials needed for assembly. *[Figure 6-91]* This table can be a folding banquet table or wheeled cart if space is limited.

Figure 6-90. *Assembly and inspection table.*

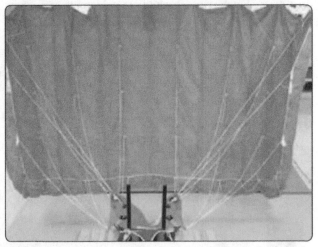

Figure 6-91. *Canopy and table layout.*

Work Area Including Layout Tables and Sewing Machines

The work and layout tables are ideally 4 × 8 feet for optimum space usage. Any canopy layout can be done on the packing table. The work tables should be adjacent to the sewing machines for minimum walking distance between them. Many lofts have a small table along the walls against which the sewing machines are placed. This allows storage of materials and other items needed during the sewing operation.

The right end of the sewing machine table is placed against this table so that the left, or open end, is available to lay canopies or containers on.

Harness Table and Machines

Because of the nature of harness work, there are many specialized materials and tools unique to harness work. The table houses the hot knife, hot glue gun, templates, and rulers. *[Figure 6-92]* The harness machine should be adjacent to the harness table for maximum efficiency.

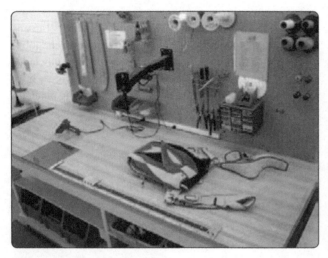

Figure 6-92. *Harness work table.*

Cutting Table

The cutting table is used for cutting canopy fabric for canopy repairs, para-pak or Cordura® for container repairs, or for cutting anything for general manufacturing. Ideally, this cutting table has a glass surface for use with a hot knife. One of the best designs utilizes a 4 × 4 feet glass surface that is hidden below a wooden cover that can be removed when needed and protects the glass when not in use. This table serves dual duty as a work table. *[Figure 6-93]* If space is limited, a smaller piece of glass can be used. If available, use a thick laminated piece of glass that is less prone to breaking.

Metal Working Area

It is important to segregate the metal working area from the rest of the loft because metal working creates considerable contamination with metal shavings and other particles injurious to parachute fabrics. The metal working area has drills, grinders, swaging tools, Nicopress® tools, and other tools needed for repairing or overhauling metal components. *[Figure 6-94]* The grommet area should be adjacent to the metal working area, since several of the tools used to remove grommets are found there. *[Figure 6-95]* The grommet machine or handsets are kept in this area. Parachute containers or other parts needing grommets are brought to this area for work. A metal working cart with drawers for

Figure 6-93. *Glass top table with cover.*

Figure 6-94. *Metal working area.*

tools may be used, provided it is kept away from any fabric that could be damaged.

Office Area

The office area handles the administrative and record keeping functions of the loft. It should have a desk, file cabinets, library or bookshelves, telephone/fax machine, and computer. All work orders are processed through here.

Figure 6-95. *Grommet area.*

Materials Storage Area

The storage area may be a separate room, a pegboard, or cabinets on the walls where thread, tapes, and webbing are stored. *[Figure 6-96]* Rolls of fabric may be stored under the work or packing tables or on wall racks.

Figure 6-96. *Thread storage area.*

All of the above may be practical for the full-time professional loft, but for the individual rigger there may be certain space constraints. Many riggers take over their garage or basement, which makes a perfectly suitable loft with some cleaning and remodeling.

Chapter Summary

This chapter contains information on the different types of sewing machines, component parts and there function, stitch formation, needles, and troubleshooting and hand tools used while performing the work of senior and Master Parachute Riggers. Having the correct tools for parachute rigging cannot be over emphasized. When the rigger is brought a parachute to be inspected, repaired, and repacked anything less than the best is unacceptable. The customer trusts the rigger with his life and no effort should be spared to provide the best.

It takes time to accumulate all the tools available. With any given task, the correct tools and space to perform the job is a must. Most important is that the rigger has the knowledge to do the work for which he or she is rated. The rigger must also have access to information, such as parachute manuals, manufactures contact information, and other riggers with more experience.

Chapter 7

Repairs, Alterations, and Manufacture

Introduction

Inspection requirements are the mainstay of the parachute rigger, but of equal importance is the repair and maintenance of the parachute and its related systems. When the parachute is new, it is expected to function as designed. As it is used and ages, however, it begins to wear and its condition changes, which over time could result in a malfunction of the system. It is the rigger's responsibility during inspections to identify any condition that might result in the parachute being considered non-airworthy and dangerous. In the course of training, the rigger candidate learns to identify those conditions that may be unsafe. The trainee also learns how to undertake the necessary repairs to return the parachute to its original, airworthy configuration. As we look at repairs it becomes very evident that inspection is the initial part of the process of any repair.

Size	MLW	MARK A-B-C	FINISH
XXS	12.00	4.75-11.00-15.75	5.25
XS	13.00	5.00-11.50-16.50	5.50
SM	14.00	5.75-13.25-19.00	6.38
MED	15.00	7.12-15.88-23.00	7.62
LG	16.00	8.00-17.75-25.75	8.62
XL	17.00	9.00-19.5-28.50	9.25
XXL	18.00	10.00-21.50-31.50	10.25

As stated in Chapter 1 of this handbook, Regulations and Human Factors, it is imperative that riggers be able to distinguish between minor and major repairs. This ensures that riggers do not exceed the limitations of their certificate or endanger the parachute user. The basic rule for repairs is to return the damaged parachute or component to its original airworthy configuration. However, in many instances, the remanufacture of the parachute may not be practical or cost effective. In these cases, there are approved repair techniques riggers can use to return the parachute to service. These techniques form an important part of the rigger's store of knowledge. To make a decision as to the confirmation for the possible need for repairs, we must first understand the Federal Aviation Administration (FAA) requirement of inspection.

Inspection Process

Chapter 5 of this handbook, Inspection and Packing, addresses the purpose of the 180-day cycle as required by the FAA. This action insures that the approved/certificated parachute assembly meets the standards and conditions for safe return to service; it also become the cornerstone of the maintenance and repair process.

The confirmation of wear or damage is critical in the determination of actions that may be needed as set forth in Title 14 of the Code of Federal Regulations (14 CFR) part 43 and key in the assessment of actions and clarity of the repair that may need to be performed.

As is the character of any device or object, use and physical location conditions (heat, moisture, sand, dirt) over time cause wear to an item and, on occasion, misuse or improper actions during use result in damage. Certain parts or areas of a device incur more wear or damage according to use, action of handling, and contact with other components. Knowledge of this aspect should require increased or location specific consideration during the inspection process.

This recognition possibility of high-wear components or areas does not decrease or eliminate the inspection of any other part of the parachute assembly. It only identifies that the wear or damage probabilities are greater at these locations. These areas are referred to as common wear or damage patterns and apply to both round and square parachutes and parachute assemblies. These types of common wear/damage pattern applies in greater detail to the parachute that is utilized as the main parachute and deployed on each jump in sport use.

The inspection of a reserve canopy after deployment should be very concise and complete. Much care should be taken for a very thorough inspection of the parachute and related components. Parachutes are manufactured in two categories: approved (certificated) and non-approved

(non-certificated). All reserve emergency use parachutes are approved (certificated) and are tested to FAA-required Technical Standard Order (TSO) standards. They are used and maintained by FAA standards (inspection and repaired by FAA-ceticated rigger or the manufacturer) as airframe and powerplant (A&P) mechanics are used.

Non-approved or non-certificated parachutes are generally main parachutes, and related components, which can be packed, used, and repaired outside of FAA maintenance and repair requirements. Rigger inspections and rigger repairs are highly recommended but not required. Inspection of and approved (certificated) parachute calls for inspection of all related components, which are listed below. Related components are parts of the parachute, deployment system, harness, and container system, and any item that has responsibility for containment, deployment, or operation of an approved (certificated) parachute and are a critical part of the assembly. They must be inspected for use the same as the reserve parachute.

- Deployment bag (freebag, safety stow)
- Bridle and pilot chute
- Slider, slider fabric, and grommets
- Rapid links (soft links)
- Rapid link covers (soft link covers)
- All seams and seam fabric
- Suspension lines and line attachments
- Ripcord housing and attachments
- Ripcord assembly
- Upper and lower skins of canopy, all load and non-load bearing ribs, all cross ports

All of these areas can sustain wear or damage during normal use. The event of use at very high speeds can be contributed to the possibility of increased damage from exceeding the maximum speed allowed during deployment.

During inspection of certificated/approved parachutes, it is advisable to map related damage found on a chart which is shown in *Figure 7-1*. This chart can be used to describe the location of needed repair to a customer, assist in quickly locating the damage, and answer questions that the manufacturer may have relating to possible repair. *[Figure 7-1]*

If a rigger were to receive a damaged sport main canopy for repair, it would be advantageous to gain as much information as possible as to the cause and situation that created the damage. Inspection of the canopy should be as follows:

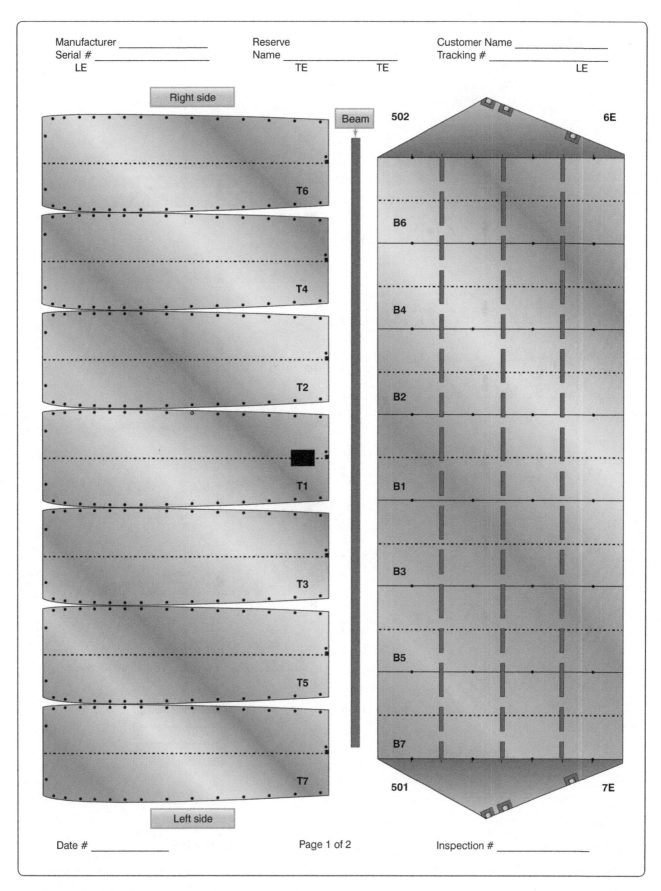

Figure 7-1. *Generic damage chart (page 1).*

Manufacturer _____
Serial # _____

Reserve
Name _____

Customer Name _____
Tracking # _____

Right side

6E

6-4

4-2

2-1

1-3

3-5

5-7

7E

Left side

R6

R4

R2

R1

R3

R5

R7

Slider

Figure 7-1. *Generic damage chart (page 2).*

1. Links—condition and confirmation of barrel condition (not cracked or stripped), soft links, installation, condition, tacked in place. *[Figure 7-2A and B]*

2. Slider—check fabric for rips and burns; grommets for dents, nicks, or damage. *[Figure 7-3A, B, C, and D]*

3. Grommet protectors—confirm they are installed correctly and in good condition. *[Figure 7-4A and B]*

4. Lines—check for burns, continuity, trim, and wear at lower section of steering lines. *[Figure 7-5A and B]*

5. Stabilizers—check attachments, signs of excessive stress, fabric damage or stress, and line attachment stitch. *[Figure 7-6A and B]*

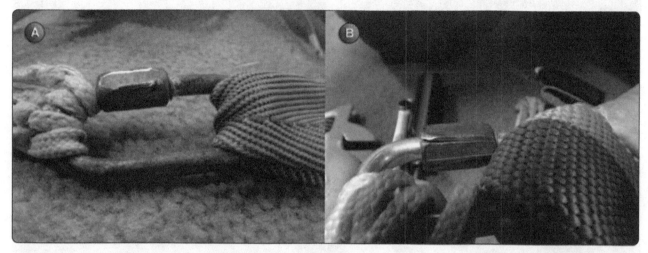

Figure 7-2. *Link damage.*

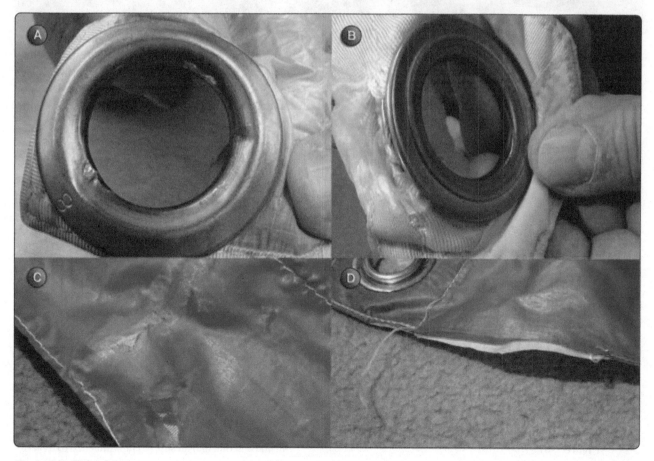

Figure 7-3. *Slider damage.*

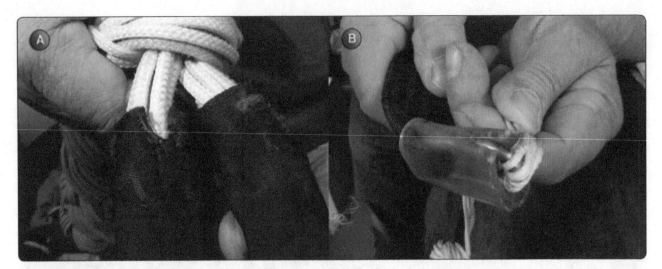

Figure 7-4. *Protector damage.*

Figure 7-5. *Line damage.*

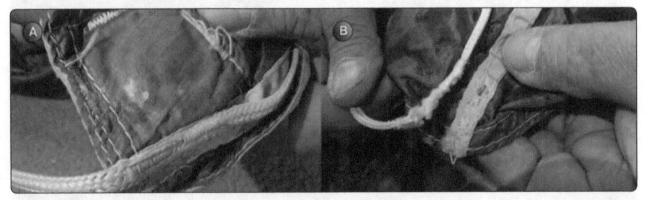

Figure 7-6. *Stabilizer damage.*

6. Line attachments—check for stitch, material fatigue, paying close attention for damage behind the line tab. *[Figure 7-7A and B]*

7. Seam starts—look for back stitching failure or fraying. *[Figure 7-8]*

8. Seam work—check for snags, pulls, loose stitches. *[Figure 7-9]*

9. Fabric—check entire canopy for burns, snags, rips, and tears and check inside cells, cross port condition, and rib damage. *[Figure 7-10A and B]*

10. Pilot chute attachment—check this area excessively, inside and out, and all support tape attached to it on rib. The damage here is not always obvious. *[Figure 7-11]*

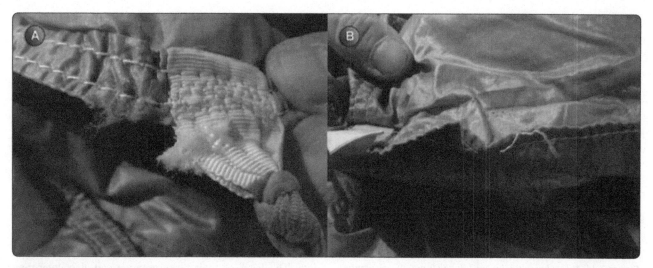

Figure 7-7. *Line attachment damage.*

Figure 7-8. *End seam damage.*

Figure 7-9. *Long seam damage.*

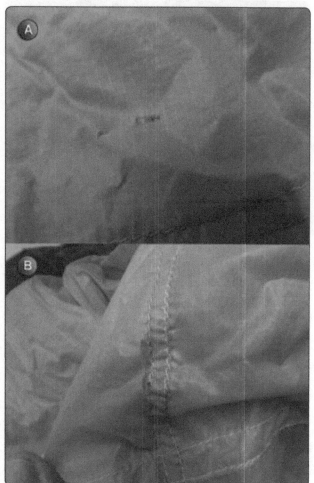

Figure 7-10. *Fabric damage.*

11. Center cell top skin (from pilot chute attachment down to tail seam)—inspect skin for snags, dirt, discoloration, body oil/sweat transfer. Body contact is very high and sweat transfer and contact cause much faster deterioration of fabric. *[Figure 7-12]*

A damage chart similar to the reserve chart can be created to address main canopy inspections also.

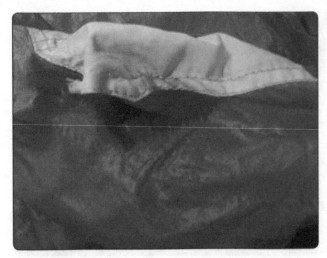

Figure 7-11. *Pilot chute attachment damage is not always obvious.*

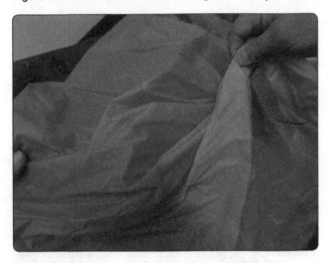

Figure 7-12. *Top rear skin damage.*

Major or Minor Repairs

It is an age-old question among rigging technicians, one that is yet to receive a clear, understandable answer. The distinction between a major repair and a minor repair is clouded by regulations and guidance material as created and applied to the repair of aircraft. The FAA classifies repairs into two categories: major and minor. Following is the FAA's definition of both:

Major repair means a repair:

1. That, if improperly done, might appreciably affect weight, balance, structural strength, performance, powerplant operation, flight characteristics, or other qualities affecting airworthiness; or

2. That is not done according to accepted practices or cannot be done by elementary operations.

Minor repair means a repair other than a major repair. It is recognized and allowed by the FAA, that the weight and balance and powerplant reference as stated in paragraph (1) under major repair is not applied to parachute repairs, but all other standards are mandatory.

So, the person performing the maintenance as applies to parachutes in the view of the FAA is the one who decides if the repair or alteration is major or minor, and that person could be a rigger, a repairman (who must be employed by a manufacturer), or a person under the direct supervision of an appropriately-rated and qualified rigger (person with appropriate facilities, machines, tools, and materials).

The manufacturer can determine if a repair is major or minor and delegate authority to rated riggers or lofts in the field to perform repairs to their required standards and approved data. The FAA or their representative can also determine what category the task may be. Often, these authorizations considered by manufacturers are a one-time only allowance or limited to a specific certificated or an approved TSO piece or type of equipment.

Now we know who is responsible to make the determination on whether a repair or alteration is major or minor, but how will they decide?

For some time, the FAA has published in Advisory Circular (AC) 120-77, Maintenance and Alteration Data, a chart to assist the technician in determining what type of repair qualifies and in which category as it applies to aircraft repair. Shown in *Figure 7-13* is an example repair decision chart that riggers can use (both senior and master) to determine the processes that need to be followed when excessive wear or damage is identified during the inspection process.

It allows for consideration of repair for both TSO equipment and non TSO. It also brings into effect the need for verification of the possibility of existing Safety Bulletin's (SBs) or Airworthiness Directives (ADs) that may apply to the items found to be damaged during the inspection process.

Contamination Conditions

During the inspection process, in many cases the focus is to locate and identify material damage, tears, rips, broken stitches, pulled tread, and burns, which generally are very apparent should they exist. Damage can exist in forms that are less apparent to the material properties/assembly. Much less obvious, but just as important, is contamination.

Contamination conditions can be critical to the repair process and have a direct effect as to the decision of the repair type (major/minor) status. Listed below are common types of contamination conditions, their visual verification properties, and the manufacturer recommended processes to

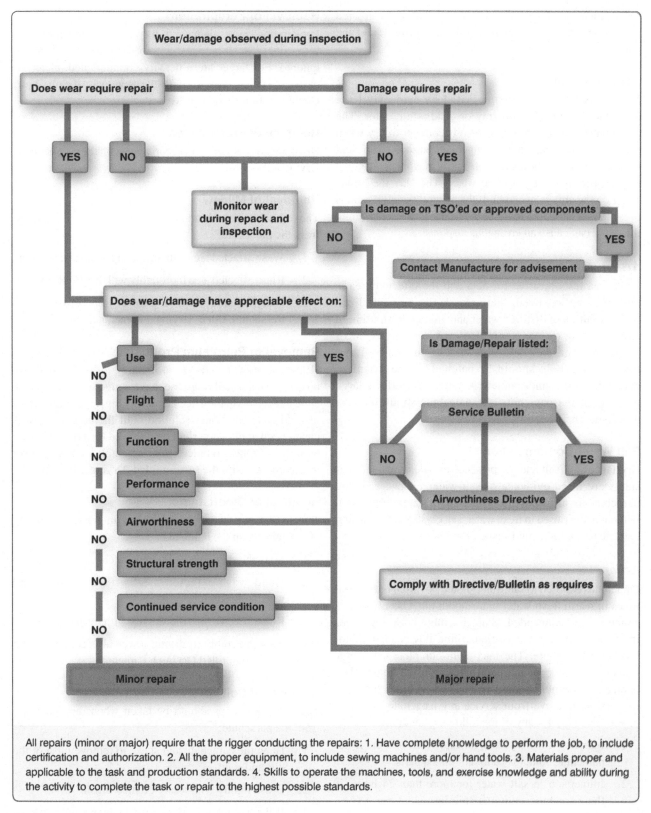

All repairs (minor or major) require that the rigger conducting the repairs: 1. Have complete knowledge to perform the job, to include certification and authorization. 2. All the proper equipment, to include sewing machines and/or hand tools. 3. Materials proper and applicable to the task and production standards. 4. Skills to operate the machines, tools, and exercise knowledge and ability during the activity to complete the task or repair to the highest possible standards.

Figure 7-13. *Parachute repair decision chart.*

repair. Identification of these conditions and rigger-applied repairs determine their effect on the airworthiness of the parachute assembly.

Acid Contamination

Nylon that has been contaminated by acid may have irregular shaped spots of gray or dead white color. The acid-contaminated fabric may also become powdery when scraped lightly. Parachute components suspected of acid contamination may be tested with blue litmus paper. Dampen the suspect area with distilled water. Then lay the litmus paper on the area in question. If the paper turns pink, acid is present. Be careful not to touch the litmus paper, as touching the paper can cause an erroneous response.

Action

If an area tests positive for acid and the effected area is known to be localized, that area should be neutralized with a solution of distilled water and ammonia. Household ammonia works. Ammonia does not damage nylon or hardware. The damaged area should be removed and the resulting hole should be patched. If the extent of contamination cannot be determined or if it effects large portions of the parachute, the parachute should be first destroyed, then disposed of.

Salt Water Contamination

Crystals of dry salt and the presence of pale brown circular stains are often evidence of salt-water exposure. If the parachute is allowed to dry after salt-water immersion without being rinsed in fresh water, salt crystals form causing damage to the fabric and suspension lines.

Action

Parachutes exposed to salt water should be rinsed out several times in warm fresh water in a smooth tub. Use of a water softener is recommended. Hang assembly in drying tower in accordance with the section within this chapter titled, Drying a Parachute. The maximum complete salt-water immersion limits for the parachute are listed below. The parachute assembly should be cleaned within 8 hours of immersion. Remove from service any parachute assembly or sub-assembly for any of the following conditions:

1. Immersion in salt water for more than 6 hours if the parachute contains cadmium plated parts.

2. Immersion in salt water for more than 24 hours if the parachute contains stainless steel parts (i.e., slider stops).

3. Immersion in salt water and cannot be cleaned for 36 hours.

Removal of Perspiration

Perspiration causes damage to the parachute much like salt water does. Small amounts are not significant and may be ignored. For larger areas heavily contaminated, clean the parachute in accordance with the Removal of Salt Water Contamination section above.

Removal of Fresh Water

Dry parachute assembly in accordance with the section titled, Drying a Parachute.

Removal of Mildew

The following steps should be taken when removing mildew from the parachute:

1. Wash affected area with mild soap and water solution.

2. Rinse affected area thoroughly with fresh, clear water.

3. Hang assembly in drying tower in accordance with the section titled, Drying a Parachute.

Removal of Petroleum Products

Hydrocarbons usually do not harm nylon. Petroleum products, such as oil or grease, have a greenish or brownish appearance. Wash the affected area by repeated applications of mild soap and water solution until the affected area is clean. Each application shall be followed by a rinse in clean fresh water. Once complete, hang assembly in drying tower in accordance with the section titled, Drying a Parachute.

Removal of Bloodstains

The following steps should be taken when removing bloodstains from the parachute:

1. Soak the stained area in cold water.

2. Hand wash affected area with mild soap and water solution.

3. Rinse affected area thoroughly with fresh clean water.

4. Hang assembly in drying tower in accordance with the section titled Drying a Parachute.

Removal of Soil

The following steps should be taken when removing soil from the parachute:

1. Hang the parachute and shake to remove most of the dirt and sand.

2. Brush lightly with a soft-bristled brush.

3. If the assembly is extremely contaminated, perform the following:

a. Wash only the soiled areas in warm water with a mild soap.

b. Rinse affected area thoroughly with fresh clean water.

4. Hang assembly in drying tower in accordance with the section titled, Drying a Parachute.

Drying a Parachute

The procedure for drying a parachute is critical. Asymmetric shrinkage may occur if the parachute is dried unevenly. Perform the following steps:

1. Remove pilot chute assembly and/or drogue/slider control line.

2. Hang parachute full-length or the seams may experience uneven shrinkage creating a built in turn.

3. Hang reserve parachute assembly by all four connector links for the same time.

Cleaning the Parachute

Sometimes during the inspection process, excessive amounts of dirt or debris are found caused from misuse or poor landing. Also, there are occasions when the customer may request that the assembly be cleaned.

Washing a parachute is not recommended unless deemed absolutely necessary because washing it can weaken and/ or increase the permeability of the fabric. Washing can also cause shrinkage in the nylon fabric, tapes, and the other components. Do not dry clean parachutes. Parachute components may be spot cleaned or cleaned as a unit, and care must be taken that the cleaning process does not do more damage than the original soiling.

Hand Washing (If Absolutely Necessary)

The following considerations/steps should be used when hand washing the parachute:

1. A mild soap or soap solution and a water softener may be used.

2. Immerse the parachute into clean, fresh water contained in a smooth vessel, such as a bathtub.

3. Do not wring the parachute fabric. Damage to fabric permeability will result.

4. Gently move items by hand until all air pockets are removed. Agitate as little as possible or damage to fabric permeability will result.

5. Empty the vessel of dirty water and refill with fresh, warm, clear water.

6. Rinse the parachute several times in warm, fresh water until rinse water is clear.

7. Hang assembly in drying tower in accordance with the section titled, Drying a Parachute.

Washing the parachute is not recommended and should be avoided if at all possible. Many times more damage can be caused to the assembly with an improper wash as opposed to the dirty condition of the equipment.

Approved Data

Now that we have determined through inspection and use of the chart what category of repair may be required, we must obtain the needed data. This can sometimes verify our determination as to the category of repair and inform us of processes or standards. Approved is the data issue or version of data that has been identified by the developer/supplier as being the master issue or version of the data subject. It is required on major repair. This data is a key element and offers the base line of all standards that must be met for completion of the task of returning the equipment to the user in a safe, continued service condition.

Riggers under FAA jurisdiction are responsible for ensuring that repairs are accomplished according to all applicable regulations under title 14 CFR part 43. Repair of damage can be classified as either major, minor, or alteration. This assessment is based on the scope and complexity of the repair, end result of the task, and the experience and capability of the operator.

As we know, the responsibility for determining whether a repair is major or minor rests with the rigger. The document needed to complete an inspection and subsequent repack is the manufacturers owners manual. The documents that offer standards for a repair are found in 14 CFR part 43 and are worded with direct application to aircraft. This allows for confusion of FAA position of repair as it applies to manufacturers and riggers. In the U.S., all repairmen (riggers and mechanics) have authority to use acceptable repair data for minor repairs without additional FAA approval. These processes are not addressed in 14 CFR part 43 as major, minor, or alteration, and no reference is found for use on parachutes or related components.

Because of this rather gray area of current repair classifications under 14 CFR part 43, many times approved data identifies directly the classification of the repair and sets forth all needed guidelines and requirements.

The standards for approved or certificated equipment apply to the reserve parachute, harness/container, and related components, and these standards can also include any Automatic Activation Device (AAD) that may be used in an approved system. With the installation of the AAD, it must meet all manufacturer service and use standards and

FAA inspection limitations. This information can be found in the Rig Manufacturers Owners Manual and the AAD Manufacturers Owners Manual.

Acceptable data is often times confused with approved data. Acceptable data has been allowed under the FAA system and generally used for minor repair. It can be applied to many minor repair practices of different types and application. It is general in its nature and not a required process for an approved repair procedure. It is used by the FAA when considering approval for alteration and usually does not fall under the standard of certificated or approved (TSO and major repairs). Acceptable data is applied in a very broad manner and is not to be a replacement for use of approved data when addressing the FAA major repair process.

Types of Approved Data

Approved data to be used for major repairs and alterations may be one or more of the following. This data can only be obtained from the manufacturer or the FAA Administrator. This data applies to:

1. Model, size, version

2. Manufacturer specifications (approval for repairs, requirements)

3. TSO C23b, C23c, and C23d

4. ADs

5. Manufacturer's SB's

6. Drawings, information, or repair standards from manufacturers research & development (R&D) engineers

7. Designated alteration data offered by the FAA

8. Manufacturer's manuals (including installation and assembly instructions)

The rigger is responsible to confirm the information of model, type, serial number, and date of manufacture when requesting or attempting to obtain any of the above data. It is very important when confirming the following:

- Appropriate to the product being repaired;

- Directly applicable to the repair being made; and

- Not contrary to manufacturer's data.

When contacting the manufacturer or FAA Administrator with request for information as listed for possible major repairs, it is advisable to confirm the following:

a. FAA certification required

b. Equipment (sewing and tools)

c. Materials, quantity, quality, and Mil-Spec

d. Skills, prior knowledge, and experience with type of repair

e. Advisability of attempting this repair

In many situations, it is a better decision, economically and for the end repair, to return the damaged equipment to the manufacturer. This answers all questions as to the quality, manufacturer/FAA repair requirements, and airworthiness of the item when returned to service and confirms that the repair meets the continued service condition.

Repair Techniques

The following procedures use a format that provides the rigger with all of the necessary information to complete the repair properly. It has been used by at least one manufacturer to provide the necessary documentation to riggers in the field to perform major repairs or alterations on that manufacturer's equipment. The procedures provide the following information to the rigger:

1. Applicable products—those parts of the parachute that the procedure addresses.

2. Description—brief explanation of the repair or alteration.

3. Materials—those items needed to perform the procedure.

4. Machines—those machines required to do the procedure. In addition to the machines, there may be special attachments required to do the work properly.

5. Equipment—additional tools needed (in addition to the sewing machines).

6. Procedure—the step-by-step guide through the repair. This may include a disassembly and reassembly procedure. Disassembly may be straightforward, but the reassembly instructions may provide special tips or procedures to accomplish the task.

7. Inspection—the final inspection of the finished repair. This is a very critical part. In many cases, the rigger is doing the work alone. Within the manufacturing environment, the persons doing the work generally do not inspect their own work. This is given over to dedicated inspection personnel. For the private rigger, there may be no one around to inspect the work. In the case of simple repairs, it is easy for the rigger to inspect the finished job. For more extensive repairs, such as a harness main lift web replacement, there can be several areas that need to be addressed, such as dimensions, stitching, and hardware orientation. By having an inspection checklist, the rigger can be assured of not missing any critical area.

Each of the seven sections in this chapter has a list that describes common repair procedures today's rigger might use. While not necessarily encompassing everything, the techniques used in these repairs can be expanded upon to address almost any other scenario that might be encountered. This is acceptable data as referred to earlier in the chapter. If the rigger encounters a repair that he or she is not familiar with, then the rigger should contact the manufacturer for further direction and guidance. The rigger should also remember that each procedure is just one method of accomplishing a given repair. There might be more than one or an individual might develop a different technique to achieve the same results. The exception to this is approved data that requires a specific procedure, rating, equipment, materials, or repair process.

No matter what techniques or procedures that are followed, remember that there are three basic requirements to follow for any proper repair procedure.

1. Knowledge to do the job, to include the required certification and authorization

2. Proper equipment, such as sewing machines or hand tools

3. Availability of the proper materials

The individual may be a master rigger with a complete parachute loft at his or her disposal but, without the materials as used in the original manufacture, the correct repair cannot be made. By following these simple guidelines, riggers are always able to determine whether or not they can do the job properly.

Most of today's manufacturers provide guidance for the repair and maintenance of their products. These instructions are the official guidelines that the rigger must follow. The four primary areas of parachute repair and maintenance are: canopy and lines; container; harness and risers; and accessory components. These areas are summarized within the seven sections of this chapter as follows:

- Section 1—Canopy and lines
- Section 2—Container
- Section 3—Harness and Risers
- Section 4—Accessory Components
- Section 5—Alterations
- Section 6—Manufacturing
- Section 7—Miscellaneous

Section 1, Canopy and Lines

There are two general categories of canopies: round and square. While there are other canopy types, their construction and repair techniques generally follow those of the round and square canopies. *Figure 7-14* shows a round canopy repair table, created from current military manuals, and describes the types and limits of canopy repairs, most of which pertain to military or surplus canopies. It must be mentioned that all of the services differ in their approach to methods of repair. Those called out in this book are methods that have been proven to be practical and efficient and commonly accepted throughout the parachute industry. The techniques are similar with only minor differences in seam dimensions and tolerances. While these limits are practical from the technical point of view, the economic cost may not be in many cases.

NOTE: Ripstop tape is listed in the table as an acceptable repair for certificated round canopies; this table comes from military manuals that have not been addressed or updated

Round Canopy Repairs and Limitations		
Type	Limits	
	Certificated	Non-certificated
Restitching	No limit as to length and number.	No limit as to length and number.
Ripstop tape	Holes or tears not exceeding .5" and snags. Limit: 3 per panel, 10 per canopy.	No limit as to size or number.
Basic patch	Size limit: 50% of panel. Limit: 3 per panel, 15 per canopy.	No limit as to size or number.
Panel patch	Limit: 9 per canopy.	No limit.
Radial seams	Size limit: 12". No more than 4 per canopy.	No limit as to size or number.
Lateral bands upper	Damage size limit: 2". Limit: 1 per canopy.	No limit as to size or number.
Lower	Damage size limit: 36". Limit: 4 per canopy.	No limit as to size or number.
V-tabs	No limit.	No limit.
Pocket bands	No limit.	No limit.
Vent collar ring	No limit.	No limit.
Vent collars	No limit.	No limit.
Suspension lines		
Continuous line	No limit.	No limit.
Noncontinuous line	No limit.	No limit.
Line splice	Not allowed.	Limit: 1 per line, 8 per canopy.

Figure 7-14. *Table of round canopy repairs and limitations.*

for many years but are currently still in use. Contact with current certified parachute manufacturers has proven that none currently recognize or accept this type of repair as an approved procedure and do not recommend the use of ripstop tape on any parachute in production. It is highly advised that before affecting any type of repair with the use of ripstop tape on an approved parachute that the manufacturer be contacted for confirmation and the request of an approval document before completing this type of repair.

Figure 7-15 shows a table of square canopy repairs and limitations. These are for reference only. Not all manufacturers recognize the same types of repairs. The information in this table is an excepted cross-section of allowable repairs. The rigger should consult with the manufacturers to confirm what repairs are allowed on any particular canopy.

Detailed Information on Square Canopy Repairs

Holes or snags smaller than the size of one ripstop box (⅛ inch, 3.2 mm) may remain unrepaired as long as no more than one hole exists within any 10-inch (25.4 cm) circle. A maximum of three such holes or snags per cell are allowed.

Ripstop tape is not authorized for use on parachutes. If the damage is enough to warrant a repair, a sewn repair must be performed. Darning is not a means of repairing any parachute currently in production.

Any hole or tear up to 10 inches (25.4 cm) in length may be repaired by a Senior Rigger as long as the closest area of the completed repair is at least 1 inch from the nearest seam and at least 5 inches from the nearest tape or line attachment. These are minor repairs. Any damage or hole larger than 10 inches (25.4 cm) may be repaired by a Master Rigger, in either direction or involving a seam or tape. This is a major repair.

Any damage that requires a repair of an area that is larger than 50 percent of the total area of a cell skin (upper or lower) requires cell skin replacement and should be returned to the manufacturer.

Master riggers may perform repairs that do not involve taking apart any bartacks on the canopy unless they have the correct bartack machine or equivalent. Special bartack patterns are used that are not normally found in the field. In addition, removal and replacement of these stitch patterns usually weakens the fabric to the point that it is necessary to replace or reinforce portions of the panels. This should also be considered in the repairs of load bearing and non load bearing ribs as most have these types of bartack stitches located at the ends.

Before performing a repair, contact with the canopy manufacturer is very important, as some of these repair standards and limitations may vary slightly.

Materials

Certified canopies should only be repaired using certified materials or equivalent. All replacement materials should come from the manufacturer or meet production quality and shelf life standards. Under-strength thread and fabric is frequently found in the field. The only way to be sure the material meets manufacturer standards is to obtain them directly from manufacturer or locate materials recognized by the manufacturer as acceptable for the repair needed.

The following are the repairs found in Section 1, Canopy and Lines:

- Seam re-stitching
- Canopy ripstop tape repair
- Round and square canopy—basic patch
- Round canopy—panel replacement
- Square canopy—partial panel replacement
- Square canopy—rib repair
- Square canopy—pilot chute attachment point repair
- Round canopy—non-continuous line replacement
- Square canopy—main line replacement
- Square canopy—control line replacement
- Square canopy—crossport repair
- Square canopy—trim check and re-trim

Square Canopy Repairs and Limitations		
Type	**Limits**	
	Certificated	**Non-certificated "Recommendations"**
Restitching	No limit to length and number overstitch 4 to 6 inches from start.	No limit to length and number overstitch 4 to 6 inches from start.
Ripstop tape	Not allowed.	Not allowed.
Basic patch	Size limit 10 inches, senior rigger.	Size limit 10 inches, senior rigger.
Panel patch	50% cell skin, master rigger. Senior rigger, not allowed.	50% cell skin, master rigger. Senior rigger, not allowed.
Suspension lines	Master rigger, no limit. Senior rigger, not allowed.	Master rigger, no limit. Senior rigger, not allowed.
Line splice	Not allowed.	Not allowed.

Figure 7-15. *Table of square canopy repairs and limitations.*

Some methods are covered with older processes and procedures of repair; some include the newest methods as are used by most riggers today. All methods are acceptable to provide a safe and airworthy repair, but it should always be the focus of the rigger to understand all methods and strive to utilize the best possible technique to allow for repairs to be completed to the highest possible standards.

Seam Restitching

- Applicable products: All canopies—round and square; main and reserve

- Description: Replacement of broken or damaged seam threads.

- Authorized repairmen: FAA Senior or Master Parachute Rigger

- Materials: E thread—color to match original

- Machines: 301 straight stitch—light duty 7–11 stitches per inch (SPI), 308 zigzag—medium duty 7–11 SPI

- Equipment: Scissors, seam ripper

Procedure

On lightweight material, the rigger should first set up the machine with similar material and thickness to set the tension of the machine before sewing the actual parachute.

1. Inspect the damaged thread or seam area. If the thread is merely broken or frayed, overstitch the seam with a minimum of 4 to 6 inches at each end.

2. If the seam is gathered or bunched up, it may be necessary to cut the thread in order to smooth out the seam and then overstitch the damaged area with a minimum of 4 to 6 inches at each end. *[Figure A* and *Figure B]*

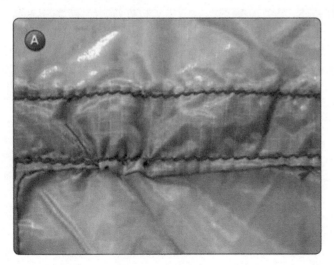

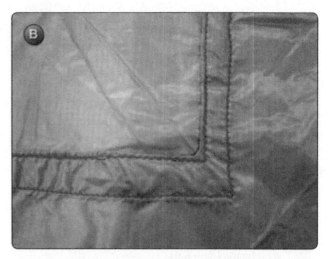

3. If the restitching was done on a radial seam of a round canopy, which has a tape or suspension line within the seam, make sure you did not catch the tape or line in the stitching.

4. For zigzag stitching, such as on suspension lines, a .25 inch overstitch on each end is standard. *[Figure C]*

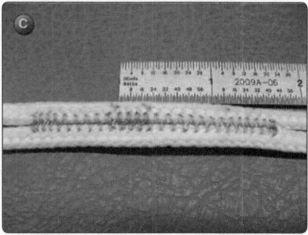

Inspection

- Check that the seam tension and stitch length match the original. Make sure to check top and bottom.

- Make sure that you have not captured any adjacent fabric in the seam. This is a common mistake on square canopies where you may have three panels joining together.

- On radial seams, slide the seam material up and down over the tape or line to check for free movement.

Canopy Ripstop Tape Repair

- Applicable products: All main canopies. Reserve canopies as specified by the manufacturer

- Description: Using ripstop tape for temporary or minor canopy repairs

- Authorized repairmen: FAA Senior or Master Parachute Rigger

- Materials: Ripstop tape—color to match fabric E thread (optional)

- Machines: 301 straight stitch—medium duty 7–11 SPI (optional)

- Equipment: Scissors, shot bags, wallpaper roller, and scotch tape (optional)

Procedure

1. Spread out the canopy on a smooth surface.

2. Smooth out the damaged area and hold in place with the shot bags. *[Figure A]*

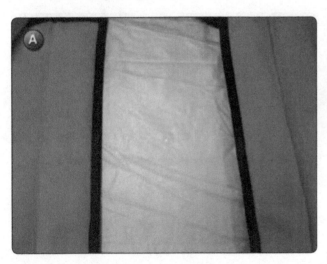

3. Inspect the damaged area.

4. Trim any loose threads and smooth any loose fabric back into place.

5. For small holes, a single-side patch will suffice. For holes up to .5-inch in diameter or a tear, a double-sided patch is necessary.

6. If the damage is a tear, the two sides must be positioned so the edges touch. Use scotch tape to temporarily hold the edges together. *[Figure B]*

7. For a hole, cut a piece of ripstop tape 2 inches square. For a double-sided patch, cut two pieces. *[Figure C]* For a tear, cut the tape approximately 2 inches longer than the length of the tear and cut two pieces.

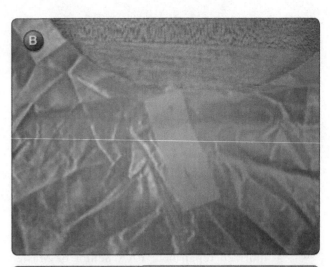

8. For the single-side patch, round the corners with approximately a ⅛ inch radius. For the double-sided patches, place the two pieces face to face and round the corners of both pieces at the same time. This ensures a perfect match and alignment. *[Figure D]*

9. For the 2 × 2 inch patch, peel back one edge of the paper backing and center the tape over the damaged area. Press the exposed adhesive side of the tape to the fabric and smoothly peel the rest of the paper from the fabric with one hand while smoothing the fabric with the other hand. *[Figure E]*

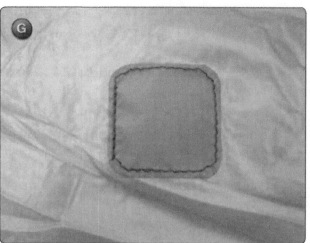

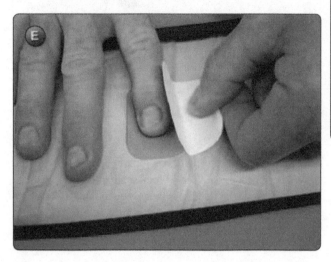

10. Use the wallpaper roller to smooth out the patch and remove any air bubbles from the patch. *[Figure F]*

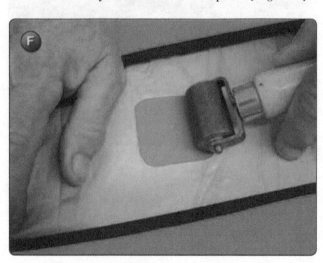

11. For a double-side patch, turn the canopy or damaged material inside out. Align the second piece of ripstop with the edges of the first and repeat the process. Again smooth out the tape with the roller.

12. If the patch is to be a temporary one, the repair is complete. If, however, it is to be permanent, it may be advisable to sew around the edge of the patch. In this case, use the single-needle machine and sew approximately ⅛ inch in from the edge of the tape. Overstitch a minimum of 1.25 inches. *[Figure G]*

NOTE: Ripstop tape has in the past been a commonly used repair material, on F-111 materials, as a short-term repair. Time has shown, however, that the adhesive used can be detrimental to the strength of the fabric over the long term. Consequently, manufacturers do not recommend its use on certificated canopies. In addition, some of the modern, coated fabrics do not accept the use of the ripstop tape without additional sewing to help hold it in place. If the damage requires the use of a sewing machine to complete the repair, it is required of certified parachutes and advised on non- certificated parachutes to utilize the Parachute Patch method, to perform the required repair.

Inspection

- The ripstop should be centered over the damaged area.

- The tape should be smooth with no air bubbles.

- Double-sided patches must be aligned.

- If sewn, tension, edge spacing, and overstitch must be correct.

Round and Square Canopy—Basic Patch Repair

In 1986, R.D. Raghanti, a Production Engineer working as a Master Parachute Rigger , created a new method of parachute repair utilizing the ripstop box configuration as observed on parachute material during production. By utilizing the material "map" ripstop box lines, he created the process of placing repair patches and confirming material replacement during repairs to match the existing grid and establish proper placement of the repair. This process greatly improved parachute repair techniques and is recognized today by most as the industry standard.

- Applicable products: All canopies—round and square; main and reserve

- Description: Application of a basic canopy patch

- Authorized repairmen: FAA Senior or Master Parachute Rigger

- Materials: E thread—color to match; fabric—type and color to match

- Machines: 301 straight stitch—light duty 7–11 SPI

- Equipment: Canopy or material to be repaired, marking pencil, single-needle sewing machine with E thread, ruler, hemostat, scissors, and nippers

Procedure

1. Be sure you have found all the damage.

2. Mark the boundaries of the damage.

3. Allow 2 inches for repair and fudge factor from each boundary.

4. A 6-inch patch will cover approximately 2 square inches of damage. A 7-inch square piece of fabric will be needed to make a 6-inch patch, using ½-inch seam allowance. Always put the patch on the inside of the parachute.

5. Find the center of the damage on the 13½-inch square piece.

6. Measure half the patch size or 3 inches out to the left of the center of damage following one ripstop line in the fabric.

7. Make a center mark and a left border mark (this will look like a T laying on its side).

8. Measure half the patch size or 3 inches up the left border ripstop line from the center line and mark the top border and left border (this will look like an upside down L). *[Figure 7-16]*

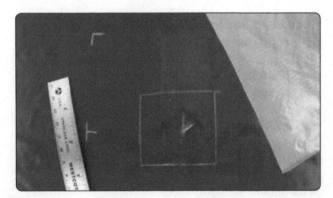

Figure 7-16. *Patch layout.*

9. Count down 10 ripstop boxes from the top border and make a mark. This is the start mark.

10. Count down 14 ripstop boxes from any corner of the 7-inch square piece and make a start mark. *[Figure 7-17]*

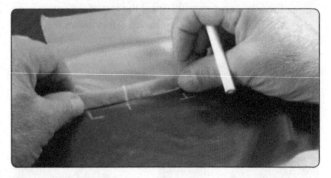

Figure 7-17. *Start point.*

11. Place the 2 start marks on top of each other using the hemostat to hold the 4 block seam allowance in place and sink the needle. Always sew counter clockwise around patches so that the bulk of the parachute does not have to go through the bed of the machine. *[Figure 7-18]*

Figure 7-18. *Start patch to damage.*

12. Count up 4 blocks from the bottom edge of the patch and use the hemostat to form a corner, line up the ripstop boxes, and load each piece with the same pressure. Then, sew to the corner. *[Figure 7-19]*

13. Repeat this step until the first two corners are sewn down. At this point, check the last corner to assure that it will fall in the top and left border marks (upside down L) were made when you the measurement step was completed. Then, sew the last two corners down. *[Figure 7-20]*

14. While sewing, it is important to pull the fabric at the same speed the machine is going and to set the hook in the stitch loop before lifting the foot to turn a corner. Always make a four to six-inch oversew. *[Figure 7-21]*

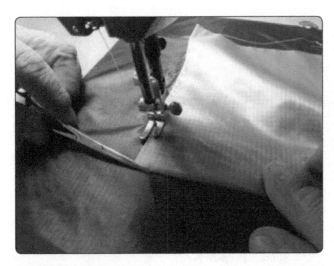

Figure 7-19. *Corner fold.*

Figure 7-20. *Confirming patch alignment.*

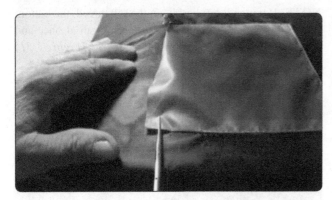

Figure 7-21. *Correct patch tension.*

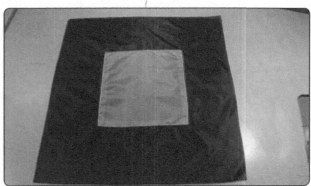

Figure 7-22. *One side inspection.*

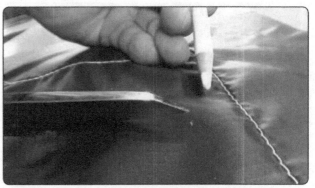

Figure 7-23. *Cutting out damaged area.*

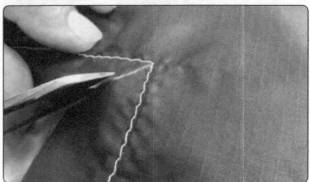

Figure 7-24. *Corner seam cut.*

15. If the fabric was loaded correctly, the patch will be square and will lay flat with no bubble. *[Figure 7-22]*

16. Using the scissors, cut the damage out along the rip stop lines 7 boxes in from the stitching that holds the patch on. Placing your hand between the patch and parachute while trimming prevents damaging your patch with the scissors. *[Figure 7-23]*

17. Make a diagonal cut in each corner to 3 ripstop boxes from the corner. *[Figure 7-24]*

18. Place the work under the sewing machine and, using the hemostat, grab one ripstop box in from the cut edge. Place the parachute fabric behind the fold back of the patch forming a French fell seam. Do this in two places and seat the one box fold back against the patch stitch row with the tip of the hemostat. Sew around the parachute patch repeating this process on each side. *[Figures 7-25 and 7-26]*

19. Take care that each corner is fully seated and square. *[Figure 7-27]*

20. Use the side of the presser foot as a gauge for stitching. *[Figure 7-28]*

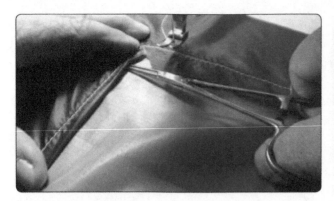

Figure 7-25. *Seam fold.*

Figure 7-26. *Seam corner.*

Figure 7-27. *Correct fold corner seam.*

Figure 7-28. *Correct stitch gauge.*

21. Always make a 4 to 6 inch oversew or turn the next corner on a short legged patch. *[Figure 7-29]*

Figure 7-29. *Correct oversew.*

22. Inspect the work thoroughly. Hold over available light source. *[Figure 7-30]*

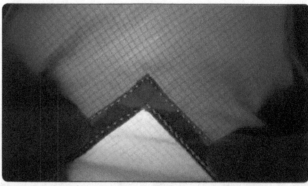

Figure 7-30. *Patch inspection.*

NOTE: If you pull up sharply on the top thread, the bottom thread forms a loop allowing you to cut both at once and remove the bottom thread through the fabric. *[Figure 7-31]*

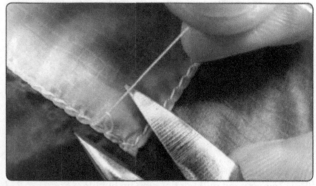

Figure 7-31. *If you pull up sharply on the top thread, the bottom thread will form a loop allowing you to cut both at once and remove the bottom thread through the fabric.*

NOTE: Wear the damaged parachute as if it were a mitten while cutting and you will not cut the patch that was just carefully placed. *[Figure 7-32]*

Figure 7-32. *Wear the damaged parachute as if it were a mitten while cutting and you will not cut the patch that was just carefully placed.*

NOTE: Always grab the work by the threads and remove directly to the rear when removing it from the machine to avoid bunching. *[Figure 7-33]*

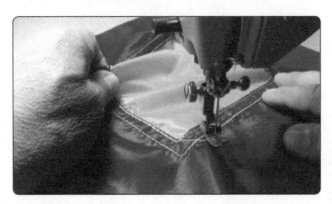

Figure 7-33. *Always grab the work by the threads and remove directly to the rear when removing it from the machine to avoid bunching.*

Round Canopy—Panel Replacement

- Applicable products: All round canopies—main and reserve

- Description: Complete replacement of a panel section of a gore of a round canopy

- Authorized repairmen: FAA Master Parachute Rigger

- Materials: E thread—color to match; fabric—type and color to match

- Machines: 301 straight stitch—light duty 7–11 SPI

- Equipment: Scissors, seam ripper, marking pencil, 6-inch ruler, large pin board, and straight pins

Procedure

This process of replacing the panel is in reality a panel patch and is similar to that used in making a basic canopy patch. Because of the time and difficulty involved in removing and replacing the actual panel, that technique is best left to the canopy manufacturer. This technique is the more commonly accepted practice for major panel repair. The major issue to be

dealt with in this technique is that of the amount of shrinkage that occurs during the repair. The larger the area of the panel, the more shrinkage occurs. The following procedure describes a panel replacement on a block constructed, non-continuous line canopy. A bias constructed canopy is similar but more "fullness" needs to be allowed for in the cutting of the panel and sewing.

1. Lay the canopy inside out on the pin board. Pin the canopy by placing tension on the seams and making sure they are straight.

2. Cut a piece of fabric larger than the damaged panel by approximately 6 inches around all sides. Make sure that the weave of the panel matches that of the canopy. For a block constructed canopy, the bolt of fabric runs parallel down the radial seams of the canopy. For a bias constructed canopy, the bolt runs parallel to the diagonal seams.

3. Trim one side of the panel to align the ripstop weave with the cross seam.

4. Fold over the edge of the panel fabric approximately ¾ inch and pin in place aligning the edge with the outside of the cross seam. *[Figure A]*

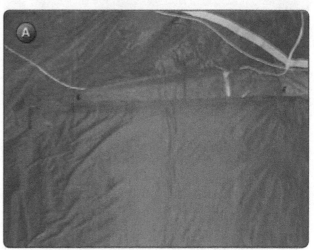

5. Smooth out the panel fabric over the damaged area and align the opposite edge over the opposite cross seam. Cut the panel fabric approximately 1 inch wider than the panel. Fold the edge under and pin in place. You now have the top and bottom cross seams of the panel in place. *[Figure B]*

6. Stitch the outside row of stitching starting and finishing approximately 1 inch short of the radial seams.

7. Take the panel fabric along the radial seam and trim approximately ¾ inch from the outside edge of the radial seam. Fold under and pin in place. Repeat for the opposite radial seam. *[Figure C]*

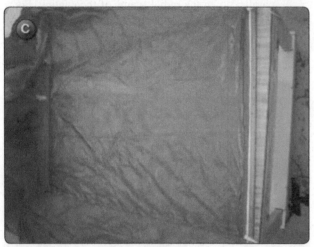

8. Overstitch the end of the cross seam that was left open a minimum of 2 inches and proceed to and down the radial seam and then overstitch the open end of the cross seam. Repeat for the opposite side. It is advisable to hold a bit of tension on the seams as you sew to minimize the shrinkage.

9. Turn the canopy right side out. Trim out the damaged panel along the seams, leaving approximately ⅝ inch. *[Figure D]* Also trim the excess edge of the panel as needed.

10. Fold the edge of the canopy under the panel to create the seam and pin in place.

11. Sew the inside of the panel seam in place. Again, hold tension on the fabric as you sew to minimize shrinkage.

12. Remove the canopy from the machine being careful not to pull on the threads. Trim the threads. Inspect the panel.

Inspection

- Check the weave alignment of the fabric panel to the canopy.

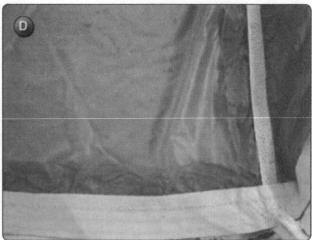

- Check for proper thread tension all around.

- Seams should be straight and parallel.

- The resulting size of the panel should match approximately that of adjacent panels allowing for shrinkage.

Square Canopy—Partial Panel Replacement

- Applicable products: Most main and reserve canopies

- Description: Replacement of a partial panel(s) in a canopy where the extent of the damage necessitates more than a single large or multiple small patches.

- Authorized repairmen: FAA Master Parachute Rigger

- Materials: E thread, fabric—type and color to match

- Machines: 301 straight stitch—light duty 7–11 SPI, 308 zigzag—medium duty 7–11 SPI (optional), 1 inch × 42 stitch bar tack (optional)

- Equipment: Scissors, seam ripper, marking pencil, 36-inch ruler, pin board or large cardboard box folded flat, straight pins, scotch tape or equivalent

Procedure

The method of repair presented in this section is an acceptable data method. It is advised if possible to utilize the R.D. Raghanti process as viewed in the Basic Patch Repair section to allow for higher quality of repair.

NOTE: The repair described in the following procedure is a major tear across the bottom surface of the canopy and includes damage to a non-loadbearing rib.

Disassembly

1. Determine the extent of the damage. Mark out the damaged area across the panel, following the weave of the fabric. Unpick the loaded seams that hold the damaged fabric for at least 8–10 inches past the

damage area mark. It is always easier to unpick more of the seam to allow better access to the damaged area. Restitching the seam is one of the easiest operations. Fighting the canopy is not.

2. Unpick the non-loaded seam the same distance as the loaded seams.

3. Lay the canopy on the floor, take the pin board or cardboard box and position it under the damaged area. Take the scotch tape and tape the raw edges of the tear together to stabilize the panel. *[Figure A]*

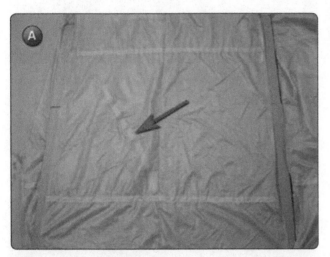

4. Pin the damaged panel to the pin board. Do not overstretch the fabric, but make sure to take all the slack out so the panel is square. In this instance, the canopy had spanwise reinforcing tapes, which were used to stabilize the canopy; however, one of them was damaged and requires replacement.*[Figure B]*

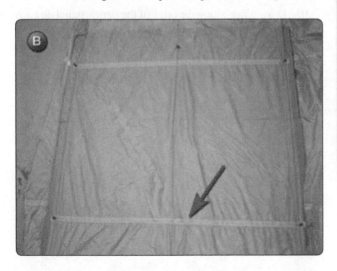

5. Mark a line on the fabric at least 2 inches from the damage area on both sides of the damaged panel. *[Figure C]*

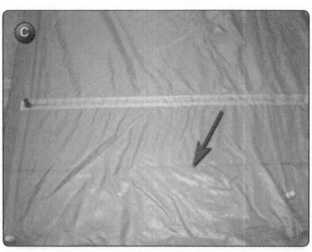

Reassembly

1. Cut a piece of fabric approximately 6 inches wider and longer than the damaged panel area. Make sure that one of the edges is straight and even with the weave of the fabric. Trim one of the adjacent sides at 90 degrees to the straight edge.

2. Mark a line parallel to the straight edge at ¾ inch from the edge. Center the new panel on the damaged one. Fold the fabric on this line and pin in place along the damage line. *[Figure D]* Smooth the new panel fabric over the damaged panel to the opposite side. Trim the new panel ¾ inch longer than the damage line. Fold the fabric at the line and pin in place. *[Figure E]*

3. Check the tension of the two panels. They should be equal.

4. Take a straightedge and mark the location of the spanwise reinforcing tape. *[Figure F]*

5. Sew the panel along the outer edge at .12 inch from the folded edge.

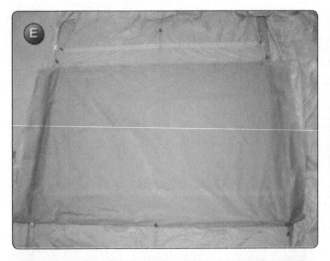

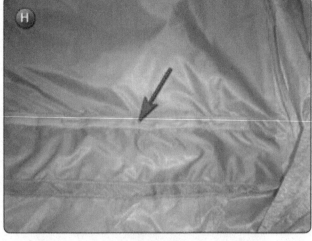

9. Repair the non-loadbearing rib with a three-sided patch. *[Figure I]*

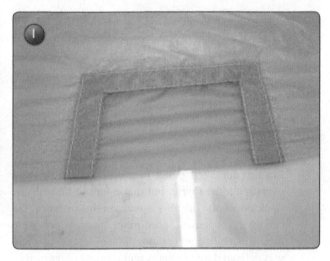

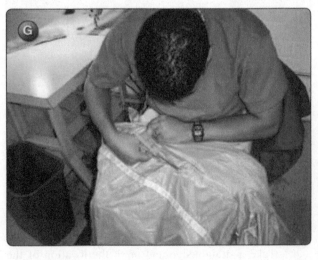

6. Turn the panel inside out. Trim the damaged panel at .62 inch from the edge of the panel edge. *[Figure G]*

10. Draw a line along the edge of the partial panel on each side from the point where the old panel meets the new one. Trim the fabric along this line. *[Figure J]*

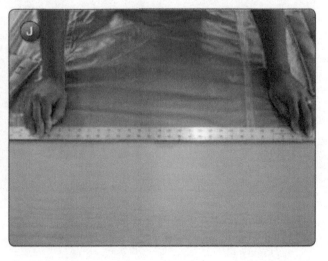

7. Fold the fabric under to create a French fell seam. Sew a stitch row .12 inch from the folded edge.

8. Sew a piece of reinforcing tape on the bottom of the replacement panel along the line for the spanwise reinforcing tape. *[Figure H]*

11. Check the tension of the new partial panel piece against the edges of the other panels that formed the original seam. They should all be equal. *[Figure K]*

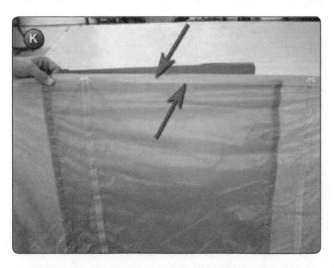

12. Refold the original seam with the three panel edges and stitch as per the original seam. *[Figure L]* Overstitch a minimum of 2 inches on each end.

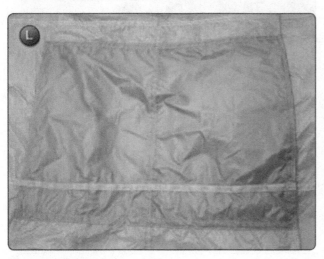

13. If a line attachment has been removed for the repair, the tab must be replaced. Make sure that the line/tab does not have a twist in it. Locate it at the correct location and reattach as per original.

Inspection

- Check the fabric tension of the replaced panel. It should be equal to that in the remainder of the cell.

- Spanwise reinforcing tape should be straight and sewn.

- Seams should be folded correctly and thread tension even along both rows of stitching.

- Line should be attached correctly and have no twists.

Square Canopy—Rib Repair

- Applicable products: square canopies; main and reserve

- Description: Rib repair on a square canopy

- Authorized repairmen: FAA Master Parachute Rigger —mains and reserves; FAA Senior Parachute Rigger—mains

- Materials: E thread; fabric—type and color to match, reinforcing tape—type and color as per original

- Machines: 301 dtraight dtitch—medium duty 7–11 SPI, 1 inch × 42 stitch bar tack, double needle with puller attachment (optional) and SPI to match original

- Equipment: Scissors, seam ripper, marking pencil, ruler, pin board, straight pins, and patching square

Procedure

Repairing a rib of a square canopy is similar to doing a partial panel repair. The biggest difference comes when the rib is either:

1. A "loaded" rib or one with support tapes for the line attachment points, or

2. A crossport is damaged and needs to be repaired and recut. In this case, the crossport area needs replacement. *[Figure A]*

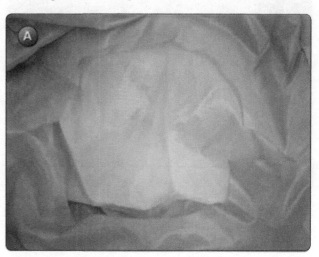

Disassembly

1. Determine the extent of the damaged area and unpick the top and bottom seams to access the rib. *[Figure B]* In most cases, restitching the rib to the top and bottom panels is fairly straightforward. Because of this, opening up the seam for a good distance (18 inches plus either side of the proposed patch) allows easier access and sewing.

2. Pin the damaged rib to the pin board to stabilize the material for marking. Mark out the damaged portion of the panel, following the weave of the fabric.

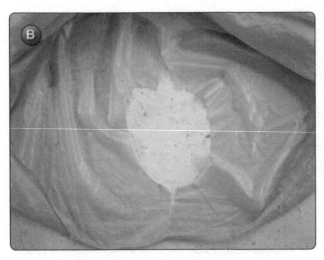

[Figure C] This will be the patch fold lines and the limits of the partial rib panel. **NOTE:** The tears of the crossports have been taped together and that the crossport has been pinned down to stabilize the fabric during the marking process.

4. Fold the new fabric outwards at the patch fold mark and pin in place. Use the patching square to mark a line at .75 inch in from the fold line. *[Figure E]*

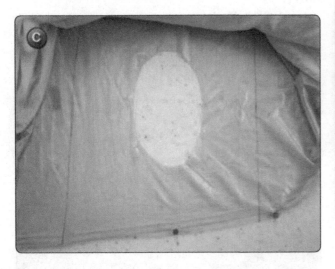

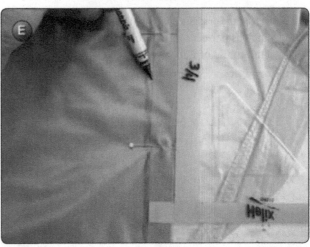

5. Trim the repair panel at the inner line, fold under and pin in place. *[Figure F]*

3. Using the patching square, mark a parallel line .75 inch inside the patch fold lines and then another one .62 inch inside the second line. *[Figure D]* The inner lines are the trim lines for the rib patch.

Reassembly

1. Cut a piece of fabric approximately 4 inches wider and longer than the damaged panel area. Make sure that one of the width edges is straight and even with the weave of the fabric.

2. Fold the straight edge .75 inch from the edge and pin in place across the damage line. Make sure the fabric is centered on the existing panel.

3. Remove the pins from the crossport area and smooth the new panel fabric over the damaged panel.

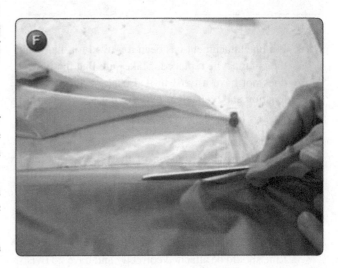

6. Check the tension of the two panels. They should be equal. Mark the top and bottom edges and the crossport location. *[Figure G* and *Figure H]*

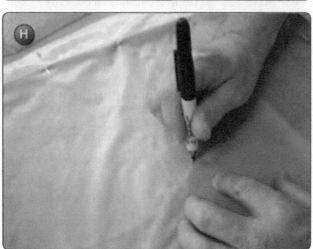

7. Remove the rib from the pin board. Sew the two outboard seams approximately .06 inch from the edge with the single needle. *[Figure I]*

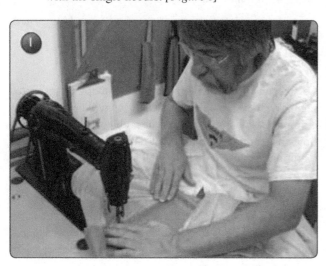

8. Trim the original damaged panel to the trim lines. *[Figure J]* Fold the fabric under to create a French fell seam. Repeat with the opposite seam. *[Figure K]*

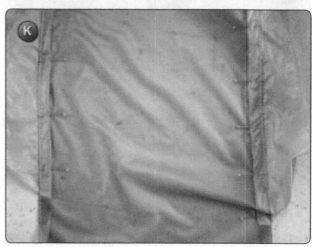

9. Sew the inside row to complete the seam. *[Figure L]*

10. Cut the new crossport to match the original location and shape. *[Figure M]*

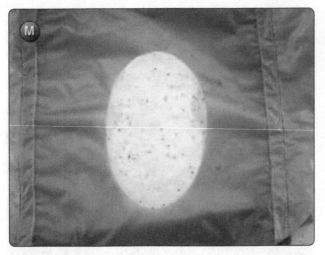

11. Trim the top and bottom edges as marked. *[Figure N]*

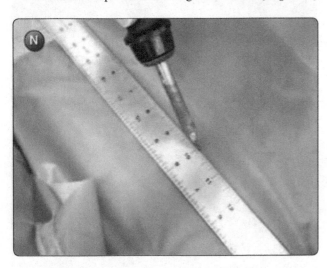

12. Pin the top seam back onto the top panel. Sew in place with either the single needle or if available, with the double needle machine and puller. *[Figure O]* Repeat with the bottom seam.

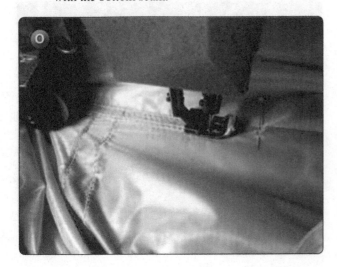

13. Inspect finished work. *[Figure P]*

Inspection

- Seam alignment should be straight.
- Check the tension of the replaced rib material.
- Make sure the seams are restitched correctly.
- Verify that the crossport is cut correctly.
- The line attachment tape must be replaced correctly with no twists in the suspension line.

Square Canopy—Pilot Chute Attachment Point Repair

- Applicable Products: Square main canopies
- Description: Repair of the main canopy pilot chute attachment point.
- Authorized Repairmen: FAA Master Parachute Rigger
- Materials: E thread; fabric—type and color to match, reinforcing tape—type and color to match, reinforcing fabric—type and color to match
- Machines: 301 straight stitch—medium duty 7–11 SPI, 308 zigzag—medium duty 7–11 SPI, 1 inch × 42 stitch bar tack
- Equipment: Scissors, seam ripper, marking pencil, and 12–inch ruler

Procedure

This repair is quite common. If the canopy is inspected regularly, the beginnings of the damage will be noticed and a simple re-stitching will solve the problem. However, many times it is not and the resultant damage is quite extensive requiring repair of the rib, as well as the top panel.

Disassembly

1. Inspect the area to determine the extent of the damage. *[Figure A]* If the stitching that holds the attachment point to the canopy is simply coming loose, re-stitch as per the original.

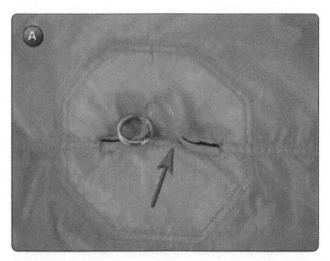

2. If the canopy fabric is damaged, then turn the canopy inside out. The center rib should have a reinforced area that brackets the attachment point. *[Figure B]*

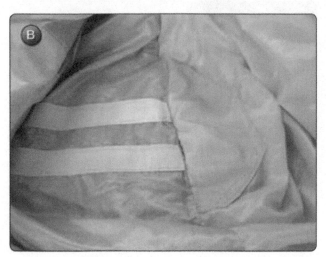

3. Detach the top of the rib from the top surface of the cell where the attachment point is located. *[Figure C]* If the rib is damaged, then a rib repair is needed.

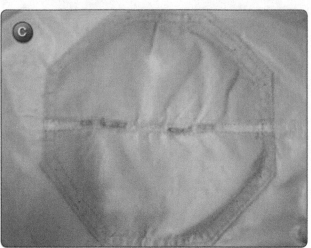

4. Usually the top skin of the cell needs to be repaired. Again, depending on the extent of the damage, either perform a patch on the panel or a partial panel replacement.

Reassembly

1. After the top skin is repaired, a new reinforcement patch needs to be installed on the center of the cell so that it is centered over the attachment point.

2. Take the pre-cut reinforcement panel and sew it in place with two rows of the single-needle machine. The corners should be folded in at a 45 degree angle to eliminate any point loading on the corners. *[Figure D]*

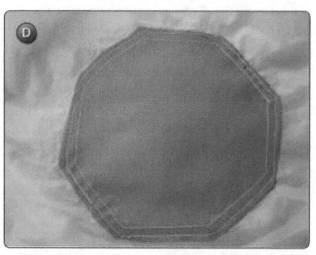

3. Reattach the rib to the top surface of the canopy as per the original configuration.

4. Install a new pilot chute attachment tape and ring at the appropriate location. *[Figure E]*

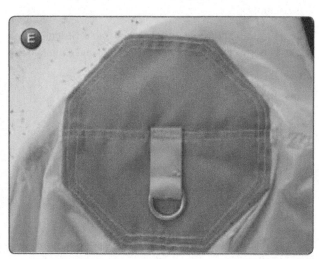

Inspection

- Check that rib and panel repairs have been made as needed.

- Verify the new top reinforcing panel is in place with two rows of single-needle stitching.

- Check the new attachment tape and ring for the appropriate stitch pattern.

Round Canopy—Non-continuous Line Replacement

- Applicable products: Round canopies—main and reserve.

- Description: Replacement of a suspension line on a round canopy with non-continuous line configuration.

- Authorized repairmen: FAA Master Parachute Rigger

- Materials: E thread; Suspension line—type and color to match

- Machines: 308 zigzag—medium duty 7–11 SPI, 1 inch × 42 stitch bar tack (optional)

- Equipment: Packing table, scissors, seam ripper or scalpel, marking pencil, 6-inch ruler, 60-pound fish scale or equivalent, and finger-trapping needle

Procedure

The most common need for this type of repair today is as a result of the suspension line of the reserve being damaged during packing or occasionally during use after landing. The newer, lightweight braided lines are very susceptible to being snagged on the hook portion of Velcro® closures on the container if care is not taken by the rigger.

Disassembly

1. Lay the canopy out on the packing table. Straighten the canopy ensuring the apex is straight and even tension on the lines.

2. Remove the damaged line from the canopy.

Reassembly

1. Cut a new line from the same material as the original approximately 36 inches longer than the damaged line.

2. Pre-stretch the line by applying approximately 10 percent of its rated strength for a minimum of 15 minutes.

3. Attach the line to the connector link in the same manner as the original. Most of the newer canopies use braided line and a finger-trap attachment technique. *[Figure A]*

4. Zigzag or bar tack the line, whichever is appropriate.

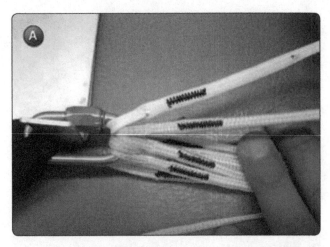

5. Run the free end of the line to the canopy. If the canopy utilizes a V-tab configuration, route the line through the V-tab. *[Figure B]*

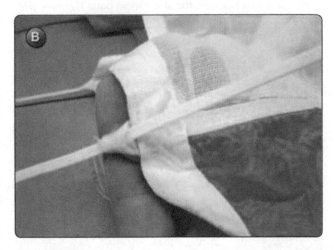

6. Pull the V-tab down until it is even with the rest of the skirt. Mark the line at the edge of the skirt and pin in place. *[Figure C]*

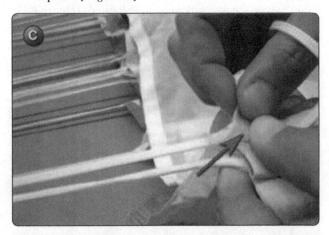

7. Sew the line to the canopy with the zigzag machine duplicating the original manufacture. *[Figure D]* Trim the excess line from the canopy.

8. Return the canopy to the packing table, straighten, and apply tension. Check the trim of the replaced line against the others.

Inspection

• Verify the line length is the same as the original with the same tension.

• The connector link and canopy ends must be sewn correctly.

Square Canopy—Main Line Replacement

• Applicable products: Square main canopies.

• Description: Replacement of main suspension lines of square canopies.

• Authorized repairmen: FAA Senior or Master Parachute Rigger

• Materials: E thread

• Machines: 308 zigzag—medium duty 7–11 SPI, 1 inch × 42 stitch bar tack (optional)

• Equipment: Scissors, seam ripper or scalpel, marking pencil, 6-inch ruler, finger-trapping needle, and 60-pound fish scale or equivalent

Procedure

Many of the modern canopies are using Spectra® or other aramid fibers in place of nylon or Dacron lines. These materials are stronger, lighter, and less bulky. An example is the 825-pound Spectra® line common on many main canopies. The strength is higher but the bulk is smaller than the 525-pound Dacron used in the past. Accordingly, the techniques needed to work this material are more refined and precise.

Disassembly

1. Lay the canopy out on one side and straighten the lines.

2. Remove the damaged line. If the cascade is undamaged, remove the cascade line from the junction of the main line. If the cascade is damaged, remove it as well.

Reassembly

1. Cut a new main line approximately 24 inches longer than the old one.

2. Finger-trap a loop at the connector link end. *[Figure A]* Make sure that the size of the loop duplicates the original or adjacent lines. If the loop is made too small, there may be difficulty in changing connector links or risers as needed. Sew the fingertrap with either a zigzag or bar tack.

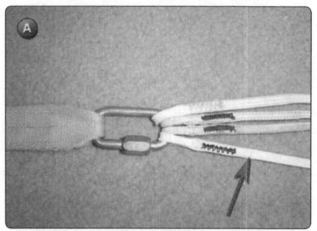

3. Pre-tension the line. With Spectra®, load the line with approximately 30 pounds for 30 seconds. Place the line on the connector link.

4. Feed the running end of the line through the slider and directly to the line attachment tape on the canopy. Make sure that there are no twists to the line or it is around the other lines. Run through the attachment tape and re-create the original knot. *[Figure B]*

5. Tension the line using adjacent lines for reference. *[Figure C]*

6. Mark the location for the entry point for the cascade line. *[Figure D]*

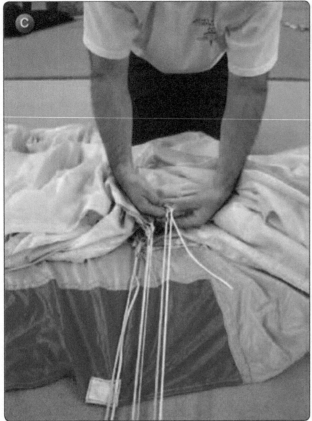

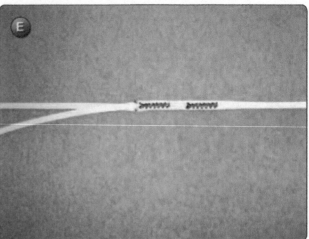

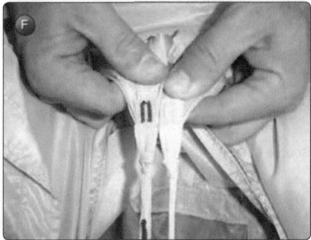

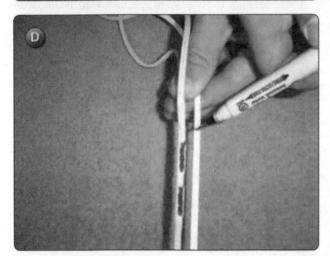

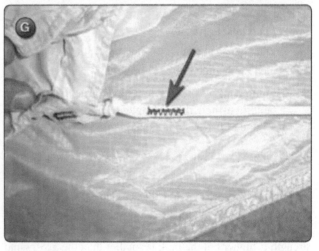

7. Cut a piece of line approximately18 inches longer than the original cascade.

8. Finger-trap the cascade into the main line and sew with either a zigzag or bar tack. *[Figure E]*

9. Attach the main line to the line attachment loop as per the original knot configuration.

10. Tension the line against the adjacent lines and secure the knot. *[Figure F]* Repeat with the cascade.

11. Finger-trap the running end of the lines and sew with either a zigzag or bar tack. *[Figure G]*

Inspection

- Check the length of the main line and the cascade line under tension against adjacent lines.

- Check stitching such as zigzag or bar tacks.

- Check line continuity.

Square Canopy—Control Line Replacement

- Applicable products: Square main canopies

- Description: Replacement of the control line assemblies on square main canopies

- Authorized repairmen: FAA Senior or Master Parachute Rigger

- Materials: E thread—color to match; suspension line—type and color to match. Most control line assemblies utilize two or more types of line: one for the upper control lines and a stronger one for the lower control lines.

- Machines: 308 zigzag—medium duty 7–11 SPI and 1 inch × 42 stitch bar tack (optional)

- Equipment: Scissors, seam ripper, marking pencil, 6-inch ruler, tape measure, and small safety pins with marker flags

Procedure

Some manufacturers provide line measurements for their canopies in their owner's manuals. If so, the rigger should thoroughly measure the control line assembly and compare the measurements against those in the manual. Over time and use, the control lines have a tendency to stretch and change dimensions. At the same time, the rigger needs to compare the right and left side assemblies against each other for any differences. It is not uncommon for the left and right control lines to be different lengths, having been changed to remove a slight turn or change the opening characteristics. *Figure A* is a sample chart that the rigger can fill in to document the various dimensions needed to repair or replace control lines.

Disassembly

1. After measuring the control lines, remove them from one side only. Leave the other side for a reference to check the new lines against both for measurements and construction.

Reassembly

1. Determine how many upper control lines there are on the canopy. Four is the most common and this procedure uses this number for the example. With four upper control lines, there are really two continuous lines forming the assembly. Each pair of upper lines is folded in the middle to form two legs of the upper assembly. Each line is therefore measured at twice the A dimension plus 12 inches. If the upper control lines have different lengths, make sure to use the longest measurement to determine the cut length for A. *[Figure A]*

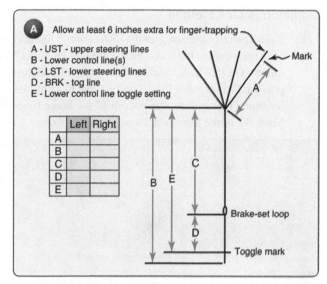

Allow at least 6 inches extra for finger-trapping — Mark

A - UST - upper steering lines
B - Lower control line(s)
C - LST - lower steering lines
D - BRK - tog line
E - Lower control line toggle setting

	Left	Right
A		
B		
C		
D		
E		

Brake-set loop

Toggle mark

2. Using a finger-trapping needle or wire, finger-trap a loop at the center of each of the lines so the result is a line with a loop at the center with two legs extending from it. *[Figure B]* The eye of the loop should be no more than .25 inch with the fingertrapped portion 1 inch long. Bar tack or zigzag the finger-trapped section.

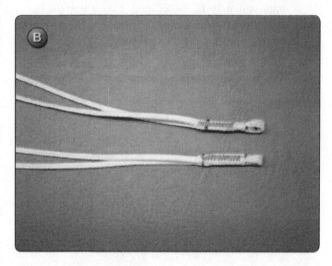

3. There are two types of lower control line configurations: a continuous line and a non-continuous line. The continuous line is one piece with a brake loop finger-trapped into it at the proper location. The non-continuous line consists of two pieces that form the upper lower and lower lower control line, as well as the brake loop. The continuous line configuration is found primarily on the older generation main canopies and on many of today's reserve canopies. The non-continuous configuration is found on most of the modern main canopies due to the ease of replacement because of wear.

Continuous Line Method

1. Take a piece of line used for the lower control line and cut a line equal to the B dimension in *Figure A* plus 12 inches. On this line, measure from one end 8 inches plus the C dimension from *Figure A* and mark at that location. This will be the bottom of the brake loop. Mark the brake loop location according to *Figure C*.

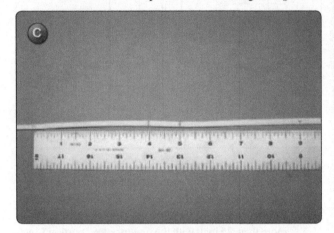

2. Take another piece of the lower brake loop line approximately 12 inches long. Finger-trap the brake loop assembly according to *Figure D*. Make sure the ends are scissor cut and tapered. Bar tack or zigzag the assembly. *[Figure E]*

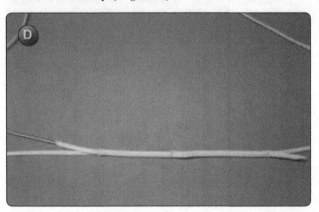

3. Measure and mark the C dimension from the bottom of the brake loop. Run the bitter end of the lower control line thru the eyes of two of the upper control lines and finger-trap the line back into itself. *[Figure F]* Adjust the finger-trap to allow for shrinkage. This completes the continuous line method of lower control line fabrication.

Non-continuous Line Method

1. Take a piece of line used for the lower control line and cut it at the C dimension from *Figure A* plus 12 inches. Mark at 6 inches from one end and finger-trap a loop .5–1 inch long as per *Figure G*.

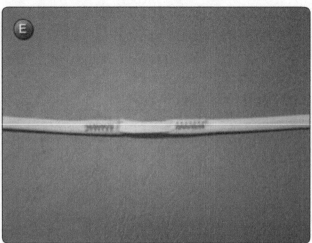

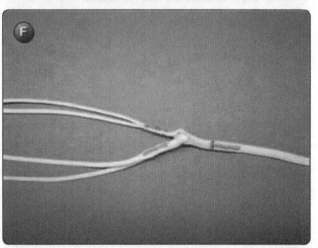

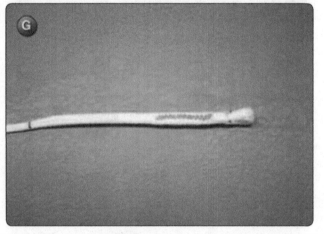

2. Take a second piece of control line material and cut it to the D dimension from *Figure A* plus 12 inches additional. Mark at 6 inches from one end.

3. Finger-trap this line thru the loop at the end of the upper lower control line. Make sure there is a minimum of 4 inches finger-trapped in the line and that the lower loop is tight against the upper loop.

4. Bar tack or zigzag the finger-trapped portions to secure them. *[Figure H]*

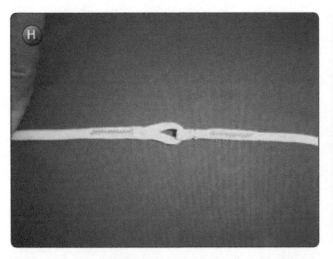

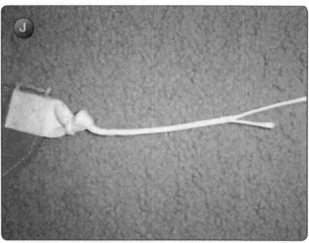

5. Measure and mark the C dimension from the bottom of the brake loop. Run the bitter end of the lower control line thru the eyes of two of the upper control lines and finger-trap the line back into itself. Adjust the finger-trap to allow for shrinkage. This completes the non-continuous line method of lower control line fabrication.

6. Measure the upper control lines according to dimension A plus .5 inch. If the upper control lines are of uneven dimensions, make sure that they are marked accordingly.

7. Lay the canopy on the floor with the trailing edge flat and straight and the line attachment tabs exposed. Lay the upper control lines so that they run to the correct attachment points and route them through the tabs. *[Figure I]*

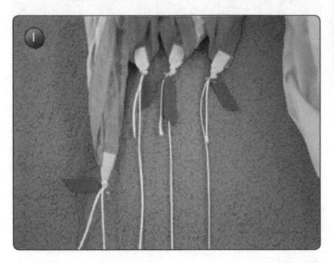

8. Make sure that the lines do not have a twist in them and finger-trap the lines back into themselves with a minimum of a 4 inches finger-trap. Leave the running ends exposed. *[Figure J]* Do not trim the excess line.

9. Anchor the brake loop securely and apply tension through the complete control line assembly. Measure the dimension A plus B starting at the outside corner of the trailing edge. Adjust the tension of the finger-trap to allow for shrinkage. Pin the finger-trapped section with a marker flag. *[Figure K]* Repeat with each upper control line until complete.

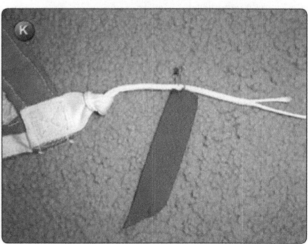

10. After setting the dimension for each upper control line, bar tack or zigzag each section. Trim the excess so that the end retreats into the line.

11. Measure the dimension D on the lower control line to set the toggle location. *[Figure L]* If the canopy is on risers, route the lower control line thru the guide ring and tie the steering toggle in place.

Inspection

- Check finished dimensions against original dimensions according to *Figure A*.

- Check that all finger-trapped junctions are secured with either a bar tack or zigzag.

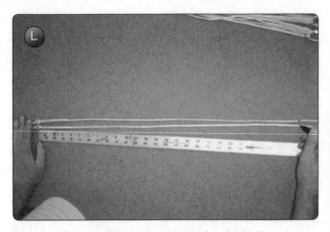

- Make sure that there are no twists in the lines.
- Check that the steering toggles (if used) are tied on securely.

Square Canopy—Crossport Repair

- Applicable products: Square main canopies with crossports
- Description: Repair of damaged crossports in square main canopies
- Authorized repairmen: FAA Senior or Master Parachute Rigger
- Materials: E thread—color to match; fabric—type and color to match
- Machines: 301 straight stitch—medium duty 7–11 SPI
- Equipment: Scissors, seam ripper or scalpel, marking pencil, 6-inch ruler, pin board, straight pins, patching triangle, and hot knife

Procedure

There is no limit as to how many crossports may be repaired on a main canopy. Reserve canopies are another matter. The number and authority to repair crossports on a reserve varies between manufacturers. Before attempting to repair the crossports of a reserve, first check with the manufacturer.

Disassembly

1. Many times, when the crossport is damaged, there is extensive gathering and distortion of the fabric. Before progressing, smooth out the fabric to reshape the rib as close as possible to its original shape.

Reassembly

1. The basic idea of the crossport repair is a three-sided patch sewn the same as a standard French fell seam patch. The fourth side is open and re-cut to the shape of the crossport. *[Figure A]* However, if the damage

is extensive enough, it may be advisable to patch the complete crossport area and then re-cut the crossport in its original shape with a hot knife.

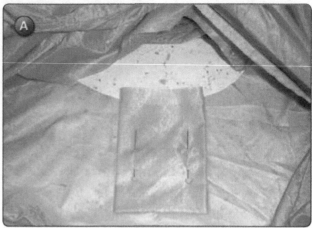

2. Pin the rib to the pin board.
3. Mark out the damaged area as you would a standard patch. Lay the patch material in place and pin.
4. Sew the patch in place with a seam $\frac{1}{16}$ inch from the edge.
5. Turn the patch over, fold the seam, and sew as a standard patch. *[Figure B]*

6. Lay the repaired rib on a suitable surface and re-cut the crossport shape in the exposed edge of the patch material with the hot knife. *[Figure C]*

Inspection

- Verify the seams of the patch are even and thread tension is correct.
- Hot knifed edge of the crossport must be smooth and even.

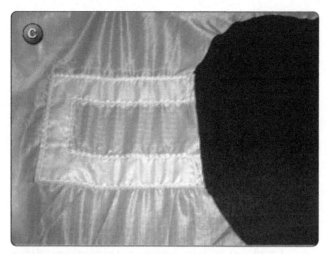

Square Canopy—Trim Check and Re-trim

- Applicable products: Square main canopies

- Description: Re-trimming the suspension lines of main canopies to return to the original trim specs

- Authorized repairmen: FAA Senior or Master Parachute Rigger

- Materials: E thread

- Machines: 308 zigzag—medium duty 7–11 SPI or 1 inch × 42 stitch bar tack (optional)

- Equipment: Scissors, seam ripper or scalpel, marking pencil, 6-inch ruler, 25-foot tape measure, and pony clamp

Procedure

Checking and re-trimming main canopies is a common requirement for riggers. All canopies and all kinds of suspension lines get out of trim in time with use. The rigger that knows how to quickly check the trim on a customer's canopy, and then determine how much work it takes to return it to the original configuration is performing a valuable service. In most cases, as long as the suspension lines are in good condition, re-trimming a canopy adds hundreds of jumps to the life of the canopy and returns the performance to almost as good as new. The chart shown in *Figure A* is tailored to apply to normal ram-air canopies. Certain designs, such as elliptical canopies, may have nonstandard trim measurements that require more detailed measurements. The rigger should consult the manufacturer's manuals or technical data for these canopies.

Disassembly

1. The first thing the rigger must do is to complete a measurement of the lines of the canopy. The chart in *Figure A* shows a matrix for measuring the lines of the canopy. Simply fill in the boxes for each dimension measured.

2. Start by laying the canopy on the left side, anchor the connector links, and flake it out as if for packing. Most canopy lines are measured from the inside of the connector links, which is called the zero point.

3. Anchor the end of the tape measure even with the zero mark at the end of the lines using the pony clamp. [*Figure B*]

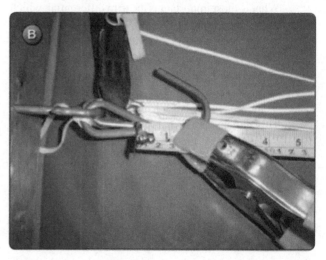

4. Start with the top outside right front corner line of the canopy. This line will be line 1A. Depending on the number of cells to the canopy, on a 7-cell canopy, the left corner line will be line 8A. On a 9-cell canopy, this line will be line 10A. Make sure that the canopy is oriented correctly so that the measurement sequence follows the boxes on the chart.

Line	10	9	8	7	6	5	4	3	2	1
A										
B										
C										
D										
UST	Left				Right					
	1	2	3	4	5	6	7	8	9	10
LST										
BK-TOG										

5. Measure all the A lines first and then proceed to the B, C, and D line groups. The lines should be measured under approximately 10 pounds of tension. As the rigger moves through the lines and changes riser groups, the end of the tape measure should be moved to the corresponding connector link and re-clamped.

6. Measure the control line groups and fill in the boxes.

Reassembly

1. Compare the measurements to the original line lengths as in the manual.

2. Depending on the type of canopy and type of line used, most canopies tend to have the center A lines stretch due to the load on opening. The outside lines that attach to the stabilizers and the control lines tend to shrink due to the friction generated by the slider on opening. The key concept to remember is that the length of the lines is not the critical dimension. What is most important is the trim differential, which determines the angle of attack of the canopy. The trim differential is the difference in the line length between the A, B, C, and D lines. The most accurate method of measuring this is to use the A lines as the base dimension and then measure A-B, A-C, and A-D. This method takes into consideration the tolerance allowed. This dimension is what makes the canopy open and fly correctly. If the overall length of the lines is 2–3 inches longer or shorter, but the trim is correct, there is probably no appreciable effect on the canopy. With this in mind, it may be desirable to "shortline" the canopy during the trim process in order to not have to replace any main lines.

3. Because of the fact that the cascaded main lines may stretch at different rates, the adjustment to be made to the lines that have stretched (i.e., gotten longer) needs to be done at the canopy end and not at the connector link.

4. Remove the bar tacks or zigzag stitching at the canopy end of the lines.

5. Adjust the line length as needed to return to the original dimensions. Re-tie the knots or finger-trap as necessary and re-sew as per the original.

6. For the lines that may have shrunk in length, it may be possible to gain as much as 2–3 inches of line adjustment by utilizing the extra line that is finger-trapped into each line attachment point. Depending on the type of line used on the canopy, the amount of excess line finger-trapped may vary. Dacron lines can have as little as 2–3 inches inserted into the finger-trap and hold securely. The smaller and more slippery Spectra® line is recommended to have at least 6 inches

of line inserted into the finger-trap. So, depending on the amount of line that is needed to be gained for the trim adjustment, the rigger may be able to adjust each end of the line to gain the necessary adjustment.

7. If this needed line can be gained, remove the bar tacks or zigzag at each end of the line and reattach after adjusting the length. Before permanently attaching, the rigger should simply tie the lines in place and check the trim. If everything is within limits, then re-tie or finger-trap and re-stitch with bar tacks or zigzag as per the original.

Inspection

- Check final trim dimensions against original

- Check continuity so there are no twists or crossed lines

- Verify all junctions are either knotted or finger-trapped and sewn as per the original

Section 2, Container

Container repairs share some techniques with canopy repairs, such as single-side patches. Most repairs, however, involve replacement of panels or flaps, Velcro®, grommets, plastic stiffeners, worn binding tape, and broken hand tackings. Even more so than canopy repairs, the cosmetic results of the container repair are most important to the customer and, thus, the rigger. A shoddy repair to the container is immediately obvious each time the user puts on the parachute. Even if it is functional, it has to look good to instill confidence in the user.

The following are repairs found in Section 2, Container:

- Container fabric panel repair

- Container grommet replacement

- Container Velcro® replacement

- Container plastic stiffener replacement

- Main container side flap replacement

- Bottom of container (BOC) pocket replacement

- 3-ring release housing replacement

Container Fabric Panel Repair

- Applicable products: All types of parachute container systems.

- Description: Application of a patch repair to container panels.

- Authorized repairmen: FAA Senior or Master Parachute Rigger

- Materials: E thread—color to match; fabric—type and color to match; nylon tapes—assorted types and widths, such as Type-3, Type-4, or Type-12

- Machines: 301 straight stitch—medium duty 7–11 SPI and 308 zigzag—medium duty 7–11 SPI

- Equipment: Scissors, seam ripper or scalpel, marking pencil, 6-inch ruler, hot knife, hot glue gun, butane lighter, ripstop tape (optional), and straight pins

Procedure

Besides holding the canopy, the container's main function is to protect the canopy from damage. To that end, a certain amount of wear and damage is to be expected. The most common repairs involve re-stitching broken threads and binding tape repairs. Other damage involves tears, punctures, and fabric abrasion. The appropriate repair varies according to need. There are five primary repair procedures to basic panel repairs: re-stitching, binding tape repair, hidden patches, overlay patches, and single-side fabric patches.

Disassembly

1. Remove all extraneous parts from the container, including canopies, handles, toggles, etc.

2. Inspect the damaged area to determine which repair method is appropriate.

Reassembly
Restitching

1. Using the same type and color of thread, sew directly over the original stitching. The amount of overstitch may vary according to location. If the affected area is completely exposed and accessible, overstitch the ends of the damaged area a minimum of 1.25 inches. If this is not possible, then backstitch a minimum of 3 stitches to lock the ends. Repair complete.

Binding Tape Repair or Splice

1. Many times the binding tape is worn through due to bridle abrasion or other wear patterns. *[Figure A]* Rather than remove the panel and rebind it, a practical and cost effective repair is to overlay a section of new binding over the damaged area.

2. Cut a piece of binding tape a minimum of 1 inch longer than the damaged area. Scissor cut the tape and then lightly sear with the butane lighter. *[Figure B]* If the tape is cut with a hot knife and then folded, the cut edge cracks at the hot-knifed end. Searing with the lighter results in a more flexible end. Fold the tape in half lengthwise to form a crease. Take a marking pencil and mark the crease. *[Figure C]*

3. Overlay the new tape over the damaged area and mark the start of where the new tape begins and covers the damaged area completely. *[Figure D]*

4. Overstitch the original tape on the inside row up to the point where the new tape is to start. Leave the needle in the material. Place the folded tape over the damaged area and hold tightly in place. Make sure that the edge is pushed up against the original and the end is against the needle. *[Figure E]* The next stitch should catch the new tape.

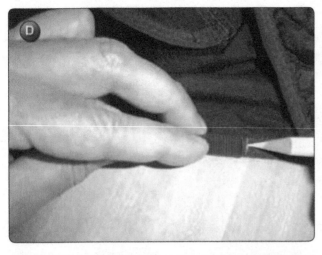

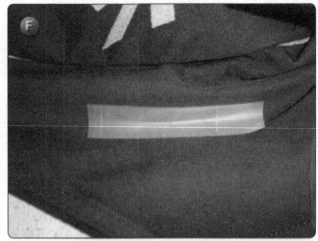

5. Stitch the new piece and overstitch the end a minimum of 1.25 inches or 3 stitches. Repeat with the outside row of stitches. Repair complete.

Hidden Patches

This type of repair has never had a name, but it is self-descriptive. It works well on tears and punctures. Done properly, it is a very cosmetic and cost effective repair.

1. Take a piece of adhesive tape and place on the outside of the damaged area to hold the edges together. *[Figure F]*

2. Turn the panel inside out, take the glue gun and glue a small piece of Type-3 tape 1 inch longer over the damaged area. *[Figure G]* Do not fold the ends under. Remove the adhesive tape from the outside.

3. Stitch around the outer perimeter of the Type-3 tape using matching colored thread to the container fabric. If necessary, increase the upper thread tension so that the outside (bottom) thread shows good tension.

4. Take the zigzag machine, again with matching color thread, and set the stitch width to its widest setting and 7–11 SPI length. Overstitch the exposed edges of the cut area to draw them together. *[Figure H]* Repair complete.

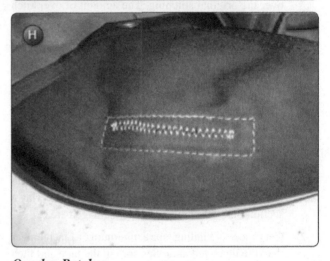

Overlay Patches

These are similar to a fabric patch but use a piece of tape or webbing to cover the damaged area. In effect, it is the same as the hidden patch but usually larger and is on the outside of the panel. It is a sturdy patch but not very cosmetic.

1. Using a hot knife, cut a piece of tape or webbing, such as Type-12, big enough to cover the damaged area. Allow enough to fold the cut ends under. Fold the ends under and glue down to itself. *[Figure I]*

2. Lay the patch in place over the damaged area and mark the corners with a marking pencil. *[Figure J]*

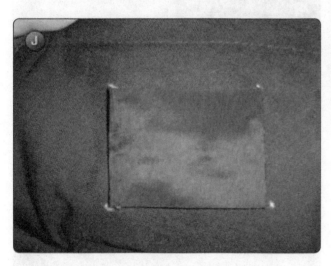

3. Take a straight pin and transfer the corners of the patch area through to the inside. *[Figure K]*

4. If on a main container, take a piece of Type-3 tape big enough to match the outside patch as marked. Cover the inside of the damaged area with the tape.

5. Pin or glue the tape patch to the inside as marked. Use the single needle to sew around the patch overstitching the ends a minimum of 1 inch.

6. Take the zigzag machine and stitch the edges of the damaged area together as described in step 4, Hidden Patches. *[Figure L]* Repair complete.

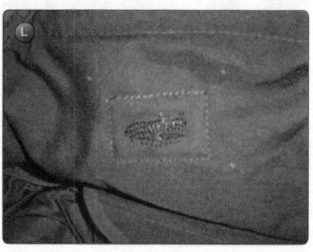

Single-Side Fabric Patches

For most fabric patches on a container panel, there is not enough area to perform a proper French fell seam patch. Consequently, the single-side patch is the most common technique used. By using matching fabric and thread, a large damaged area may be covered to affect the necessary repair. While called a single-side patch, in effect it is an enlarged version of the overlay patch. A smaller piece of webbing or fabric is used to cover the damaged area on the inside and the outside is covered with the single-side patch. This technique is used where there may be large holes or widespread damage and replacement of the panel is not practical.

1. Duplicate steps 1–5 that was used in the "Overlay Patches" section above but substitute webbing for the inside patch and use container fabric for the outside patch.

2. Fold the edges of the outside patch under a minimum of .5 inch. Stitch around the perimeter approximately .12 inch from the edge. Run a second row of stitches approximately .25 inch inside and parallel to the first. *[Figure M]* This gives added strength to the patch and an appearance of a French fell seam patch. Repair complete.

Inspection

- Check thread tensions, stitches per inch, and overstitch lengths.

- Damaged area must be covered completely.

- For the overlay and single-side patches, make sure the stitch patterns catch both sides of the patch materials completely.

Container Grommet Replacement

- Applicable products: All types of containers that use grommets

- Description: Replacement of damaged grommets of all types

- Authorized repairmen: FAA Senior or Master Parachute Rigger

- Materials: E thread—color to match; grommets—size, type, and material to match

- Machines: 301 straight stitch—medium duty 7–11 SPI, 308 zigzag—medium duty 7–11 SPI

- Equipment: Scissors, seam ripper or scalpel, marking pencil, 6 inch ruler, grommet die set—size to match grommets, leather mallet, grommet cutting board, hole punch to match grommet size, basting tip (optional), and diagonal wire cutters—8 inch minimum

Procedure

There are many types of grommets used in parachute container manufacture. Older style military surplus containers used flat grommets made of brass with a chrome finish, which were designed to work with cones. Most modern container systems use rolled rim spur grommets and washers. The most common size is the "O." For many years, regular brass grommets were used and then nickel plated ones became the norm. In recent years, stainless steel has come to be the preferred type due to the ability to resist deformation and corrosion. Today,

there are two types of "O" stainless grommets. The first is the regular or "short shank." Recently, a long shank version has become available. It has proven to be very versatile and popular. This repair procedure focuses primarily on the "O" spur grommet and washer, but the technique can be applied to all types of grommets.

Disassembly—Grommet Replacement

This is for replacing a damaged grommet or changing from brass to stainless steel. Use the cutters to remove the grommet. If the grommet is set into a fabric/webbing base, fold the material back to expose the washer. Using the diagonal cutter, cut through the washer and then peel it back from the grommet. *[Figures A and B]* Grasp the grommet and peel it from the material.

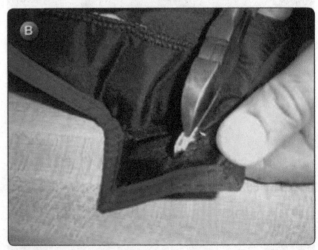

Reassembly—Grommet Replacement

If the hole is intact and undamaged, simply insert the replacement grommet into the material from the correct side, and set with the grommet die. Make sure that the grommet is set sufficiently so that there is no exposed edge to snag lines or material.

Material Repair and Grommet Replacement

If, after removing the grommet, the fabric is damaged so that the grommet cannot be set properly, use the zigzag machine to stitch around the perimeter of the hole, reducing its size. *[Figure C]*

1. Take the basting tip and pass it through the hole, searing the material. *[Figure D]* This solidifies the frayed and raw edge of the damaged material.

2. Set the grommet in the repaired hole. *[Figure E]*

Inspection

- Check the grommet orientation.
- Grommet must be set tightly.
- There should be no sharp edges on inside of grommet.

Container Velcro® Replacement

- Applicable products: Most parachute assemblies that use Velcro®

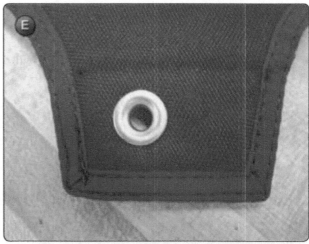

- Description: Main riser cover Velcro® replacement
- Authorized repairmen: FAA Senior or Master Parachute Rigger
- Materials: E thread—color to match; Velcro®—color, width, and type to match
- Machines: 301 straight stitch—medium duty 7–11 SPI
- Equipment: Scissors, seam ripper or scalpel, marking pencil, and 6-inch ruler

Procedure

The name Velcro® is a trade name for what is known as "pressure sensitive hook and loop fastener." It is a commonly used material for closure systems. Before the advent of Velcro®, snaps and zippers were the preferred method of closing containers. Velcro® changed how the parachute industry designed products. In the late 1970s and early 1980s, there was a tendency to overdo the use of Velcro® and problems with durability and interaction with other materials became known. Since then, the use of Velcro® has been reduced to those applications where it is superior to other methods and can be easily replaced.

Disassembly

1. Identify the nature of the use of the Velcro®. Before you remove the piece, note how it is attached to the container. Some designs are such that several layers of construction have to be reversed to get to the location where the Velcro® was sewn on. If this is the case, the rigger may have to make a very expensive repair to replace a small piece of Velcro®.

Reassembly

1. Cut the replacement Velcro® to size. Velcro® is normally scissor cut, not cut with a hot knife.

2. Position the Velcro® and stitch around the perimeter at .12 inch from the edge. For any pieces, 1 inch in width or wider, sew a row of stitching down the center. *[Figure A]* This prevents the center from being pulled up from the material and loading the outside row of stitching. *[Figure B]*

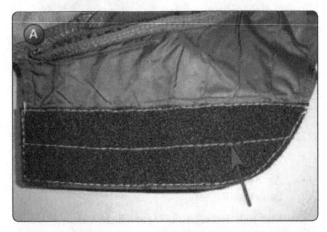

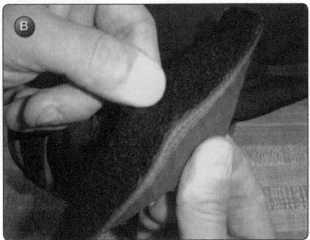

3. Some applications have the Velcro® sewn to a piece of tape for support. Again, if it is 1 inch or more wide, sew down the center to prevent lifting.

4. Depending on the application, the mating loop piece of Velcro® may be wider than the hook to provide additional protection. That is, the hook may be .75 inch wide and the loop 1 inch wide.

Inspection

- Check that thread tension is correct.
- Verify orientation is correct.
- Check that center stitching is used where needed.

Container Plastic Stiffener Replacement

- Applicable products: All types of containers that use plastic stiffeners

- Description: Replacement of damaged plastic stiffeners of all types

- Authorized repairmen: FAA Senior or Master Parachute Rigger

- Materials: E thread—color to match; grommets—size, type, and material to match; and plastic stiffeners—type and thickness to match

- Machines: 301 straight stitch—medium duty 7–9 SPI and 308 zigzag—medium duty 7–11 SPI

- Equipment: Scissors, seam ripper or scalpel, marking pencil, 6-inch ruler, grommet die set—size to match grommets, leather mallet, grommet cutting board, hole punch to match grommet size, basting tip, diagonal wire cutters—8 inch minimum, heavy shears or tin snips, electric drill and ⅜ inch drill bit, and feeler gauge—.010 inch

Procedure

The term "plastic," when used in conjunction for the materials used as stiffeners in modern parachute containers, is a misnomer. In reality, the composition of the material varies. The most common material used today is molydisulfide (MDS) nylon. In addition, Lexan®, a clear polycarbonate material and high density polyethelyne (HDPE), are also used. The most common thicknesses used are .025 inch, .040 inch, and .060 inch, which are standard commercial thicknesses commonly available. Stiffeners are used primarily as backing for grommets to spread the load placed on closing flaps. Instead of focusing the load on the diameter of the grommet, it is spread out across the length of the stiffener, resulting in a smoother flap and container. Consequently, replacing plastic stiffeners almost always requires replacing the grommet as well. Usually the plastic breaks at the grommet location because the hole for the grommet is the weak point. The following procedure shows the replacement of the bottom main flap stiffener of a Javelin container.

Disassembly

1. Unpick the stitching that holds the binding tape to the bottom flap. *[Figure A]* Remove the grommet.

2. Remove the stitching that holds the stiffener in position. Remove the stiffener.

Reassembly

1. Use the original stiffener as a template to cut a new stiffener. *[Figure B]* While many of the older containers use HDPE or other materials, most of the newer designs use MDS nylon because of its superior properties. Because of this, many riggers use MDS exclusively for replacing any stiffeners.

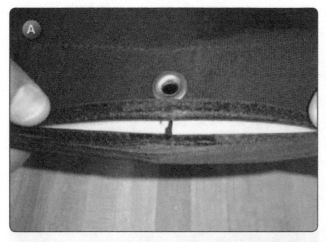

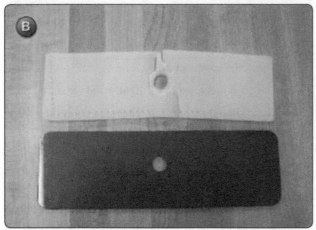

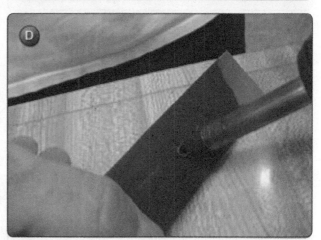

2. Mark out the outline of the original stiffener on the MDS. Mark the center of the hole for the grommet very precisely.

3. Use the basting tip to mark the center of the hole for the grommet. Push the tip through the MDS until the shoulder of the tip makes an indentation in the MDS. *[Figures C, D, and E]* This forms a pilot hole for the drill.

4. Using heavy shears or tin snips, cut the MDS nylon to shape. Clip the corners to remove the sharp ends and, if the edges are sharp or rough, sand them with sandpaper.

5. Secure the MDS against a piece of wood and drill a ⅜ inch hole. While this hole may seem big for the shank of the grommet, when installed and the material is punched, it will be the right size. A common mistake is to make the hole too small and when the grommet is set, it cracks the plastic.

6. Insert the stiffener in between the layers of fabric of the bottom flap and let it float inside.

7. Baste the two layers of fabric together with the single needle.

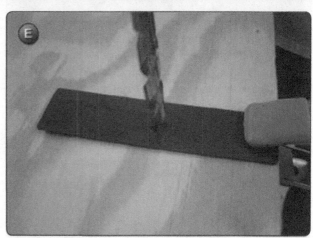

8. Restitch the binding to the bottom flap. *[Figure F]*

9. Slide the stiffener to the edge of the flap and align the hole in the stiffener with the hole in the fabric. Use an "O" grommet to align the holes. *[Figure G]*

10. Stitch the stiffener in place as per the original installation.

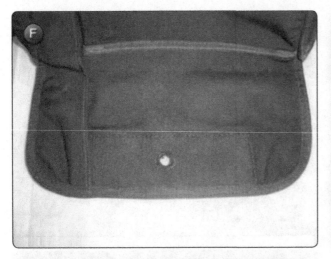

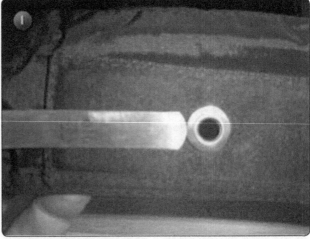

11. Insert the grommet with the correct orientation and set with the grommet set. *[Figure H]* Make sure that the grommet is set sufficiently so there is no exposed edge to snag the lines or material. Use the feeler gauge to check the gap under the edge of the grommet. *[Figure I]* It should be no more than .010 inch. If more, hit the set again to tighten the grommet.

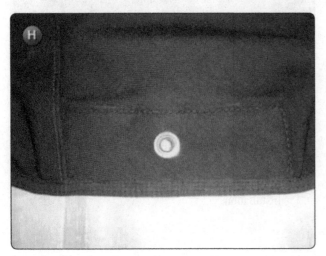

Inspection

- Verify the stiffener backing is re-sewn.
- Check the grommet orientation.
- The grommet must be set tightly and measured.
- There should be no sharp edges on the inside of the grommet.

Main Container Side Flap Replacement

- Applicable products: Most modern container systems
- Description: Replacement of a main container side flap
- Authorized repairmen: FAA Senior or Master Parachute Rigger
- Materials: E thread—color to match; Type-3¾ inch tape—color to match, replacement flap
- Machines: 301 straight stitch—medium duty 5–9 SPI, 308 zigzag—medium duty 7–11 SPI, 301 double needle with tape folder 5–9 SPI, and 1 inch × 42 stitch bar tack
- Equipment: Scissors, seam ripper or scalpel, marking pencil, 6-inch ruler, and hot knife

Procedure

The following technique is typical of many modern container systems. This procedure addresses only the disassembly of the container and replacement of the factory made part. It does not address the manufacture of a replacement part.

Disassembly

1. Remove all extraneous parts from the harness/ container assembly.
2. Open the bottom corner of the main container on the appropriate side.

3. It is necessary to remove the Type-3 binding tape on the inside seam joining the main body to the side flap. Depending on the container construction configuration, there are two options how to do this:

- Option 1: salvage method. With this method, the binding tape is left undamaged and sewn back in place after replacing the flap. A slower method, but good if the rigger does not have the necessary replacement tape.

  - Using a seam ripper, unpick the two rows of stitching that holds the side flap to the main container. *[Figure A]* Start at the lower corner and continue until approximately 2 inches past where the side flap joins the riser cover.

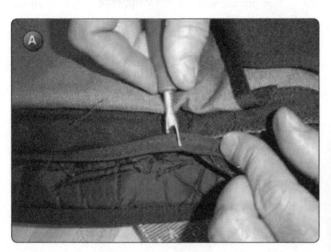

  - Remove the side flap.

- Option 2: replacement tape method. With this method, the binding tape is destroyed during the removal process and replaced with new. A faster method, but new tape is required.

  - Use a hot knife to melt the stitching that holds the binding tape that attaches the side flap to the main container. *[Figure B]* When doing this, have the side of the tape that faces the damaged side flap facing up in case you slip so the wrong flap is not damaged. Proceed to the point where the side flap stops. Trim the melted tape at this point.

  - Using a seam ripper, unpick the tape approximately 2 inches past the end of the side flap. Remove the side flap.

Reassembly

1. Take the new flap and sew it in place on the main container starting approximately .38 inch from the

corner. *[Figure C]* On this design and others like it, the lower end of the main riser cover is unstitched during removal of the main flap. When sewing the new flap in place, make sure that the side flap is sewn to the main container first and then the riser cover on top of it. Look at the opposite side to see which is on top and duplicate.

2. If option 1 was used, take the original binding tape, fold over the seam and sew in place with two rows of stitching. Note that there is a second row of stitching sewn directly on top of the inside row of stitching for reinforcement. *[Figure D]* This is very important.

3. If option 2 was used, it is necessary to replace the binding tape with new. Stitch down the loose end of the binding tape at the top and then overlap the tape by approximately 2 inches using the double needle machine and tape binder. *[Figure E]* Overstitch the inside row for reinforcement.

4. Trim the bottom end of the binding tape at the corner.

5. Note that the junction of the side flap and riser cover is overstitched and reinforced as needed. *[Figure F]*

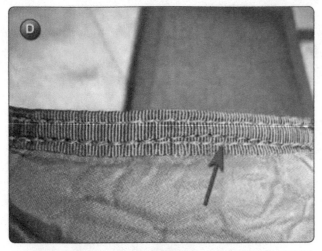

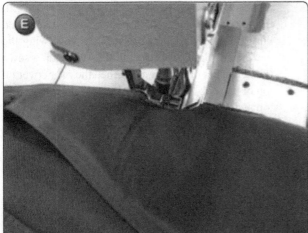

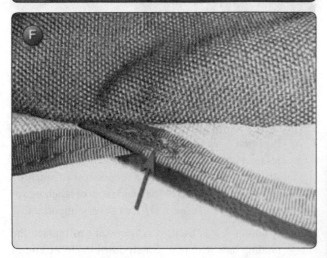

6. Close the bottom of the container as per the original and reinforce as required.

Inspection

- Check that the flap is installed correct side out.
- Check the inside binding for reinforcing stitching.
- The side flap/riser cover should be stitched and reinforced.

- The container bottom must be closed correctly and reinforced.

Bottom of Container (BOC) Pocket Replacement

- Applicable products: Any main container with a BOC pocket configuration
- Description: Installation of a BOC pocket to the main container
- Authorized repairmen: FAA Senior or Master Parachute Rigger
- Materials: E thread—color to match
- Machines: 301 straight stitch—medium duty 7–9 SPI and 308 zigzag—medium duty 7–11 SPI
- Equipment: Scissors, seam ripper or scalpel, marking pencil, and t-pins

Procedure

The following technique is typical of many modern container systems. This procedure addresses only the disassembly of the container and replacement of a factory made replacement part. It does not address the manufacture of a replacement part. Depending on the size of the container assembly, it may be possible to do the replacement of the BOC pocket with the reserve packed. However, the smaller the system, the more difficult it will be. If the container cannot be placed under the machine, then remove the reserve canopy.

Disassembly

1. Mark the location of the corners of the BOC pocket on the container with a marking pencil.

2. Open the lower right corner of the main container. *[Figure A]*

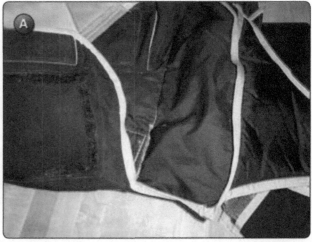

3. Remove the old BOC pocket.

Reassembly

1. Locate the new BOC pocket on the container at the marks of the old pocket and pin in place with T-pins. *[Figure B]*

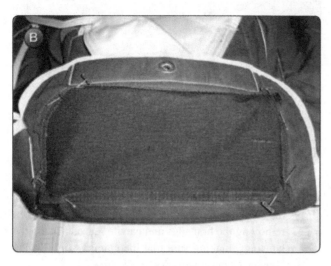

2. Stitch around the perimeter of the pocket with the single-needle machine. Backstitch at the corners for reinforcing. *[Figure C]*

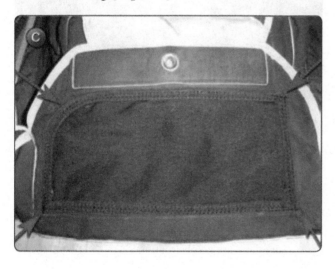

3. Restitch the corner of the main container as per the original configuration.

Inspection

- Check the orientation of the pocket with the opening to the right (unless for left-handed deployment).

- Check the stitching and corner reinforcing.

Ring Release Housing Replacement

- Applicable products: All harness and container systems equipped with a 3-ring release system

- Description: Replacement of damaged or missing 3-ring release housings

- Authorized repairmen: FAA Senior or Master Parachute Rigger

- Materials: Nylon supertack, 3-ring housings of the correct length, heat shrink tubing - ½ inch diameter, Owner's Manual for the harness and container assembly (if available)

- Machines: None

- Equipment: Scissors, seam ripper or scalpel, marking pencil, 6-inch ruler, hand tacking needle, heat gun, crimping tool (optional)

Procedure

Replacement of the 3-ring housings may be necessary due to wear, damage, or stretching of the housings. Correct installation and tacking of the housings are important to ensure proper operation of the 3-ring release system.

Disassembly

1. Inspect the original installation to determine the exact routing of the housings. Some systems have dedicated channels and/or loops through which they are routed. In others, the housings are routed under or over back straps or reserve ripcord housings. If necessary, draw a diagram of the routing or take a picture so that the replacement housings are routed correctly.

2. Remove any tackings or clamps that hold the housings together and/or to the container. Remove the housings from the system.

Reassembly

1. Install the replacement housings into their respective locations as per the original installation. Usually the longer housing is installed first and then the shorter one.

2. Make sure that the flat side of the housing terminal end is orientated outward so that it lays flat against the rear of the main riser when the 3-ring release is assembled correctly. *[Figure A]*

3. Align the handle end of the housings and secure as per the original installation. This may be with either a double clamp or hand tacking. *[Figure B] Figure C* shows a typical method of using supertack to secure the housings together.

4. If hand tacking is used, it is desirable to cover the tacking with heat shrink tubing. Place a length of tubing over the housing ends and shrink using the heat gun. *[Figure D]*

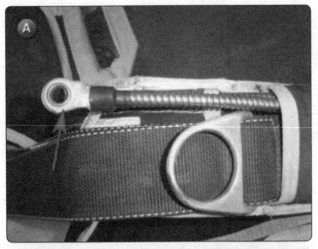

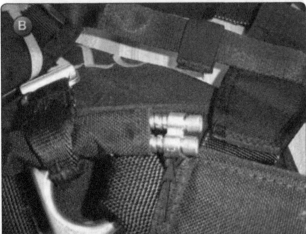

a double clamp to secure the housings together, as well as to the container or pockets. If these are used, inspect the clamp to make sure that it was not damaged when removing the housings and can be reused. Crimp the housings, making sure that the clamp is tight so the housings cannot work loose. *[Figure E]*

6.   Route the release cables through the housings to make sure there are no obstructions.

Inspection

*   Check for correct routing of the housings.
*   Verify correct orientation of the terminal ends.
*   Housings should be secured together at the handle ends.
*   Housings should be secured to the container/back pad or pockets with either clamps or supertack.
*   There should be sufficient slack or "float" in the housings.
*   Housings should be clear.

5.   Secure the double housing to the container/back pad or pocket assembly. Depending on the manufacturer, it may be necessary to provide a certain amount of "float" to the housings in order that the loop of the riser is not loaded or under tension when the main canopy is deployed. If available, consult the owner's manual for correct positioning and tacking. Some systems use

Section 3, Harness and Risers

Harness repairs are almost always a major repair. Consequently, they are master rigger work. About the only repairs open to a senior rigger are replacement of ripcord pockets and Velcro®; and replacement of hand tackings for ripcords, comfort pads, 3-ring housings, and other hardware. Major harness repairs are the most critical maintenance operations a rigger can perform on a parachute assembly. Even seemingly innocuous repairs, if done incorrectly, can have fatal consequences. Depending on the type of harness design, repairs to the harness main lift web or leg straps involve major repair or remanufacture.

According to 14 CFR part 65, section 65.129 (e) and (f), "No certificated parachute rigger may – (e) Pack, maintain, or alter a parachute in any manner that deviates from procedures approved by the Administrator or the manufacturer of the parachute; or (f) Exercise the privileges of his certificate and type rating unless he understands the current manufacturer's instructions for the operation involved..." In other words, because this operation is a major repair, the person doing the work must be a currently certificated Master Parachute Rigger with the appropriate ratings.

In the past, many master riggers felt that they were empowered to undertake almost any task. The attitude was, "We can lift the TSO label, build a new harness, and put the TSO label back on." This is not the case. Just because an individual has a master rigger license does not mean he or she is qualified to undertake a complex repair.

There are four primary areas of concern that need to be addressed in any repair program. They are as follows:

1. Inspection, damage identification, and repair planning

2. Teardown and cleanup

3. Preparation and reconstruction

4. Quality control inspection and recordkeeping

Main risers are components that are subject to extreme wear and tear. The only items that are practical for repair are the 3-ring locking loops and the toggle mounting/Velcro® assembly. Once the webbing begins to show wear, it is more practical to replace than repair them.

The following are repairs found in Section 3, Harness and Risers:

- Chest strap replacement
- Lower leg strap shortening
- Ripcord pocket Velcro® replacement
- Articulated upper leg hardware replacement
- Standard harness main lift web replacement
- Main riser 3-ring locking loop replacement
- Main riser steering toggle Velcro® replacement

Chest Strap Replacement

- Applicable products: Most standard harness configurations

- Description: Replacement of chest strap due to damage or for lengthening

- Authorized repairmen: FAA Master Parachute Rigger

- Materials: E thread—5-cord nylon thread

- Machines: 301 straight stitch—medium duty 7–11 SPI, heavy-duty harness machine—Singer 7–33 or equivalent-stitch length to match the original, and 308 zigzag—medium duty 7–11 SPI

- Equipment: Scissors, seam ripper or scalpel, marking pencil, ruler, hot glue gun, and hot knife

Procedure

This procedure deals with the longer side of the chest strap, usually the left, which is threaded through the chest adapter or through an adjustable V-ring. Replacing the opposite side would mirror this process.

Disassembly

1. Examine the chest strap/MLW junction to determine if the backpad needs to be removed from the harness to access the junction. If so, remove the pad from the harness to allow access to the junction. *[Figure A]*

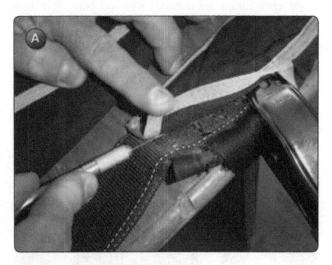

2. Many harnesses have the reserve ripcord housing located on the left side. The housing needs to be disconnected at this location. It is usually secured to a loop located at the chest strap junction. During the

replacement process, this loop is removed and may be reused if in good condition.

3. Remove the harness stitching and any other stitching from the junction making sure not to damage the main lift web. *[Figure B]*

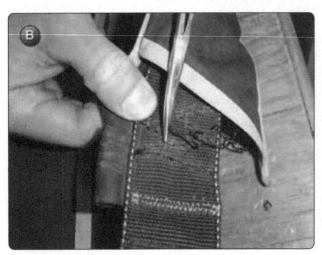

4. Remove the old chest strap webbing from the main lift web. Pay particular attention to the end of the webbing. While most chest straps are installed at right angles to the main lift web, some have an angle cut at the end for better fit. If the webbing has an angle, make sure to duplicate it.

5. Clean the junction area of old thread, as well as any glue residue on the inside of the main lift web.

6. Take the marking pencil and mark the points of the stitch pattern for the reassembly. *[Figure C]* Most chest straps are installed with a 3-point WW in a horizontal orientation, but the rigger should duplicate the original design.

7. If the procedure is a replacement of a damaged chest strap, then it should be replaced to the original length. If so, then remove the rolled stop end so that the finished length may be determined. If the chest strap is to be lengthened, then an appropriate length of webbing needs to be determined. The finished length should be measured from the outside of the main lift web plus 3.50 inches. *[Figure D]*

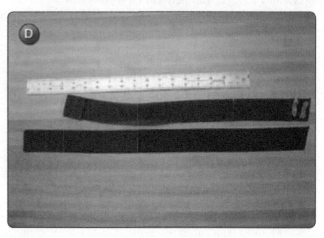

Reassembly

1. Cut a piece of webbing to the appropriate length. If needed, cut the MLW end of the strap at an angle. *[Figure E]*

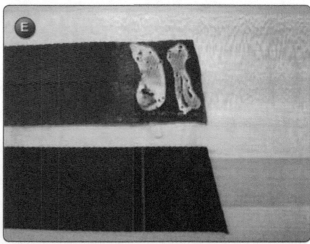

2. Insert the end of the webbing into the MLW junction. Align the end of the chest strap with the outside edge of the MLW. Insert the housing loop back into the junction as well. Lightly glue the MLW to the chest strap. *[Figure F]* Do not use too much glue.

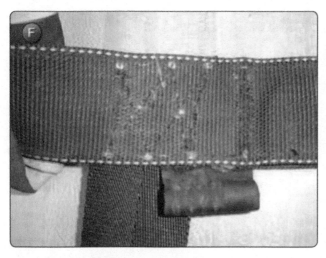

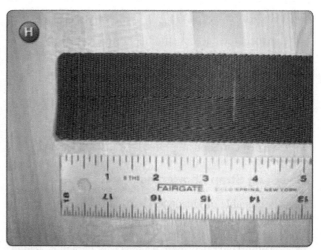

3. Some harnesses are pre-sewn along the edges with a medium duty machine and E thread. If so, duplicate this.

4. Using the harness machine and 5-cord nylon thread, sew the junction as marked with the original pattern. *[Figure G]*

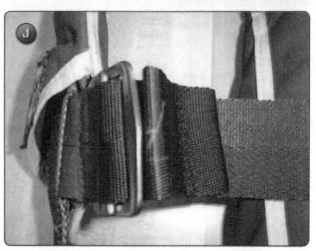

5. Mark the length of the chest strap to include enough needed for the stop end. If the chest strap is to be configured for a thread-thru adapter, an additional 3.50 inches is needed for the roll back.

6. After determining the cut length, place a mark at 3.50 inches on the BACK side of the chest strap. Fold to this mark and then fold the webbing one more time for three layers. *[Figures H and I]*

7. Using the zigzag machine, sew across the center of the stop end fold. This results in a loose fold that jams against the adapter in the event of slippage of the chest strap. *[Figure J]*

8. If the MLW was attached to the backpad assembly, reattach as per the original configuration. If the backpad is attached in such a manner that does not allow inspection of the back side of the MLW, inspect the stitching at this time before reattaching the backpad.

9. Reinstall the ripcord housing and secure.

Inspection

- Inspect the harness stitching for correct stitch length, tension, and appropriate pattern.
- Reattach the MLW to the backpad as needed.
- The stop end must be sewn and oriented correctly.
- Verify the chest strap is the correct length.
- The ripcord housing must be reinstalled and tacked.

Lower Leg Strap Shortening

- Applicable products: All harness configurations
- Description: Shortening of the lower leg straps
- Authorized repairmen: FAA Master Parachute Rigger
- Materials: 5-cord nylon thread—color to match original
- Machines: Heavy-duty harness machine—Singer 7–33 or equivalent 5–7 SPI
- Equipment: Seam ripper or scalpel, marking pencil, ruler, and hot knife

Procedure

The shortening of the leg strap, while a relatively straightforward process, is an extremely important procedure. If done improperly, it could result in the harness fitting improperly or the leg straps to come unthreaded and the user to fall out during opening.

Disassembly

1. If the leg strap is of the thread-thru configuration, unthread the webbing from the leg adapter. If the leg strap has an adjustable "V" ring used in conjunction with a snap, disconnect the "V" ring from the snap. Lay the leg strap out flat.

2. Remove the harness stitching from the rolled end of the webbing.

3. Measure the required distance from the end of the strap that is required for shortening and mark accordingly. *[Figure A]*

4. Trim the webbing at the mark using the hot knife.

Reassembly

1. For the thread-thru configuration, place a mark at 3.50 inches from the end of the webbing on the bottom of the webbing. *[Figure B]* This is the "fold to" mark for the first fold of the webbing. Fold one more time for a total of three layers of webbing. *[Figure C]*

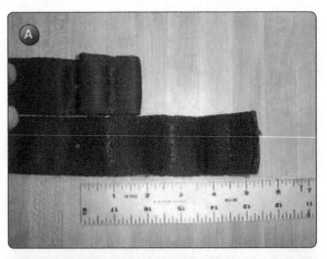

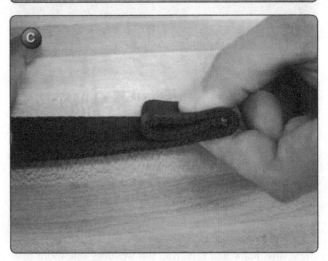

2. Sew the rolled stop end according to *Figure D* with the harness machine.

3. For the "V" ring configuration, place a mark at 2 inches from the top end of the webbing. This is also the "fold to" mark for the first fold. Make two additional folds for a total of four layers.

7-54

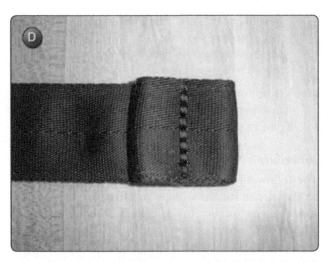

4. Sew the rolled stop end according to *Figure E* with the harness machine.

Inspection

- Check the stitching for the correct pattern and thread tension.

- For the thread-thru configuration, make sure there is no twist to the leg strap and thread the webbing through the leg adapter. The rolled end should face outward.

- For the "V" ring configuration, connect the "V" ring to the snap. The rolled stop end should also face outward.

Ripcord Pocket Velcro® Replacement

- Applicable products: Any harness configuration with a Velcro® style ripcord pocket configuration

- Description: Replacement of the Velcro® of the ripcord pocket

- Authorized repairmen: FAA Senior or Master Parachute Rigger

- Materials: E thread—color to match original; hook and loop Velcro®—width and length to match original

- Machines: 301 straight stitch—medium duty 7–11 SPI and 308 zigzag—medium duty 7–11 SPI

- Equipment: Scissors, seam ripper or scalpel, marking pencil, 6-inch ruler, and glue gun

Procedure

Disassembly

1. Depending on the configuration, it may be necessary to remove the ripcord housing from its attachment point on the harness for access to the pocket. If the harness is attached to the backpad, disconnect this as well.

2. Remove the E thread stitch pattern that forms the pocket on the MLW. *[Figure A]*

3. Mark the ends of the old Velcro® and remove from the inside of the webbing. Note which side of the webbing the hook and loop are located.

Reassembly

1. Cut the replacement Velcro® to the correct length.

2. Glue the Velcro® pieces to their respective locations on the inside of the webbing.

3. Using the single needle machine, sew around the perimeter of the Velcro®, as well as a row of stitching down the center. *[Figure B]* Repeat for the opposite side.

4. Re-sew the pocket with two rows of single needle stitching with E thread. *[Figure C]*

5. Reattach the harness to the backpad.

6. Reinstall the ripcord housing to the harness.

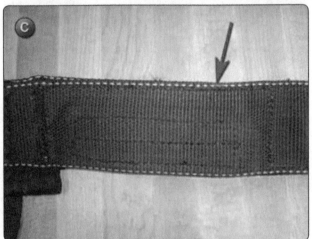

Inspection

- Verify the correct orientation of the Velcro® in the pocket.
- The correct stitch pattern must be used for the Velcro®.
- Verify the ripcord pocket is re-sewn.
- The backpad must be reattached (if needed).
- The ripcord housing must be reinstalled.

Articulated Upper Leg Hardware Replacement

- Applicable products: Most articulated harness configurations
- Description: Replacement of the upper leg strap hardware
- Authorized repairmen: FAA Master Parachute Rigger
- Materials: E thread—color to match; 5-cord nylon thread—color to match; Type-8 webbing—color to match; Type-12 webbing, Type-4 1-inch tape, replacement adapter—MS-22040

- Machines: 301 straight stitch—medium duty 7–11 SPI, 308 zigzag—medium duty 7–11 SPI, heavy-duty harness machine—Singer 7–33 or equivalent, stitch to match the original
- Equipment: Scissors, seam ripper or scalpel, marking pencil, ruler, glue gun, and 4-point W-W pattern template

Procedure

The following procedure is required when the knurling on the friction bar has worn to the point that the leg strap would slip on opening. In addition, the webbing at the ring location shows wear and is replaced at the same time. This procedure is typical for a Flexon and Talon 2 articulated harness configuration.

Disassembly

1. Remove the leg pad assembly.
2. Remove the leg strap by cutting the webbing.

Reassembly

1. Use *Figure A* to cut a replacement leg strap and parts.
2. Take the Ty-8 webbing and sew a bowtie fold with the Ty-4 tape buffer at the 3.50 inch mark. *[Figure B]*
3. Turn the adapter upside down and install the Ty-8 webbing as shown and glue in place. *[Figure C]*
4. Install the bowtie around the ring and glue in place. *[Figure D]* The picture shows the inside orientation of the harness.
5. Double check the correct orientation of the hardware. *[Figure E]*
6. Mark the stitch pattern. *[Figure F]*
7. Sew the webbing with the harness machine in a 4-point W-W pattern *[Figure G]*
8. Reinstall the leg pad. Route the upper pad flap through the adapter from the bottom and zigzag. *[Figure H]*
9. Fold the bottom pad under and zigzag in place. *[Figure I]* Note that the ends of the upper and lower pads are offset to reduce the thickness to be sewn.

Inspection

- Verify the hardware orientation is correct.
- Verify the stitch pattern is correct.
- The leg pad must be reinstalled correctly.

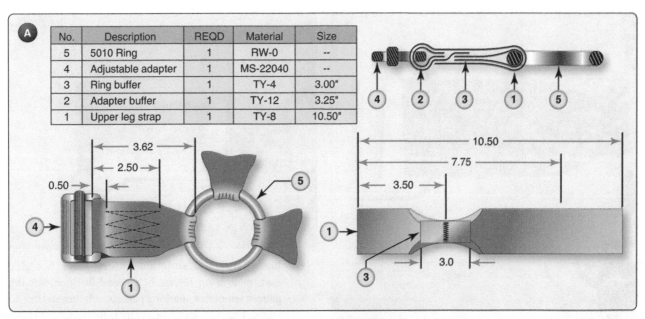

No.	Description	REQD	Material	Size
5	5010 Ring	1	RW-0	--
4	Adjustable adapter	1	MS-22040	--
3	Ring buffer	1	TY-4	3.00"
2	Adapter buffer	1	TY-12	3.25"
1	Upper leg strap	1	TY-8	10.50"

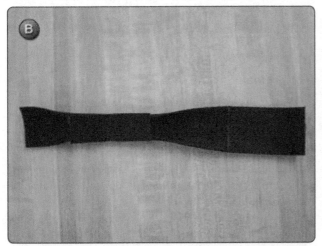

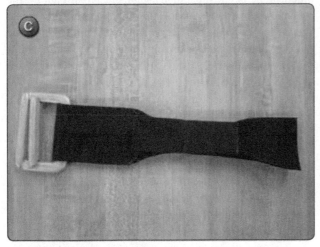

Standard Harness Main Lift Web Replacement

- Applicable products: Most standard harness configurations

- Description: Complete replacement of one side of a standard harness main lift web

- Authorized repairmen: FAA Master Parachute Rigger

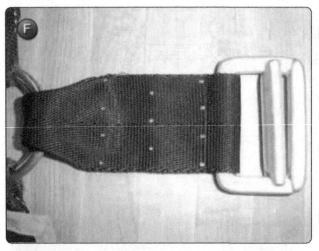

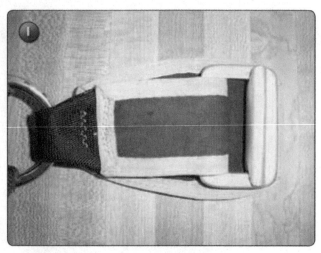

- Materials: E thread—color to match; 5-cord nylon thread—color to match; Type-7 webbing—color to match; Type-8 webbing—color to match; Type-12 webbing—color to match

- Machines: 301 straight stitch—medium duty 7–11 SPI, 308 zigzag—medium duty 7–11 SPI, and heavy-duty harness machine—Singer 7–33 or equivalent 5–7 SPI

- Equipment: Hot knife and cutting glass, hot glue gun, measuring rulers: 6, 18, and 36 inch, sewing pattern templates, marking pencils, scissors and thread snips, Exacto® knife or scalpel, hemostats, Type-4 1-inch tape—color to match; Type-3 tape—color to match; 1½ inch Velcro®—hook and loop, and 1-inch Velcro®—hook and loop

Background

The following steps provide an overview of the procedure to follow:

Step One

The first thing the rigger must do is to inspect the parachute harness to identify the make and model and determine the extent of the damage. In some cases, particularly for older designs, it may not be practical or economically feasible to repair the harness. If the rigger determines that repair is practical, he or she must then establish a repair plan for the project. There are two reasons for this: one, that the project is done logically and efficiently and two, if not having done this type of repair before, having contacted the manufacturer for guidance, the rigger can explain what he or she intends to do to affect the repair.

The rigger must make detailed measurements of the harness. *Figure A* shows a typical harness configuration and the needed dimensions. On a situation where one side of the harness is intact and can be used for reference, the rigger still needs dimensions to work against to determine how much material to order or bill to the job. If both sides of the harness are damaged, great care must be taken to ensure the correct measurements of the final repair.

Step Two

Teardown and cleanup is the second most important part of the process. It is important that all the old thread, glue, and damaged webbing are removed. Leaving any of these in place

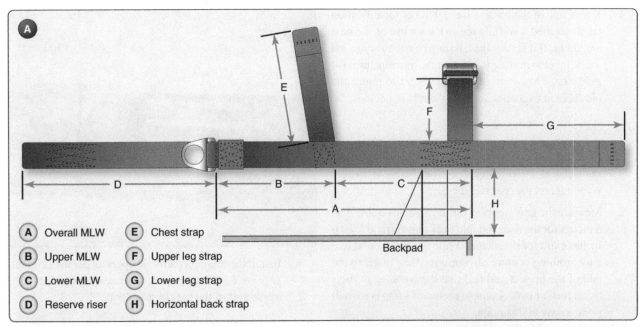

A — Overall MLW   E — Chest strap
B — Upper MLW   F — Upper leg strap
C — Lower MLW   G — Lower leg strap
D — Reserve riser   H — Horizontal back strap

and sewing over them results in a poor appearance. Also, it is not uncommon to find additional damage or wear at this point that was not identified during the initial inspection process.

Step Three

After the teardown and cleanup, the replacement webbing can be measured, cut, and pre-sewn in preparation for installation to the harness assembly. The construction sequence is followed. In certain cases, it may be desirable to replace not just damaged parts but worn ones to give the final result a more cosmetic appearance. An example is when replacing a main lift web, it does not look good to reuse the old chest strap webbing when the main lift web is new material.

Step Four

After the repair is completed, a thorough quality control program is undertaken. This is especially critical in a situation where the rigger is working alone and there is no one to rely on for crosschecking the work. All the critical points of the repair must be identified and checked as well as the finished dimensions.

Procedure

Disassembly

1. Remove all housings, leg pads, and any other parts that may interfere with the work from the harness. Disassemble the leg strap/horizontal back strap junction. *[Figure B]* Disconnect the upper MLW from the yoke portion of the backpad if necessary.

2. Disassemble the junction of the diagonal back strap and main lift web at the 3-ring attachment point. *[Figure C]* Be very careful not to damage the diagonal

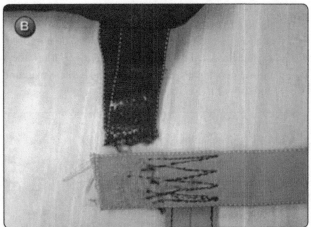

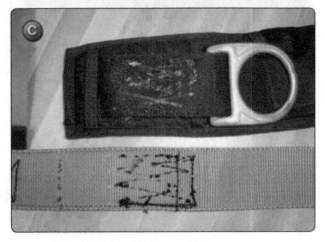

back strap. If it is damaged, it is a major project to replace this on most assemblies.

3. Lay out the main lift web assembly and check the measurements against the initial dimensions. Check against the opposite side MLW for symmetry.

4. If this side of the harness has a TSO or identification label attached, carefully remove it for use on the new assembly. If it is damaged, it may be necessary to get a new label to replace it. Contact the manufacturer for guidance. They may require the rigger to return the old label in exchange for a new one.

Reassembly

1. Note that this configuration consists primarily of two main pieces of webbing. The front MLW is Type-7 webbing and the rear is Type-8.

2. Measure the new webbing for the main lift webs. Add 5 inches for the riser end fold back and allow at least 6 inches extra for shrinkage. While this may sound like a lot, nothing is more discouraging than to get to the end of the project and find that the webbing is short by an inch or two. A couple inches of scrap is a small price to pay at this point.

3. Starting at one end of the webbing, measure the riser end configuration. Fold back and glue in place. If there is a toggle stow loop on the old harness, do not forget to glue in place before sewing. *[Figure D]* Mark the 4 point W-W pattern and sew with the harness machine and 5-cord nylon thread.

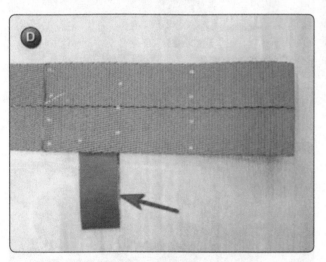

4. Install the steering line guide ring with a duplicate stitch pattern as per the original. *[Figure E]* In some instances, the manufacturer may have used a special bar tack or other stitch pattern to attach the ring. If the rigger does not have the same machine, it is necessary to contact the manufacturer for an acceptable alternative. This should have been identified in phase one. Check the distance from the end of the riser to the top of the ring. The industry standard is 4 inches, but there may be special dimensions for some applications.

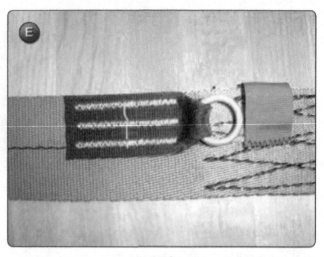

5. Install the toggle Velcro® keepers as per the original. *[Figure F]* Complete any other sewing needed, such as the end of the toggle stow loop.

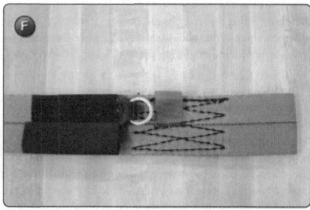

6. If needed, reattach the TSO label at the appropriate location. If the label is the original one and is made from material such as Ty-vek®, try to follow the original needle holes to avoid perforating the material. Too many holes cause the label to tear out.

7. Working from the measurement diagram in *Figure A*, mark the location of the 3-ring.

8. Working downward mark the location of the chest strap, the ripcord pocket, and the bottom of the upper leg strap. *[Figure G]*

NOTE: It is necessary to allow for a certain amount of shrinkage during the sewing process. There are four areas of shrinkage to allow for:

1. The harness stitching at the 3-ring.

2. The harness stitching at the chest strap.

3. The ripcord pocket.

4. The harness stitching at the leg strap junction.

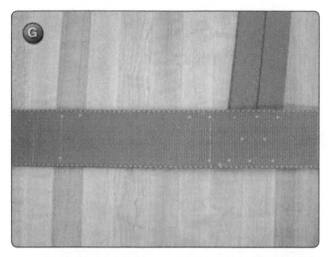

The standard rule of thumb for the sum of these patterns is approximately .75 inch for the length. In other words, the marked length of the MLW should be .75 inch longer than the desired finished length. Most of the shrinkage is in the ripcord pocket and the leg strap junction. If the rigger has not done this operation before, he or she may want to build a sample MLW to check the measurements and the resultant shrinkage.

9. Sew the Velcro® in place for the ripcord pocket. *[Figure H]*

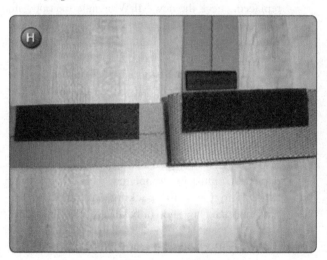

10. Glue the chest strap in place. In this instance, do not forget the housing loop.

11. Using the single needle, pre-sew the front and rear main lift webs. Use of the sewing pattern in *Figure I* accomplishes this and at the same time creates the ripcord pocket. Sew the chest strap 3-point W-W with the harness machine. *[Figure J]*

12. Reassemble the upper diagonal back strap and the 3-ring hardware by threading the rear riser through the large ring followed by the front riser.

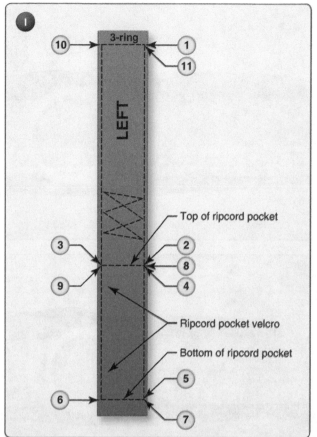

13. Position the 3-ring at the mark on the main lift web and glue in place. Install the Type-12 confluence wrap below the 3-ring and mark the 4-point W-W pattern. *[Figure K]*

14. Sew the confluence wrap with the harness machine. *[Figure L]*

15. Re-create the leg junction. Glue the upper leg strap in place first and then the horizontal back strap second. *[Figure M]*

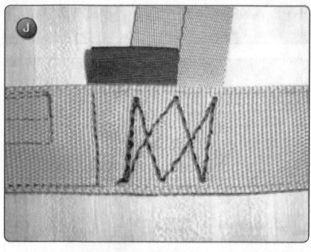

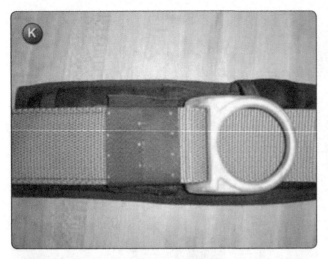

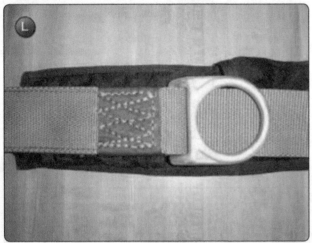

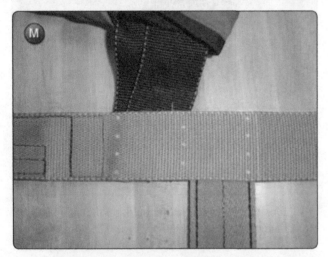

16. Mark the 4-point W-W and then sew with the harness machine. Start the stitch pattern at the front side of the MLW and complete with the overstitch the full length of the pattern. *[Figure N]* This provides additional reinforcing at the upper leg strap/MLW location.

17. Measure the length of the lower leg strap allowing 3.50 inches for the rolled stop end. Trim to length and then install the stop end with the harness machine.

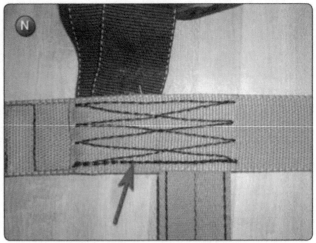

18. Reattach the backpad to the upper MLW using the 308 zigzag machine.

19. Reinstall the leg pads using the 308 zigzag machine.

20. Reinstall the ripcord and 3-ring housings and hand tack in place.

Inspection

- Check the finished dimensions against the original dimensions in *Figure A*. If only one side has been replaced, check the new MLW against the opposite side for comparison. The generally accepted tolerances for this type of construction are ± .25 inch. In particular, reserve riser length and the overall MLW length are the most important. If either of these is mismatched to their opposites, then the flight of the canopies may be affected.

- Start inspecting from the riser end working down. Use the inspection chart in *Figure O* as a guide for the inspection points. After the inspection, all appropriate paperwork must be completed. This includes the rigger's logbook, the packing data card for the parachute, and any shop or business forms or log.

Main Riser 3-Ring Locking Loop Replacement

- Applicable products: All 3-ring riser assemblies

- Description: Replacement of the 3-ring riser locking loop

- Authorized repairmen: FAA Senior or Master Parachute Rigger

- Materials: E thread; 5-cord nylon thread—color to match, Type-IIa nylon cord or equivalent

- Machines: 308 zigzag—medium duty 10 SPI and heavy-duty harness machine—Singer 7–33 or equivalent

  Equipment: Scissors, seam ripper or scalpel, marking pencil, 6-inch ruler, glue gun, and hot knife

Check	Inspection	Date	Harness Inspection
			Inspection Points
			1. Color
			2. Sizing: risers, MLW, chest, leg strap, HZ
			3. 3-ring size
			4. Leg hardware—orientation, type
			5. Reserve riser ends—4 pt. W-W, guide rings, toggle stow loops
			6. Chest strap—3 pt. W-W each side
			7. Articulated harness ring junction—buffers
			8. Upper leg strap—4 pt. W-W, buffers, hardware orientation
			9. Lower leg strap—stitch pattern, buffers, stop end
			10. TSO label and orientation
			11. Harness stitching—SPI, backstitch, stop ends, tension
			12. Ripcord pocket—present, secure fit

Procedure

Disassembly

- Mark the locking loop at the bottom edge of the confluence wrap. *[Figure A]*

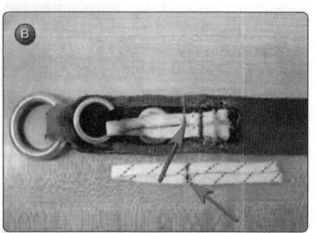

- Place a mark at the bottom of the confluence wrap and carefully remove the confluence wrap from the riser.

- Remove the old locking loop.

Reassembly

1. Cut a new loop the length of the old one plus 2 inches.

2. Fold the new loop in half and lay alongside the old loop. Transfer the marks from the old loop to the new one. *[Figure B]*

3. Align the marks on the loop with the mark at the bottom of the confluence wrap on the riser. *[Figure C]* Glue the loop in place.

4. Sew the loop with the 308 zigzag machine. *[Figure D]* Set the stitch width at approximately ⅛ inch and 10 SPI.

5. Trim the excess loop off at the top. *[Figure E]*

6. Reinstall the confluence wrap using the harness machine. *[Figure F]*

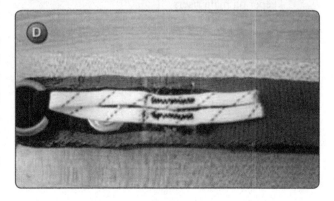

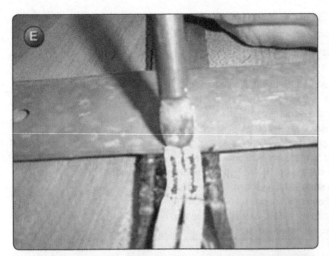

Inspection

- Before installing the confluence wrap, make sure the zigzag stitching is complete.

- The loop length should be the same as the old loop.

- The confluence wrap must be reinstalled.

Main Riser Steering Toggle Velcro® Replacement

- Applicable products: Most main risers with a Velcro® toggle installation

- Description: Replacement of the Velcro® toggle keeper on main risers

- Authorized repairmen: FAA Senior or Master Parachute Rigger

- Materials: E thread, Velcro® of the appropriate width and type

- Machines: 301 straight stitch—medium duty 7–11 SPI

- Equipment: Scissors, seam ripper or scalpel, marking pencil, and 6-inch ruler

Procedure

The term "Velcro®" is used in a generic fashion for hook and loop fastener. While the rigger should replace the Velcro® to match the original configuration. This installation has proven superior for its holding ability and the secure line stow configuration.

Disassembly

1. Mark the location of the old Velcro®. *[Figure A]*

2. Remove the old Velcro®.

Reassembly

1. Cut a new piece(s) of Velcro® to match the original.

2. Position the Velcro® to the original location.

3. Sew the hook Velcro® with a single-needle machine. Sew an additional row of stitching down the center of the Velcro®. *[Figure B]* This keeps the center from lifting during use and tearing out the edge stitching.

4. Position the loop line stow Velcro® to match the hook and sew along the edge, overstitching the ends. *[Figure C]*

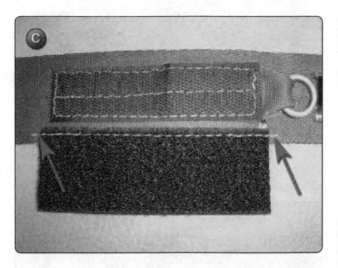

Inspection

- Check that the location of Velcro® is the same as the original.
- Check stitch patterns and center stitching.

Section 4, Accessory Components

Accessory components are comprised of the reserve pilot chute, reserve deployment bag or device, main deployment bag, main pilot chute and bridle, main and reserve toggles, reserve static line (RSL) lanyard, 3-ring release handle, and reserve ripcord.

The reserve components generally do not suffer much wear due to their infrequent use. In addition, with their frequent inspection during the repack cycle, any necessary repairs become obvious and are taken care of before they become major problems.

1. Metal ripcords usually are not repairable and must be replaced when they are damaged.
2. Reserve pilot chutes experience torn mesh, minor canopy damage, broken hand tackings, and damaged grommets in the cap.

The reserve free bag may have the grommets in the closing flap pull out of the material. The high-drag bridle is a critical area and is usually not repairable. The RSL lanyard is another critical item that is usually not repairable, except for the replacement of a defective snap shackle.

Main components, on the other hand, are subject to extensive wear and tear. Most jumpers do not take time to inspect their main components on a regular basis and generally operate on a "repair as broken" basis. By the time the rigger sees the components, it is easier and more cost effective to replace than to repair them. However, there are regular wear trends that the rigger can make their customers aware of so they can look for them and have them taken care of.

The following are repairs to accessory components, found in Section 4, Accessory Components, of this chapter:

- Reserve pilot chute repair—mesh, tackings, and bad grommet
- Reserve free bag repair—grommet pullout
- Main pilot chute repair—top canopy reinforcing
- Main pilot chute collapsible bridle replacement
- Main deployment bag repair—closing flap grommet pullout

Reserve Pilot Chute Repair—Mesh, Tackings, and Bad Grommet

- Applicable products: Most reserve pilot chutes
- Description: Replacement of cap grommet
- Authorized repairmen: FAA Master Parachute Rigger
- Materials: Nylon supertack, stainless steel sheet grommet—same as original
- Machines: None
- Equipment: Scissors, seam ripper or scalpel, hand tacking needle, grommet set, and diagonal cutters

Procedure

The canopy fabric portion of a reserve pilot chute would be repaired as necessary with similar patching techniques as used on a canopy. The mesh portion, however, may be subject to different techniques. Another area of common damage is the thru grommet in the top of the pilot chute. The following procedure describes the replacement of the grommet in the top of the pilot chute. *Figure A* shows a damaged grommet.

Disassembly

1. Remove the hand tackings used to secure the base of the pilot chute to the spring. *[Figure B]*
2. Turn the pilot chute upside down and push the canopy down until the grommet is exposed. *[Figure C]*
3. Using diagonal cutters, remove the damaged grommet being careful not to damage the fabric of the cap. *[Figure D]*

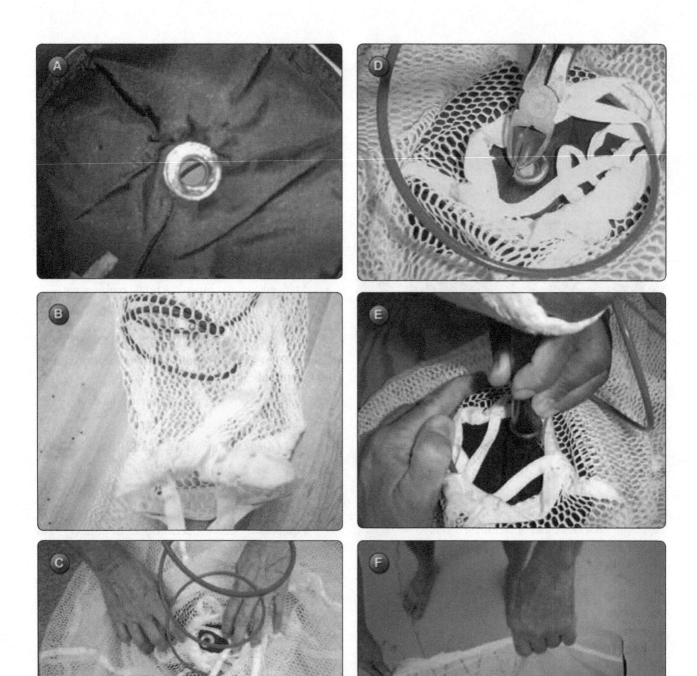

Reassembly

1. Using the handset, set a new grommet. Be careful not to catch any fabric during the process. *[Figure E]*

2. Reposition the canopy over the spring. Grasp the skirt at the bottom end of the spring. Make sure that the radial tapes run directly from the bottom to the cap in a straight line. *[Figure F]* If the tapes "barberpole" around the spring, the pilot chute may not inflate properly on launch.

3. Hand tack the bottom of the canopy to the bottom of the spring. *[Figure G]*

Inspection

• Verify the grommet is secure.

• Tapes should be straight.

• Tackings should be secure.

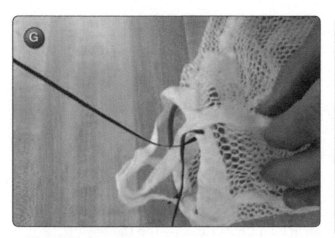

Disassembly: Mesh Repair

1. Remove the tackings used to secure the base of the pilot chute to the spring.

2. For small holes, turn the mesh inside out and zigzag the edges together.

Reassembly

1. Reattach the bottom of the pilot chute to the spring with hand tacking.

Inspection

- Tapes should be straight.

- Tackings should be secure.

Reserve Free Bag Repair—Grommet Pullout

- Applicable products: Most reserve free bags

- Description: General repair to the reserve free bag

- Authorized repairmen: FAA Master Parachute Rigger

- Materials: E thread, 1½ inch Type-3 tape, and grommets to match the original type and size

- Machines: 301 straight stitch—medium duty 7–11 SPI

- Equipment: Scissors, seam ripper or scalpel, marking pencil, 6-inch ruler, hot knife, grommet set, and hole punch

Procedure

Most reserve free bag designs are fairly robust. The most common types of damage seen are the pulling out of the grommets in the tongue of the bag and tearing out of fabric from the binding tape due to overstressing during packing. *[Figure A]* Damage to the bridle portion of the free bag is generally not repairable nor allowed by most manufacturers. Consequently, any damage in this area would necessitate the replacement of the bag. The following procedure deals with the repair of the tongue area and replacement of the grommets.

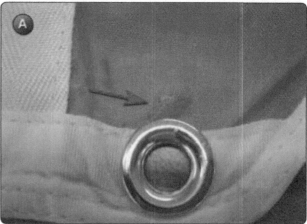

Disassembly

1. Remove the grommets from the tongue. *[Figure B]*

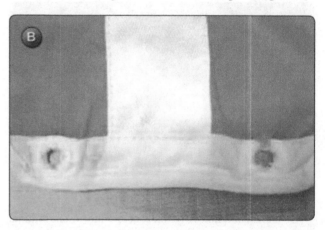

2. Remove the binding from the tongue area by unpicking the stitching. *[Figure C]*

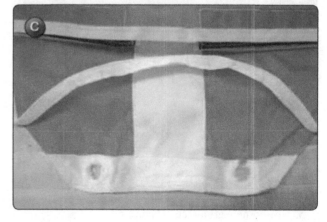

Reassembly

1. Cut two pieces of 1½ inch Type-3 tape and overlay them on each side of the damaged area. Sew around the edges of the tape and down the center to secure it. *[Figure D]*

2. Trim the ends of the tape to match the shape of the tongue.

3. Using the single needle machine, reapply the binding tape around the edge of the tongue. *[Figure E]*

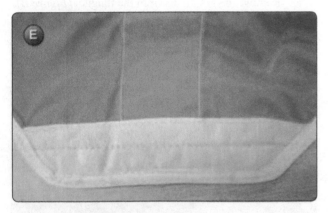

4. Punch new holes over the exact position as the original ones. *[Figure F]*

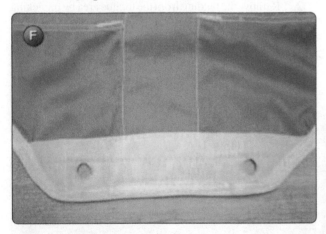

5. Insert new grommets. *[Figure G]*

Inspection

- Reinforcing tape must be secure.
- Binding must be re-sewn.
- Grommets must be set and secure.

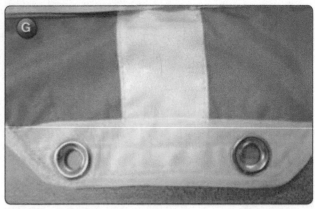

Main Pilot Chute Repair—Top Canopy Reinforcing

- Applicable products: Most main hand deploy pilot chutes
- Description: Repair of the apex area of a hand deploy pilot chute
- Authorized repairmen: FAA Senior or Master Parachute Rigger
- Materials: E thread and ¾ inch Type-3 tape
- Machines: 301 straight stitch—medium duty 7–11 SPI
- Equipment: Scissors, seam ripper or scalpel, marking pencil, 6-inch ruler, and hot knife

Procedure

Most repairs of the main pilot chute consist of fabric or mesh repairs and may be repaired similar to canopy procedures. The most common damage seen on main pilot chutes is in the area of the apex and the hand deploy handle. *[Figure A]* This area is subject to fairly severe stress and strain. The following procedure deals with the apex area repair. It should be noted that if the repair is too complex, it is probably more cost effective to replace rather than repair the pilot chute.

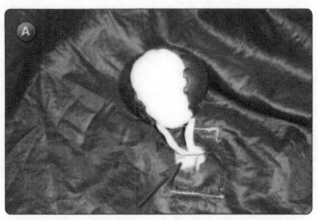

Disassembly

1. Working through the hole in the base, turn the pilot chute inside out. Unpick the seam at the junction of the canopy and mesh and between two of the radial tapes. *[Figure B]* This allows good access to the apex area.

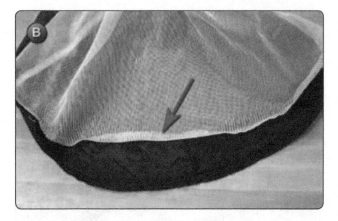

Reassembly

1. Take a piece of ¾ inch Type-3 tape and overlay the reinforcing material at the apex, covering the damaged area. *[Figure C]*

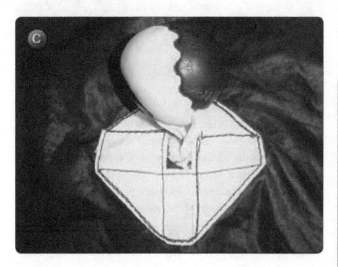

2. Re-sew the canopy and mesh panels as per the original. Turn the pilot chute right side out.

Inspection

- Damaged area must be covered.
- Canopy seam must be re-stitched correctly.

Main Pilot Chute Collapsible Bridle Replacement

- Applicable products: Most kill-line pilot chute bridle configurations
- Description: Replacement of the bridle of a kill-line collapsible pilot chute

- Authorized repairmen: FAA Senior or Master Parachute Rigger
- Materials: E thread, replacement bridle
- Machines: 301 straight stitch—medium duty 7–11 SPI and 1 inch × 42 stitch bar tack 308 zigzag—medium duty 7–11 SPI (optional)
- Equipment: Scissors, seam ripper or scalpel, green felt tip marker, 6-inch ruler, hemostats, pony clamp, and hot glue gun

Procedure

There are three basic main bridle configurations listed below:

- Standard non-collapsible bridle
- Bungee collapsible bridle
- Centerline or "kill-line" collapsible bridle

The standard bridle is a simple design and any damage usually results in the replacement of the bridle. The exception to this is if the tape attaching the curved pin is worn. The replacement of the tape is a simple task. The most common bridle in use today is the kill-line collapsible type. The replacement of the bridle is described in the following procedure.

Disassembly

1. Remove the old bridle from the pilot chute. *[Figure A]*

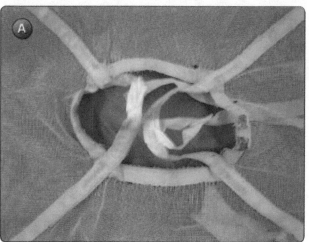

Reassembly

1. Thread the loop ends of the bridle through the bottom support tapes of the pilot chute. *[Figure B]*
2. Glue the ends in place with the glue gun. *[Figure C]*
3. Bar tack the bridle along the sides. Do not capture the centerline. *[Figure D]*
4. Align the bridle tapes on the center of the pilot chute attachment tapes and bar tack in place. *[Figure E]*

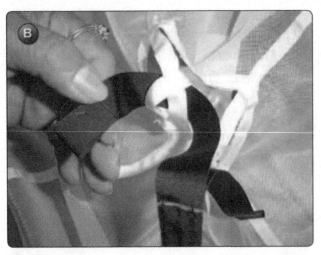

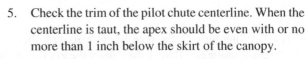

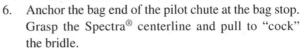

5. Check the trim of the pilot chute centerline. When the centerline is taut, the apex should be even with or no more than 1 inch below the skirt of the canopy.

6. Anchor the bag end of the pilot chute at the bag stop. Grasp the Spectra® centerline and pull to "cock" the bridle.

7. Route the free end of the Spectra® centerline up through the center of the pilot chute and through the loop of the pilot chute centerline at the apex. Grasp the handle of the pilot chute and apply tension so that the centerline of the pilot chute and the bridle are equal. Pinch the Spectra® line so that the location will not move. Secure with 2 half hitches. *[Figure F]*

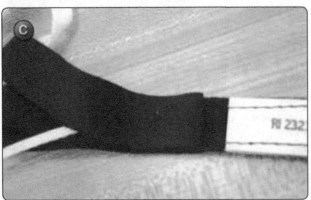

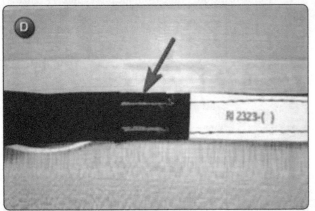

8. Change the anchor point to the end of the bridle. Stretch the bridle so that the pilot chute is collapsed. Lay the pilot chute out with the mesh exposed and secure the radial tapes with the pony clamp at the mesh/fabric seam. *[Figure G]* Pull moderate tension on the pony clamp and check the location of the apex of the pilot chute at the opening of the bridle.

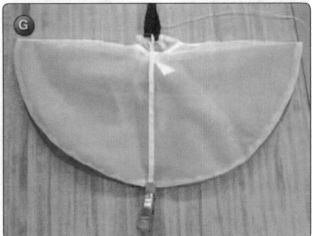

9. Again anchor the bridle at the bag stop and cock the bridle. Check the position of the apex of the pilot chute. It should be within 1 inch of the skirt. [Figure H]

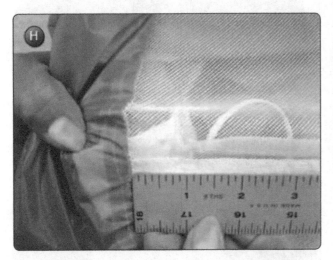

10. Finger-trap the running end of the Spectra® centerline for a distance of 3 inches. [Figure I] Bar tack or zigzag to secure. Trim the excess line.

11. Cock the bridle. Take the hemostats and grasp the Spectra® centerline at the eye of the bridle. [Figure J]

12. Pull the centerline out to expose approximately 3 inches each side of the hemostats. Take the green felt tip marker and place a mark at the hemostat location and 1 inch either side. [Figure K] Color the line between the marks and on both sides. [Figure L]

13. Pull the bridle tight to reposition the centerline and check the green color of the eye. [Figure M]

Inspection

- Check the bar tack at the pilot chute loops and at the base.

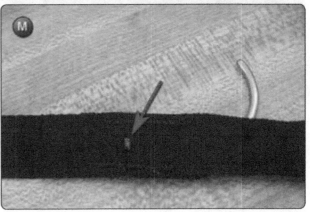

- Verify the Spectra® centerline is knotted, finger-trapped and sewn.

- Verify the colored eye location of the centerline is marked green.

Main Deployment Bag Repair—Closing Flap Grommet Pullout

- Applicable products: All main deployment bags

- Description: Repair of main deployment bag

- Authorized repairmen: FAA Senior or Master Parachute Rigger

- Materials: E thread, Type-4 tape or equivalent and grommets to match original

- Machines: 301 straight stitch—medium duty 7–11 SPI and 308 zigzag—medium duty 7–11 SPI

- Equipment: Scissors, seam ripper or scalpel, marking pencil, 6-inch ruler, grommet set, and hole punch

Procedure

The most common repair needed to a main deployment is the repair of the closing flap in the area of the grommets. The grommets work loose and pull out, damaging the material. The tongue will need reinforcing and new grommets.

Disassembly

1. Remove grommets from the tongue of the bag.

2. Unpick the binding along the edge of the grommet reinforcing tape. *[Figure A]*

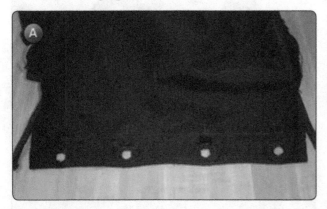

Reassembly

1. Overlay a piece of 1.5 inch Type-4 tape on the top of the bag tongue and sew down. *[Figure B]*

2. Punch new holes through the Type-4 from the back side in the same location as the original location.

3. Overlay the back side of the tongue with a piece of 1.5 inch Type-3 tape and sew down. *[Figure C]* Punch new holes through the tape.

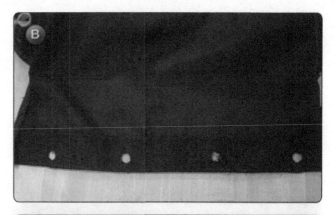

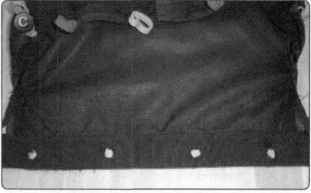

4. Sew down the binding tape and rebind as needed. *[Figure D]*

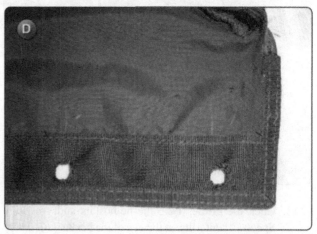

5. Set new grommets in the original locations. *[Figure E]*

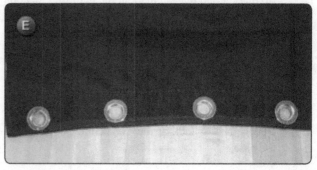

Inspection

- Verify stitching is secure.
- Verify new grommets are secure.

Section 5, Alterations

In the "old days" when military surplus equipment was common, there were a number of alterations available to make the surplus equipment suitable for sport use. Since then, however, the sport has progressed and purpose-built sport equipment is now the rule, so most equipment does not need any specialized alterations for use. Most alterations now deal primarily with harness size adjustments for individuals, or they are designed to enhance the performance of the parachute.

In the past, alterations were often done by well-intentioned individuals who knew how to do them but in most cases did not have the authority to perform them. The common attitude was, "I'm a master rigger; I can do anything." As long as the work was done reasonably well and no one got hurt, this was an accepted practice. While there may be a few individuals who still adhere to that philosophy, as a whole, the rigging profession is much more aware of limitations in regard to alterations. Under 14 CFR part 65, section 65.129(d), "No certificated parachute rigger may (d) Alter a parachute in a manner that is not specifically authorized by the Administrator or the manufacturer." In today's world, manufacturers are much more concerned with the alterations being performed on their products. With the advent of the Internet and other means of high-speed communications, riggers have much more access to the manufacturer and are more likely to communicate with them as to what can be done. Also, due to liability issues, many riggers are reluctant to undertake alterations without the manufacturer's approval.

What constitutes the manufacturer's approval for an alteration? To be safe, the rigger should always have something in writing that specifically addresses the alteration the rigger wishes to perform. There should be a two way line of communication for this. One, the rigger should specifically request from the manufacturer the authority to perform the alteration. This should include serial number, make, model of the product involved, and a description of the alteration. Two, in return, the rigger should receive written authorization to perform the alteration. The manufacturer specifies the form of this authorization, but it should have the date, the rigger's name and certificate number, and a reference to the rigger's original request. This fulfills the requirements of the regulations and protects both parties involved.

In certain cases, a rigger might want to perform an alteration on a product for which the manufacturer is no longer in business. This is commonly known as an orphaned product.

If this occurs, the rigger should obtain approval from the FAA. Refer to AC 105-2, Sport Parachute Jumping. Alterations to approved parachutes must be performed only by a certificated and appropriately rated Master Parachute Rigger, a parachute manufacturer, or any other manufacturer that the FAA considers competent. To receive approval from the FAA, a person qualified to alter a parachute would first contact the FAA Flight Standards District Office (FSDO) to discuss the proposed alteration with an FAA inspector. The inspector requires a description of the proposed alteration along with a sample, technical data and proposed test data to ensure that the altered parachute meets all applicable requirements. After discussing the proposed alteration, the two parties agree on a suitable plan of action. The individual then drafts an application, in letter form, addressed to the local FSDO. Along with the letter, the following information needs to be attached:

1. A clear description of the alteration

2. Technical information that includes drawings and photographs, materials used, stitch patterns, and location of altered components

3. A means of identifying the altered parachute, such as model and serial number, and identification of the person having performed the alteration

After the inspector reviews the application, if he or she is satisfied, he or she indicates approval by date stamping, signing, and placing the FSDO identification stamp on the letter of application. Upon receiving this approval, the master rigger can then perform the alteration.

The following are alterations found in Section 5, Alterations, of this chapter:

- *Articulated harness main lift web resizing
- Leg pad resizing
- *Automatic Activation Device (AAD) installation

NOTE: A * denotes approval needed by the Administrator or the manufacturer.

Articulated Harness Main Lift Web (MLW) Resizing

- Applicable products: Most articulated harness configurations
- Description: Resizing of an articulated harness
- Authorized repairmen: FAA Master Parachute Rigger
- Materials: E thread, 5-cord nylon thread, Type-7 webbing, or as original and Type-4 1 inch tape

- Machines: 308 zigzag—medium duty 7–11 SPI, heavy-duty harness machine, Singer 7–33 or equivalent 4-6 SPI
- Equipment: Scissors, seam ripper or scalpel, marking pencil, 18-inch ruler, and hot glue gun

Procedure

Resizing of a harness is usually considered an alteration. However, because of the simplicity of the procedure, most manufacturers do not object to a qualified master rigger performing the procedure. It would be wise, however, for the rigger to contact the manufacturer for permission before undertaking the procedure. The following procedure is shown on a Voodoo™ system.

Disassembly

1. Measure the MLW to check if the harness is even.

2. Remove the ripcord pocket/MLW cover. *[Figure A]*

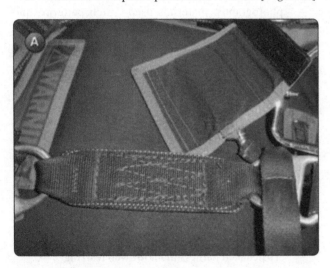

3. Measure the lower MLW. *[Figure B]*

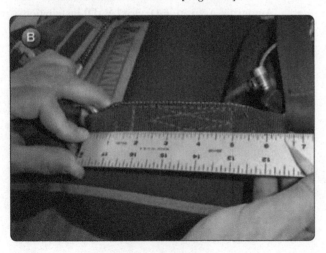

4. Remove the lower MLW. *[Figure C]*

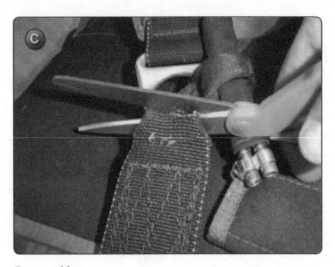

Reassembly

1. Measure the webbing for the lower main lift web. *[Figure D]*

2. Zigzag the bowtie folds as marked including the Type-4 buffers. *[Figure E]*

3. Glue the MLW in place. Make sure that the open end of the webbing is on the rear and oriented up towards the chest strap.

4. Mark the stitch pattern on the MLW and sew with the harness machine. Use a 3 inch W-W pattern at the top as shown in *Figure F*. Include a box pattern on the lower section of the MLW.

5. Reattach the ripcord pocket/MLW cover. *[Figure G]*

Inspection

- Check that the new harness dimensions are correct and symmetrical.
- Verify the harness stitching is correct for SPI and tension.
- The ripcord pocket/MLW cover must be reattached.

Leg Pad Resizing

- Applicable products: Most harness leg pad configurations
- Description: Shortening the length of the leg pad
- Authorized repairmen: FAA Senior or Master Parachute Rigger
- Materials: E thread
- Machines: 301 straight stitch—medium duty 7–11 SPI, 301 double needle with tape folder 7–11 SPI, and 1 inch × 42 stitch bar tack
- Equipment: Scissors, seam ripper or scalpel, marking pencil, 6-inch ruler, and hot knife

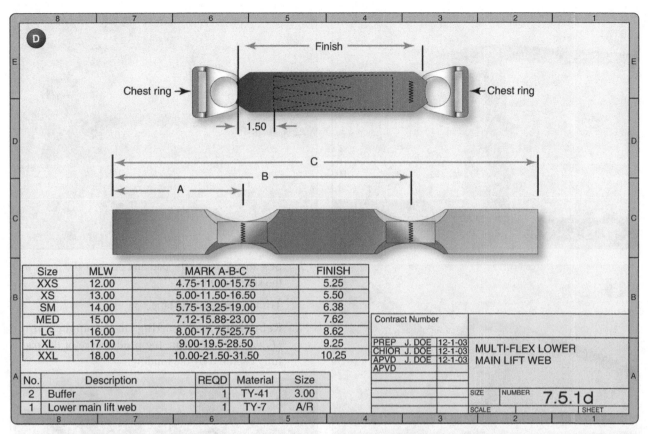

Size	MLW	MARK A-B-C	FINISH
XXS	12.00	4.75-11.00-15.75	5.25
XS	13.00	5.00-11.50-16.50	5.50
SM	14.00	5.75-13.25-19.00	6.38
MED	15.00	7.12-15.88-23.00	7.62
LG	16.00	8.00-17.75-25.75	8.62
XL	17.00	9.00-19.5-28.50	9.25
XXL	18.00	10.00-21.50-31.50	10.25

Finish

Chest ring →   ← Chest ring

1.50

C
B
A

Contract Number

PREP	J. DOE	12-1-03
CHIOR	J. DOE	12-1-03
APVD	J. DOE	12-1-03
APVD		

MULTI-FLEX LOWER
MAIN LIFT WEB

| SIZE | NUMBER | 7.5.1d |
| SCALE | | SHEET |

No.	Description	REQD	Material	Size
2	Buffer	1	TY-41	3.00
1	Lower main lift web	1	TY-7	A/R

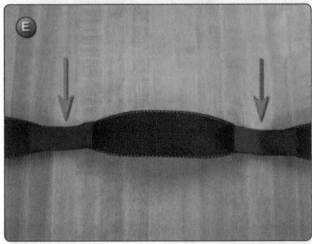

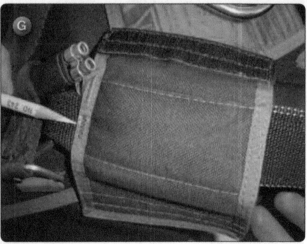

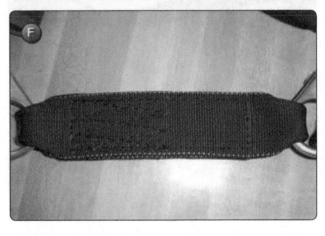

Procedure

Disassembly

1. Measure the amount that the pad is to be shortened and mark on the sleeve of the pad. *[Figure A]*

2. Remove all bar tacks or zigzag stitching from the binding.

3. Using the hot knife, remove the binding from the pad. *[Figure B]*

4. Unpick the sleeve from the body of the pad. Fold the pad under and using the hot knife, shorten the sleeve by the required amount.

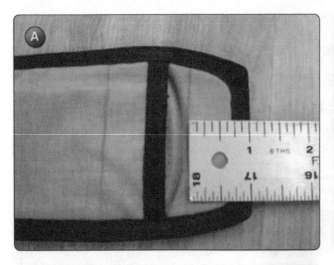

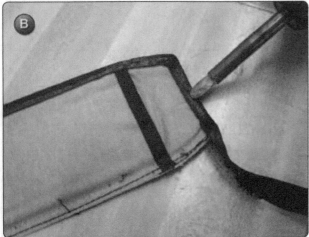

5. Measure the pad and mark. Trim with the hot knife. *[Figure C]*

Reassembly

1. Using the double needle machine and binder, bind the end of the sleeve. *[Figure D]*

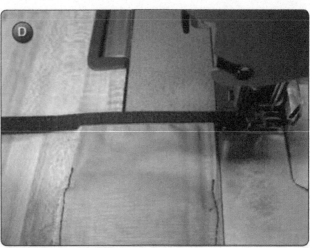

2. Sew the sleeve to the pad and pre-sew the foam with the single needle.

3. Trim the ends of the tape.

4. Rebind the pad starting at the upper corner. *[Figure E]* Make sure the inside curve of the pad is fully captured by the binding.

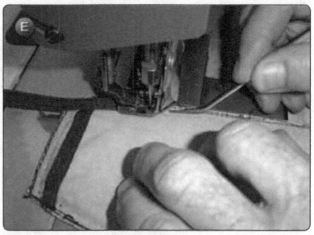

5. Bar tack at the original locations. *[Figure F]*

Inspection

- Verify the length is correct.
- Check that the bar tacks are at the original location.

Automatic Activation Device (AAD) Installation

- Applicable products: Most 1-pin sport piggyback systems
- Description: Installation of a CYPRES® AAD to a 1-pin sport piggyback harness and container system
- Authorized repairmen: FAA Master Parachute Rigger
- Materials: E thread—color to match, CYPRES® installation kit, and Spandex® fabric (optional)
- Machines: 301 straight stitch—medium duty 7–11 SPI and 308 zigzag—medium duty 7–11 SPI
- Equipment: Scissors, seam ripper or scalpel, marking pencil, 12-inch ruler, hot knife, and wallpaper roller

Procedure

The following procedure is representative of a typical installation of the CYPRES® AAD into a modern 1-pin reserve container system. While providing guidance for this operation, it is imperative that the rigger possesses the proper instructions from both the harness-container manufacturer and the AAD manufacturer.

Disassembly

Open the right side corner of the reserve container. *[Figure A]* While this might not be needed on some size containers, it generally makes the installation of the pocket easier and it is not that hard to close the corner back up.

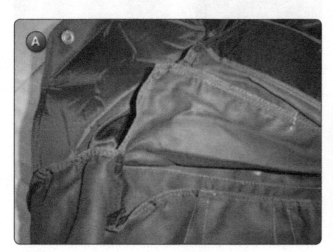

Reassembly

1. Mark the center of the container wall at the bottom. *[Figure B]*

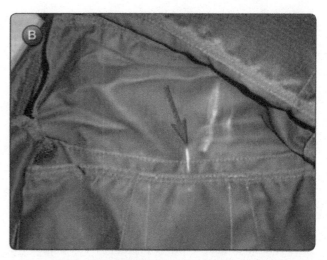

2. Mark the center of the Spandex® portion of the CYPRES® pocket. *[Figure C]* Do not mark the center of the entire pocket. The Spandex® must be centered on the wall to allow for the correct positioning of the CYPRES® processing unit.

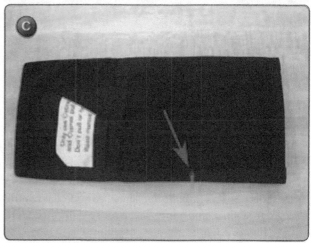

3. Align the marks and the pocket as close to the bottom of the wall as possible. *[Figure D]*

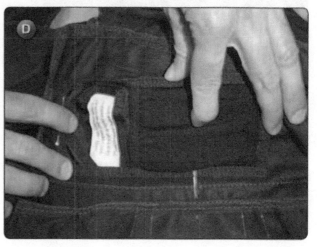

4. Sew around the pocket with the single needle machine. Backstitch .5 inch at each of the corners for reinforcing.

5. Next, install or create a cable channel for the control cable. Some systems, such as the one shown in *Figure F*, can be modified to provide the channel. Others need to use the adhesive backed channel provided with the CYPRES® kit.

Built-In Channel Modification Configuration

1. Mark the bottom and top of the pack tray cover as shown. *[Figure E]* Place a hand tack at the A position. Unpick the stitching between the corner bar tack and the hand tack at the A position. Also, unpick the stitching between the B bar tacks.

2. There is now a built-in channel to slide the control cable thru and stow the excess cable as well. *[Figure F]*

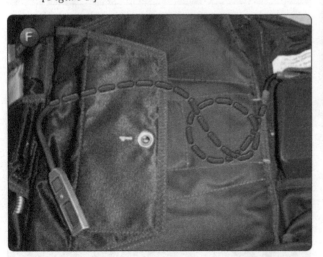

Adhesive Channel Installation

1. Measure the distance along the long axis of the reserve container from the bottom of the pocket location to the top of the container near the planned location for the control unit. *[Figure G]*

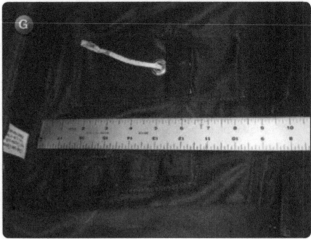

2. Cut a piece of the adhesive backed channel to the same length. Remove the adhesive covering and position the channel in place. Roll the channel with the wallpaper roller to secure the adhesive.

3. Locate the position for the control pocket. Unpick the stitching that holds the main container to the backpad. *[Figure H]*

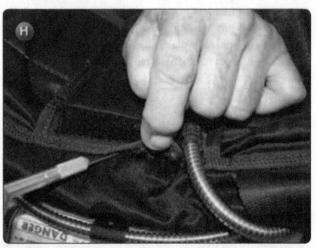

4. Insert the pocket with the mouth towards the channel opening and restitch the container to the backpad. *[Figure I]* Make sure the control head fits into the pocket.

Cutter Channel and Elastic Installation

The location of the cutter is specified by the container manufacturer's instructions and should be strictly adhered to. The following location is specified for the Talon system.

1. Lay the CYPRES® unit on the pocket and route the cutter/cable assembly out the top of the pocket and in as direct a line to the side flap as possible. It is necessary to cut a hole in the bottom launching flap to access the side flap.

2. Where the cable passes through the bottom launching flap as close to the wall as possible, place a line approximately .5 inch long. *[Figure J]* Take the hot knife and cut a single slit the length of the mark. DO NOT CUT ANY OTHER MATERIAL.

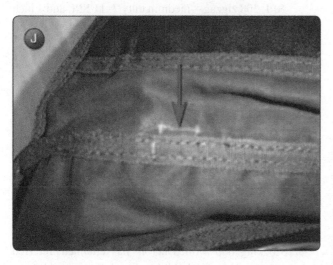

3. Route the cable through the slit and then along the side flap as shown. *[Figure K]*

4. Place marks along the binding showing the start and finish locations for the cable channel. Again, the rigger can use the adhesive backed channel or make a channel out of the Spandex® material as shown. *[Figure L]*

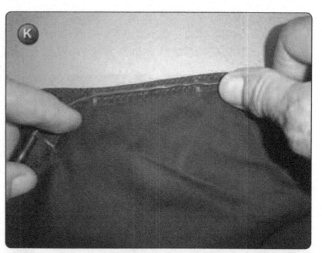

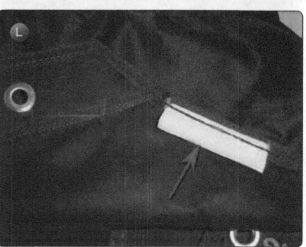

5. Route the cutter thru the channel and out the end nearest the side flap grommet.

6. Slide the cutter elastic over the cutter and position the cutter over the grommet with the hole to the outside of the grommet and the elastic facing inwards on the flap. Mark the corners of the cutter as shown. *[Figure M]*

7. Remove the CYPRES® from the container completely. Position the elastic sleeve to the marks and sew in place with the zigzag machine. *[Figure N]*

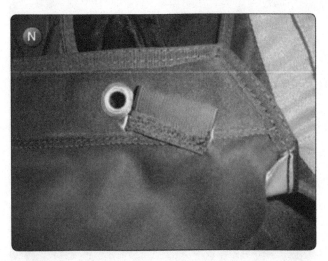

8. Re-close the corner of the reserve container as per the original.

Inspection

- Verify the CYPRES® pocket is sewn with the Spandex® pocket centered on the wall.

- Control cable channel must be installed.

- Control unit pocket must be installed.

- Cutter cable channel must be installed.

- Cutter elastic must be installed.

- Verify the reserve container corner is closed, as necessary.

- Check the fit of CYPRES® in the entire installation.

- Log installation data on the packing data card. Remember, this is an alteration.

Section 6, Manufacturing

There might come times when it is more practical for the rigger to manufacture replacement parts in order to return a system to operation. The items listed in this section are those that are either main component parts or the reserve closing loop, which is simple to make and usually within the purview of the senior rigger to do so. It is important for the rigger to recognize just what parts are legal to make. One item some riggers make, but one in which they are not usually approved to do so, is the Safety Stow™ for the reserve free bag. As part of the TSO-C23d component, it is manufactured from approved materials and under an approved Quality Control system. As simple as this item is, if it is not manufactured according to the original configuration. There is a very good chance for a failure of the reserve deployment system. The best rule of thumb to follow is this: If the component is part of the approved assembly, then it is probably not something that may be manufactured in the field. The common exception to this rule is the reserve closing loop.

The rigger who is undertaking the manufacture of these components needs to have, at the minimum, the following sewing machines: medium duty, single-needle, double needle machine with a binding attachment and a zigzag machine. In addition, the rigger needs grommet setting tools and a basic selection of webbings, materials, and fabrics.

The following are outlines of construction procedures for the manufacture of the listed items found in Section 6, Manufacturing:

- Main and reserve closing loop manufacture

- Main deployment bag

- Bottom of Container (BOC) pocket

Main and Reserve Closing Loop Manufacture

- Applicable products: All harness and containers that utilize a fabric closing loop configuration

- Description: Fabrication of fabric closing loops

- Authorized repairmen: FAA Senior or Master Parachute Rigger

- Materials: E thread, loop material—725# Spectra®

- Machines: 301 straight stitch—medium duty 7–11 SPI, 308 zigzag—medium duty 7–11 SPI, and 1 inch × 42 stitch bar tack (optional)

- Equipment: Scissors, seam ripper or scalpel, marking pencil, 18-inch ruler, hot knife, finger-trapping needle or fid, and finger-trapping wire

Procedure

The terms "locking loops" and "closing loops" are synonymous and used interchangeably. Fabric locking loops have become the preferred method of closing most modern parachute containers. Dating from the mid 1970s, the most common material was Type-III suspension line. It was soon recognized that other materials, such as Dacron® were superior for this use. Today, Spectra® is widely used for reserve locking loops while Dacron® has remained preferred for main loops due to its durability. The following technique demonstrates the fabrication of a 1-pin and a 2-pin loop.

Preparation: 1-Pin Loop

1. Measure the length of the original loop. If the stop knot is too tight to untie, allow extra length (you can always cut it down, but you cannot glue it back on).

2. Cut an appropriate length of material and hot knife one end on an angle.

Fabrication

1. Fold the line in half and mark the center. *[Figure A]*

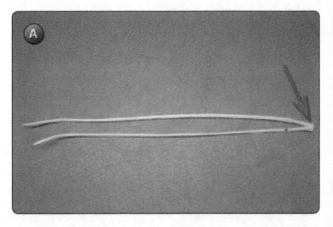

2. Place a mark at 1 inch from the center on the hot knifed end.

3. Take the finger-trapping fid and screw it onto the hot knifed end. *[Figure B]*

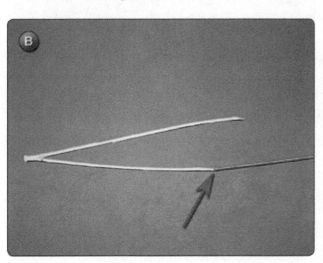

4. Insert the pointed end of the fid into the line at the farthest mark by separating the weave of the material so that the fid then passes through the length of the braided line and out the scissor cut end. *[Figure C]*

5. Draw the line through until the two marks are aligned. This results in a loop eye of approximately .5 inch. *[Figure D]*

6. Pinch the eye of the loop with one hand and smooth the material from the eye to the end. Hot knife the running end.

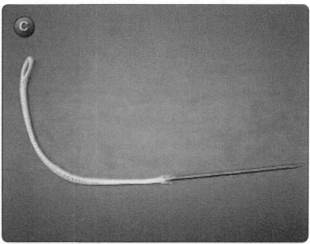

7. For short loops used with a main container, simply tie an overhand knot in the loop for the required length. A metal washer is used to keep the loop from pulling through the grommet. *[Figure E]*

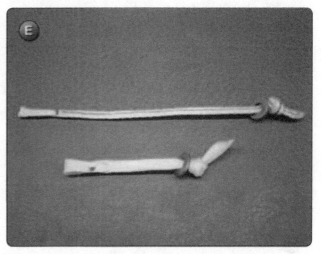

8. If the loop is to be used with a reserve container, it may be required to sew the finger-trapped part of the loop for security. If this is the case, simply sew the length of the finger-trapped portion of the loop with a single-needle machine before hot knifing the end. Start at the running end and sew towards the eye of the loop. Stop sewing approximately .12 inch from the eye and then backstitch a minimum of 1 inch. *[Figure F]* Trim the end with the hot knife.

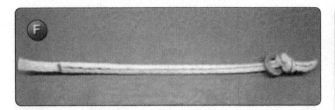

Fabrication: 2-Pin Loop

1. Measure and mark the line according to *Figure G.* Cut both ends with the scissors.

2. Using the finger-trapping wire, finger-trap one end to form the loop and have the running end exit approximately 1 inch past the center mark. *[Figure H]*

3. Repeat with the opposite end. Exit again past the center so that the two lines overlap at the center. *[Figure I]*

4. Pull the loop tight to remove any slack.

5. Bar tack or zigzag the loop ends. *[Figure J]*

6. Trim the running ends. *[Figure K]*

7. Bar tack or zigzag the center overlap junction. *[Figure L]*

8. Measure the finished loop.

Inspection

- Check the loop length.
- Verify stitching is secure and backstitched.

Main Deployment Bag

- Applicable products: All sport systems that utilize a main deployment bag

- Description: Fabrication of a main deployment bag

- Authorized repairmen: FAA Senior or Master Parachute Rigger

- Materials: E thread, Nylon para-pak fabric, Type-3 ¾ inch nylon binding tape, Type-1 ⁹⁄₁₆ inch nylon tape,

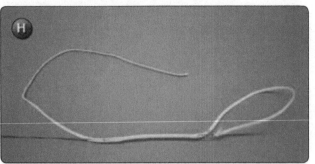

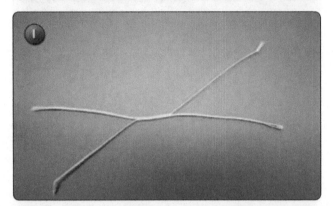

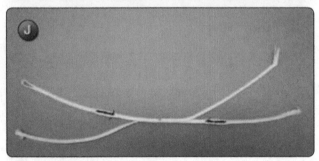

Type-4 1 inch nylon webbing, Type-4 1½ inch nylon webbing, Type-12 nylon webbing, #3 rolled rim spur brass grommets, #5 rolled rim spur grommet

- Machines: 301 straight stitch—medium duty 5–9 SPI, 301 double needle with tape folder 5–9 SPI, 1 inch × 42 stitch bar tack

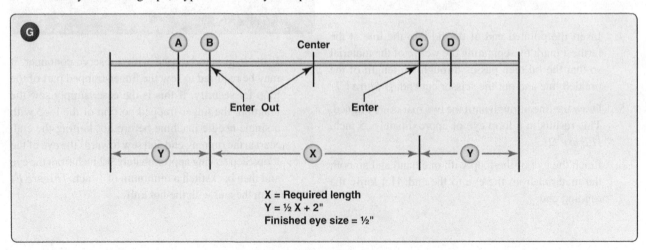

X = Required length
Y = ½ X + 2"
Finished eye size = ½"

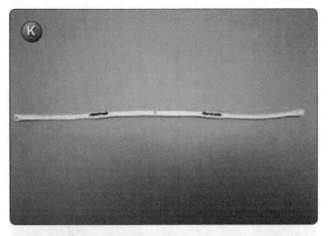

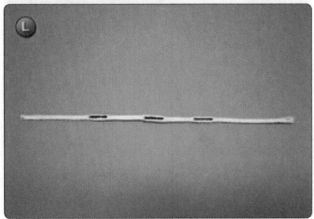

- Equipment: Scissors, marking pencil, 36-inch ruler, carpenter's square, hot knife, and #3 & #5 spur grommet sets

NOTE: This procedure allows for either (1) duplicating an existing main bag, or (2) measuring a container to determine the correct size bag required.

Procedure

Layout

1. Measure the container according to *Figure A* or measure an existing bag according to *Figure B*.

2. Transfer these dimensions to *Figure C*.

3. Lay out bag pattern on the para-pak according to *Figure C*.

4. Cut para-pak and all required tapes and webbings.

Assembly

1. Fold Type-12 to center and sew to the inside of the bag fabric at the top grommet location. *[Figure D]*

2. Sew 1½ inch Type-4 tape at the outside tongue location. *[Figure E]*

3. Sew 1 inch Type-4 tape at the outside mouth location. At the same time, sew down the two side stow band tapes and the three mouth stow band tapes. *[Figure F]*

4. Bind the mouth of the bag with the double needle binding machine. Leave the tapes long at the ends.

5. With the bag inside out, match the edge of the mouth with the alignment marks on the tongue. *[Figure G]* Sew along edges to form bag.

6. Trim the excess tapes at the edge of the bag.

7. Starting at the inside corner of the bag, bind the inside seam. *[Figure H]*

8. Trim the inside ends of the binding leaving a 2 inch tail. *[Figure I]* Double the tail back and bar tack.

9. Bar tack the stow loops at the appropriate locations. *[Figure J]*

10. Install a #5 grommet at the top center of the bag. Orient the grommet from the inside with the washer on the outside. *[Figure K]*

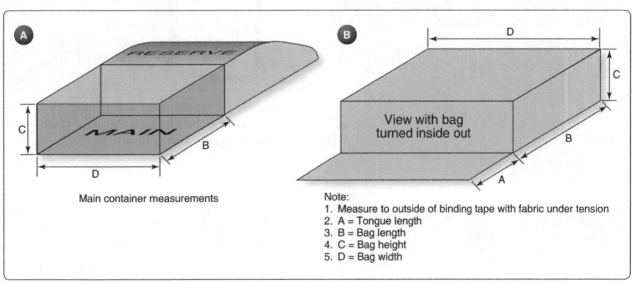

Main container measurements

Note:
1. Measure to outside of binding tape with fabric under tension
2. A = Tongue length
3. B = Bag length
4. C = Bag height
5. D = Bag width

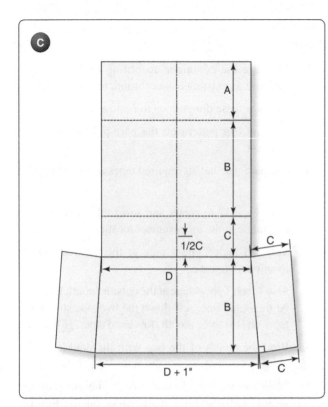

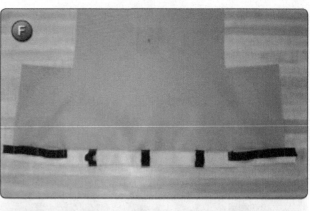

11. Install the three #3 grommets in the tongue of the bag with the grommets from the outside and the washers on the inside. *[Figure L]*

Inspection

- Sewing should be straight.
- Binding should be secure.
- Verify all bar tacks are in place.
- Grommets should be oriented correctly and secure.

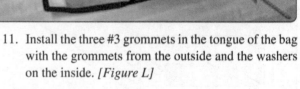

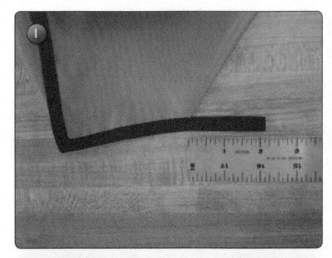

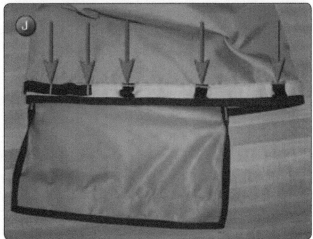

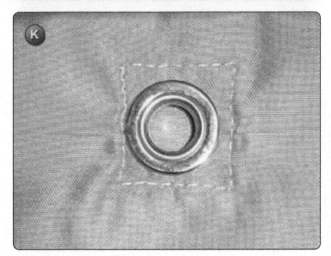

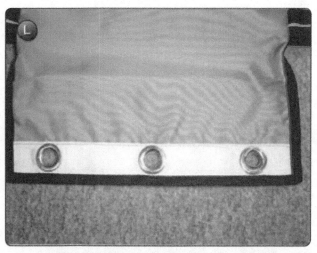

- Materials: E thread, Para-pak fabric, Spandex® or equivalent elastic fabric, ⅝ inch elastic tape, and Type-3¾ inch binding tape

- Machines: 301 straight stitch—medium duty 7–11 SPI, 301 double needle with tape folder 7–11 SPI, and 1 inch × 42 stitch bar tack

- Equipment: Scissors, marking pencil, 18-inch ruler, carpenter's square, and hot knife

Procedure

Layout

1. Draw the shape of the BOC pocket on the para-pak fabric to the size required to fit the pilot chute. This will be the base panel.

2. Fold the Spandex® fabric in half and cut to the same size as the base panel. This will be the pocket panel. Make sure the grain of the fabric is parallel with the length of the pocket for stretch. Trim ½ inch off the end opposite the fold. *[Figure A]*

Bottom of Container (BOC) Pocket

- Applicable products: All containers that have a BOC pocket configuration

- Description: Fabrication of a BOC pocket

- Authorized repairmen: FAA Senior or Master Parachute Rigger

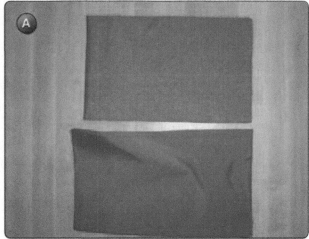

Assembly

1. Open the sides of the pocket at the folded end and insert the length of elastic tape. Sew the tape in place with the single needle on both sides.

2. Mark the center of the mouth and bar tack the elastic reinforcing as shown. *[Figure B]*

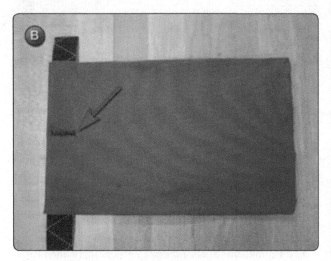

3. Lay the pocket on the para-pak base and sew in place. *[Figure C]* (Sewing with the Spandex® on the bottom and the para-pak on top minimizes stretch from the presser foot.)

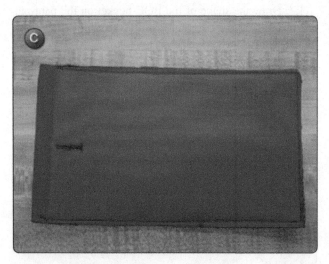

4. Bind the pocket, starting at the bottom corner opposite the mouth of the pocket. *[Figure D]*

5. Bar tack the mouth of the pocket securing the elastic reinforcing on both sides. *[Figure E]*

6. The pocket is now complete and ready for installation.

Inspection

- Verify that the size is correct.

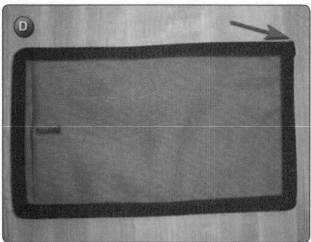

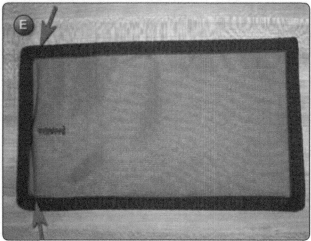

- Binding should be secure.
- Verify the bar tacks are in place at the center of the pocket and at the sides.

Section 7, Manufacturing

The following are miscellaneous procedures used in repairs and alterations found in Section 7, Manufacturing, of this chapter:

- Hand tacking techniques
- Cleaning and washing procedures

Hand Tacking Techniques

- Applicable products: Any systems requiring hand tacking
- Description: Securing housings, hardware, etc., with hand tackings
- Authorized repairmen: FAA Senior or Master Parachute Rigger
- Materials: Nylon supertack tacking thread
- Machines: None

- Equipment: Scissors, assorted hand tacking needles, and modified navy end tab

Procedure

Hand tacking is an integral part of rigging skills. There are numerous places where components or parts are joined. Hardware, housings, cones, and other parts require hand tacking to secure them to their positions. The following figures show typical tacking techniques.

Pilot Chute

1. Take the needle and supertack and pass it through the reinforcing tape at the bottom of the pilot chute mesh capturing the spring coil. *[Figure A]*

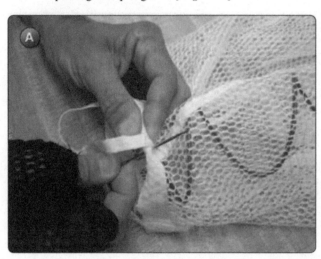

2. Cross over the radial seam reinforcing tape and again pass the needle through the reinforcing tape and capturing the spring coil as before. *[Figure B]*

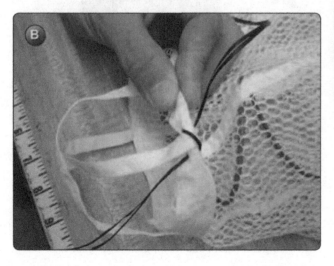

3. Secure the ends of the supertack with a surgeon's knot and locking knot. *[Figure C]* Trim to a ¾ inch tail.

Housing

1. Position the housing end flush with the end of the housing channel.

2. Take the needle and supertack and tie an overhand knot approximately 1 inch from the end.

3. Pass the needle through the inside of the housing channel and then around the outside below the housing end. *[Figure D]* The purpose is to choke the end of the channel so that the housing does not protrude from the end.

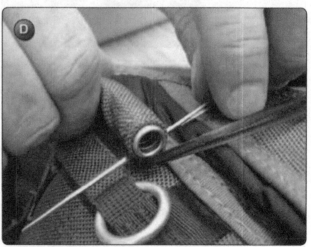

4. Next take the needle and pass it through the top of the channel fabric over the housing. *[Figure E]*

5. Take the needle and locate the grooves in the housing. *[Figure F]* Make three loops through the channel, trapping the supertack in the grooves. *[Figure G]*

6. Secure the running end with a surgeon's knot and locking knot.

7. Twist the supertack together and trim with a ¾ inch tail.

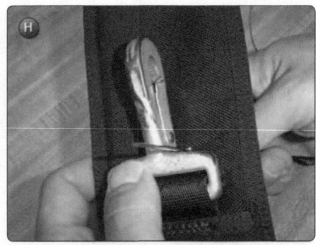

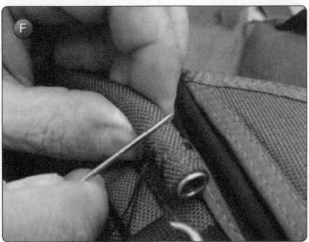

3. Continue with two more turns over the bar keeping the tackings next to each other. *[Figure J]*

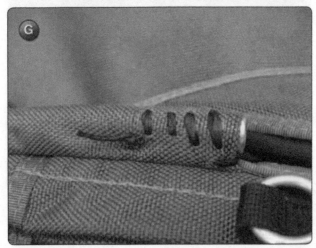

Hardware

1. Take the needle and doubled supertack and pass it through the leg pad from the bottom next to the edge of the leg snap. *[Figure H]*

2. Pass the supertack over the bar of the snap and down through the pad. *[Figure I]*

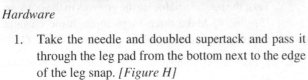

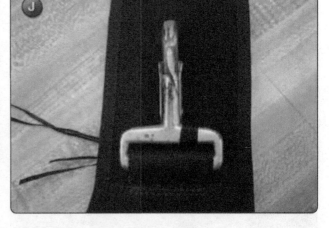

4. Secure the two ends on the bottom of the pad with a surgeon's knot and locking knot. *[Figure K]*

5. Twist the ends together and trim to a ¾ inch tail.

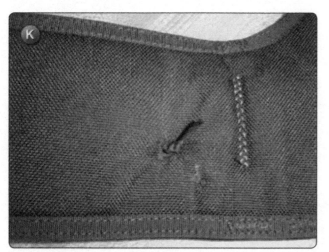

Cleaning and Washing Procedures

- Applicable products: Most harness and container systems

- Description: Cleaning and washing parachute components

- Authorized repairmen: FAA Senior or Master Parachute Rigger

- Materials: Woolite® or similar mild liquid soap and a lot of clean fresh water

- Machines: Jumbo tumbler type commercial washing machine. It is not recommended to do this in your home washing machine.

- Equipment: Medium stiffness scrub brush, large pillowcase or laundry bag, wash tub, assortment of rags, and extra laundry

Background

This procedure applies only to harness and container systems. Most canopy manufacturers do not approve of washing their products to clean them. Doing so may alter the performance characteristics of the canopy. Follow the instructions in the owner's manual for each make and model of canopy.

Colorfastness

It is important to check for colorfastness of certain types of materials. Colored E thread and Type-3 binding tape have shown a tendency for their colors to run when wet or damp. Red is particularly prone to doing so. Before using the following procedures, the rigger or owner should check for colorfastness. Do so by wetting a small area of the container including the binding tape and then lay a damp piece of white cotton t-shirt on the wet area. Leave for 30 minutes. Check to see if any color has transferred to the cotton fabric. If not, then it is probably alright to wash the rig. Remember, this procedure in no way guarantees that the colors will not run.

Procedure

Disassembly

1. Remove all canopies, AADs, and component parts, such as toggles, RSL, ripcords, bags, and elastic keepers, as well as the packing data card.

Handwashing

1. Soak the rig in lukewarm water. Apply straight Woolite® or soap onto the dirtiest areas and scrub with the brush. Soak in lukewarm water for 20 minutes.

2. Scrub the rig vigorously all over. Soak for another 20 minutes.

3. Continue scrubbing vigorously and soak for another 20 minutes. For particularly dirty rigs, empty the first batch of soapy water and wash in a fresh batch of soapy water.

4. Squeeze out as much soapy water as possible. Immerse in fresh, clean, cool water and rinse several times until no further soap comes out.

5. Hang to dry out of direct sunlight. The use of a fan directly onto the rig will greatly speed up the drying process.

Machine Washing

1. Wrap the hardware of the rig with the rags to pad them so they do not beat the inside of the machine.

2. Soak the rig in lukewarm water and apply Woolite® or other soap directly onto the dirtiest parts. Scrub these parts vigorously. Allow these parts to absorb the Woolite® during the time traveling to the Laundromat.

3. Place the rig into the pillowcase or laundry bag and add extra padding, such as extra laundry. Levi's® work exceptionally well for this. Tie off the pillowcase or bag to hold everything in. Place in the washing machine adding more washing soap and Woolite® and wash in warm water.

4. Run through at least two rinse cycles or hand rinse several times until no soap comes out.

5. Hang to dry out of direct sunlight. The use of a fan onto the rig will greatly speed up the drying process.

Scotchgard®

The use of Scotchgard® brand fabric protector has become commonplace in recent years. This fabric treatment seals the pores of the fabric against dirt and other stains. Scotchgard® is not a magical "silver bullet" against dirt. However, it has shown good results in keeping lighter-colored fabric cleaner longer under normal use. Grinding in on grass or asphalt or other heavy abuse still stains and/or damages the rig materials. Scotchgard® is not harmful to today's container fabrics, such as para-pak and Cordura®. There are currently several Scotchgard® formulas. The standard fabric and upholstery formula is in the red can. *[Figure A]* Do not use the rug and carpet formula in the blue can. After the rig is completely dry, hang it in a well ventilated location.

Following the directions on the can, apply the protector to the entire outer surface of the rig. For those areas, such as the inside of the leg pads, backpad, and bottom of the main container, and light colored panels, such as white, etc., apply a second coat after the first has dried. Do not intentionally spray the hardware, housings, and clear vinyl CYPRES® window. After the rig has dried, it may then be reassembled and placed back into service.

Chapter Summary

It is very important that any repairs or maintenance of the parachute and its related systems are done correctly so that the parachute is always airworthy. This chapter provides detailed step-by-step procedures for many repairs and alterations that can be done by both senior and master riggers. All riggers must learn to identify conditions that may be unsafe and learn how to undertake the necessary repairs to return the parachute to its original, airworthy configuration.

Appendix A
Technical Documents

Standardized Nomenclature for Ram-Air Parachutes

Introduction

This Technical Standard was adopted by the Parachute Industry Association (PIA) on March 27, 2015. Input concerning revisions and additions should be submitted to:

Parachute Industry Association, Inc.
Attention: Technical Committee Chair
3833 West Oakton Street
Skokie, IL 60076
Telephone: 847-674-9472
Fax: 847-674-9743
Email: TechComChair@pia.com

Definitions

Airlock: On a canopy, a valve which permits air flow more easily in one direction, and restricts airflow in the opposite direction. In most case, airlocks are installed in the nose of the canopy to permit air to enter during deployment and flight, and restrict air from flowing out the nose to ensure better pressurization in turbulent air.

Angle of

> **Attack:** The angle formed between the flight path and the chord line. The Greek letter alpha (α) is used to denote the angle of attack. See Figure 3.

> **Trim:** The angle formed between the horizontal reference line and the trim line. The Greek letter theta (θ) is used to denote the angle of trim. Used instead of the somewhat analogous aircraft term "angle of incidence." See Figure 1b.

Area,

> **Airfoil Section:** The finished cross sectional area of a given rib (airfoil) section. When ribs are not identical, the specific rib must be identified. Used for calculations of pack volume and internal volume of canopy.

> **Planform:** The product of the average chord times the average span of the canopy.

> **Projected:** The area of an inflated canopy as viewed from above, perpendicular to the chord line at the centerline of the parachute. Due to canopy curvature and cell inflation bulging the projected area is always smaller than the planform area.

Aspect Ratio: Span^2/Area, which for a rectangular planform reduces to Span/Chord.

Attachment Point: A loop of tape, webbing, or the functional equivalent, for attaching something to the surface of the canopy.

> **Pilot Chute**. An attachment point for the pilot chute or pilot chute bridle, including any reinforcement to reduce the effects of abrasion, and also including any additional rib- or canopy-reinforcing tapes intended to distribute the load from the pilot chute to the canopy.

> **Suspension Line.** An attachment point for a suspension line or control line. Some canopies use extensions of rib-reinforcing or flare-reinforcing load tapes to form line attachment points. See also **Flare, Suspension Line Attachment**.

Cell: The chamber formed by upper and lower surfaces and two adjacent loadbearing ribs.

Channel,
> **Drawstring:** A fabric or tape channel that encloses a drawstring, most often found on main canopy sliders.

> **Pilot Chute Reefing:** A channel that runs through the center of the canopy, from upper surface to the lower surface, to allow the pilot chute bridle to connect to the slider.

Chord: The distance from the farthest forward point to the farthest aft point on an airfoil section. If the canopy airfoil sections are not identical, an average chord may be specified. Airfoil dimensions are assumed to be finished dimensions unless otherwise specified. See also **Span**, and **Line (Design), Chord.**

Construction,
> **Chordwise:** A construction method in which upper and lower surfaces are assembled from panels which run from front to rear (chordwise) and are joined to the ribs and each other using a variety of sewn seams. The most common type of ram-air parachute construction.

> **Spanwise:** A construction method in which the upper and lower surfaces are assembled from panels that run from side to side (spanwise) across the full width of the canopy. Personnel parachutes usually require three or four panels each for the upper and lower surfaces.

Crossports: Holes cut in the rib sections to balance the air pressure between adjacent chambers.

Drawstring, Slider: A length of tape or line which may be pulled to collapse or remove a slider after deployment.

Flare, Suspension Line Attachment: An extension of a load bearing rib used on some canopies to distribute suspension line loads along the lower rib seams. A suspension line attachment flare may be integral with the rib or may be sewn to it.

Line (Design),

> **Chord:** A line drawn through the farthest forward point and the farthest aft point on an airfoil section. See Figure 3.

> **Reference, Horizontal:** A line drawn at a right angle to the Vertical Reference Line. Usage is equivalent to the practice of using the aircraft longitudinal axis as an aircraft reference line. See Figure 3.

> **Reference, Vertical:** A line drawn through the links and the quarter chord point.

Trim: A line drawn through the farthest forward and farthest aft line attachment points (excluding control line attachment points). See Figure 1b.

Line (Rigging),

Cascade: A line attached with one end at the canopy and the other end to an intermediate point of an adjacent line. Contrast with **Continuous.**

Continuous: A line attached with one end at the canopy and the other end at the riser of connector link. Contrast with **Cascade.**

Control: A line fastened to the trailing edge of the canopy, used to steer and modulate the forward speed and descent rate of the parachute. Also known as steering or brake line.

Flare: A control line intended primarily for flaring the canopy for landing, but which may also for steering. Also known as **Secondary** control lines, in which case the remaining control lines are known as **Primary** control lines.

Brake-Toggle: When a control line is constructed in sections, that portion of the line between the toggle and the deployment set eye ("cat-eye").

Lower: When a control line is constructed in sections, that portion of the line between the deployment set eye and the upper portion.

Upper: When a control line is constructed in sections, that portion of the line between the canopy and where it converges with other lines attached to the canopy.

Identification System for:

Suspension lines: lettered "A," "B," "C," . . . from front to rear along each load-bearing seam. Numbered from outboard to inboard (outboard lines numbered "1"; see Figure 2a) or inboard to outboard (lines on center load-bearing seams numbered "1"; see Figure 2b).

Control lines: numbered by rib seam, including non-load-bearing ribs, from outboard to inboard. See Figures 2a and 2b.

Suspension: One of the lines that carries the load from the canopy surface to the risers. Control lines are usually not considered suspension lines.

Pilot Chute Controlled Reefing (PCR): A parachute reefing system that uses the drag of the pilot chute to modulate the opening rate of the canopy.

Planform: The overall shape of the wing as viewed from above, perpendicular to the chord line.

Quarter Chord Point: a point on the chord line one quarter of the distance from the nose to the tail of an airfoil.

Removable Deployment System (RDS): A slider variation that permits the slider to be removed and stowed separately after deployment. "Full RDS" is a further variation that also permits the pilot chute, bridle, and deployment bag to be removed and stowed after deployment.

Rib: A section of fabric installed between the upper and lower surfaces of a canopy. Used to establish the airfoil shaped of the canopy. Rib numbering systems (for example, from outboard to inboard, or from inboard to outboard) vary from manufacturer to manufacturer.

Page 3 of 8

Rib, crossbrace: A rib or partial rib installed at an angle other than a 90° angle to the upper and lower surfaces of a canopy.

Rib, loadbearing: A rib to which suspension lines are attached, installed at a 90° angle to the upper and lower surfaces of a canopy.

Rib, non-loadbearing: A rib without attached suspension lines, installed at a 90° angle to the upper and lower surfaces of a canopy.

Rib, stabilizer: A stabilizer-end rib assembly with line attachments along the lower edge.

Rigging,
> **Crown:** A suspension line length pattern in which all "A" lines are the same length across the span of the canopy, all "B" lines are the same length across the span of the canopy, and similarly all "C" and "D" lines, etc.

> **Flat:** A suspension line length pattern in which the lines in the center of the canopy are shorter than the lines farther outboard. In flight, the center part of the airfoil is flatter and creates more vertical lift than a crown-rigged canopy, which generates lift along the radius of the spanwise arc.

Setting,
> **Deployment:** The position of the trailing edge when the control lines are pulled down to their deployment position.
> **Full-Flight:** The position of the trailing edge when the control lines are fully extended.

Slider: A parachute reefing device usually consisting of a rectangular section of canopy cloth reinforced on the edges with lightweight webbing or tape, and with a large grommet or D-ring installed at each corner. Sliders may have fabric removed from the rectangular section or may have fabric edge extensions installed to change opening characteristics. Slider variations include:
- Domed, with a planform similar to a flat rectangular slider, but with fabric pleated along the edges.
- Split, capable of being disassembled into halves after deployment.
- Spider, made of two lengths of webbing sewn in an "X," and usually used with pilot chute controlled reefing. See **Pilot Chute Controlled Reefing (PCR).**
- Removable. See **Removable Deployment System.**

Slider Bumper: A small device, typically made from vinyl/silicon tubing, Type-4 tape, or Type-12 webbing, installed at the lower end of the suspension lines to prevent damage to the slider grommets caused by the slider contacting the connector links.

Slider Stop: A small piece of rigid material (metal, plastic, phenolic, etc.) normally covered in tape or light webbing, installed on the lower edge of a stabilizer panels to prevent a slider grommet from riding up over the stabilizer material and damaging the stabilizers or the slider.

Slider Stop Chafing Pad: A tape or fabric reinforcement installed on a stabilizer at a slider stop to reduce wear from abrasion.

Soft link: A connector link constructed primarily of fabric or tape.

Span: The distance from one side of a canopy to the opposite side. Measurements taken at various distances aft of the nose will yield different results, Measurements taken across the upper surface will typically be longer than those taken across the lower. An average span, or separate leading and trailing edge dimensions, may be specified. Airfoil dimensions are assumed to be finished dimensions unless otherwise specified. See also **Chord.**

Stabilizer: A fabric panel installed at the end of a canopy, intended primarily to reduce wingtip vortices (much as an end plate on an aircraft wing), and to provide some directional stability. Some stabilizer designs are ram-air pressurized for additional rigidity.

Tapes, Reinforcement: A tape installed in the canopy to provide additional strength or dimensional stability. Tapes are identified by location.

> **Cross Tapes:** A reinforcing tape that runs spanwise on the upper or lower surface to distribute loads through the canopy. With chordwise construction, a cross tape typically runs from a line attachment point to laterally adjacent line attachment point, although some may run from a suspension line attachment point diagonally to a control line attachment point. With spanwise construction, a cross tape may be rolled into a seam joining spanwise panels.

> **Leading Edge Tape:** A tape applied to or rolled into the leading edge of a upper or lower panel. May be continuous across the span of the canopy.

> **Line Attachment Reinforcement Tape:** A tape sewn chordwise into a seam at a line attachment point.

> **Load Tape:** A tape applied to a rib section and used to distribute the load from a line attachment to the canopy. When applied in a "V" may also be known as a "**V-tape**." In some canopies, load tapes may extend through the lower seam to become line attachment points.

> **Rib Leading Edge Tape:** A tape applied to or rolled into the leading edge of a rib section.

> **Trailing Edge Tape:** A tape applied to or rolled into the trailing edge seam. Usually continuous across the span of the canopy.

Toggle, Control: A grip attached to the end of the control line to allow the user an adequate handhold on the line. Most commonly consists of a tape/webbing loop or a hard plastic dowel. Typically supplied as part of the container assembly.

Trim: The arrangement of differential line lengths to produce a desired trim angle and anhedral. See also **Angle of Trim**. See Figures 1a and 1b.

Vent, Lower Surface: An opening in the lower surface to provide an alternate path for pressurization during deployment ("inflation vent") or depressurization during flight ("accuracy vent").

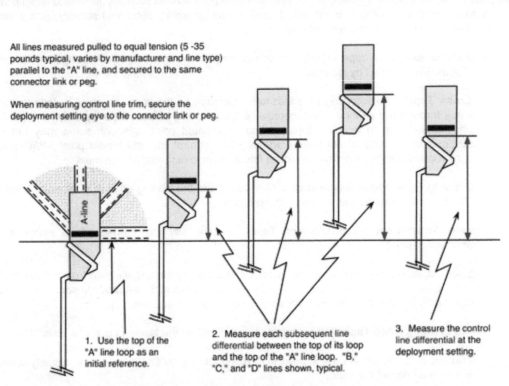

All lines measured pulled to equal tension (5 -35 pounds typical, varies by manufacturer and line type) parallel to the "A" line, and secured to the same connector link or peg.

When measuring control line trim, secure the deployment setting eye to the connector link or peg.

1. Use the top of the "A" line loop as an initial reference.

2. Measure each subsequent line differential between the top of its loop and the top of the "A" line loop. "B," "C," and "D" lines shown, typical.

3. Measure the control line differential at the deployment setting.

Figure 1a. Measuring line length trim.

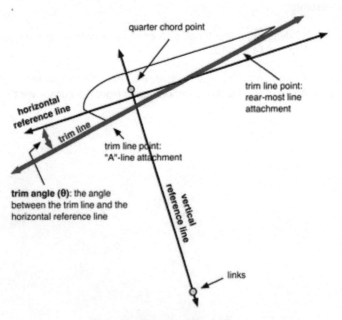

quarter chord point

trim line point: rear-most line attachment

horizontal reference line

trim line

trim line point: "A"-line attachment

vertical reference line

trim angle (θ): the angle between the trim line and the horizontal reference line

links

Figure 1b. Measuring trim angle.

Page 6 of 8

A-8

Change 1 (December 2015)

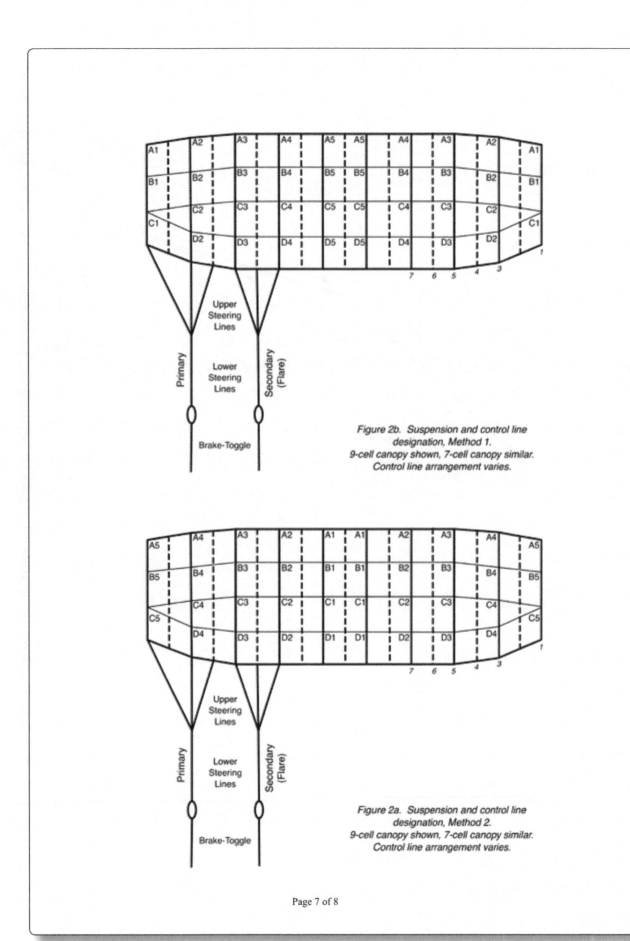

Figure 2b. Suspension and control line
designation, Method 1.
9-cell canopy shown, 7-cell canopy similar.
Control line arrangement varies.

Figure 2a. Suspension and control line
designation, Method 2.
9-cell canopy shown, 7-cell canopy similar.
Control line arrangement varies.

Page 7 of 8

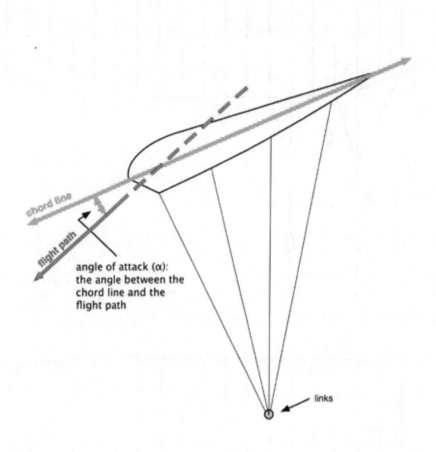

chord line

flight path

angle of attack (α): the angle between the chord line and the flight path

links

Figure 3. Angle of attack.

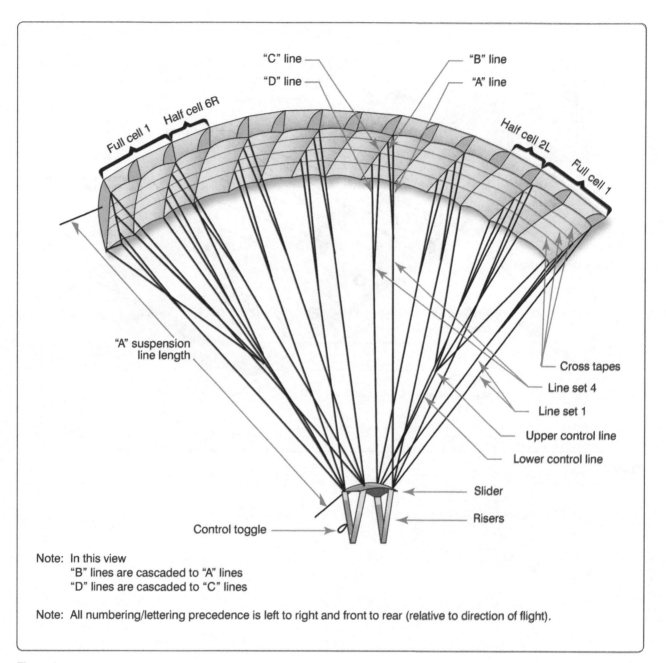

"C" line
"D" line
"B" line
"A" line

Full cell 1
Half cell 6R
Half cell 2L
Full cell 1

"A" suspension
line length

Cross tapes
Line set 4
Line set 1
Upper control line
Lower control line

Slider
Risers

Control toggle

Note: In this view
"B" lines are cascaded to "A" lines
"D" lines are cascaded to "C" lines

Note: All numbering/lettering precedence is left to right and front to rear (relative to direction of flight).

Figure 1.

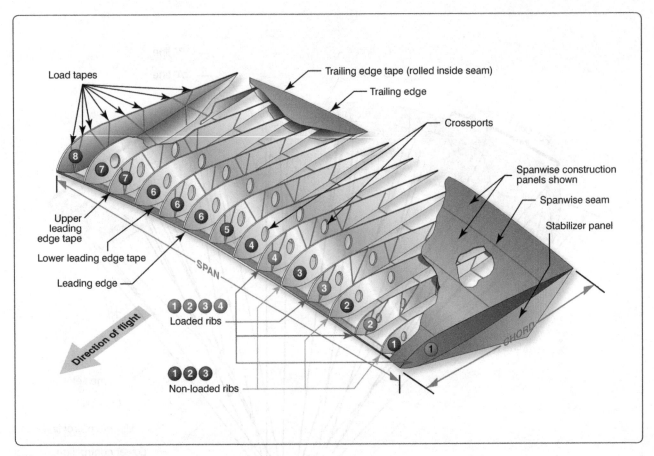

Load tapes

Trailing edge tape (rolled inside seam)

Trailing edge

Crossports

Spanwise construction panels shown

Spanwise seam

Stabilizer panel

Upper leading edge tape

Lower leading edge tape

Leading edge

SPAN

CHORD

Direction of flight

① ② ③ ④
Loaded ribs

① ② ③
Non-loaded ribs

Figure 2.

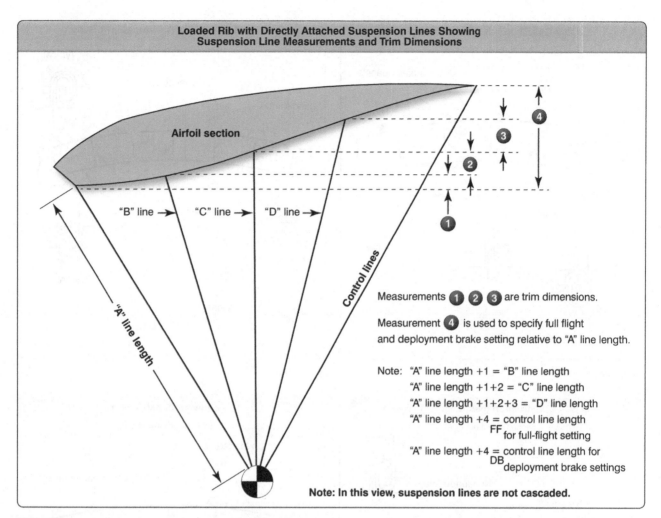

Loaded Rib with Directly Attached Suspension Lines Showing Suspension Line Measurements and Trim Dimensions

Airfoil section

"B" line → "C" line → "D" line →

"A" line length

Control lines

Measurements ① ② ③ are trim dimensions.

Measurement ④ is used to specify full flight and deployment brake setting relative to "A" line length.

Note: "A" line length +1 = "B" line length
"A" line length +1+2 = "C" line length
"A" line length +1+2+3 = "D" line length
"A" line length +4 = control line length
$_{FF}$ for full-flight setting
"A" line length +4 = control line length for
$_{DB}$ deployment brake settings

Note: In this view, suspension lines are not cascaded.

Figure 3A.

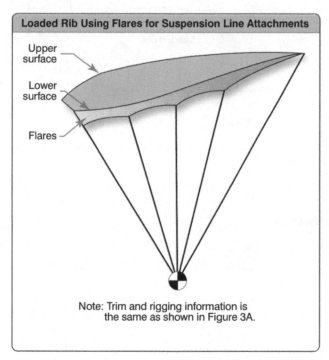

Loaded Rib Using Flares for Suspension Line Attachments

Upper surface

Lower surface

Flares

Note: Trim and rigging information is the same as shown in Figure 3A.

Figure 3B.

Half Cell Chordwise Construction
Section view from front
Upper surface panels
Non-loaded ribs
Loaded ribs
Typical
Lower surface panels

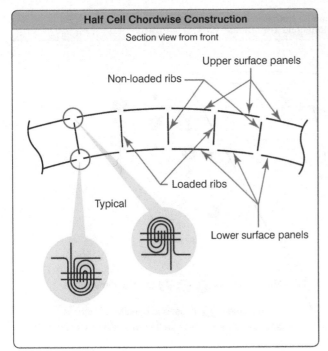

Figure 4A.

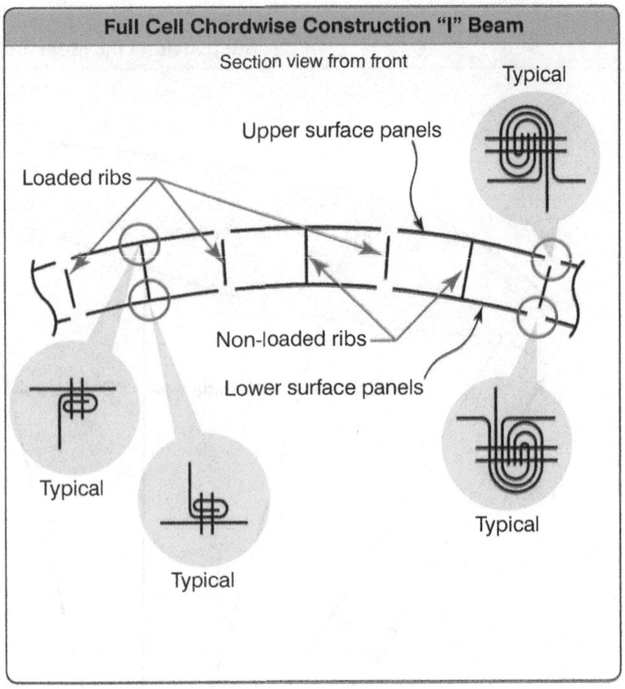

Full Cell Chordwise Construction "I" Beam
Section view from front
Typical
Upper surface panels
Loaded ribs
Non-loaded ribs
Lower surface panels
Typical
Typical
Typical

Figure 4B.

Full Cell Construction Interlocking "T" Beam
Section view from front
Typical
Non-loaded ribs
Upper surface panels
Loaded ribs
Lower surface panels
Typical
Typical
Typical

Figure 4C.

Spanwise Construction
Section view from front
Non-loaded ribs
Upper surface panels
Loaded ribs
Lower surface panels
Typical
Typical

Figure 4D.

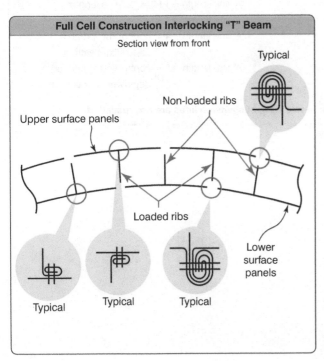

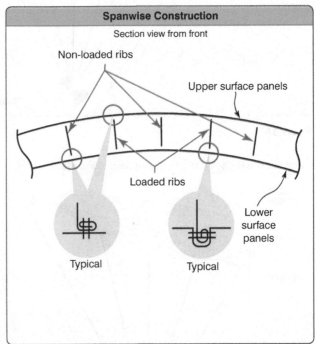

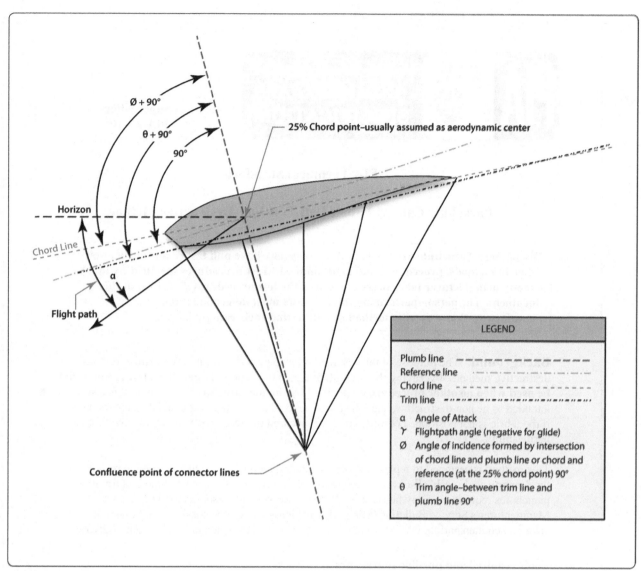

Figure 5.

LEGEND

Plumb line	— — —
Reference line	—·—·—
Chord line	———
Trim line	—··—··—

α   Angle of Attack

γ   Flightpath angle (negative for glide)

Ø   Angle of incidence formed by intersection of chord line and plumb line or chord and reference (at the 25% chord point) 90°

θ   Trim angle–between trim line and plumb line 90°

Ø + 90°

θ + 90°

90°

Horizon

Chord Line

α

Flight path

25% Chord point–usually assumed as aerodynamic center

Confluence point of connector lines

PIA-TS-108.1
15 January 2010

**Superseding
PIA-TS-108**
12 December 1992

PIA Technical Standard

Parachute Canopy Fabric Pull Test Non-Destructive Method

Disclaimer: Parachute canopy manufacturers may have pull test requirements that differ in methods, procedures, and loads applied. Test procedures specified by the canopy manufacturer takes precedence over the test procedures described in this document. The person performing the pull tests must determine if the canopy manufacturer has a specific method of pull testing their canopy fabric.

Background: The purpose of this test method is to provide a simple, standardized, non-destructive method of verifying the strength of parachute canopy fabric. **This test method may be used when no other procedure is specified by the manufacturer.** Although this test is intended to be non-destructive, caution should be exercised as this test could damage the fabric, if the fabric is not positioned correctly or is not secured tightly. It may also affect the fabric permeability.

This method is designed to replace the old "Riggers' Thumb Test", first devised in response to the "canopy acid-mesh" discovery in the mid-1980's. It is now the accepted method for all parachutes requiring canopy fabric strength tests. Reasons for testing may include: Manufacturer's Service Bulletins (SBs), Airworthiness Directives (AD's), aging material, chemical contamination, UV exposure or discoloration of a suspicious origin, such as grease.

Tools required and possible sources are as follows:

2 ea. Locking Fabric Clamps   Figure 1

        Para-Gear Equipment Co.   800-323-0437   (P/N S7989)
        3839 W. Oakton St.   www.para-gear.com
        Skokie, IL 60076-3438

        Aerostar International, Inc.   605-331-3500   (P/N 51406M)
        1814 N.   www.aerostar.com
        Sioux Falls, SD 57117-5057

Ink, Marking (for parachutes and other textile items)
A-A-59211 (21Jul/98) Supersedes MIL-I-6903C (5Mar/68)

        American Writing Ink Co.   781-762-0026
        33 Endicott St.
        Norwood, MA 02062

Strata Blue P/N 7510-00-286-5362   Available in 1 pint container
Orange-Yellow P/N 7510-00-634-6583   Available in 1 pint container

Hitt Marking Devices, Inc.   714-979-1405
3231 W. MacArthur Blvd.   800-969-6699 (toll free)
Santa Ana, CA 92704   www.hittmarking.com

Sharpie Pen- black

1 ea. Calibrated Spring Scale, 50 lb. (23 kg.) minimum capacity

This scale should be calibrated at least once a year to an accuracy of +/- 3 lbs. It should be identified with a serial number and written verification of calibration must be kept on file. An adhesive label (or similar) should be affixed to the scale showing the date calibrated and the date next calibration is due. If the scale is damaged in any manner, such as dropping, it must be pulled from service and tagged as unserviceable until its recalibration.

Test Procedures: The following procedures do not take precedence over a manufacturer's test procedures for their products. Before testing make sure you have the manufacturer's most current test procedures.

A minimum of 2 areas should be tested on a canopy, but not less than 2 pull tests on each separate color (1 in the warp direction and 1 in the fill direction). When testing look for areas of contamination and/or discoloration. If possible remain approximately 6 inches (150mm) from any seam.

Proceed as follows:

NOTE: Steps 1 and 2 apply to cases involving acid-mesh pull testing.

1. Locate the mesh vents in the canopy and determine the fabric areas which are in contact with the mesh when the canopy is packed. These areas are shown as the diagonally shaded lines in typical tri-vent canopies (see FIGURE 2).

2. Perform one 40 lb. (18 kg.) pull test on each panel of material that comes in contact with the mesh when the canopy is packed. Alternate tests from the warp to fill direction on the panels. This could be as few as four tests or as many as twelve tests on some bias constructed canopies.

CAUTION: Never attach fabric clamps or perform pull tests on the mesh covered areas of any canopy. Extensive damage will result.

NOTE: Steps 3 through 6 apply to all pull tests (not just acid-mesh).

3. The area to be tested must be visibly marked for future reference. Refer to FIGURE 3 for examples of how to mark the parachute to be tested.

4. After the marking ink has dried, attach the locking fabric clamps to the ripstop fabric as shown in FIGURE 4. The distance between the clamps should be 3 inches (76.2mm) plus or minus ¼

inch (6.35mm) and the clamps must be aligned so that the ripstop pattern is parallel (not on bias) to the edge of the jaws. Lock the clamps **VERY SECURELY**. This will prevent slippage and possible damage to the fabric.

NOTE: If the area to be tested is too small to allow 3 inches (76.2mm) plus or minus ¼ inch (6.35mm) between the jaws of the fabric clamps (such as the apex area of a round canopy), the distance between the jaws may be reduced to 2 inches (50.8mm) plus or minus ¼ inch (6.35mm).

5. Secure one clamp to the packing table or other object which will allow a sufficient load to be applied without movement of the fabric clamp. Attach the spring scale hook to the other fabric clamp and apply the load very smoothly and steadily. Hold the load for 3 seconds.

6. Record test results on the tested areas in contrasting ink as shown in FIGURE 5. Information should include the following:

- The amount of loading pulled to in pounds or kilograms
- The date tested
- The word PASS or FAIL
- The name and certificate number of the individual performing the test.

After completing the tests record the information in your rigger logbook and on the packing data card.

(THIS SPACE LEFT INTENTIONALLY BLANK)

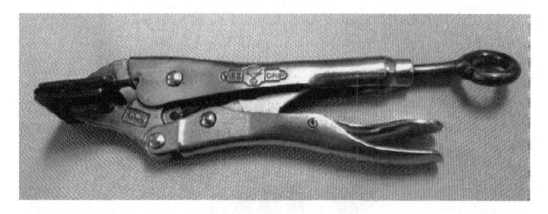

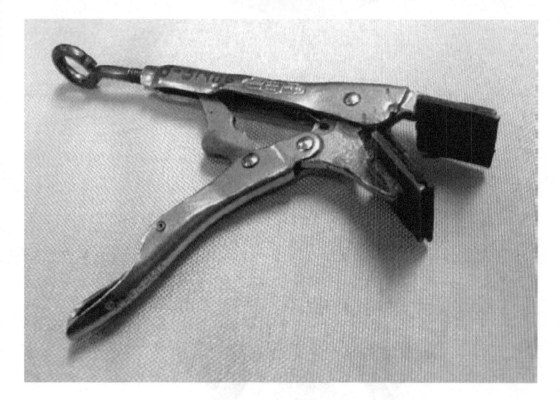

Fabric clamp (rubber padded/square jaw)

FIGURE 1

NOTE: Use only approved fabric clamps. Improvised or homemade clamps may increase the chances of damaging the area to be tested.

Below are diagrams of typical tri-vent modifications.

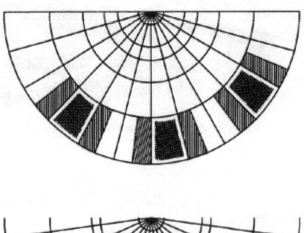

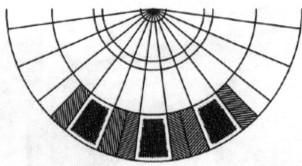

NOTE: Diagonally shaded areas show examples of fabric that comes in contact with mesh or may contact mesh.

FIGURE 2

> ___LB/KG PULL TEST:
>
> DATE:
>
> RIGGER'S NAME AND CERTIFICATE NUMBER

NOTE: This method uses either the corners of the box (above) or
the dots (below) as guides for the fabric clamps.

> ___LB/KG PULL TEST:
>
> DATE:
>
> RIGGER'S NAME AND CERTIFICATE NUMBER

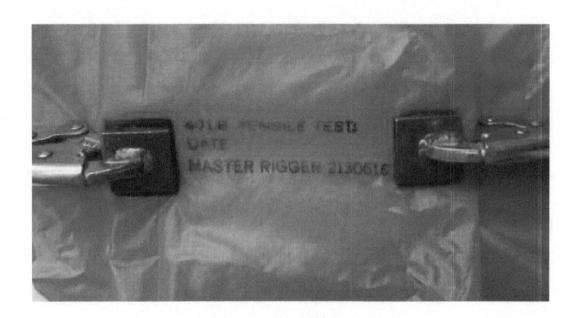

Examples of canopy markings

FIGURE 3

NOTE: Use only a rubber stamp and approved ink or a black Sharpie™ pen to mark the
areas to be tested. Do not use a ballpoint pen, pencils or similar items to mark the test
area. This could result in damaging the fabric being tested.

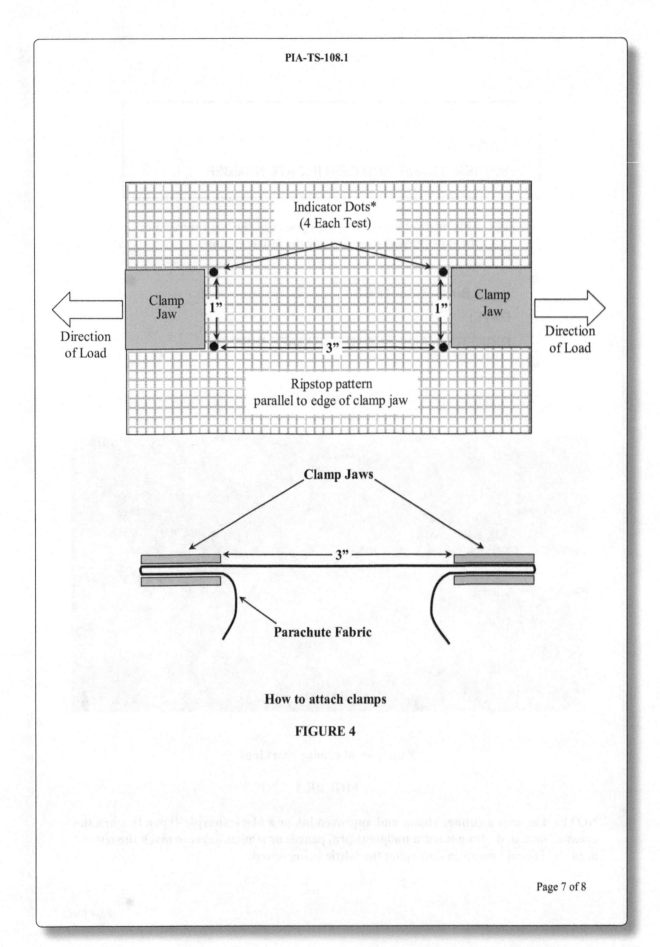

Indicator Dots*
(4 Each Test)

Clamp Jaw

Clamp Jaw

Direction of Load

Direction of Load

1"

1"

3"

Ripstop pattern
parallel to edge of clamp jaw

Clamp Jaws

3"

Parachute Fabric

How to attach clamps

FIGURE 4

40 LB PULL TEST: PASSED

DATE: 14 JUN 2009

MASTER RIGGER: JOE RIGGER 1234567

Example of completed test

FIGURE 5

Department of Transportation
Federal Aviation Administration
Aircraft Certification Service
Washington, DC

| TSO-C23d |

Date: 6/1/94

Technical Standard Order

Subject: TSO-C23d, PERSONNEL PARACHUTE ASSEMBLIES

a. <u>Applicability.</u>

(1) <u>Minimum Performance Standards</u>. This technical standard order (TSO) prescribes the minimum performance standard that personnel parachute assemblies must meet in order to be identified with the applicable TSO marking. New models of personnel parachute assemblies that are to be so identified and that are manufactured on or after the date of this TSO must meet the standards set forth in Society of Automotive Engineers, Inc. (SAE) Aerospace Standard (AS) Document No. AS 8015B, "Minimum Performance Standards for Parachute Assemblies and Components, Personnel," dated July 7, 1992.

b. <u>Marking</u>. Each personnel parachute assembly or separate sub-assembly must be marked in accordance with 14 CFR part 21, section 21.607(d) and paragraph 4.2 of SAE AS 8015B. This marking requirement applies to any previously approved major component/sub-assembly used in this TSO.

c. <u>Data Requirements</u>.

(1) In addition to the requirement in part 21, section 21.605, the manufacturer shall furnish the manager of the Aircraft Certification Office (ACO), FAA having geographical purview of the manufacturer's facilities, one copy each of the following technical data:

(i) A complete description of the personnel parachute assemblies, including detail drawings, material identification and specifications.

(ii) Operating instructions and limitations, to include donning, retention, adjustment, and deployment.

(iii) Installation instructions and limitations.

(iv) A report of the tests conducted in accordance with SAE AS 8015B for qualification and approval of personnel parachute assemblies.

DISTRIBUTION: ZVS-326; A-W(IR)-3; A-X(CD)-4; A-FFS-7, 8(LTD); A-X(FS)-3;
AFS-600 (2 cys); A-FAC-0(MAX)

(v) Detailed maintenance instructions, including specific guidance on the limits of wear and damage permissible to webbing material that would warrant replacement.

(vi) The quality control inspection and functional test specification to be used to ensure each production article complies with this TSO, as required by part 21, section 21.605(a)(3) and part 21, section 21.143(a)(3).

(2) The manufacturer must furnish to the user of the article one copy of the data and information specified in paragraphs c(1)(ii) and c(1)(v). This data and information is necessary for proper installation and use and for continued airworthiness of the product or article.

"The conditions and test required for TSO approval of this article are minimum performance standards. It is the responsibility of those desiring to install the article either on or within a specific type or class of aircraft to determine that the aircraft installation conditions are within the TSO standards. The article may be installed only if further evaluation by the applicant (user/installer) documents an acceptable installation and is approved by the Administrator."

d. Availability of Referenced Documents.

(1) Copies of SAE AS 8015B may be purchased from the Society of Automotive Engineers, Inc., Department 331, 400 Commonwealth Drive, Warrendale, PA 15096.

(2) Federal Aviation Regulations, part 21, subpart O, may be purchased from the Superintendent of Documents, U.S. Government Printing Office, Washington, DC 20402-9325.

(3) Advisory Circular 20- 110, "Index of Aviation Technical Standard Orders," may be obtained from the U.S. Department of Transportation, General Services Section, M-443.2, Washington, DC 20590.

/S/ John K. McGrath
Manager, Aircraft Engineering Division
 Aircraft Certification Service

Page 2

PIA TS 135

Parachute Industry Association (PIA)

TECHNICAL STANDARD 135

PERFORMANCE STANDARDS
FOR
PERSONNEL PARACHUTE ASSEMBLIES
AND
COMPONENTS

1.   SCOPE:

This document defines the performance standards for personnel parachute assemblies (and components thereof) to be carried in aircraft for emergency use by aircrew and those reserve parachutes worn by parachutists for intentional jumping.

This document covers three types of personnel carrying parachute assemblies and the operating limitations for each:

1.1   PARACHUTE TYPES:

1.1.1   Single harness reserve parachute assembly.

1.1.2   Single harness emergency parachute assembly.

1.1.3   Dual harness reserve parachute assembly.

1.2   MAXIMUM OPERATING LIMITS, GENERAL:

1.2.1   A single harness parachute assembly (or components thereof) may be certified for any maximum operating weight and for any maximum pack opening speed equal to or greater than 150 KTAS (277.8 km/h).

1.2.2   A dual harness reserve parachute assembly (or components thereof) may be certified for any maximum operating weight greater than 500 lb (227.3 kg) (with 250 lb (113.6 kg) in each harness) and any maximum pack opening speed equal to or greater than 175 KTAS (324.1 km/h). Note that the maximum operating weight need not be the same for each harness.

PIA TS 135

1.3 LIST OF TECHNICAL STANDARDS, TABLES AND FIGURES:

2. DEFINITIONS AND GENERAL REQUIREMENTS

2.1 GENERAL DEFINITIONS:

For the purposes of this document, the following definitions are used:

a. "Administrator" – The FAA Administrator or equivalent chief executive of the cognizant agency and/or his designated subordinate personnel and/or designated subordinate organization acting on his behalf and with his authority in the matter concerned.

b. "Airspeed, Calibrated" (KCAS) means the indicated airspeed of an aircraft, corrected for position and instrument error. Calibrated airspeed is equal to true airspeed in standard atmosphere at sea level.

c. "Airspeed, Equivalent" (KEAS) means the calibrated airspeed of an aircraft corrected for adiabatic compressible flow for the particular altitude. Equivalent airspeed is equal to calibrated airspeed in standard atmosphere at sea level.

d. "Airspeed, Indicated" (KIAS) means the speed of an aircraft as shown on its pitot static airspeed indicator calibrated to reflect standard atmosphere adiabatic compressible flow at sea level uncorrected for airspeed system errors.

e. "Airspeed, True" (KTAS) – means the airspeed relative to undisturbed air. True airspeed is equal to equivalent airspeed multiplied by $(\rho_0/\rho)^{1/2}$ where ρ_0 is the air density at standard day conditions and ρ is the air density at the local altitude.

f. "Approved", unless used with reference to another person, means approved by the Administrator for use within the limits specified by the manufacturer and verified by compliance with the requirements of this standard.

g. "Canopy"- The part of the parachute that opens up and fills with air and provides the lift and/or drag required to decelerate the payload to the desired value.

h. "Certified", unless used with reference to another agency, means certified by the cognizant agency as having met the requirements of this standard.

i. "Cognizant Agency" – The governmental agency or other organization tasked with oversight or regulation of aviation activities within a given geographical area or country. e.g. the Federal Aviation Administration (FAA) within the United States, the Joint Airworthiness Authorities (JAA) within the European Union and similar agencies worldwide. In some cases, the cognizant agency may delegate part or all of its authority to a subordinate agency such as a national aero club.

j. "Drogue" – A small aerodynamic decelerator towed behind a falling body to slow its velocity.

k. "Manufacturer" – The person (or business/corporate entity) who controls the design and quality of the article produced including the parts of them, and any processes or services related to them that are procured from an outside source.

l. "Main Assisted Reserve Deployment (MARD) device" – An automatically releasable connection between the main parachute and the reserve deployment system which uses a malfunctioned main canopy to speed reserve deployment upon breakaway.

PIA TS 135

m. "Parachute" means a device used or intended to be used to retard the fall of a body or object through the air.

n. "Parachutist in Command" – means the person making a tandem jump who:
(1) Has final authority and responsibility for the operation and safety of the jump;
(2) Has been designated as parachutist in command before the jump; and
(3) Holds the appropriate rating for the conduct of the jump.

o. "Passenger parachutist" means a person who boards an aircraft, acting as other than the parachutist in command of a tandem parachute operation, with the intent of exiting the aircraft while in-flight using the forward harness of a dual harness tandem parachute system to descend to the surface.

2.1.1 **MAJOR COMPONENTS:**
For purposes of this document a parachute assembly normally, but not exclusively, consists of the following major components:

a. Deployment control device such as a sleeve, bag, diaper, or functional equivalent.
b. Deployment initiation device (pilot chute, drogue, or functional equivalent) and bridle.
c. Canopy(s) including suspension lines, reefing device, and connector links (if used).
d. Riser(s), when not integral with harness and/or canopy.
e. Stowage container(s) or stowage pack(s).
f. Harness (es).
g. Primary actuation device (ripcord or functional equivalent).
h. Reserve static line.
i. Drogue canopy and bridle (if used with reserve and/or emergency parachutes).
j. Drogue release device (if used with reserve and/or emergency parachutes).

2.1.2 **SINGLE HARNESS RESERVE PARACHUTE ASSEMBLY:**
A certified parachute assembly that is worn in conjunction with a main parachute assembly and used by one person for premeditated jumps. This includes, as applicable, the reserve deployment initiation device, deployment control device, canopy, risers, stowage container, harness, primary actuation device, and reserve static line.

2.1.3 **DUAL HARNESS RESERVE PARACHUTE ASSEMBLY:**
A certified parachute assembly used for premeditated jumps by two people: a parachutist in command and a second parachutist (each in his/her own harness), utilizing one main parachute assembly and one reserve parachute assembly. This assembly includes, as applicable, the reserve deployment initiation device, deployment control device, canopy, risers, stowage container, harness, primary actuation device, and reserve static line.

2.1.4 **MAIN PARACHUTE ASSEMBLY:**
A non-certified parachute assembly that is worn in conjunction with a certified reserve parachute assembly as the primary parachute (the one intended for use) for premeditated jumps. The main parachute assembly shall consist of the main container and all associated parts of the main parachute that are not permanently attached to the certificated harness assembly.

2.1.5 **SINGLE HARNESS EMERGENCY PARACHUTE ASSEMBLY:**
A certified parachute assembly that is worn by one person for emergency, (unpremeditated) use only. This assembly includes, as applicable, the deployment initiation device, deployment control device, canopy, risers, stowage container, harness, and primary actuation device.

2.1.6 FAILURE OF A PARACHUTE ASSEMBLY OR COMPONENT:
The term "failure" in this document shall mean any change in a component or assembly that adversely affects its airworthiness. However, the use of consumable, frangible or single use parts shall be permitted in all assemblies and shall not be considered a failure if they function as designed.

2.1.7 FUNCTIONALLY OPEN:
Functionally open shall mean a parachute sufficiently deployed and inflated to provide a rate of descent of not more than 24 ft/s (7.3m/s). This condition may be demonstrated by video, film or electronic data of the test in a manner determined by the manufacturer.

2.1.8 RESERVE STATIC LINE (RSL):
A device connected to the main parachute assembly that is capable of actuating the reserve parachute assembly following a breakaway from the main canopy.

2.1.9 MAIN PARACHUTE BREAKAWAY DEVICE:
A device used by the parachutist in command to separate the main parachute from the harness of a single or dual-harness reserve parachute assembly. The parachutist in command shall be able to operate the main parachute breakaway device for dual harness reserve parachute assemblies.

2.1.10 MAXIMUM OPERATING WEIGHT (MOW):
The maximum operating weight is the total (gross) weight of all individuals or dummies and their equipment including the parachute assembly itself. MOW is also known as the "placard weight".

2.1.11 MAXIMUM PACK OPENING SPEED (MPOS):
The maximum pack open speed in KTAS (knots true airspeed) is the maximum speed at which the (reserve/emergency) parachute pack (container) is designed to be opened. This definition specifically allows for the wearing of parachutes in freefall and/or in aircraft at speeds higher than the maximum pack opening speed. MPOS is also known as the "placard speed".

NOTE: In order to provide an inherently greater margin of safety without requiring that tests be conducted at all possible altitudes, all test conditions in this document are stated in KEAS and that all maximum pack opening speeds are stated in KTAS. In the event that a manufacturer elects to conduct further testing at higher altitudes, the placard limits may be changed to reflect any test conditions successfully conducted.

2.1.12 MINIMUM OPERATING WEIGHT (MinOW)
The minimum operating weight is the lowest allowed total (gross) weight of an individual or dummy (or all individuals or dummies in the case of a tandem) and their equipment including the parachute assembly itself. The **MinOW** shall be specified by the manufacturer and may be any weight demonstrated to be appropriate by the manufacturer for the system.

2.1.13 SERVICE LIFE RESTRICTED ITEMS:
Materials or products that, by design, are service life restricted for any reason (environmental, structural, chemical, etc.) may be used in any manner chosen by the manufacturer. Each such item must be marked in a manner that will allow maintenance personnel to determine the serviceable status of the part.

PIA TS-135, Revision 1.4, Issued April 22, 2010, Page 4 of 18

3. **MATERIALS AND WORKMANSHIP:**
Materials and workmanship shall be of a quality that documented experience and/or tests have conclusively demonstrated to be suitable for the manufacture of, and appropriate for the intended use in, personnel parachute assemblies. All materials shall remain functional for storage from -40 to +200°F (-40 to +93.3 °C), and from 0 to 100% relative humidity. All plated ferrous parts shall be treated to minimize hydrogen embrittlement.

4. **DETAIL REQUIREMENTS**

4.1 **DESIGN AND CONSTRUCTION:**

4.1.1 **MATERIALS:**
All materials shall be designed to support the proof loads specified in the applicable specification, drawing, or standard, without failure. In the absence of an applicable specification, drawing, or standard for a particular material, successful completion of the qualification tests listed under section 4.3 shall be considered adequate evidence of suitability.

4.1.2 **STITCHING:**
Stitching shall generally be of a type that will not ravel when broken. Note that this is not required for consumable or frangible parts.

4.1.3 **MAIN PARACHUTE ASSEMBLY:**
When installed but not deployed, the main parachute assembly shall not interfere with the proper function of the reserve parachute assembly. Ref: Table 2

4.1.4 **PRIMARY ACTUATION DEVICE/RIPCORD:**
The primary actuation device/ripcord, including all joints, shall withstand the test loads of 4.3.2 without failure. The primary actuation device/ripcord shall meet the human-factors requirements of 4.3.3., if applicable.

4.1.5 **RESERVE STATIC LINE (RSL):**
The reserve static line, if used, including all joints shall withstand the test loads of 4.3.2 without failure and shall meet the functional requirements of 4.3.8.2.

4.1.6 **HARNESS RELEASE:**
The harness shall be so constructed that, after landing, the parachutist can separate himself from the main and reserve canopies and/or harness assembly unaided. On a dual harness, reserve parachute assembly, the parachutist in command must be able to separate himself <u>and</u> the second parachutist from the reserve canopy and/or harness assemblies unaided.

4.1.7 **DROGUE PARACHUTE ASSEMBLY & RELEASE:**
For reserve or emergency parachute assemblies, incorporating a drogue, the drogue release shall be tested at an equivalent force to the drag force generated at the MOW and MPOS. The human release force shall not be less than 5 lbf (22.2N) and must not exceed 22 lbf (97.9N). The release shall meet the human-factors requirements of 4.3.3.

4.1.8 **DATA CARD POCKET; STOWAGE CONTAINER:**
The stowage container shall be provided with a parachute data card pocket constructed such that the card will not be easily lost and will be readily accessible, when the parachute is packed in the container.

PIA TS 135

4.2   MARKING REQUIREMENTS:
Marking requirements are listed in Table 1.

NOTE: The data items listed in Table 1 need not be marked at the same location on the component as long as all of the pertinent information is permanently marked.

4.2.1   MARKING, STOWAGE CONTAINER - OPERATING LIMITS:
The minimum and maximum operating limits in Table 1 shall be marked/placarded on or attached to the outside of the parachute stowage container (pack). The marking/placard may refer to the owner's manual for the minimum operating weight. The lowest maximum operating weight of any component in the assembly (canopy, harness, etc.) and the lowest maximum pack opening speed of any component (canopy, harness, etc.) shall be marked on the outside of the stowage container (pack) in such a location as to be readily available to the user during donning of the parachute assembly and subject to a minimum of obliteration during use.

This information may alternately be placed in a pocket marked with the legend 'Operating Limitations Inside'; the pocket must be readily available to the user during donning of the parachute assembly and subject to a minimum of obliteration during use.

NOTE: The maximum pack opening speed and minimum and maximum weight markings shall be in a block typeface, in a minimum size of 0.375 inch (9.5 mm) tall (27 point type). The other information required by Table 1 may be marked in another location, if desired.

4.2.2   MARKING, CANOPY - STATEMENT OF USE:
Each certified canopy shall be marked to show its approved use as follows:

4.2.2.1   "Single Harness Emergency Parachute Canopy"
"Single Harness Reserve Parachute Canopy"
"Single Harness Emergency/Reserve Parachute Canopy"
"Dual Harness Reserve Parachute Canopy"

4.2.2.2   Each canopy (single harness types only) that has not been tested in accordance with the breakaway tests of Section 4.3.8.2 shall be marked as follows:

"**LIMITATION**: May not be used with main parachute breakaway device".

4.3   QUALIFICATION TESTS:
The minimum performance standards listed in Tables 2, 3 and 4 shall be met. There shall be no failure to meet any of the requirements during the qualification tests of this section. In case of a failure, the cause must be found, corrected, and all affected tests repeated.

4.3.1   PACKING METHOD:
The packing method must be specified and the identical packing method must be used for all of the functional and structural tests.

4.3.2   PRIMARY ACTUATION DEVICE/RIPCORD TEST:
(a) The ripcord, including all joints, shall not fail under a straight tension test load of 300-lbf (1337.7 N) applied for not less than 3 seconds.

(b) If the reserve is to be static line actuated by releasing the main canopy, the reserve static line, if used, must not fail under a straight tension test load of 300-lbf (1334.5 N) applied for not less than 3 seconds.

(c) If the reserve ripcord is to be static lined from an aircraft the reserve ripcord/static line, must not fail under a straight tension test load of 600-lbf (2668.9 N) applied for not less than 3 seconds.

(d) Rigid pins, if used, shall not yield under a load of 8-lbf (35.6 N) applied to the cable (or equivalent) perpendicular to the axis of the pin, for not less than 3 seconds. The pin shall be supported for 0.5 in (12.7-mm) maximum at the end farthest from the cable attachment. All 4.3.3 human factors tests shall be performed using a primary actuation device/ripcord that has passed this test.

4.3.3   HUMAN FACTORS AND ACTUATION FORCE TESTS:
An anthropometrically diverse group of individuals (consisting of a representative group of no less than 3 males and 3 females) from the intended user group shall be employed for all human factors tests in 4.3.3. All individuals shall be able to operate the subject device without any undue difficulty. Table 2 lists the required test conditions and number of tests for each particular component. Additional information for the component tests is listed below.

TESTS: Under normal design operating conditions, all devices tested under this paragraph shall result in a positive and quick operation of the device within the following load range applied to the handle:
(a) a load applied at the handle of not less than 5 lbf (22.2 N), applied in the direction giving the lowest pull force,
(b) a load applied at the handle of not more than 22 lbf (97.9 N), applied in the direction of normal design operation,
(c) for chest type parachute assemblies, the maximum pull force shall be 15 lbf (66.7 N),
(d) the primary actuation device shall be tested in accordance with Table 2,
(e) the emergency/reserve drogue release (if used) shall be tested in accordance with Table 2.

NOTE: For these tests, the primary actuation device (ripcord or equivalent) shall be equipped with a tamper-indicating device (i.e. seal thread or equivalent) of the same type that will be required for production articles in service.

4.3.4   HUMAN FACTORS TESTS, HARNESS:
Harnesses shall demonstrate that they will perform the basic function of retaining the body at the end of the parachute suspension system in an inherently secure manner.
This requirement shall be demonstrated by passing all live drop tests in Table 3.

4.3.5   ENVIRONMENTAL TESTS:
Three drops shall be made at 60 KEAS except that prior to the test the parachute assembly shall be subjected to the following preconditioning: (These tests may be combined with other tests.)

4.3.5.1   Precondition for 16 hours at not less than +200 °F (93.3 °C), stabilize to ambient and test drop.

4.3.5.2   Precondition for 16 h at not greater than -40 °F (-40 °C), stabilize to ambient and test drop.

PIA TS-135, Revision 1.4, Issued April 22, 2010, Page 7 of 18

4.3.5.3 Precondition for not less than 400 continuous hours with a 200 lbf (889.6 N) or greater load applied to compress the pack in a manner similar to that most likely to be encountered in actual use. Test drop within 1 hour after removing the load.

4.3.5.4 **Alternate preconditioning.** The preconditioning requirements for 4.3.5.1 and 4.3.5.3 may be combined as follows: The complete test parachute assembly may be placed in a vacuum bag and preconditioned at +180 °F (82.2 °C) for 18 hours at a constant vacuum of not less than 25" Hg (0.846 bar). Stabilize to ambient and drop.

4.3.6 **STRUCTURAL OVERLOAD TESTS:**
No material(s) or device(s) that attenuates shock loads and is not an integral part of the parachute assembly or component being certified may be used. Tests may be conducted for either a complete parachute assembly or separate components. There shall be no evidence of material, stitch, or functional failure that will affect airworthiness. For reusable items the same items shall be used for all 4.3.6 tests. Peak opening force shall be measured on all 4.3.6 tests. The parachute must be functionally open within the number of seconds calculated for 4.3.8 tests. Parachute assemblies shall be tested in accordance with the following schedule:

(a) Test weight = Maximum operating weight x 1.2
Test speed = Maximum pack opening speed x 1.2

-OR-

(b) Test weight = Maximum operating weight multiplied by the factor from Figure 1
Test speed = Maximum pack opening speed multiplied by the factor from Figure 1

However, the test speed must not be less than 180 KEAS (333.4 km/h) for reserve and emergency parachute assemblies and the test weight must not be less than 264 lb. (120 kg).

For dual harness parachute assemblies the test weight must not be less than 600 lb. (272.7 kg) and the test speed must not be less than 200 KEAS (370.4 km/h).

4.3.6.1 **STRENGTH TEST, COMPLETE PARACHUTE ASSEMBLY:**
Three drops shall be made with weight and speed in accordance with 4.3.6. When using test method (b), in 4.3.6 a 4th drop must be added using the same parachute under the same conditions in the first three drops. Where non-positive locking hardware is used to attach the canopy or riser(s) to the harness, a cross connector must be used and one of the above drops shall be with only one attachment engaged to test the cross connector and hardware.

4.3.6.2 **STRENGTH TEST, ALTERNATE MEANS OF COMPLIANCE CANOPY (ONLY):**
Three drops shall be made with a gross weight and speed in accordance with 4.3.6. When using test method (b), in 4.3.6 a 4th drop must be added using the same canopy under the same conditions in the first three drops. A test vehicle (e.g., a bomb) may be used. The canopy and any required additional components (i.e., deployment device, pilot chute, and risers) shall be tested as a unit. The connector links (if used) shall be attached to the risers in the same manner as the intended use and the riser(s) should be secured to the test vehicle in a manner appropriate to the test objective. For example, if the parachute risers are to be tested on the bomb drop, it should be arranged in a manner as to duplicate the loading found on the personnel parachute harness. Where non-positive locking hardware is used to attach the canopy or riser(s) to the harness, a cross connector must be used and one of the above drops shall be with only one attachment engaged to test the cross connector and hardware.

PIA TS-135, Revision 1.4, Issued April 22, 2010, Page 8 of 18

4.3.6.3   STRENGTH TEST, ADDITIONAL MEANS OF COMPLIANCE HARNESS (ONLY):
A harness may, at the manufacturer's option, be placarded with a higher average peak opening force than what was measured in 4.3.6 tests by performing additional tower drop tests as outlined below:

The harness shall be drop tested using a torso shaped dummy, three (3) times for each of four (4) different loading conditions.
The dummy weight shall be not less than 75% of harness maximum operating weight and the drop distance shall be as necessary to generate the required forces.
Up to three (3) separate harnesses may be used; however each harness shall be subjected to a minimum of one test at each of the following four test conditions.

    (a) Test condition one – All risers loaded to a combined load of at least 100% of placard maximum load.
    (b) Test condition two – Only left side harness/canopy attachment point(s) loaded to a combined load of at least 66% of placard load.
    (c) Test condition three – Only right side harness/canopy attachment point(s) loaded to a combined load of at least 66% of placard load.
    (d) Test condition four – Each unique brake setting shall be tested to a minimum of 16.7% of placard load if applicable.

4.3.6.4   STRENGTH TESTS, ALTERNATE MEANS OF COMPLIANCE, DROGUE CANOPY (ONLY)
For parachute assemblies in which a drogue parachute canopy is an integral part of the reserve or emergency parachute assembly, the drogue may be separately tested at the conditions determined in 4.3.6. The drogue canopy itself and all related components of the drogue assembly must be tested as a functional subsystem of the parachute assembly.

4.3.7   FUNCTIONAL TESTS (Twisted Lines):
A minimum of 5 drops shall be made with a weight not more than the maximum operating weight dummy or person[1] in each harness. The airspeed at the time of pack opening shall be 60 KEAS (111.1 km/h)

Procedural Note: The suspension lines shall be twisted together (360 degrees) three times in the same direction within the upper one third of the suspension line length beginning immediately below the attachment point to the canopy. The twists shall be placed in the lines before the suspension lines are stowed.

Performance Requirement: The parachute must be functionally open within 133% of the time calculated in 4.3.8 from the time of pack opening.

4.3.8   FUNCTIONAL TESTS (Normal Pack - All Types):
Opening Time or Altitude Loss: Using the MOW in pounds and the MPOS in KTAS for all 4.3.8 tests the maximum allowable opening time and the maximum allowable altitude loss on any drop shall be determined from the following formulas..

    (a) The greater of 3.00 seconds or the value determined as follows:

---

[1] A person's or individual's body weight may be increased to equal the maximum operating weight by using a weight belt or similar device.

PIA TS-135, Revision 1.4, Issued April 22, 2010,   Page 9 of 18

Opening Time Allowed (sec.) = (MOW – 250) * 0.01 + (MPOS/150 * 3.0)

-OR-

(b) The greater of 300 feet or the value determined as follows:

Altitude Loss Allowed (ft) = (MOW-250) + (MPOS/150 * 300)

4.3.8.1   DIRECT DROP TESTS:

There shall be a minimum of 48 tests at weights and airspeeds (at the time of pack opening) as outlined in Table 3. The test condition airspeeds are in KEAS. From the time of pack opening, the parachute canopy must be functionally open within the allowed time or altitude as calculated in 4.3.8.

(a) The manufacturer shall specify the Maximum Operating Weight and the Minimum Operating Weight.
(b) The Maximum Pack Opening Speed (MPOS) shall not be less than 150 knots.
(c) The MPOS and MOW shall be established by successful completion of the structural overload testing in Paragraph 4.3.6
(d) The manufacturer will be allowed to select whether to measure altitude loss or opening time, but within each block on the test grid the same method must be used.
(e) The maximum allowable opening time shall be calculated using the formula in 4.3.8(a): there shall be a minimum of 4 successful tests for each block; the opening times will be averaged and presented to the Administrator in the format shown in Figure 2.
(f) The maximum allowable altitude loss shall be calculated using the formula in 4.3.8(b): there shall be a minimum of 4 successful tests for each block; the altitude loss must be averaged and presented to the Administrator in the format shown in Figure 2.
(g) The opening times and/or altitude loss for each test block will be averaged and published in the format shown in Figure 2 in the owner's manual or in some other readily available location.

NOTE:

If a "MARD device" option is offered, an additional 8 drops at weights and airspeeds (at the time of pack opening) must be performed as outlined in the Table 3 with the MARD attached.

4.3.8.2   BREAKAWAY DROP TESTS (systems with main canopy release):

Eight drop tests shall be made by breaking away from an open and normally functioning main parachute canopy and actuating the reserve parachute within 2 seconds of the breakaway. These tests shall be conducted by a person (or suitable other devices) weighing not more than the maximum operating weight. The initial vertical velocity shall be less than 20 ft/s (6.1 m/s) and the total velocity less than 36 ft/s at the time of breakaway. From the time of pack opening, the parachute canopy must be functionally open within the altitude or within the allowed time as calculated in 4.3.8.

NOTE:

(a) If a reserve static line is part of the assembly, then 4 of the breakaway drops shall be made with the reserve static line actuating the reserve pack.
(b) If a "MARD device" option is offered, an additional 16 drops at weights and airspeeds (at the time of pack opening) must be performed as outlined in the Table 3 with the MARD attached.

PIA TS-135, Revision 1.4, Issued April 22, 2010,   Page 10 of 18

4.3.9   RATE OF DESCENT TESTS (METHOD 1):
Per Table 3, there shall be not less than 6 drops, with an individual and/or dummy in each harness weighing not less than the maximum operating weight[2]. The average rate of descent shall not exceed 24 ft/s (7.3 m/s) and the total velocity shall not exceed 36 ft/s (11.0 m/s) in an unaltered post deployment configuration, corrected to standard day sea level altitude conditions. The rate of descent measurement shall be taken over a minimum interval of 100 ft (30.5 m). These tests may be combined with other tests in this section.

4.3.9.1   RATE OF DESCENT TESTS (METHOD 2):
The rate of descent corrected to standard day sea level altitude conditions shall not exceed 5 ft/sec (1.5m/sec) at touchdown with appropriate control manipulations and the average rate of descent shall not exceed 24 ft/sec (7.3 m/s) in the unaltered post deployment configuration over a minimum interval of 100 ft (30.5m). These tests may be combined with other tests in this section.

NOTE: If the total velocity exceeds 36 ft/sec at maximum certified weight, the container or harness (if integral to the container) must be marked in an area readily visible to the user: "For experienced parachutists only. The owner's manual contains experience requirements."

4.3.10   STABILITY TESTS:
Per Table 3, there shall be not less than 6 drops, at the minimum operating weight. The oscillations shall not exceed 15° from the vertical, in an unaltered post-deployment configuration. These tests may be combined with other tests in this section.

4.3.11   LIVE TESTS:
Per Table 3, there shall be a minimum of 4 live tests with an individual weighing not more than the maximum operating weight in each harness. Two drops shall include a freefall of not more than 3 seconds and 2 drops shall include a freefall of at least 20 seconds. These tests may be conducted in conjunction with functional and/or rate of descent tests when practical. The user(s) must suffer no significant discomfort from the opening shock and must be able to disengage himself (themselves) unaided from the harness after landing. For this test the standard harness may be altered to permit attachment of a certified reserve parachute assembly (less harness) provided that such alteration does not interfere with the normal operation of the parachute assembly being tested. Reserve parachute assemblies shall be tested with the main compartment(s) full and empty, with a minimum of two tests each.

NOTE: Live tests for Dual Harness Reserve Parachute Assemblies may be tested with the parachutist in command and a dummy payload in the passenger harness.

5.   COMPONENT QUALIFICATIONS:
Any single component, assembly of components, group of components or group of assemblies may be certified. Table 4 lists the appropriate test paragraphs for each of the major components. Any components not listed in Table 4 shall be tested according to all applicable sections of this document based on the components function.

---

[2] A person's or individual's body weight may be increased to equal the maximum operating weight by using a weight belt or similar device.

PIA TS 135

5.1   COMPONENT COMPATIBILITY:

The component manufacturer shall provide a means of determining compatibility and shall provide specific guidance to ensure that form, fit and function of all components, as assembled, are within acceptable limits for each individual component and the assembly as a whole.

5.2   COMPONENT QUALIFICATION BY GROUP:

Components may be qualified as a group consisting of a range of scaled sizes. Separate elements of the component design may be linearly scaled at different rates as specified in the component drawings provided that fit, form, and function are not adversely affected. For canopies, the range may consist of scaled sizes to a maximum area of three times the smallest size.

When certifying components as a group, only the largest and the smallest members of the group must be tested in accordance with the appropriate sections of this document.

5.3   MAINTENANCE REQUIREMENTS:

The manufacturer of each component is responsible for developing and disseminating the maintenance requirements for each component, specifically including the inspection interval, repack cycle, service life, criteria for continued airworthiness and the qualifications required of maintenance personnel.

5.4   FITTING REQUIREMENTS:

The manufacturer is responsible for developing and disseminating instructions identifying the correct method of fitting the equipment to the user.

PIA TS 135

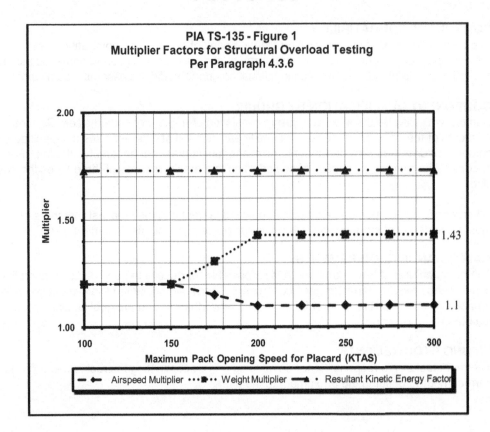

PIA TS-135 - Figure 1
Multiplier Factors for Structural Overload Testing
Per Paragraph 4.3.6

- — ◆ — Airspeed Multiplier   ··· ■ ··· Weight Multiplier   — ▲ · Resultant Kinetic Energy Factor

---

PIA TS-135 Figure 2
Direct Drop Tests
Per Paragraph 4.3.8.1

Test Weight	Test Speed			
	60 KEAS	85 KEAS	MPOS x 80%	MPOS x 100%
Minimum Operating Weight	4	4	4	4
Averaged Operating Weight*	4	4	4	4
Maximum Operating Weight	4	4	4	4
Minimum Total (direct drop) Functional Tests Required				48

*Averaged Operating Weight is defined as (Maximum Operating Weight + Minimum Operating Weight)/2
Average test weights shall be +/- 5%
Minimum test weights shall be +1%/-10%.
Maximum test weights shall be +10%/-1%

PIA TS 135

PIA-TS-135 - Table 1.												
Data Marking Requirements												
Marking Data Requirements	Reference Paragraph	Deployment Initiation Device (Pilot Chute, etc.)	Deployment Control Device (d-bag, etc.)	Reserve Emergency Canopy	Stowage Container	Primary Actuation Device (Ripcord or Equivalent)	Reserve Static Line (if used)	Harness (if not integral with container)	Risers (if not integral with harness)	Reserve/Emergency Drogue Canopy & Riser (if used)	Reserve/Emergency Drogue Release Device (if used)
Manufacturers Name, Code or Symbol		X	X	X	X	X	X	X	X	X	X
Part Number (w/dash numbers)		X	X	X	X	X	X	X	X	X	X
Serial or Lot Control Number		X	X	X	X	X	X	X	X	X	
Date of Manufacture (month and year minimum)		X	X	X	X	X	X	X	X	X	
Date to Be Removed from Service (if applicable)		X	X	X	X	X	X	X	X	X	
Maximum Pack Opening Speed (KEAS)	4.3.6	X		X	X				X	X	
Maximum Gross Weight (lb) if applicable	4.3.6				X				X	X	
Minimum Gross Weight (lb)	4.2				X						
Average Peak Force Measured during 4.3.6 tests	4.3.6				X				X		
Appoved for Use Statement	4.2.2			X							
Statement of Authorization Under TS0-C-23e and/or (J) TSO-C-23e if applicable		X	X	X	X			X	X	X	
Operators Warning Label with Maximum Operating Limits	4.3.6			X				X			
Operators Warning Label and location for component operating limitations	4.2.1				X						
Operators Warning Label with Maximum Total Velocity for intended use (Student, Tandem, Emergency Air Crew or Other).	4.3.9			X							
Maximum Drogue deployment speed	4.3.6									X	

For ripcords, either lot control number or date of manufacture may be marked provided that tracabillity is maintained

At a minimum, Maximum Operating Limitations must include maximum pack opening speed and maximum gross weight. Manufacturer may voluntarily derate operating limitations.

Redundant marking may be eliminated for components which are permanently joined at the time of manufacture. If this is the case, the marking will be located on the most visible component, normally the container.

PIA TS 135

PIA-TS-135 - Table 2
Human Factors and Actuation Force Tests
Primary Actuation Device / Ripcord

	Data Required	Test Condition	Load Factor	Second Parachutist	Suspended by	Pack Condition	Emergency Parachute Assembly		Single Harness Reserve Parachute Assembly		Dual Harness Reserve Parachute Assembly	
							Male	Female	Male	Female	Male	Female
Primary Actuation Device / Ripcord	P/F Force	Standing Upright	N/A	N/A	N/A	N/A	6	6				
	P/F Force	Standing Upright	N/A	none/with	N/A	Full			3	3	3/3	3/3
	P/F Force	Standing Upright	N/A	none/with	N/A	Empty			3	3	3/3	3/3
	P/F Force	Suspended Harness	1g	none	Main Risers	Empty			3	3	3	3
	P/F Force	Suspended Harness	1 g	with	Main Risers	Empty					3	3
	Additional tests if emergency/reserve drogue is used:											
	P/F Force	Suspended Harness	4.1.7	N/A	Drogue	N/A	6	6				
	P/F Force	Suspended Harness	4.1.7	none	Drogue	Full			3	3	3	3
	P/F Force	Suspended Harness	4.1.7	none	Drogue	Empty			3	3	3	3
	P/F Force	Suspended Harness	4.1.7	with	Drogue	Full					3	3
	P/F Force	Suspended Harness	4.1.7	with	Drogue	Empty					3	3
	Total Tests Required in This Section (drogue / no drogue)						24/12		30/18		60/36	

4.1.7 - The drogue release shall be tested at an equivalent (or greater) force to the drag force generated at the MOW and MPOS.

Notes:
1. All tests must be conducted with a reserve/emergency canopy assembly packed for intended use.
2. N/A = Not Applicable
3. P/F = Pass/Fail

Change 1 (December 2015)

PIA TS 135

PIA TS-135 Table 3
Required Qualification Tests

Notes on Data Required	Test Description	Reference Paragraph	Speed at Pack Opening (KEAS)	Test Weight	Main Pack Condition	Emergency Parachute Assemblies		Single or Dual Harness Reserve Parachute Assembly	
						Dummy	Live	Dummy	Live
1, 8, 5	*Primary Actuation Device/Ripcord Test*	**4.3.2**	IAW 4.3.2 (a) through (d)						
1,2,5	*Human Factors and Actuation Force Tests*	**4.3.3**	IAW Table 2 and as described in paragraphs 4.3.3(a) through (e)						
	Human Factors Tests, Harness	**4.3.4**	Demonstrated by successful completion of live jumps per paragraph 4.3 .11						
	Environmental Tests	**4.3.5**							
1, 3, 5	Precondition to +200 F	**4.3.5.1**	60 KEAS	<= MaxOW		1		1	
1, 3, 5	Precondition to -40 F	**4.3.5.2**	60 KEAS	<= MaxOW		1		1	
1, 3, 5	Precondition - compressed pack	**4.3.5.3**	60 KEAS	<= MaxOW		1		1	
1, 3, 5	Precondition - alternate to 4.3.5.1 & 4.3.5.3	**4.3.5.4**	60 KEAS	<= MaxOW		1		1	
	Structural Overload Tests	**4.3.6**							
1,2,3,5	Complete Assemblies	**4.3.6.1**	Fig. 1	Fig. 1	N/S	3		3	
1,2,3,5	Alternate Means of Compliance, Canopy Only	**4.3.6.2**	Fig. 1	Fig. 1	N/S	3	N/A	3	N/A
1,2,3,5	Alternate Means of Compliance, Harness Only	**4.3.6.3**	Fig. 1	Fig. 1	N/S	3		3	
1,2,3,5	Drogue (if applicable)	**4.3.6.4**	Fig. 1	Fig. 1	N/S	3		3	
1, 3 (or 4), 5,	*Functional Tests, Twisted Lines*	**4.3.7**	60 KEAS	<= MOW	N/S	5		5	
1, 3 (or 4), 5,	*Functional Tests, (Normal Pack all types)*	**4.3.8**	Opening Time allowed shall be calculated IAW paragraph 4.3.8 (a). Opening Altitude allowed shall be calculated IAW paragraph 4.3.8 (b)						
1, 3 (or 4), 5,	Direct Drop	**4.3.8.1**	60 KEAS	MinOW	Empty	4		2	
1, 3 (or 4), 5,	Direct Drop	**4.3.8.1**	60 KEAS	AvOW	Full	N/A		2	
1, 3 (or 4), 5,	Direct Drop	**4.3.8.1**	60 KEAS	MaxOW	Empty	4		2	
1, 3 (or 4), 5,	Direct Drop	**4.3.8.1**	60 KEAS	MinOW	Full	N/A		2	
1, 3 (or 4), 5,	Direct Drop	**4.3.8.1**	60 KEAS	AvOW	Empty	4		2	
1, 3 (or 4), 5,	Direct Drop	**4.3.8.1**	60 KEAS	MaxOW	Full	N/A		2	
					Total Drops at 60 KEAS	12		12	
1, 3 (or 4), 5,	Direct Drop	**4.3.8.1**	85 KEAS	MinOW	Empty	4		2	
1, 3 (or 4), 5,	Direct Drop	**4.3.8.1**	85 KEAS	AvOW	Full	N/A		2	
1, 3 (or 4), 5,	Direct Drop	**4.3.8.1**	85 KEAS	MaxOW	Empty	4		2	
1, 3 (or 4), 5,	Direct Drop	**4.3.8.1**	85 KEAS	MinOW	Full	N/A		2	
1, 3 (or 4), 5,	Direct Drop	**4.3.8.1**	85 KEAS	AvOW	Empty	4		2	
1, 3 (or 4), 5,	Direct Drop	**4.3.8.1**	85 KEAS	MaxOW	Full	N/A		2	
					Total Drops at 85 KEAS	12		12	
1, 3 (or 4), 5,	Direct Drop	**4.3.8.1**	80% MPOS	MinOW	Empty	4		2	
1, 3 (or 4), 5,	Direct Drop	**4.3.8.1**	80% MPOS	AvOW	Full	N/A		2	
1, 3 (or 4), 5,	Direct Drop	**4.3.8.1**	80% MPOS	MaxOW	Empty	4		2	
1, 3 (or 4), 5,	Direct Drop	**4.3.8.1**	80% MPOS	MinOW	Full	N/A		2	
1, 3 (or 4), 5,	Direct Drop	**4.3.8.1**	80% MPOS	AvOW	Empty	4		2	
1, 3 (or 4), 5,	Direct Drop	**4.3.8.1**	80% MPOS	MaxOW	Full	N/A		2	
					Total Drops at 80% MPOS	12		12	

PIA TS-135, Revision 1.4, Issued April 22, 2010,   Page 16 of 18

PIA TS 135
PIA TS-135 Table 3 continued
Required Qualification Tests

1, 3 (or 4), 5,		Direct Drop	4.3.8.1	100% MPOS	MinOW	Empty	4		2	
1, 3 (or 4), 5,		Direct Drop	4.3.8.1	100% MPOS	AvOW	Full	N/A		2	
1, 3 (or 4), 5,		Direct Drop	4.3.8.1	100% MPOS	MaxOW	Empty	4		2	
1, 3 (or 4), 5,		Direct Drop	4.3.8.1	100% MPOS	MinOW	Full	N/A		2	
1, 3 (or 4), 5,		Direct Drop	4.3.8.1	100% MPOS	AvOW	Empty	4		2	
1, 3 (or 4), 5,		Direct Drop	4.3.8.1	100% MPOS	MaxOW	Full	N/A		2	
					Total Drops at 100% MPOS		12		12	
					Total Direct Drop Tests		**48**		**48**	

1, 3 (or 4), 5, 10, 11		Direct Drop "MARD device"	4.3.8.1	60 KEAS	<= MaxOW	Full	N/A		4	
1, 3 (or 4), 5, 12		Direct Drop "MARD device"	4.3.8.1		<= MaxOW	Full	N/A		4	
1, 3, 5, 9	*Functional Tests, Breakaway*		4.3.8.2	< 20 fps Vv	<= MaxOW	Empty	N/A		8	
1, 3, 5, 9, 13	Functional Tests, Breakaway "MARD device"		4.3.8.2		<= MaxOW	Empty	N/A		4	
1, 3, 5, 9, 14	Functional Tests, Breakaway "MARD device"		4.3.8.2		<= MaxOW	Empty	N/A		4	
1, 3, 5, 9, 15	Functional Tests, Breakaway "MARD device"		4.3.8.2		<= MaxOW	Empty	N/A		4	
1, 3, 5, 9, 12, 16	Functional Tests, Breakaway "MARD device"		4.3.8.2		<= MaxOW	Empty	N/A		4	

1, 5, 7	*Rate of Descent Tests*		4.3.9	N/A	MaxOW	N/S	6		6	
1, 5, 6	*Stability Test*		4.3.10	N/A	MinOW	N/S	6		6	
1, 3, 5, 11	*Live Jumps*		4.3.11	< 60 knots	<= MaxOW	N/S		2		2
1, 3, 5, 12	*Live Jumps*		4.3.11	> 120 knots	<= MaxOW	N/S		2		2

Abbreviations used above:

IAW	In accordance with
MPOS	Maximum pack opening speed
MaxOW	Maximum operating weight
AvOW	Average operating weight
MinOW	Minimum operating weight
N/A	Not Applicable
N/S	Not Specified

Notes on Test Critera

1 Record Pass/Fail
2 Record Riser Force
3 Record Opening Time
4 Record Altitude Loss
5 Video Record
6 Record Oscillation Angle
7 Record Rate-of-Descent
8 Record Ripcord Pull Force
9 If an RSL used, then half of the cutaway test shall be connducted with the RSL - a total of 8 tests is required
10 Jumps may be performed concurrently with similar direct drops outlined in table 3
11 Shall include a freefall of not more than 3 seconds
12 Shall include a freefall of at least 20 seconds
13 Breakaways from stable main
14 Breakaways from forward spinning main. Half left spin, half right spin
15 Breakaways from BACKWARDS spinning main. Half left spin, half right spin
16 Breakaways from bag lock malfunction

PIA TS 135

PIA-TS-135 - Table 4.
Performance Test Requirements for Component Qualification

Description of Test	Reference Paragraph for PIA-TS-135	Complete Parachute Assembly	Deployment Initiation Device (Pilot Chute, etc.)	Deployment Control Device, (dbag, etc.)	Canopy, lines, links, and reefing device (if used)	Stowage Container	Primary Actuation Device (Ripcord or Equivalent, Except Static Line)	Primary Actuation Device (Static Line)	Reserve Static Line (if used)	Harness	Risers (if not integral with harness)	Drogue, Canopy & Riser (if used)	Drogue Release Device (if used)	MARD (if used)
Ripcord Strength Tests	4.3.2	X					X	X	X				X	
Human Factors	4.3.3	X				X	X					X	X	X
Environmental	4.3.5	X	X	X	X	X				X	X	X	X	X
Structural Overload Test	4.3.6	X	X	X	X	X				X	X	X	X	*1
Functional Tests - Twisted Line	4.3.7	X		X	X									
Functional Tests - Normal Pack, Direct Drop	4.3.8.1	X	X	X	X	X						X	X	
Functional Tests - Normal Pack, Breakaway	4.3.8.2	X	X	X	X	X	X		X					X
Rate of Descent	4.3.9	X			X									
Stability	4.3.10	X			X									
Live Drops	4.3.11	X	X	X	X	X	X	X	X	X	X	X	X	X

*1 MARD installation shall not degrade strength or tensile loads on any reserve deployment devices or subassemblies on which it is installed. The manufacturer shall prove equivalent strength between similar devices or subassemblies with and without the MARD installed. This can be done with a bench/pull test or tensile test. For example, the strength of a free bag bridle with MARD parts installed but not hooked up should not be less than a bridle without a MARD installation.

Department of Transportation
Federal Aviation Administration
Office of Airworthiness
Washington, D.C.

TSO-C23c

Date 4/25/84

Technical Standard Order

Subject: TSO-C23c, PERSONNEL PARACHUTE ASSEMBLIES

(a) <u>Applicability</u>

(1) <u>Minimum Performance Standard</u>. This Technical Standard Order (TSO) prescribes the minimum performance standard that personnel parachute assemblies must meet in order to be identified with the applicable TSO marking. This TSO has been prepared in accordance with the procedural rules set fourth in Subpart O of the Federal Aviation Regulations, Part 21. Personnel parachute assemblies that are to be so identified and that are manufactured on or after the date of this TSO must meet the standard set fourth in society of Automotive Engineers, Inc. (SAE), Aerospace Standard (AS) 8015A, Minimum Performance Standard for Parachute Assemblies and Components, Personnel, dated September 30, 1982, as amended and supplemented by this TSO.

(b) <u>Markings</u>. None in addition to the marking specified in Federal Aviation Regulations (FAR)/21.607(d).

(c) <u>Data Requirements</u>.

In addition to FAR/21.605, the manufacturer must furnish the Manager, Aircraft Certification Office (ACO), Federal Aviation Administration (FAA), having purview of the manufacturer s facilities, one copy each of the following technical data:

(1) Operating instructions.
(2) Equipment limitations.
(3) Inspection and test procedures applicable to this product.
(4) Specifications.
(5) Maintenance procedures.
(6) Manufacturer's TSO qualification test report.

(d) <u>Previously Approved Equipment</u>. Personnel parachute assemblies approved prior to the date of this TSO may continue to be manufactured under the provisions of the original approval.

A-37

(e)   <u>Availability of Reference Documents</u>.

(1)   Copies of SAE AS 8015A may be purchased from the Society of Automotive Engineers, Inc., Department 331, 400 Commonwealth Drive, Warrendale, Pennsylvania 15096.

(2)   Federal Aviation Regulations, Part 21, Subpart O and Advisory Circular 20-110, Index of Aviation Technical Standard Orders, may be reviewed at the FAA Headquarters in the Office of Airworthiness, Aircraft Engineering Division (AWS-110) and at all ACO s.

M.C. BEARD
Director of Airworthiness

A-38

FEDERAL AVIATION AGENCY

Washington 25, D. C.

TECHNICAL STANDARD ORDER

Regulations of the Administrator

Part 514

SUBJECT: **PARACHUTES**   **TSO-C23b**

Technical Standard Orders for Aircraft Materials, Parts, Processes, and Appliances

Part 514 contains minimum performance standards and specifications of materials, parts, processes, and appliances used in aircraft and implements the provisions of sections 3.18, 4a.31, 4b.18, 6.18 and 7.18 of the Civil Air Regulations. The regulation uses the Technical Standard Order system which, in brief, provides for FAA-industry cooperation in the development of performance standards and specifications which are adopted by the Administrator as Technical Standard Orders, and a form of self-regulation by industry in demonstrating compliance with these orders.

Part 514 consists of two subparts. Subpart A contains the general requirements applicable to all Technical Standard Orders. These provisions are summarized below for the convenient reference of the public. Subpart B contains the technical standards and specifications to which a particular product must conform, and each Technical Standard Order is set forth in the appropriate section of Subpart B. The subject Technical Standard Order is printed below. ANY TECHNICAL STANDARD ORDER MAY BE OBTAINED BY SENDING A REQUEST TO FAA, WASHINGTON 25, D. C.

SUBPART A--GENERAL

This subpart provides, in part, that a manufacturer of an aircraft material, part, process, or appliance for which standards are established in Subpart B, prior to its distribution for use on a civil aircraft of the United States, shall furnish a written statement of conformance certifying that the material, part, process, or appliance meets the applicable performance standards established in this part. The statement of conformance must be signed by a person duly authorized by the manufacturer, and furnished to the Chief, Engineering and Manufacturing Division, Bureau of Flight Standards, Federal Aviation Agency, Washington 25, D. C.

Subpart A also requires appropriate marking of materials, parts, processes, and appliances as follows:

(a) Name and address of the manufacturer responsible for compliance,

(b) Equipment name, or type or model designation,

(c) Weight to the nearest pound and fraction thereof,

(d) Serial number and/or date of manufacture, and

(e) Applicable Technical Standard Order (TSO) number.

In addition, Subpart A provides that no deviation will be granted from the performance standards established in Subpart B, and that the Administrator may take appropriate action in the event of noncompliance with Part 514.

A-45

§ 514.33 Parachutes - TSO-C23b--(a) Applicability--(1) Minimum performance standards. Minimum performance standards are hereby established for parachutes which are to be used in civil aircraft of the United States. New models of parachutes manufactured for use in civil aircraft of the United States on or after March 29, 1962, shall meet the minimum performance standards of National Aircraft Standards Specification 804 dated August 24, 1949,[1]/ with the exceptions covered in subparagraph (2) of this paragraph. Parachutes approved prior to March 29, 1962, may continue to be manufactured under the provisions of the original approval.

(2) Exceptions. (i) The auxiliary parachute used in combination with a standard parachute shall be designed for use in combination with the specific main parachute.

(ii) For the purpose of testing an auxiliary type parachute used in combination with a standard parachute the speed specified in Section 4.3.8 of NAS Specification 804 shall be 25 feet per second instead of 21 feet per second.

(b) Marking. The auxiliary parachute and its pack shall be marked "Auxiliary Parachute" in addition to the other marking requirements contained in Subpart A.

(c) Data requirements. (1) The manufacturer shall maintain a current file of complete design data.

(2) The manufacturer shall maintain a current file of complete data describing the inspection and test procedures applicable to his product. (See paragraph (d) of this section.)

(d) Quality control. Each parachute shall be produced under a quality control system, established by the manufacturer, which will assure that each parachute is in conformity with the requirements of this section. This system shall be described in the data required under paragraph (c)(2) of this section. A representative of the Administrator shall be permitted to make such inspections and tests at the manufacturer's facility as may be necessary to determine compliance with the requirements of this section.

(e) Effective date. March 29, 1962.

1/Copies may be obtained from the National Standards Association, 616 Washington Loan and Trust Building, Washington 4, D. C.

- 2 -

(3/27/62)

Department of Transportation
Federal Aviation Administration
Aircraft Certification Service
Washington, D.C.

TSO-C23f

Effective
Date: *09/21/2012*

Technical Standard Order

Subject: Personnel Parachute Assemblies and Components

1.   PURPOSE. This technical standard order (TSO) is for manufacturers applying for a TSO authorization (TSOA) or letter of design approval (LODA). In it, we the Federal Aviation Administration (FAA), tell you what minimum performance standards (MPS) your personnel parachute assembly and components must first meet for approval and identification with the applicable TSO marking.

2.   APPLICABILITY. This TSO affects new applications submitted after its effective date.

   a. All prior revisions to this TSO are no longer effective. Generally, we will not accept applications for the previous revision after the effective date of this TSO. We may do so, however, up to six months after it, if we know that you were working against the prior MPS before the new change became effective.

   b. Personnel parachute assemblies and components approved under a previous TSOA may still be manufactured under the provisions of its original approval.

3.   REQUIREMENTS. New models of personnel parachute assemblies and components identified and manufactured on or after the effective date of this TSO must meet the MPS qualification and documentation requirements in Parachute Industry Association (PIA) Technical Standard 135 TS-135 Revision 1.4 issued April 22, 2010 *"Performance Standards for Personnel Parachute Assemblies and Components"* as modified by appendix 1 of this TSO.

   a.   Functionality. This TSO's standards apply to equipment intended to be used as a reserve or emergency parachute.

   b.   Failure Condition Classifications.

      (1) Lose of the function defined in paragraph **3.a** is a catastrophic failure condition.

    c. Functional Qualification. Demonstrate the required performance under the test conditions in Appendix 1 of this TSO.

    d. Deviations. We have provisions for using alternate or equivalent means of compliance to the criteria in the MPS of this TSO. If you invoke these provisions, you must show that your equipment maintains an equivalent level of safety. Apply for a deviation under the provision of 14 CFR § 21.618.

4. MARKING.

    a. Mark at least one major component permanently and legibly with all the information in CFR § 45.15(b). The marking must include the serial number.

    b. Also, mark the following permanently and legibly, with at least the manufacturer's name, subassembly part number, and the TSO number:

        (1) Each component that is easily removable (without hand tools), and

        (2) Each subassembly of the article that you determined may be interchangeable.

5. APPLICATION DATA REQUIREMENTS.
You must give the FAA aircraft certification office (ACO) manager responsible for your facility a statement of conformance, as specified in 14 CFR § 21.603(a)(1), and one copy each of the following technical data to support your design and production approval. LODA applicants must submit the same data (excluding paragraph **5.f**) through their civil aviation authority.

    a. A manual(s) containing the following:

        (1) Operating instructions and equipment limitations sufficient to describe the equipment's operational capability.

        (2) Describe in detail any deviations.

        (3) Installation procedures and limitations sufficient to ensure that the personnel parachute assembly and component, when installed according to the installation procedures, still meets this TSO's requirements. Limitations must identify any unique aspects of the installation. The limitations must include a note with the following statement:

"This article meets the minimum performance and quality system standards required by a technical standard order (TSO). Installation of this article requires separate approval."

    b. Schematic drawings, wiring diagrams, and any other documentation necessary for assembly, installation, donning, and operation of the personnel parachute assembly and component

Page 2

c. Instructions covering periodic maintenance, calibration, and repair, for the continued airworthiness of personnel parachute assemblies and components. Include recommended inspection intervals and service life, as appropriate.

d. A drawing depicting how the article will be marked with the information required by paragraph **4** of this TSO.

e. Identify functionality or performance contained in the article not evaluated under paragraph **3** of this TSO (that is, non-TSO functions). Non-TSO functions are accepted in parallel with the TSO authorization. For those non-TSO functions to be accepted, you must declare these functions and include the following information with your TSO application:

(1)   Description of the non-TSO function(s), such as performance specifications, failure condition classifications, software, hardware, and environmental qualification levels. Include a statement confirming that the non-TSO function(s) do not interfere with the article's compliance with the requirements of paragraph **3**.

(2)   Installation procedures and limitations sufficient to ensure that the non-TSO function(s), meets the declared functions and performance specification(s) described in paragraph **5,e.(1).**

(3)   Instructions for continued performance applicable to the non-TSO function(s) described in paragraph **5.e.(1).**

(4)   Interface requirements and applicable installation test procedures to ensure compliance with the performance data defined in paragraph **5.e.(1).**

(5)   Test plans, analysis and results, as appropriate, to verify the function and performance of the hosting TSO article is not affected by the non-TSO function(s).

(6)   Test plants, analysis and results, as appropriate, to verify the function and performance of the non-TSO functions(s) as described in paragraph **5.e.(1).**

f. The quality system description required by 14 CFR § 21.608, including functional test specifications. The quality system should ensure that you will detect any change to the approved design that could adversely affect compliance with the TSO MPS, and reject the article accordingly. (Not required for LODA applicants.)

g. Material and process specifications list.

h. List of all drawings and processes (including revision level) that define the article's design.

i. Manufacturer's TSO qualification report showing results of testing accomplished according to paragraph **3.c** of this TSO.

6.   MANUFACTURER DATA REQUIREMENTS. Besides the data given directly to the responsible ACO, have the following technical data available for review by the responsible ACO:

   a. Functional qualification specifications for qualifying each production article to ensure compliance with this TSO.

   b. Equipment calibration procedures.

   c. Schematic drawings.

   d. Wiring diagrams.

   e. Material and process specifications.

   f. If the article contains non-TSO function(s), you must also make available items **6.a** through **6.e** as they pertain to the non-TSO function(s).

7.   FURNISHED DATA REQUIREMENTS.

   a. If furnishing one or more articles manufactured under this TSO to one entity (such as an individual jumper or a drop zone operator), provide one copy or on-line access to the data in paragraphs **5.a** through **5.c** of this TSO. Add any other data needed for the proper installation, certification, use, or for continued compliance with the TSO, of the personnel parachute assembly and components.

   b. If the article contains declared non-TSO function(s), include one copy of the data in paragraphs **5.e.(1)** through **5.e.(6).**

8.   HOW TO GET REFERENCED DOCUMENTS.

   a. You can download a free copy of PIA TS-135 Revision 1.4 issued April 22, 2010 *Performance Standards for Personnel Parachute Assemblies and Components* at:

   http://www.pia.com/piapubs/TSDocuments/TS-135v1.4.pdf

   b. You can find a current list of technical standard orders and advisory circulars on the FAA Internet website Regulatory and Guidance Library at http://rgl.faa.gov/. You will also find the TSO Index of Articles at the same site.

/S/
Susan J. M. Cabler
Assistant Manager, Aircraft Engineering Division

APPENDIX 1. MINIMUM PERFORMANCE STANDARD FOR PERSONNEL PARACHUTE ASSEMBLIES AND COMPONENTS

This appendix prescribes the MPS for a personnel parachute assembly and component. The applicable standard is PIA TS-135 Revision 1.4 issued April 22, 2010 *Performance Standards for Personnel Parachute Assemblies and Components,* as modified for this TSO:

1. Page 2, replace Para, 2.1.i. to read as follows:

   "Cognizant Agency" - The Federal Aviation Administration (FAA) or civil aviation authorities recognized in bilateral agreements by the FAA,

2. Page 5, Para. 4.1.2. delete: "generally".

   Stitching should not ravel when broken. "Generally" reduces the requirement for stitch choice, and adversely impacts the current standard.

3. Page 5, Para. 4.1.3.delete: "Ref: Table 2".

   Table 2 is not relevant to this requirement. Testing of a packed assy will show if the main parachute will interfere with the proper function of the reserve parachute.

4. Page 9, Para. 4.3.7. in first sentence delete: "a weight not more than".

   The worst case is the maximum operating weight.

5. Page 11, disregard paragraph 4.3.9.1., Rate of Descent Tests (Method 2).

        We omitted the Method (2) testing, for not providing an equivalent level of safety to current standard. This method is directed at high performance and experience parachutists in sport and skydiving activities. Novice or less experienced parachutists in emergency conditions due to incapacitation, panic, etc., may not be able to safely deploy and land.

We have to consider the safety of all jumpers, not just the highly skilled, highly experienced. It is argued that the risks the experienced jumpers are exposing themselves to, are mitigated by their skill and experience.

To allow the increased velocity may improve the safety of highly skilled, highly experienced jumpers, but it erodes the safety for the beginner, incapacitated, panicked, or a jumper who has gotten himself into a treacherous landing area.

Page 5

We do not agree that a canopy manufacturer can demonstrate that a jumper can safely land with an appropriate control manipulation while performing a flare before touchdown. This approach relies on jumper's experience to meet the MOPS that parachutes have been certified to. This approach does not provide an equivalent level of safety.

6. Page 14, Table 1, under Marking Data Requirements, replace:

Statement of Authorization under TS0-C-23e and/or (J) TSO-C-23e if applicable.

With

Statement of Authorization. Under TSO-C23f and/or ETSO-C23f if applicable.

TSO-C23e has been cancelled

Page 6

NATIONAL AIRCRAFT STANDARDS COMMITTEE

AIRCRAFT INDUSTRIES ASSOCIATION OF AMERICA, INC., 610 SHOREHAM BUILDING, WASHINGTON 5, D. C.

SPECIFICATION - PARACHUTES

This specification defines the minimum performance and safety standards for parachutes to be used in certificated aircraft.

1. APPLICABLE SPECIFICATIONS

    1.1 None.

2. TYPES

    2.1 This specification covers two types of man-carrying parachutes for use in certificated civil aircraft

        Standard Type Parachute
        Low Speed Type Parachute (Up to 150 miles per hour).

3. MATERIAL AND WORKMANSHIP

    3.1 Materials shall be of a quality which experience and/or tests have conclusively demonstrated to be suitable for use in parachutes. Workmanship shall be consistent with high-grade parachute manufacturing practice.

        3.1.1 Canopy Material: The fabric used in the canopy construction shall be free from harmful gums, starches and other foreign material. It shall also be free from avoidable inperfections in manufacture and from defects or blemishes affecting its strength or durability and shall have been finished without application of excessive heat. The canopy material shall have sufficient resilience to insure proper opening of the canopy under conditions outlined in 4.3.5.

        3.1.2 Fitting Materials: Fittings shall be fabricated from carbon steel, alloy steel, or corrosion-resisting material. Fittings made from metals that are not corrosion-resisting shall be plated or otherwise protected, to resist corrosion during the normal life of the parachute. The use of dissimilar metals, expecially brass, copper, or steel in intimate metal-to-metal contact with aluminum or aluminum alloy, shall be avoided, wherever possible.

4. DETAIL REQUIREMENTS

    4.1 Design and Construction

        4.1.1 Fittings: All fittings shall be designed to carry their full rated load without yielding.

APPROVAL DATE 8-24-49   REVISION

TITLE	CLASSIFICATION SPECIFICATION
SPECIFICATION - PARACHUTES	NAS 804 Sheet 1 of 5

THIS DRAWING SUPERCEDES ALL ANTECEDENT STANDARD DRAWINGS FOR THE SAME PRODUCT, AND SHALL BECOME EFFECTIVE FOR VENDOR MANUFACTURERS NOT LATER THAN 6 MONTHS AFTER THE LATEST DATE OF APPROVAL SHOWN.

A-47

NATIONAL AIRCRAFT STANDARDS COMMITTEE

AIRCRAFT INDUSTRIES ASSOCIATION OF AMERICA, INC., 610 SHOREHAM BUILDING, WASHINGTON 5, D. C.

4.1.2 <u>Suspension Lines</u>: All suspension lines of a given model parachute shall be marked under equal tension to show points of attachment.

4.1.3 <u>Stitching</u>: Stitching shall be of a type that will not ravel when broken.

4.1.4 <u>Rip Cord</u>: The rip cord, including joints between the handle and the release, shall be designed to withstand the tension test load of 4.3.1.

4.1.5 <u>Pack Opening Device</u>: No more than 22 pounds pull shall be required to cause the positive and quick functioning of the pack opening device.

4.1.6 <u>Harness Release</u>: The harness shall be so constructed that the rider can release himself and drop clear in case of a water landing, but a quick-attachable or quick-releasing device between the harness and the parachute is not mandatory.

4.2 <u>Marking</u>

4.2.1 <u>Pack</u>: The following information shall be legibly and permanently marked on or attached to the outside of the parachute pack by use of a name plate, identification label or stenciled letters.

> Manufacturer's name
> Model number or model name*
> Parachute serial number
> Date of manufacture
> National Aircraft Standard Number (NAS804)

*Note: Special designation or identification of low speed type parachutes must be indicated on the outside pack by stenciling in red letters one inch high the following: "Low Speed Parachute" and in red letters one-half inch high, "Limited to Use in Airplane Under 150 MPH."

4.2.2 <u>Canopy</u>: Each parachute canopy shall be legibly and permanently marked, preferably adjacent to the skirt, with the same information as in 4.2.1.

4.2.3 <u>Harness</u>: The parachute model number or model name and date of manufacture shall be stenciled on all harnesses. This marking shall be placed inside the back strap of the harness or other suitable location where it will be subject to minimum of obliteration.

REVISION		TITLE	CLASSIFICATION
APPROVAL DATE 8-24-49			SPECIFICATION
		SPECIFICATION - PARACHUTES	**NAS 804** Sheet 2 of 5

THIS DRAWING SUPERCEDES ALL ANTECEDENT STANDARD DRAWINGS FOR THE SAME PRODUCT, AND SHALL BECOME EFFECTIVE FOR VENDOR MANUFACTURERS NOT LATER THAN 6 MONTHS AFTER THE LATEST DATE OF APPROVAL SHOWN.

NATIONAL AIRCRAFT STANDARDS COMMITTEE

AIRCRAFT INDUSTRIES ASSOCIATION OF AMERICA, INC., 610 SHOREHAM BUILDING, WASHINGTON 5, D. C.

4.2.4 <u>Inspection Data Pocket</u>: Each parachute outfit shall be provided with an inner and an outer pocket for keeping a record card containing space for recording the date of repacking or repair and the rigger's name and serial number. The inner pocket shall be located in the center of the packed container, tray or frame and the outer pocket placed externally in an easily accessible position. If the inner record card can be read from the outside of the pack because of the use of transparent materials, only the inner pocket need be provided.

4.3 <u>Qualification Tests</u>: 100% performance in qualification tests 4.3.1 through 4.3.8 is required.

4.3.1 <u>Rip Cord Tension Test</u>: The rip cord, including joints between the handle and the release, shall not fail under a straight tension test load of 300 pounds applied for not less than three seconds.

4.3.2 <u>Pull Test - Pack Opening Device</u>: The pack opening device shall be tested by use of an accurate spring balance to indicate its positive and quick-functioning with no more than 22 pounds pull.

4.3.3 <u>Functional Test (Normal Pack)</u>: Twelve drops at least six of which shall be from an airplane with a 170-pound dummy man, from an altitude of not more than 500 feet. The indicated air speed at the time of release shall be 70 miles per hour. No twists shall purposely be packed in the suspension lines. The parachute must be fully open within three seconds from time of release.

4.3.4 <u>Functional Test (Twisted Lines)</u>: Five drops with a 170-pound dummy man, from an altitude of not more than 500 feet. The indicated air speed at the time of release shall be 70 miles per hour. Three twists shall purposely be packed in the suspension lines near the skirt. The parachute must be fully open within four seconds from time of release.

4.3.5 <u>Compressed Pack Test</u>: This test is required only when canopy materials other than pongee, silk or nylon are used (Ref. 3.1.1). Three drops with the conditions stated in 4.3.3 except that prior to the tests the parachutes completely packed shall be subjected continuously to a 200-pound weight for 400 hours and then dropped without being repacked.

APPROVAL DATE 8-24-49   REVISION

TITLE	CLASSIFICATION SPECIFICATION
SPECIFICATION - PARACHUTES	**NAS 804** Sheet 3 of 5

THIS DRAWING SUPERCEDES ALL ANTECEDENT STANDARD DRAWINGS FOR THE SAME PRODUCT, AND SHALL BECOME EFFECTIVE FOR VENDOR MANUFACTURERS NOT LATER THAN 6 MONTHS AFTER THE LATEST DATE OF APPROVAL SHOWN.

A-49

NATIONAL AIRCRAFT STANDARDS COMMITTEE

AIRCRAFT INDUSTRIES ASSOCIATION OF AMERICA, INC., 610 SHOREHAM BUILDING, WASHINGTON 5, D. C.

4.3.6 <u>Strength Test</u>

4.3.6.1 <u>Standard Type Parachute:</u> Three drops with a parachute of the same type at an altitude of not more than 500 feet shall be made with a dummy weight and indicated air speed to give the equivalent of 5000 lbs. shock load. (See Table I.) No twists shall purposely be packed in the suspension lines. The weight shall be attached to the harness. No external shock absorbers or material which may act as such shall be permitted. The parachute shall show no failure of any material.

Table I
Launching Speeds & Total Weights for Approx. 5000# Shock Load *

Speed – MPH	Total Weight (Incl. Chute) – Lbs.
150	660
175	500
200	400
225	325
250	275
275	225
300	200
325	175
350	160
375	150

* Data computed for 28 ft. Standard Flat-Type Parachute based on USAF Parachute Handbook Section V.

4.3.6.2 <u>Low Speed Type Parachute:</u> Three drops with a parachute of the same type at an altitude of not more than 500 feet shall be made with a dummy weight and indicated air speed to give the equivalent of 3000 lbs. shock load. No twists shall purposely be packed in the suspension lines. The weight shall be attached to the harness. No external shock absorbers or material which may act as such shall be permitted. The parachute shall show no failure of any material.

Table II
Launching Speeds & Total Weights for Approx. 3000# Shock Load *

Speed – MPH	Total Weight (Incl. Chute) – Lbs.
100	750
125	525
150	375
175	300
200	235
225	200

* Data computed for 28 ft. Standard Flat-Type Parachute based on USAF Parachute Handbook Section V.

APPROVAL DATE 8-24-49   REVISION

TITLE	CLASSIFICATION
	SPECIFICATION
SPECIFICATION - PARACHUTES	**NAS 804** Sheet 4 of 5

NATIONAL AIRCRAFT STANDARDS COMMITTEE

AIRCRAFT INDUSTRIES ASSOCIATION OF AMERICA, INC., 610 SHOREHAM BUILDING, WASHINGTON 5, D. C.

4.3.7 <u>Live Drop Tests</u>: Two live drop tests from an airplane with a man weighing approximately 170 pounds, including the weight of an additional certificated auxiliary parachute, from an altitude of 2000 feet on a comparatively still day. The rider must suffer no discomfort from the opening shock and must be able to disengage himself unaided from the harness after landing. For this test the standard harness may be altered to permit attachment of an auxiliary parachute provided that such alteration does not interfere with the normal operation of the parachute and harness equipment being tested.

4.3.8 <u>Rate of Descent Test</u>: At least six drops from an airplane with a 170-pound dummy man. The average rate of descent shall not exceed 21 feet per second for the last 100 feet under standard sea level altitude conditions. A method shall be employed for direct and accurate measurement of rate of descent for the last 100 feet, such as the use of a weighted cord or cable by which the descent may be timed from the time of ground impact of the weight to ground impact of the parachute.

APPROVAL DATE 8-24-49   REVISION

TITLE	CLASSIFICATION
	SPECIFICATION
SPECIFICATION - PARACHUTES	**NAS 804** Sheet 5 of 5

THIS DRAWING SUPERCEDES ALL ANTECEDENT STANDARD DRAWINGS FOR THE SAME PRODUCT, AND SHALL BECOME EFFECTIVE FOR VENDOR MANUFACTURERS NOT LATER THAN 6 MONTHS AFTER THE LATEST DATE OF APPROVAL SHOWN.

A-51

EXAMPLE OUTLINE FOR SENIOR RIGGER TRAINING, CLASSES, DEMONSTRATIONS AND PROJECTS.

A. Introduction

1. FAA rules and regulations
2. Part 105, 91, 65, and basic facilities to practice rigging, (packing table, inspection, drying area)
3. Responsibility as a licensed rigger, privilages, and rating limitations
4. Paperwork, FAA, logbook, datacard, ADs, service bulletins, (binder with all ADs and SBs)
5. Filling out inspection log book, filling out data cards

B. Rigging Techniques and Tools (VIDEO)

1. Modem rigging technics and methods
2. Packing tapes (Square reserves)
3. Vector
4. Racer
5. Javelin
6. Talon
7. Vector tandem, strong, racer

C. Round Canopy

1. Construction and materials
2. Aerodynamics
3. Inspection procedures, (bridle attaching methods)
4. Line continuity (two and four riser systems) (round to riser assembly)
5. Canopy layout (on packing table)
6. Canopy sections, gore numbers, panel designations.
7. Data panel information
8. Alterations or repairs listed on data panel (is it approved? where do we look?)
9. Diapers, full stow, two stow, vertical stow, etc.
10. Flaking the canopy for packing
11. Diaper and line stowing
12. Acid test and inspection

D. Square Canopy

1. Construction and materials
2. Aerodynamics
3. Inspection procedures, (layout on carpet) (hanging by tail)
4. Line continuity (cascaded and continuous lines) (assembly to risers)
5. Canopy sections (nose, tail, upper and lower skins, ribs, load bearing ribs, crossports)
6. Data panel infonnation
7. Steering toggles (types installation sand stowing methods)
8, Deployment systems (freebags, etc.) (inspection of these systems)
9. Packing methods (side pack, stack pack, pro pack, hanging pro pack)
10. Folding canopy (to place indeployment bag) (freebag types, vector, racer, molar, etc.)
11. Line stowing (methods and tools)

E. Harness and Containers

1. Construction and materials
2. Hardware (types, inspection, values of types, ADs or SBs, proper installation)
3. Gromets (types, inspection)
4. Snaps (types, inspection)
5. Cable housings (types, inspection)
6. Attachment links (types, inspection, main and reserve)
7. Pilot chute (types, inspection, both main and reserve, including retract and collapsible)
8. Hand tacking (materials, methods, inspections)
9. Ripcords and release handles (types, materials, inspection procedures)
10. Pins and cones (types, inspection)
11. Harness and container inspection (as a unit)

F. Sewing Machines

1. Manufactures and types (uses of different types) (straight locking, zig zag, bar tack, harness)
2. Sewing machine components (table, head, motor, clutch/brake, bobbin winder, etc.)
3. Threading the machine (needle and bobbin) (thread types and values)
4. Basic operating of machine (foot, knee, hands, and effects, sew, brake, lift foot, set needle, etc.)
5. Types of sewing stitches (301-304-308)

G. Tools (Demonstrations and Applications for all Types)

1. Pull up cords
2. Packing weights
3. Line seperator (round/square)
4. Through the bag cord with friction lock
5. Molarstrap
6. Rifle cleaning rod
7. Velcro covers
8. Temporarypins
9. Knee plate
10. T-Bar
11. Packing paddles (long/short)
12. Bodkins
13. Seam ripper
14. Scissors (nippers)
15. Finger trap fids
16. Positive closing device
17. Hand sewing needles
18. Razor knife
19. Tailoring pencils (correct type dixon)
20. Seal press
21. L-Bar seperator
22. Weight scale (pull test)
23. Pull test clamps
24. Hot knife
25. Gromet hole cutters
26. Gromet sets
27. Snap setting tools
28. Hot glue gun

H. Automatic Activation Devices

1. Makes models and applications
2. Setting and calibration (all makes and models)
3. Discription of activation types (ballistic, spring, etc.)
4. Care and maintainence (testing operations, replacing batterys, replacing cutters, cocking unit, changing catridges, etc.)
5. Installations (different applications using optional numbers of cutters, pinpullers, powerplates, pull cables, etc.)
6. Responsibility (who can install, remove, replace, maintain, and what are the liabilities connected with these situations?)

I. Materials

1. Presentation of all types, with reference to idertification and strength values (material sample book)
2. Cordura, parapack (denier weights)
3. Suspension line (dacron, spectra, kevlar)
4. F-111, zero porosity, different weight ripstops 1.5, etc.
5. Marquisette netting, high drag netting
6. Velcro (½-¾-1½-2 inch)
7. Elastics (l inch, 1½-inch)
8. Shock cord (⅛-³⁄₁₆-¼)
9. Tubular nylon (½-⁹⁄₁₆-⅝-¾-1 inch)
10. Kevlar tape
11. Nylon stiffener plate
12. Nylon binding tape (⅜-¾-1 inch)
13. Nylon support tape (1 inch square weave)
14. Webbing (type4, type6, type7, type8 , type9, typel2, type 13, type17, type24)
15. Threads and cords (nylon and cotton)

J. Demonstrations

1. Packing B-12
2. Packing NB-6
3. Packing wonderhog (2 stow)
4. Packing centarus (wide full stow para-innovators)
5. Packing vector II (full stow vertical strong lopo)
6. Packing javelin (national full stow)
7. Packing racer square (side and pro)
8. Packing vector I square (side and pro)
9. Packing talon square (side and pro)
10. Packing flex on square (pro)
11. Packing javelin square (pro)
12. Packing vector tandem
13. Packing strong tandem
14. Packing racer tandem
15. Packing security back pack
16. Packing softie back pack
17. Packing briefcase
18. Packing sprint
19. Packing strong hawk
20. Packing EOS

J . Demonstrations (continued)

21. Tangled round
22. Tangled square
23. Complete inspection (round reserve)
24. Complete inspection (square reserve)
25. Assembly complete (round)
26. Assembly complete (square)
27. Hand sewing and tacking (comfort pads, connector links, cones, reserve cable housing, eyelets)
28. Needle fold (reserve bridles)
29. Installing toggles (main and reserve)
30. Installing gromets and snaps
31. Finger trapping suspension line
32. 4-line release systems
33. Nylon mesh acid test
34. Pull test (description warp and fill thread to selvege edge)
35. Pull test (using scale check pull tension on reserve ripcord)
36. Installing a 6-inch patch in F-111

K. Projects

1. Install to airworthy standards around reserve
2. Install to airworthy standards a square reserve
3. Round canopy inspection locate and verify defects
4. Square canopy inspection locate and verify defects
S. Square reserve side pack
6. Square reserve pro pack
7. Harness and container inspection locate and verify defects
8. Pack B-12
9. Pack NB-6
10. Pack round reserve with 2 stow diaper
11. Pack round reserve with vertical full stow diaper
12. Pack round reserve with full stow diaper
13. Pack round reserve with vertical full stow diaper parallelto bottom of pack tray
14. Pack square reserve in Vector-type freebag (using through bag cord)
15. Pack square reserve in Javelin-type free bag (molar)
16. Untangle round reserve using proper technique
17. Untangle square reserve using proper technique
18. Demonstrate knowledge of 4-line release systems
19. Hand sew ripcord housing, tack comfort pad, Hand sew cone and eyelet
20. Tie knots, overhand, square, clove hitch, double half hitch, slip loop, bowline, surgeon's & locking.
21. Install proper seal on closing pin
22. Perform proper needle fold
23. Machine sewing 1 (build shot bags using templates and perform sewingpractise drills)
24. Machine sewing 2 (install a six inch patch to exceptable and airworthy standards)
25. Using proper tools (cut hole and set gromets in parapack and install snaps)
26. Install steering toggles using recognizedmethods
27. Finger-trap suspension line to a finished length by calculating shrinkage of traped area
28. Perform dryrun reserve inspection and repack to airworthy standards meeting all FAA requirements
29. Locate correct information for compatability, assembly and inspection of a sport rig and reserve
30. Perform at least 20 complete inspections and repacks to standards of back type reserves

Example Training Syllabus for Master Rigger Training, Classes, Demonstrations, and Projects

A. Introduction

1. Federal Aviation Administration (FAA) regulations and rating privileges
2. Review Title 14 Code of Federal Regulations (CFR) parts 105, 91, detail part 65 required facilities, equipment, tools, materials, record keeping, repair testing
3. Mil-Spec materials and values
4. Technical Standard Order (TSO) standards and who creates them. Current standards, categories, and limitations and who maintains them
5. Skills, responsibilities, and ethics of a master parachute rigger
6. Record keeping
7. Alterations, manufactures, FAA authorization process, records and documentation

B. The Parachute Loft

1. Facilities
2. Work areas, round canopies, square canopies, suspended, table
3. Material storage, and support, conditions for material quality
4. Inspection areas and lighting
5. Hand tools, types, uses, control, maintenance
6. Sewing machines
7. Parachute equipment storage, short and long term
8. Project tables, layout and cutting

C. Harness & Container Systems

1. Reserve system deployment types, (internal pilot chute) (external pilot chute)
2. Harness types, (standard harness) (partial articulated harness) (fully articulate harness)
3. Hardware, current manufactures, (standard cadmium plated) (stainless steel) (rapide links, "galvanized" "stainless") (Slinks – Manufactured by Performance Design and Precision Aerodynamics)
4. 3-ring release systems, ring sizes, maintenance, riser sizes, lengths, construction
5. Reserve ripcord systems, types, housings, ripcords
6. Main canopy deployment systems, ripcord, throwout, pullout, bottom of container (BOC), PUD system
7. Freebag systems, deployment bag types and cuts, line stow types, bridles and bridle assists, reserve pilotchute types
8. Main canopy release systems, housing types, duel action systems (student equipment)

D. Square Parachute Systems

1. Modern construction
2. Materials
3. Airfoil types (elliptical, semi elliptical, tapered, multi cell)
4. Cell construction types (I-beam, interlocking T-beam, half cell, spanwise)
5. Suspension line types and line attachments types (Spectra, Kevlar, Vectran, HMA, Dacron)
6. Canopy suspension line trim
7. Modern canopy repair methods and limitations (Chapter 7 FAA Parachute Rigger Handbook) (RD Raghanti repair method)
8. Square canopy design and flight definitions
   - (A) Airfoil section area
   - (B) Angle of attack
   - (C) Angle of trim
   - (D) Angle of incidence
   - (E) Aspect ratio
   - (F) Cascade line
   - (G) Cell
   - (H) Chord
   - (I) Control line
   - (J) Control line deflection

(K)   Construction chordwise

(L)   Construction full-cell chordwise

(M)   I-beam

(N)   Interlocking T-beam

(O)   Half-cell chordwise

(P)   Construction spanwise

(Q)   Cross ports

(R)   Deployment brakes

(S)   Flares, suspension line attachments

(T)   Full flight settings

(U)   Glide path (flightpath) angle

(V)   Pilot chute controlled reefing

(W)   Planform

(X)   Planform area

(Y)   Plumbline

(Z)   Projected area

(AA)   Quarter chord area

(BB)   Reference line

(CC)   Ribs

(DD)   Riser specs

(EE)   Slider

(FF)   Slider stops

(GG)   Stabilizer panels

(HH)   Span

(II)   Suspension lines (A) (B) (C) (D)

(JJ)   Suspension line length

(KK)   Trim line

(LL)   Toggles control

(MM) Final trim measurements

E. Authorized/Certificated Parachute Components and Compatibility

1. Manufactures inspection and packing instructions
2. Approved data
3. Acceptable data
4. Methods to confirm compatibility

F. Automatic Activation Devises

1. Types
2. Service requirements (life, battery service, trouble codes, inspections)
3. Control and calibration
4. Installation
5. Service during FAA 180-day inspection cycle
6. Compatibility to TSOed equipment
7. Airworthiness Directives (AD) or Service Bulletins (SB)

G. Commercial Sewing Machines

1. Machine types and stitch requirements for production of components and major repairs
2. Sewing machine maintenance

    (A)   Tools

    (B)   Lubrication

    (C)   Needles, sizes, types, uses

    (D)   Inspections

    (E)   Thread pick-up types (oscillating, rotating vertical, and rotating horizontal)

     (F)   Shuttle timing

     (G)   Feed dog, tooth type and feed adjustment

     (H)   Walking foot feed

     (I)   Stitch length adjustment

     (J)   Thread tension adjustment

     (K)   Thread tension disk adjustment

     (L)   Motor type, speed, clutch adjustment and application

     (M)   Double needle applications and stitch width

     (N)   Setting up machine to run .75 inch nylon binding tape and double and single needle installation

     (O)   Bar tack machines, stitch patterns and lengths

     (P)   Free arm machines, operation and uses

3. Harness geometry and junctions

4. Harness machine use and operation (7 class)

     (A)   3 and 4 point harness junction stitch patterns

     (B)   Calculating pattern and stitch numbers to exceed webbing strength

     (C)   Chaffing strip uses and installation in harness junctions

     (D)   Main lift web confluence wrap at 3 ring

5. Double needle binding tape machine use and operation

     (A)   Appling binding tape to component edge

     (B)   Turning 90 degree corner appling tape

6. 304 zig zag stitch machine use and operations

     (A)   Stitch length adjustment

     (B)   Stitch width adjustment

7. Bar tack machine use and operation

    Stitch width and length adjustment

H. Master Parachute Rigger Applicant Projects

Listed below are possible, projects or tasks you may be required to perform, during the master rigger practical test phase. They may require only the repair or replacement of a single item, or possible construction and replacement of the entire assembly. All projects are to be performed to return to service safety and manufacture standards.

1. Webbing joint construction / replace main lift web

2. Chest strap replacement

3. Partial top/bottom skin replacement (ram air canopy)

4. Line set repair or replacement, (round or ram air)

5. Complete panel replacement (round reserve canopy)

6. Main parachute riser, major repair or construction

7. Main parachute deployment bag construction

8. Installation of AAD in container system not factory ready

9. Construction of slider ram air canopy

10. Construct replacement leg pads for container system

11. Alter riser from l-bar to rapide link

12. Construct lower steering line assemblies and replacement toggles

13. Construct 32-inch hand deploy pilotchute

14. Construct and replace main side flap on container

15. Replace plastic stiffener and grommet reserve flap assembly

16. Build and install BOC pocket on container

17. Construct pull lines and channel for collapsible slider

18. Construct and replace lower leg straps on articulated harness

19. Replace parcel rib ram air

20. Construct collapsible pilotchute bridle assembly

These are just a few of the possible projects or task you may be required to perform during the practical portion of the master parachute rigger test. It is important that you learn use of the proper machines, materials, construction methods, obtain the skills, and knowledge to complete these projects to a return to service standard for safe use.

Glossary

A

Accordion folding. The folding of the canopy for stacking in the container prior to closing.

Administrator. The Federal Aviation Administrator (FAA) or any person to whom he and/or she has delegated his and/or her authority in the matter concerned.

Advisory circular (AC). The FAA issues advisory circulars (ACs) to provide guidance and information in a designated subject area or to show a method acceptable to the Administrator for complying with a related Title 14 of the Code of Federal Regulations (14 CFR). Each AC is issued with a number corresponding to the subject it addresses in the 14 CFR. Unless incorporated into a regulation by reference, the contents of an AC are not binding on the public.

Aerodynamics. The study of the behavior of moving air and the forces that it produces as it passes over or around certain shaped objects, such as wings, propellers, or parachute canopies.

AGL. Above ground level.

Airframe and powerplant mechanic (A&P). Any person certificated by the FAA to perform maintenance or inspections on an aircraft's airframe or powerplant.

Airworthiness Directives (ADs). Issued by the FAA to notify owners and users of aeronautical products of unsafe conditions and the mandatory corrections under which the product may continue to be used. Each AD is an amendment to 14 CFR part 39, as such, it is part of the Federal Public Laws.

Airworthiness. A complete parachute assembly is considered airworthy when it conforms to its Technical Standard Order (TSO) and/or properly altered condition and is in condition for safe operation.

Alteration. A change to the original configuration or any other major change to any portion of the parachute from its original manufacture's specifications.

Apex. The center and topmost point of a round parachute canopy.

Approved. An item, which in its present form, has received official certification from the FAA.

Assistor pocket. Air scoops at the top of a sleeve that provide drag and aid in anchoring the sleeve as the canopy is pulled out. Also, fabric pockets on the bridle of a free bag that aid in the deployment of the bag in the event of a horseshoetype malfunction.

Automatic activation device (AAD). A device for automatically releasing the reserve or emergency parachute; utilizes barometric and rate of descent sensors.

Auxiliary parachute. A reserve parachute.

B

Back parachute. A parachute that is worn on the back.

Backstitch. Used to anchor a row of stitching by turning the material and sewing over the stitching for a short distance.

Back strap. A part of the harness that extends across the wearer's back. It may be diagonal, horizontal, or vertical and may or may not be adjustable.

Backpad. A foam-filled pad placed between the harness and the wearer that provides comfort and/or holds the harness in place.

Bar tack. A concentrated series of zigzag-like stitches used to reinforce points of stress.

Barometric pressure release. A device of the automatic opening of a free-fall parachute operating on the differences of barometric pressure.

Becket. A piece of tape or webbing sewn to a parachute or pack to form a loop through which a cord or thread may be passed.

Beeswax. A wax, usually mixed 1:1 with paraffin and heated. Webbing is dipped into it to prevent fraying.

Bellyband. A reserve tiedown strap.

Bias construction. Construction where the warp and filler threads of the material are at 45 degrees to the centerline of the gore.

Bias cut. A diagonal cut across a piece of fabric. Canopy fabric may be cut on the bias and assembled so that both warp and fill threads run at a 45 degree angle to the vertical centerline of the gore.

Block construction. An arrangement of the gores such that the warp threads are parallel to the peripheral hem.

Bobbin. A small spool used to hold thread. Commonly found in sewing machines.

Bodkin. A large-eyed needle, flat or round, and usually blunt, used to draw tape, ribbon, elastic, or cord through a loop or hem. Used to pull pack opening bands through containers.

Bolt. A compact package or roll of fabric.

Break tie. Any tie or tacking designed to break under a specified amount of stress.

Breakaway. The jettisoning of the malfunctioned main parachute by activating riser releases and deployment of the reserve parachute; also known as cutaway.

Breakcord. A thread or tape tied between parachute components that is intended to break under the desired load during deployment.

Bridle. A line that attaches the pilot chute to the apex of the canopy or to a sleeve or bag.

Bungees. Pack opening bands.

Burble. The turbulent and unstable airflow behind a falling object, such as a skydiver in free fall.

C

Cable ripcord. A flexible metal cable 3/32" diameter made of 49 strands of stainless steel wire. The cable runs from the ripcord grip to the locking pins. It is housed in a flexible, protective tube.

Calendering. The process where a machine with heated rollers is used to finish fabric. The heat and pressure process lowers permeability by forcing the fibers between each other and flattening them.

Canopy. The umbrella-like surface of a parachute and its framework of cords, called suspension lines, from which the load is suspended. The drag surface of the decelerator.

Canopy fabric. The fabric used in the fabrication of parachute canopies. It is lightweight and woven to withstand the impact of air pressure when the parachute opens. The canopy fabric is woven from nylon yarns usually in a ripstop weave.

Canopy relative work (CRW). A skydiving discipline where the parachutists fly their open canopies in a formation formed by grasping the canopies or lines using the hands or legs.

Canopy releases. Devices that allow immediate release of the parachute canopy. They disconnect the harness main lift webs from the risers.

Center pull. A ripcord design for chest parachutes.

Centerline. Lines that run from the risers to the apex of a canopy and are used to pull the apex down, such as on a Para Commander.

Certificated. A personnel parachute holding an FAA TSO certificate. Also used to refer to other FAA-approved parachutes, such as Government surplus personnel models, which were manufactured under military contract.

CFM. Cubic feet per minute. A measure of permeability.

Chafing strip. A light piece of webbing positioned between the load bearing webbing and a piece of hardware that acts as a buffer between the two.

Chest parachute. A parachute worn on the wearer's chest.

Chuck. The upper part of the tool used to install fastener or grommet parts.

Chute. A contraction of the term "parachute," and used interchangeably with it.

Clamp. A medical hemostat used by riggers for picking threads or retrieving small objects.

Closing loops. Fabric or cord loops used to secure the container closed. Used in place of locking cones.

Cloth. A pliable fabric that is woven, felted, or knitted from any filament; commonly fabric of woven cotton, woolen, silk, nylon, rayon, or linen fiber.

Clove hitch knot. A type of knot used for attaching the suspension lines of a parachute to the connector links.

Cloverleaf handle. A ripcord handle with a cloverleaf shape. Commonly found on chest parachutes.

Cocking. Setting the collapsible bridle for operation.

Confluence wrap. A piece of webbing that wraps around the confluence of two or more pieces of webbing. Prevents the stitching from splitting. Most common use is on main risers and the 3-ring harness ring installation.

Connector link. Usually identified as a small, rectangular metal fitting used to connect ends of risers or lift webs to suspension lines. The suspension lines are tied and sewn above one part of the link, the webs being stitched about the lower part. The design of the link may vary in size and shape according to the intended use.

Connector link separable. Any connector link comprised of readily separable elements, which may be used to facilitate assembly of parachute canopies to a riser system.

Container. The portion of the parachute assembly that holds the canopy in place after being folded. This is not to be confused with the term "pack."

Contamination. Where foreign materials or substances come into contact with parachute materials and possibly cause degradation or weakening of the materials.

Cords. Suspension lines.

Cross connector strap. A webbing strap attached between the risers to prevent the collapse of the canopy in the event one riser becomes disconnected.

Cross seam. A seam joining sections of a panel.

Cutaway. The cutting of risers or suspension lines to release the deployed canopy while the parachutist is still in the air. Also known as breakaway.

D

D-ring. A metal fitting shaped like a D into which snap connectors are hooked.

Daisy chain. A method of gathering the suspension lines when field packing a parachute so as to reduce the possibility of their becoming entangled.

Damage chart. A graphic representation of a canopy used to identify and mark damaged areas for repair.

Dart. A short, tapered seam.

Data pocket. Small patch pockets sewed to the inside and outside surfaces of a parachute container for carrying the parachute record card.

Decelerate. To slow down. A free-falling body decreases its rate of descent due to pressure of the atmosphere against its frontal area. This resistance gradually increases as the falling body nears the earth due to increasing atmospheric pressure.

Denier. A unit of measurement of silk in which the size of yarn is quoted as its weight per length. This is determined by weighing 9,000 meters and quoting the size of the yarn in grams. Thus, if 9,000 meters weigh 30 grams, the size of the yarn is then known as 30 denier.

Deployment. That portion of a parachute's operation occurring from the moment of pack opening to the instant the suspension lines are fully stretched but prior to the inflation of the canopy. Also known as development.

Deployment bag. A container, typically fabric, and usually enclosed in a parachute pack containing a parachute canopy.

Deployment device. A sleeve or bag.

Designated parachute rigger examiner (DPRE). A master parachute rigger appointed by the Administrator to conduct oral and practical tests required for the certification of parachute riggers.

Diagonal seam. A French fell seam of the canopy that joins two sections of a gore. Diagonal seams meet the centerline of the gore at angles of 45 degrees and 135 degrees.

Diameter. The greatest distance across a flat canopy, from skirt to skirt, measured when the canopy is lying flat. This measurement designates the size of the parachute in feet.

Diaper. Generally, a fabric panel secured by the suspension lines, which is sewn to and wrapped around the canopy. Used to control and reduce opening forces. Found mostly on round reserves.

Die. The lower part of the tool used in a press to install snap fasteners or grommets.

Direct bag static line system. A static line deployment system where the bag is attached to the static line and the canopy deploys free into the airstream.

Double throw zigzag stitching. Stitching in which the needle makes a center stitch between each left and right stitch. Also known as a No. 308 stitch.

Double-W. A three-point cross-stitch.

Drop test. Dropping a dummy or other load from an aircraft in flight or otherwise simulating a live jump to prove serviceability of a parachute.

Drop zone (DZ). A specified area upon which personnel or equipment are dropped by parachute.

Drying tower. A facility where parachutes are suspended for airing and drying.

Dual parachute packs. A sport assembly consisting of a main and a reserve parachute.

Dummy (parachute). Torso-shaped dummy of variable weight used for testing parachutes; may be of fixed or articulated construction.

Dummy drop. A parachute test using a dummy as the suspended load.

Durable dot fastener. The common snap fastener used for closing flaps, etc.

E

Ejector type snap harness. A harness snap that attaches to the V-ring to secure two parts of the harness together. An ejector arm expels the V-ring when the finger-grip lever is pulled outward.

Emergency parachute. A certificated parachute intended for emergency use.

End flap. The fabric on the end of a pack as opposed to the side, used to enclose and protect the canopy.

End tabs. Metal tabs on the end flap of the pack (principally chest and seat containers) used to secure it closed.

Eye. A small steel-wire loop attached to the parachute pack into which a hook on a pack-opening elastic is fastened.

F

Fastener slide. Zipper.

Federal Aviation Administration (FAA). An organization within the Department of Transportation. The FAA establishes aviation rules and regulations, as well as enforces those policies. The purpose of the FAA is to set the standards for civil aircraft in the interest of public safety.

Feed dog. A mechanical device located under the throat plate of a sewing machine that feeds the material through a sewing machine.

Ferrule. Device that provides a strong and smooth finish on the ends of a ripcord housing.

Fid. A small, flat, tapered bar of metal or wood used to insert the corner flaps into the container when packing.

Finger trap. A method of attaching or splicing lines by inserting one line into another. Used primarily on hollow braided lines.

Finish. The condition of the parachute fabric caused by the application of heat and pressure whereby the fibers are forced closer together. This treatment is used to determine the permeability of the fabric.

Fish scale. A spring scale used to measure the ripcord pull force or fabric strength test.

Folder. A device used as an attachment to a sewing machine to guide and fold fabric.

Force. A push or pull that tends to change the velocity or direction of a body's motion.

Forging. A high-pressure shaping of hot metal. The process used to make parachute hardware.

Forward speed. The rate at which a parachute moves horizontally in a mass of air.

Four line check. On a round canopy, the four lines that run to the top center and bottom center gores. Used to check the line continuity. On a 28-foot canopy, they are lines 1, 14, 15, and 28.

FPS. Feet per second.

Free bag. A type 5 reserve deployment device used with ram-air canopies. Not attached to the canopy, it is designed to allow deployment of the canopy in the event of a horseshoe-type malfunction.

Free fall. A parachute jump in which the parachute is activated manually at the discretion of the parachutist.

French fell seam (LSC-2). A plain overlap where material is folded over on itself and stitched to prevent raveling.

Friction burns. The result of two textile surfaces rubbing together rapidly and generating frictional heat, which reduces the tensile strength of the textile and causes deterioration of the individual threads; it occurs primarily during parachute deployment and initial inflation.

G

G force. The measure or value of the gravitational pull of the earth as modified by the earth's rotation, equal to acceleration of a freely moving body at the rate of 32.16 feet per second. Example: If a 100-pound load places a 300-pound stress on the parachute during opening, the shock is 3 Gs.

Gauge. The space between needles on a sewing machine.

Glide. The horizontal movement of the canopy.

Gore. The portion of the canopy contained between two adjacent suspension lines and the area between them, extending from the apex of the canopy to the skirt.

Grommet. A metal eyelet used as a reinforcement around a hole in fabric. Grommets are used on pack flaps to fit over locking cones or loops.

Gross weight. The complete weight of the parachute assembly.

Guide or control line. One or more parachute lines that run from a slot or orifice in a steerable canopy to the harness providing better steerability.

H

HALO. High Altitude, Low Opening.

Handle. Ripcord handpull or grip.

Hardware. All metal parts associated with parachutes, parachute systems, and their suspended loads.

Harness. An arrangement of cotton, linen, or nylon webbing designed to conform to the shape of the load to be carried in order to secure it properly so that the opening shock and the weight of the load are evenly distributed during descent.

Harness keeper. Elastic webbing used to hold harness straps in place.

Harness main sling. The main load-carrying member of the harness formed by two lengths of webbing, beginning at the shoulder adapter or D-ring, continuing down across the seat and up the other side, ending at the opposite adapter or Dring.

Hesitator loop. One of a series of webbing loops that hold the suspension lines in an orderly position in the container when the parachute is packed and which pay the lines out in sequence (hesitate) for orderly deployment.

Hot knife. An electrically-heated cutting tool used to cut and sear webbing and fabrics.

Housing clamp stiffener. A metal plate sewn to the top flap of the main parachute container and used to hold the ripcord cable housing in place and to give rigidity to the housing. Designed to provide stiff separation between the housing and the top cone for an automatic opener.

Hygroscopic. A substance or material that absorbs water readily from its surroundings.

I

Initial layout. Process in which the canopy is stretched out on the table with the top center gore on top in preparation for securing proper layout.

Inspection. A step-by-step procedure for examining a parachute prior to packing to identify any damage or non-airworthy condition.

Inversion. State in which the canopy has been turned completely inside out. Also see partial inversion.

J

Joint efficiency. The comparison of the strength of the junction or joining materials against the original materials.

Jumping. To engage in a premeditated parachute jump.

K

Kicker plate. A launching disc which is placed under the pilot chute.

Kill-line collapsible bridle. A main pilot chute bridle configuration whereby the pilot chute is collapsed by use of a retractable centerline after it has deployed the parachute.

L

L/D. Lift to drag ratio.

Lap parachute. A parachute that rests in the lap of the wearer and attaches to the harness with risers to snaps and D-rings on the front. Resembles a chest parachute with long risers. Not in current use.

Lateral band. Lower (in the periphery) or upper (in the vent hem), a reinforcement web.

Launching disc. A kicker plate placed under the pilot chute.

Leg strap. That part of the harness webbing that encircles the wearer's leg. The leg straps can be adjusted to fit the user.

Life cycle. Service life. The time that a parachute may be considered usable.

Lift web (main). The portion of the harness from the shoulder to the hip area; generally from the canopy releases to the leg strap junction.

Lift webs. The front portion of the harness from the shoulder to the leg strap junction; includes the risers if there are no riser releases.

Lift. The force perpendicular to drag that helps reduce vertical descent.

Line extension. When the lines are fully deployed; prior to line stretch.

Line separator. A tool used to separate and hold the lines of a round parachute during the packing process.

Line stowing. The process of drawing the suspension lines into suspension line retaining loops in the parachute pack; accomplished to prevent entanglement or twisting of the lines during opening of the parachute. Stows may be held by retaining loops or rubber bands.

Line stretch. Occurs during deployment, after the lines are fully extended. Follows snatch force and line extension.

Line-over. A type of deployment malfunction that occurs when one or more suspension lines pass over the top of the canopy during deployment preventing complete, normal inflation. Not to be confused with "partial inversions."

Locking cone. A cone shaped metal device used in conjunction with end tabs and ripcord pins to hold the container flaps closed.

Locking pins. Straight or curved metal pins used with a throwout or pull-out pilot chute for securing the container closed.

Locking ripcord pin. A small metal prong, slightly smaller in diameter than the ripcord cable and fastened to it by means of a swage fitting or serving and solder. One pin is attached to the end of the cable and the others (when two or more are used) are set at intervals on the cable. The spacing of the pins is dependant on the distance between the cones on the container flap. The locking pins pass through the locking cones of the flaps and thus serve to lock the container until such time as the pins are withdrawn.

Lockstitch. Type of stitching used in manufacturing parachutes. This type of stitch is formed by two threads. A loop of the thread is passed through the material where it is entered by the supply of the other thread. The loop of the first thread is drawn into the material to the extent that the loop or lock is approximately halfway between the two surfaces of the material. Also known as a type 301 stitch.

Loft. A facility for the repair and maintenance of parachutes.

Logbook. A format for complying with 14 CFR part 65, subsection 65.131(a) in regards to recording the work done by the rigger on parachutes.

M

Machine head. The entire metal housing that supports the moving parts and bearings of the machine.

Main parachute. A parachute assembly, excluding the harness, that is used in conjunction with a reserve parachute assembly as the primary assembly for a premeditated jump.

Main seam. That which joins two adjacent gores in a canopy; also known as a radial seam.

Maintenance. Inspection, overhaul, repair, preservation, and replacement of parts but excludes preventative maintenance.

Major repair. A repair that, if improperly done, might appreciably affect weight, balance, structure strength, performance, powerplant operation, flight characteristics or other qualities affecting airworthiness; or that is not according to accepted practices or cannot be done by elementary operations.

Malfunction. The complete or partial failure of the parachute canopy to effect proper opening and descent. Some malfunctions are canopy damage, twisted suspension lines, inversion or semi-inversion of the canopy, a line over, etc.

Malfunction or Defect Report, FAA Form 8330-2. A form used to report serious defects or other recurring unairworthy conditions of parachutes or aircraft.

Marquisette. Netting.

Mass. The quantity of matter in an object.

Master Parachute Rigger. An individual certified by the FAA to pack, maintain, and alter parachutes. The highest classification of parachute rigger.

Maximum operating weight. The total weight of the parachutist and all equipment that exits the aircraft with the jumper.

Mildew. A type of fungus or mold that forms on fabric and leather in damp environments. Mildew weakens some materials and if it appears on a parachute canopy, the areas must be cleaned, repaired, or replaced.

Military specification (MIL-SPEC). A specification set by military agencies and used for the procurement of military supplies and equipment.

Minor repair. A repair other than a major repair.

Modification. 1. A change. 2. Often refers to the removing of canopy area to effect steerability and forward glide.

Mouth lock. A device that holds the mouth of the canopy closed until the lines are deployed.

MPH. Miles per hour.

MSL. Mean sea level.

MS. Military Specification under the MS system.

N

NAS-804. National Aircraft Standards Specifications Number 804; this is the minimum performance standards required by Technical Standard Order, TSO-C23b, for parachute assemblies manufactured under this TSO.

National Airspace Standards (NAS). National Aircraft Standards.

Needle. A small, slender, pointed piece of steel with a hole for thread used for sewing.

Nicopress. A copper sleeve used to join cables to form loops or splices.

Nylon. A synthetic material of protein-like structure derived from coal, air, and water, which is adapted for fashioning into filaments of extreme toughness, strength, and elasticity and used in the manufacture of parachutes.

O

Opening shock. The decelerating force exerted on the load following that of the snatch force. Caused by the acceleration of the canopy and the air mass associated with it.

Opening time. The time elapsing between the opening of a parachute pack and the opening of the canopy to its fullest extent.

Oscillation. Pendulum-like swinging of the suspended load beneath the inflated canopy; usually the result of trapped air escaping under the lower lateral band.

Outboard. Facing to the outside, such as a ripcord facing to the side of the jumper rather than toward the breastbone.

Overhand knot. A simple knot tied separately in each end of a piece of cord above a square, surgeon's, or other knot to prevent the end from slipping through the lower knot.

P

Pack. A synonymous term for the parachute container.

Pack opening band. A cloth-covered steel spring assembly with hooks at each end used to expedite the opening of the pack by rapidly pulling the flaps away from the canopy.

Pack stiffener. Generally, metal stiffeners used in military assemblies to give shape and form to the pack.

Pack tray. The portion of the container or deployment device where the lines are stowed.

Packing bar. A long, flat bar of metal or wood used in the folding of the canopy of a parachute during the packing process and to aid in closing the container; also known as a long bar, paddle, or fid.

Packing hook. A special hook-like tool used to draw the suspension lines into place in the hesitator loops. Pull-up cords are sometimes used for this purpose.

Packing paddle. A flat, narrow piece of metal or wood used to form the packed container; also known as a packing bar or fid.

Packing table. A table used in packing parachutes, normally 3 feet wide by 40 feet long with a smooth top surface.

Packing. The operation of folding the canopy and enclosing it in the container.

Panel. A subdivision of a gore; also known as a section.

Parachute. An umbrella-like device designed to trap a large volume of air in order to slow the descent of a falling load attached to the parachute. The word "parachute" is formed from the French words "para," for shield, and "chute," to fall. Thus, "parachute" literally means "to defend from a fall."

Parachute Industry Association (PIA). An international trade organization composed of parachute manufacturers, dealers, riggers, and others involved in the parachute industry.

Parachute pack. Such as a back pack or chest pack, means the parachute assembly less the harness. It means the container, canopy, suspension lines, pilot chute risers and connector links. The terms "pack" and "container" are not synonymous in the terminology of this part.

Parachute record card. A card kept in the record pocket that records the packing intervals of the parachute and other important information as required under 14 CFR part 65, subsection 65.131(c). Also known as the "packing data card."

Parachute rigger. A person certified by the FAA to perform packing and maintenance on parachutes.

Parachute rigging. The process of inspecting, repairing, and replacing minor parts of a parachute assembly and of repacking the parachute so that it is ready for immediate use. Parachute rigging also includes fitting and adjusting the harness.

Parachute standard (PS). PIA specification for parachute materials.

Partial inversion. A type of deployment malfunction that occurs when one or more gore sections near the skirt become inverted during deployment and form a small pocket which inflates, causing a partial inversion of the canopy. The condition may or may not work out or may become a complete inversion (i.e., the canopy turns completely inside-out). It is the skirt, not the line, which is "over;" not to be confused with a "line-over." Also known as a "Mae West."

Patching. Method of repair by covering a hole or tear in a canopy or pack.

Performance standards. The specifications that define the minimum performance and safety standards for certificating parachutes. There are three standards that have been used or are in use: NAS-804, AS-8015A, and AS-8015B.

Permeability. The mass rate of flow or the volume rate of flow per unit projected area of cloth for a prescribed pressure differential. In the U.S., permeability is measured in cubic feet of air through one square foot per minute at ½" of water pressure. Sometimes confused with porosity.

Personnel parachutes. Parachutes designed expressly for human use as opposed to cargo drops or aircraft deceleration.

Piggyback. A single harness, dual parachute system used for intentional parachute jumping where both parachutes are mounted on the back of the jumper.

Pilot chute assist system. A connection of breakcord or Velcro® between the static line and the pilot chute of a sport parachute, which pulls the pilot chute out of the pack and then separates.

Pilot chute. A small parachute used to accelerate deployment; constructed in much the same manner as the main canopy and from similar material. Some types of pilot chutes are equipped with a spring-operated, quick-opening device. The frame is compressed so as to open immediately when released from the pack.

Pin protector flap. A flap that covers the locking pins and cones to prevent the pack from being opened by any means other than the ripcord.

Pleat. A fold sewn in the fabric.

Pocket ripcord handle. Elastic or spring-edged pocket that holds ripcord handle in an accessible position on the harness. The chest-type pocket consists of a piece of straight elastic webbing serving the same purpose.

Porosity. The ratio of void or interstitial area to total area of a cloth expressed in percent. The ratio of open space to covered area of a drag surface. Used for ring slot, ribbon, ring sail, and rotafoil canopies. Not to be confused with permeability.

Premature opening. Any accidental opening of the parachute prior to the intended time.

Prepack inspection. The inspection made on the parachute prior to its packing.

Presser foot. The part of the sewing machine above the feed dog that holds the fabric in place.

Preventative maintenance (PM). The systematic care, servicing, and inspection of equipment and facilities for the purpose of maintaining them in a serviceable condition and detecting and correcting incipient failures. Simple or minor preservation operations and the replacement of small standard parts not involving complex assembly operations.

Proof load. The testing of an item for conformance with strength requirements.

Proper layout. Process by which the canopy and suspension lines are arranged on the packing table for inspection and packing.

Pull the dot. A particular type of snap fastener that can only be opened or closed by pulling in one direction designated by an indented dot on the button.

Pull-up cords. Nylon cords of varying length used to pull up the sides and ends of the container flaps over the container cones and to pull the cones through the grommets. They are also used to pull the suspension lines into place in some types of containers.

Q

Quality control. A method of describing the inspection and test procedures necessary to ensure that each article produced conforms to the type design and is in a condition for safe operation.

Quick connector snap. A large hook-shaped, spring-loaded snap, two of which are used to quickly attach the chest-type parachute to the two D-rings on the harness.

R

Radial seam. A seam extending from the skirt to the apex, joining two gores. A portion of the suspension lines may be concealed in the tube formed by the radial seam.

Ram-air parachute. Generally, a rectangular, double-surface canopy with airfoil shaped ribs inflated by the air flowing into the front openings to produce an airfoil shape.

Rate of descent. The vertical velocity, in feet per second, of a fully-opened parachute.

Rating. A statement that, as a part of a certificate, sets forth special conditions, privileges, or limitations.

Ravel (unravel). To separate, untwist, or unwind, leaving a frayed or ragged edge. "Unravel" is often used with the same meaning, although grammatically incorrect.

Raw edge. The unfinished edge of the material; liable to raveling.

Reefing. A temporary restriction of the skirt of a parachute to a diameter less than the fully inflated diameter. Reefing is used to decrease drag area and/or to obtain stability.

Reinforcements. Commonly strong tape or webbing used to strengthen parts of the canopy, container, or harness.

Relative humidity. Ratio of the amount of water vapor present in the air to that which the air would hold at saturation at the same temperature.

Repack cycle. The time that a certificated parachute is considered to be airworthy before being inspected and repacked. The current U.S. repack cycle is 180 days.

Reserve parachute. The second or "auxiliary" parachute worn by a person making a premeditated jump.

Reserve static line (RSL). A backup device for activating the reserve after a cutaway. Usually a line, webbing, or cable that connects the main risers with the ripcord handle, housing, or cable.

Restitching. The process of sewing directly over base or broken stitching.

Retainer band. A rubber band used to hold folded suspension lines or static lines to the parachute pack.

Rig. 1. To pack. 2. A set of sport parachute equipment. 3. To assemble a parachute.

Rigger roll. To prepare an unpacked parachute for storage by rolling the canopy into a ball with the suspension lines around it.

Ripcord. A locking device that secures the pack in a closed condition and by which the release of the parachute is effected. It may consist of a handle, cable, locking pins, and a cable swage.

Ripcord cable. A flexible cable joining the locking pins and the ripcord handle.

Ripcord housing. A flexible tubing in which the ripcord is installed for protection and to provide a free path for the ripcord.

Ripcord housing clamp. A metal clamp located on the outside of the end flap of back and seat-type parachutes. The clamp secures the ripcord cable and power cable of the actuator.

Ripstop nylon. A type of weave designed to prevent tears from spreading. Extra numbers of yarns are closely woven into the cloth intermittently across the width and across the length.

Ripstop tape. Ripstop nylon fabric with a pressure sensitive adhesive. Used to repair small tears in canopies.

Riser. The portion of the suspension system between the lower end of a group of suspension lines and the point of attachment to the load.

Riser release. A canopy release.

Roll packing. A method of packing a ram-air parachute whereby the nose and the tail are rolled towards the center of the canopy.

Routine inspection. A visual inspection of all parts of a packed parachute that may be checked without opening the parachute.

S

S.A.E. Society of Automotive Engineers.

Saddle. The part of the harness positioned under the seat of the wearer.

Safety tie. The thread used in sealing a parachute.

Scissors. A cutting instrument with two opposing blades.

Seal press. A mechanical press used for compressing lead seals to seal parachutes in accordance with 14 CFR part 65, subsection 65.133.

Seam ripper. A small tool used for picking or cutting threads in sewing operations.

Seams. Where two pieces of fabric are joined together.

Sear. Damage to fabric or lines by heat generated through rubbing. The melting of webbing, fabric, or line of nylon to prevent fraying.

Seat parachute. Parachute positioned below the back of the wearer. Forms part of the seat cushion in the aircraft.

Section. Any one of the pieces of cloth which, when assembled, form one gore of a parachute canopy. Also known as a panel.

Selvage edge. The edge of cloth which is so woven as to prevent raveling.

Senior Parachute Rigger. An individual certified by the FAA to pack and maintain parachutes. A journeyman level classification of parachute rigger.

Sewing machine. A machine with a mechanically-driven needle used for sewing.

Sewing machine knee lifter. A knee-operated mechanism that lifts the presser foot of a sewing machine.

Sewing machine uprise. The uprise is the upright part of the head (generally located on the right side of the head) that houses a portion of the moving parts that transmit motion through mechanical shafts and linkages to the mechanisms in the base of the machine.

Sewing pattern. A design outlined in drawings for joining parts.

Shock cord. A straight elastic cord comprised of continuous strands of rubber encased in a braided cover. Used today primarily for Safety Stow® loops on free bags.

Shock load. The maximum force exerted on the canopy by inflation. This maximum force may be the snatch force or it may be the opening shock.

Shot bag. A parachute packing tool. A rectangular bag filled with shot and used to hold folded gores in position during packing.

Shoulder strap. The part of the harness webbing that crosses the wearer's back diagonally between the shoulder blades and the horizontal backstrap.

Side flap. Fabric extensions on each of the long sides of the pack that fold over to enclose the canopy.

Silk. A fiber produced by the silk worm.

Single point release. A harness release that has a single closure, such as the T-10 type; also a canopy release system operated by one hand or action.

Single throw zigzag. A machine zigzag stitch from left to right to left, etc. Also known as a 304 stitch.

Skirt. The reinforced hem forming the periphery of a canopy.

Skydiving. A popular name for sport parachuting.

Slag. A type 6 deployment device. A short sleeve configuration used on ram-air parachutes.

Sleeve. A tapered, fabric tube in which the canopy is placed to control deployment. A deployment device.

Sliders. A reefing device usually for ram-air canopies. Comprised of a fabric panel with grommets at the corners through which pass the suspension lines of the canopy.

Snag. A fabric imperfection.

Snap fastener. Metal fastening device that usually consists of four parts: button, socket, stud, and eyelet. Device is manufactured in various shapes and sizes.

Snatch force. The shock produced on the load when the parachute assembly fully strings out and becomes suddenly accelerated to the same speed as the load. Comes just prior to opening shock.

Sniveling. Slow opening of a parachute.

SPEC. Specification and/or MIL-SPEC (military specification).

Spiral vane pilot chute. A pilot chute with a cone-shaped, cloth-covered coil spring used in free-type parachute assemblies.

Splicing. The process of joining together, as the interweaving of strands, overlapping and stitching of materials.

Split saddle. The lower part of a harness that has independent leg straps; no saddle cross strap.

Sport parachuting. The making of premeditated parachute jumps for pleasure.

Sport rig. A skydiving harness and container system.

Square knot. A strong knot for joining two cords or lines, which does not slip or loosen easily.

Square parachute. A gliding or ram-air canopy having a square or rectangular shape.

Stand. A sewing machine table.

Static line. A line, cable, or webbing, one end of which is fastened to the pack, the other to some part of the launching vehicle; used to open a pack or to deploy a canopy.

Static line operated parachute. A parachute operated by a length of webbing after a jumper has fallen the length of the static line. The ripcord pins are pulled from the pack, the parachute opens, and a "break tie" breaks, freeing the parachute.

Static line system. A parachute system that is attached to the aircraft with a line and automatically deploys the parachute.

Straps. The webbing components of a harness.

Surgeon's knot. A type of knot commonly used for tying nylon threads or cords in place of a square knot to prevent mis-tying.

Suspension lines. Cords or webbing of silk, nylon, cotton, rayon, or other textile materials that connect the drag surface of the parachute to the harness. They are the means by which the wearer or weight is hung or suspended from the inflated canopy.

Swages. The ball or other device used at the end of a ripcord to secure the cable to the handle.

T

Tail pocket. A deployment device sewn onto the tail of a ram-air canopy used to stow the suspension lines.

Tandem. A dual harness, dual parachute system for use by two people under the same main parachute.

Tapes. Narrow woven ribbons used for reinforcing parachutes.

Tape fastener. Velcro®.

Technical standard order. A minimum performance standard for specified articles, such as materials, parts, processes, or appliances used on civil aircraft.

Tension plate. A device hooked into the connector links in order to put tension on the canopy while packing.

Thread. A thin continuous filament made by spinning fibers and combining the strands.

Title 14 of the Code of Federal Regulations (14 CFR). The rules, regulations, and guidelines established by the FAA to govern the operation of aircraft, airways, airmen, and the safe operation of civil aircraft.

Toggle. A knob or webbing loop at the end of the steering line for grasping by the parachutist.

Trimming. Clipping or paring to reduce to a neat orderly state.

Tubular nylon. Sleevelike weave, seamless, and pressed flat, similar in appearance to tape, but stronger and hollow in the center.

Tuck. A shortening of material caused by pulling fabric up in folds and stitching across the gathered fabric.

U

Ultimate load. Maximum load that can be applied without causing any part of the structure to fail.

Ultraviolet light damage. Degradation of nylon fabric by exposure to sunlight or fluorescent lights. Identified by a yellowish color on white fabric or excessive fading to colored fabric.

United States Parachute Association. A nonprofit division of the National Aeronautic Association (NAA) that governs sport parachuting activities in the U.S.

V

V-ring. A metal fitting shaped in the form of a closed letter V, used with snaps to secure or attach a load to a parachute.

Velcro®. The commercial name for hook and pile nylontape fastener.

Velocity. A vector quantity that includes both magnitude (speed) and direction relation to a given frame of reference; also the time rate of change of position.

Vent. The opening at the top, or peak, of the canopy.

Vent cap. A piece of fabric sewn to the upper lateral band and covering the vent; also known as a vent patch.

W

Warp. The threads that run parallel to the selvage edge of cloth; those which are crossed by the filling threads.

Weave. The forming of a textile by interlacing yarns. The making or manufacturing of cloth on a loom by interlacing warp and filling yarns.

Webbing. A stout, closewoven tape used for straps, belts, harnesses, etc.

Weight (fabric). The weight of fabric measured in ounces per square yard.

Weight. Gravitational force on a mass.

Wrinkles. A series of small pleats.

Z

Zigzag. A stitch formation of alternating left and right throw stitches, usually made on a sewing machine that moves the needle bar alternately left and right during sewing.

Zipper. A slide fastener.

Index

Made in the USA
Las Vegas, NV
16 December 2023

82983639R00195